# Latinx Media

**Edited by Rielle Navitski and Leslie Marsh**

*Latinx Media* is licensed under a Creative Commons Attribution-NonCommercial-ShareAlike 4.0 license.

This license allows you to remix, tweak, and build upon this work under noncommercial circumstances, as long as you credit this original source for the creation and license the new creation under identical terms.

If you reuse this content elsewhere, in order to comply with the attribution requirements of the license, please attribute the original source to the University System of Georgia.

NOTE: The above copyright license which the University System of Georgia uses for their original content does not extend to or include content which was accessed and incorporated, and which is licensed under various other CC Licenses, such as ND licenses. Nor does it extend to or include any Special Permissions which were granted to us by the rightsholders for our use of their content.

Image Disclaimer: All images and figures in this book are believed to be (after a reasonable investigation) either public domain, carry a compatible Creative Commons license, are used under fair use, or permissions were granted by the copyright owner. If you are the copyright owner of images in this book and you have not authorized the use of your work under these terms, please contact the University of North Georgia Press at ungpress@ung.edu to have the content removed.

ISBN: 978-1-959203-00-1

Produced by:
University System of Georgia

Published by:
University of North Georgia Press
Dahlonega, Georgia

Cover Design: Ariana Adams and Sarah Mikhail
Layout Design: Corey Parson

For more information, please visit http://ung.edu/university-press
Or email ungpress@ung.edu

# Table of Contents

Preface .................................................... iv

## PART I: MEDIA FORMS     1

### Chapter 1: Film............................................ 2
Rielle Navitski (University of Georgia)

### Chapter 2: Television .................................... 13
Crystal Camargo (Northwestern University)

### Chapter 3: Digital Media................................ 27
Javier Rivera (University of Southern California)

## PART II: IDENTITIES     37

### Chapter 4: Defining Race and Ethnicity between Latin America and the United States ............................... 38
Rielle Navitski (University of Georgia)

### Chapter 5: Afro-Latinx Identity and Media ................ 52
Keara K. Goin (University of Virginia)

### Chapter 6: Diasporic Indigenous Latinx Identity and Media .... 66
Argelia González Hurtado (St. Mary's College of Maryland)

### Chapter 7: Feminist Perspectives in Latinx Media ............ 81
Myra Mendible (Florida Gulf Coast University)

### Chapter 8: Latina/o/x LGBTQ Identities .................... 93
Gilberto M. Blasini (University of Wisconsin, Milwaukee)

## PART III: HISTORIES     105

### Chapter 9: Latino Images and Audiences to 1960............ 106
Laura Isabel Serna (University of Southern California)

### Chapter 10: Spanish-Language Television and Pan-Latinidad...118
Craig Allen (Arizona State University)

### Chapter 11: The Mexican American Experience Onscreen ......131
Libia Jiménez Chávez (University of Georgia)

### Chapter 12: The Puerto Rican Experience Onscreen .......... 145
Dalina A. Perdomo Álvarez (Eli and Edythe Broad Art Museum) and Pedro Noel Doreste (University of Chicago)

**Chapter 13: The Cuban American Experience Onscreen** . . . . . . . . 157
    Ana M. López (Tulane University)

**Chapter 14: The Dominican American Experience Onscreen** . . . 172
    Sharina Maillo-Pozo (University of Georgia)

**Chapter 15: The Central American Experience Onscreen** . . . . . . 184
    Jonathan Peraza Campos (Georgia State University)

# PART IV: LATINX MEDIA TODAY AND TOMORROW: A ROUNDTABLE     199

   Moderated and transcribed by Leslie L. Marsh and Rielle Navitski

# PART V: KEY CREATIVES     211

## Sample Profiles:

### Lourdes Portillo . . . . . . . . . . . . . . . . . . . . . . . . . . . . 212
   Rielle Navitski (University of Georgia)

### Alex Rivera . . . . . . . . . . . . . . . . . . . . . . . . . . . . . . . . . 219
   Sarah Ann Wells (University of Wisconsin, Madison)

### Robert Rodriguez . . . . . . . . . . . . . . . . . . . . . . . . . . . . 226
   Charles Ramírez Berg (University of Texas at Austin)

## Student Key Creatives Profiles:

### Aurora Guerrero . . . . . . . . . . . . . . . . . . . . . . . . . . . . 233
   Katie Morgan

### Lin-Manuel Miranda . . . . . . . . . . . . . . . . . . . . . . . . 237
   Grace Kennedy

### Gregory Nava . . . . . . . . . . . . . . . . . . . . . . . . . . . . . . 241
   Zayna Khan

### Danny Trejo . . . . . . . . . . . . . . . . . . . . . . . . . . . . . . . 246
   Chris Borg

### Luis Valdez . . . . . . . . . . . . . . . . . . . . . . . . . . . . . . . . 250
   Andrew Phipps

# GLOSSARY     254

# Preface

The creation of this textbook was made possible by Affordable Learning Georgia, an initiative of the University System of Georgia; the Latin American and Caribbean Studies Institute at the University of Georgia, with funding from the Title VI National Resource Centers Program (US Department of Education); the University of Georgia Provost's Affordable Course Materials Grant program administered by the University of Georgia Libraries and the Center for Teaching and Learning; and Georgia State University's Center for Latin American and Latino/a Studies. We deeply appreciate their support.

Our utmost gratitude to our authors, who agreed to contribute to this open-access textbook in the midst of a pandemic and a very difficult time for higher education; to Éric Morales-Franceschini and our two anonymous readers for their constructive feedback; and to Director Dr. Bonnie "BJ" Robinson, Managing Editor Corey Parson, and Assistant Managing Editor Elizabeth Odom at the University of North Georgia Press for all their work in bringing the project to fruition. Rielle is grateful to Dr. Megan Mittelstadt, Director of the Center for Teaching and Learning at UGA, and Mariann Samuel of UGA Libraries for their encouragement regarding the project. Leslie would also like to thank the Latino/a/x Studies Working Group at GSU.

The text of this book is licensed under a [Creative Commons Attribution-NonCommercial-ShareAlike 4.0 license](). It can be freely reproduced with attribution, provided the use is noncommercial. Any derivative works must be distributed under this same license.

The images in the textbook are either in the public domain; appear via a Creative Commons license whose terms allow for reproduction (see details in the corresponding image captions); are screen captures utilized in keeping with the principle of fair use (academic analysis/interpretation of the image constituting a transformative use); or are copyrighted by a contributor and used with permission. Images in the textbook thus should not be understood to be licensed under Creative Commons except where explicitly indicated.

Contributors to the textbook have the discretion to use their preferred term(s) for referring to people of Latin American origin living in the United States, so usage varies. Generally, we have tried to avoid historical anachronism by not applying the term "Latinx," which was coined only recently, when discussing eras when it would not have been used.

Terms that are bolded in the text appear in the glossary at the end of the book.

We welcome feedback about the textbook. If you use it in a class, we'd be grateful if you could let us know so we can document the impact of the project. We can be reached by email at rnavitsk@uga.edu and llmarsh@gsu.edu.

# Part I: Media Forms

The first section of this textbook provides an overview of key concepts and approaches used to analyze works of film, television, and digital media and the social contexts in which they are produced and consumed. Chapter 1 provides an overview of the fundamentals of film style as well as the processes of film production, distribution, and exhibition. Chapter 2 addresses the narrative structure, aesthetics, history, and production of television, seen as a form of mass communication that is woven into the fabric of everyday life and a space where ideas about Latinx people are increasingly present. The final chapter in this section, Chapter 3, examines digital media, which have become increasingly important venues of expression for Latinx creatives and consumers to reflect on their experiences and create alternative public spheres online.

After completing this section, students should be able to do the following:
- Use tools from film and media studies to analyze works of Latinx film, media, and television.
- Identify the most important issues concerning production, distribution, exhibition, and reception for different types of media (film, television, digital media).

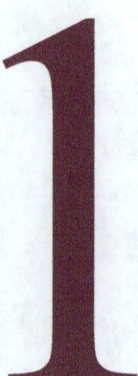

# Film
Rielle Navitski
(University of Georgia)

Cinema, which was perhaps the single most popular medium of the twentieth century, has faced growing competition in the twenty-first from online media. Digital technologies offer forms of entertainment that differ fundamentally from the feature film, from social networks to fifteen-second videos. They have also transformed the movie business in both obvious and subtle ways. These include filming with digital cameras instead of celluloid ones and projecting films from digital files stored on hard drives rather than from 35mm reels. These technological shifts open up new possibilities but have not dramatically changed the look of films in most cases. By contrast, the ability to stream films without leaving home poses a threat to the financial health of movie theaters. Yet this concern is not new but rather dates back to the widespread introduction of television in the 1950s. Despite the availability of new forms of audiovisual entertainment, films have continued to play a major role in our routines and emotional lives.

Even with such significant changes, many aspects of the movie business, including the racial and ethnic makeup of film industry workers both in front of and behind the cameras, continue to be shaped by long-established practices. Understanding its history can help us understand why change in the film industry can be so slow, despite many audience members calling for greater diversity. To give a sense of the current situation, a 2020 study found that of the one hundred top-grossing films released in 2019, less than 5% of the characters were Latinx or Hispanic (*Inequality* 2). When top-grossing films from 2007 to 2019 were examined, under 4% of directors were Latinx or Hispanic (*Inequality* 4). In 2020, the US population was 18.7% Latinx ([Jones et al].). Top-grossing films would need to include three and a half times more Latinx characters than they currently do to accurately represent the US population.

This chapter seeks to shed light on the factors behind those numbers. It will provide you with basic tools developed by the academic area of film studies to make sense of multiple dimensions of the movies, including audiovisual style, the economics and technology of the industry, and cinema as a social experience.

Writing in film studies often overlaps with everyday conversations about cinema, including the comments we make about films online or to friends and family, reviews by influential critics, and industry buzz in newspapers, magazines, television, and social media. Yet it also differs from these conversations in important ways. Our ordinary discussions of films tend to focus on story, stars, and directors. We often consider first how the characters and events depicted in a movie make us feel and whether or not we find them believable. We might also think about the physical attributes or acting abilities of its performers and how the film fits with our understanding of its director's personal style based on their other work. Without neglecting story, stars, or directors, the academic study of film explores dimensions of cinema that may be less high-profile but nevertheless are key for understanding why movies look and sound the way they do and how they affect us.

When considering individual films, film studies devotes as much attention to **film style** (visual and audio choices) as to story. It also looks at the impact of all aspects of the film industry—business practices, technology, and audience experiences—rather than focusing on the most prominent film industry workers, namely stars and directors. While many but not all film scholars accept the widespread idea that movies reflect their directors' personal vision, taking a broader view of cinema makes it clear that this vision is not the final word on a film's meaning and impact. Most films would never be successfully made and screened without the labor of hundreds of people on both the business side and the creative side. And without the engagement of critics and audiences, who may find significance in a film in ways that differ from or even go against the creators' intentions, the film would not take on a meaningful existence in a broader world.

## FILM STYLE

In paying attention to style, film studies seeks to grasp what is unique about the medium. Movies can and often do take their plots from novels, plays, and other sources, but they use artistic resources specific to film and television to bring these stories to the screen. Analyzing film style means focusing not only on *who* and *what* is shown onscreen (characters, performances, dialogue, and plot) but also on *how* it is shown. Audiovisual style can reveal or withhold important information about the plot and create a tone or mood, all without the actors uttering a word. This section offers an introduction to the elements of film style.

Film, television, and digital video create the illusion of movement by presenting a series of images (usually twenty-four or thirty per second) in rapid succession. Since the brain is unable to process images individually when shown at this speed, they begin to blur together, giving the impression of smooth motion. Through this illusion, live-action films offer a realistic reproduction of events that unfold over time in a three-dimensional space, rendered in a two-dimensional frame. (The term **frame** refers both to the fixed dimensions of the image and to an individual photographic image or its digital equivalent). Both animation and computer-generated imagery (CGI) use the same illusion of motion but create fictional worlds from scratch.

While watching a movie, we as viewers can make educated guesses about why the creative team made specific choices affecting each of these aspects: the three-dimensional world created or selected to be placed in front of the camera; the two-dimensional frame (what we actually see onscreen); and the dimension of time. Of course, in the vast majority of films, time is not presented continuously. Rather, **editing** is used to assemble various **shots** (unbroken runs of the camera) recorded at different times and in different places to construct a fictional time and space. Finally, **film sound** (dialogue, noise, and music), recorded at the time or added later, is incorporated, shaping our interpretation of the images. All of these dimensions of film work together and are interconnected.

Before filming begins, the creative team must assemble a group of actors (**casting**) and create or adapt a three-dimensional space to be filmed via set design, location scouting, costume design, and lighting. These are all aspects of what is sometimes called **mise-en-scène**, meaning the elements of cinema borrowed from theater.

Before and during the shooting of a film, directors and cinematographers work to design the two-dimensional space of the film frame as it changes over time. This aspect of film style is referred to as framing or composition. It is defined by choreographing the movement of the camera and the actors in relation to the setting. Directors and cinematographers consider the camera's position relative to the subjects: **camera angle** (low, high, or straight-on) and **camera distance** (the apparent distance between the camera and the main subject in the frame, usually a human figure, ranging from extreme close-up to extreme long shot).

*Screen captures from* Bird of Paradise *(1932). The film stars Mexican actress Dolores del Río in the role of a Pacific Islander woman, indicating Hollywood studios' fascination with "exotic" non-White characters portrayed in highly stereotypical ways and cast with little regard for cultural differences.*

**Figure 1.1: An extreme close-up—a shot in which a detail of an object (in this case, a pictorial message sent by del Río's character) or human face fills the frame.**

Source: *Bird of Paradise*
Attribution: King Vidor
License: Public domain

**Figure 1.2: A close-up—a shot in which the apparent size of the human face is roughly equal to the height of the frame.**

Source: *Bird of Paradise*
Attribution: King Vidor
License: Public domain

**Figure 1.3: A medium close-up—a shot in which an actor's face and shoulders are visible.**

Source: *Bird of Paradise*
Attribution: King Vidor
License: Public domain

**Figure 1.4: A medium shot—a shot in which an actor is visible from the waist up.**

Source: *Bird of Paradise*
Attribution: King Vidor
License: Public domain

**Figure 1.5: A medium-long shot—a shot in which an actor is visible from the knees up.**

Source: *Bird of Paradise*
Attribution: King Vidor
License: Public domain

**Figure 1.6: A long shot—a shot in which the actor's full body is roughly equal to the height of the frame.**

Source: *Bird of Paradise*
Attribution: King Vidor
License: Public domain

**Figure 1.7: An extreme long shot—a shot in which the actor appears tiny in relation to the setting.**

Source: *Bird of Paradise*
Attribution: King Vidor
License: Public domain

They also take into account the visual effects of **camera movement**, or a change in the camera's position in the course of a shot. Types of camera movement include **pans** (side-to-side movements of the camera pivoting on a fixed point, typically a tripod), **tilts** (up-and-down movement of the camera pivoting on a fixed point, typically a tripod), **tracking shots** (movement forward, backward, or parallel to the plane of the frame using train-like tracks or a dolly with wheels), **crane shots** (movements that involve the camera being lifted through space and moving freely on a device similar to a construction crane), and **traveling shots** (shots that combine two or more types of camera movement). They also plan a shot's **composition**; that is, how shapes, colors, and contrasts of light and shadow will appear within the final image. In some cases, storyboarding is used to sketch out the composition of shots in advance.

While films occasionally manipulate the unfolding of time directly using slow motion, fast motion, or reverse motion, most simply combine takes using editing. Editing can show a staged event from different angles, but it can also bring together objects or people that were never anywhere near each other during shooting (known as creative geography) to create new meanings. The pace of editing—that is, how many cuts, or changes from one take to another, happen per minute—can also impact the mood of a scene, with rapid editing often creating tension and a slow pace of editing lending a relaxed feel. In conventional fiction films, editing is specifically designed *not* to be noticed by the viewer, which makes it particularly challenging to observe and comment on. Several strategies, such as cutting in the midst of an onscreen movement (a match on action) are used to conceal edits and make the flow of images appear smooth.

In some cases, viewers can make sense of spatial relationships across cuts in an intuitive way. For example, in a **shot-reverse shot structure** often used for dialogue scenes, the camera might film one character (A) from behind the other character (B) in an **over-the-shoulder shot**. A sliver of B's shoulder is visible in a close-up of A. When the scene cuts to a **reverse angle** (a 180-degree change in perspective), a sliver of A's shoulder is included in a close-up of B, allowing us to understand that the characters are facing each other.

Other editing patterns are conventions; that is, they don't necessarily make sense on their own, but they are an accepted practice in filmmaking that we can absorb from watching many movies. Take the example of a **point-of-view shot structure**. First, we see a character looking. Then we see what they are looking at. It is a convention of film style that we are seeing through the character's eyes. Like shot-reverse shot, point-of-view shot structure often uses reverse angles, but the subjective nature of the shot is an important difference. Another example is **parallel editing**, when a scene cuts back and forth between actions happening in different locations. The viewer understands that these actions are happening at the same time because it is a convention of film editing, although there may be nothing to indicate it directly.

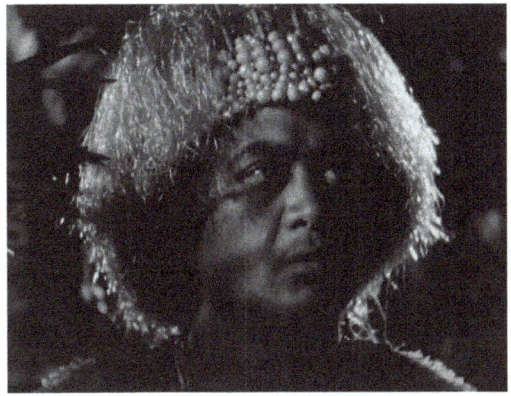 

**Figure 1.8 and 1.9:** Shot-reverse shot structure in *Bird of Paradise*; Luana (Dolores del Río) looks anxiously at the local prince she is to marry (uncredited) despite her feelings for a White sailor played by Joel McCrea. The character's gazes intersect in an *eyeline match*, helping to create a clear sense of spatial relationships. Screen captures.

Source: *Bird of Paradise*
Attribution: King Vidor
License: Public domain

**Figure 1.10 and 1.11:** Point-of-view shot structure in a scene from *Bird of Paradise* featuring Joel McCrea (right) and Dolores del Río. Screen captures.

Source: *Bird of Paradise*
Attribution: King Vidor
License: Public domain

Sound works with the visual aspects of film style to provide story information and create atmosphere. Dialogue informs us about situations, characters, and relationships, while noise tells us about the physical characteristics of the environment. In discussing sound, critics make two distinctions. First, is the source of the sound visible or not (**onscreen sound** vs. **offscreen sound**, including voiceover)? Second, does the sound believably belong to the fictional world or diegesis of the film (**diegetic sound** vs. **non-diegetic sound**)? The most common form of non-diegetic sound is the musical score included in many films. Usually, we are not meant to imagine that musicians are playing just out of sight. That is, they do not inhabit the same fictional world as the characters.

The next section goes beyond what we see and hear while watching a film to consider what needs to be in place for a film to get made and consumed by audiences. This context helps us understand cinema's broader impact.

## THE LIFECYCLE OF A MOVIE: PRODUCTION, DISTRIBUTION, EXHIBITION

Critics often divide the lifecycle of a film into three stages: production, distribution, and exhibition. Since they are happening simultaneously for different films, production, distribution, and exhibition can also be considered distinct sectors of the movie business. Defined broadly, **production** includes everything that happens from the original idea for a movie to a finished product that can be passed on to distributors. **Distribution** refers to the business deals, marketing, and logistics needed for films to be shown to the public. **Exhibition** refers to the presentation of films in theaters and (usually later) on television, home video, and streaming services. We could also include the film's **reception**—the response of critics and audiences—as part of its lifecycle.

The way that each of these phases typically unfolds in Hollywood helps explain why it remains rather unwelcoming to groups that have historically been marginalized from the industry. Beginning in the 1920s, major Hollywood studios have limited the success of competitors by cooperating closely and integrating all stages of a film's lifecycle. Until the late 1940s, the "Big Five" studios (MGM, Paramount, RKO, Universal, and Warner Bros.) had achieved **vertical integration,** meaning they not only produced movies but also had control over distribution and exhibition. Owning theaters gave them guaranteed venues for their slate of releases and allowed them to shut out independent films. Studios could also oblige independent theaters to screen their entire line-up of films. In 1948, the Supreme Court ruled that the studios' business practices unfairly stifled competition in violation of US law. Studios were forced to sell off their movie theater chains, but they still controlled distribution, meaning that the range of films available to audiences did not change radically. In 2020, this ruling was reversed at the federal government's request ("[Federal Court](#)"). By this time, Netflix, which was not covered under the earlier ruling, had already started to purchase its own movie theaters while also being involved in the production of films.

Production is the phase of a film's lifecycle that typically gets the most attention; we usually think less about what is involved in getting a film in front of audiences once it is complete. Production can be divided into four phases: development, pre-production, shooting, and post-production. Development refers to the process of going from an idea to a complete script and then to a viable film project with a director, main actors, and financing lined up. The film's producer works to bring these elements into place. In pre-production, casting is completed and the other aspects of the mise-en-scène are created to prepare for shooting. Post-production refers to the processes like editing, color correction, and sound mixing, which are necessary to assemble and polish the footage created during shooting to create a finished product.

As practiced in Hollywood, the production of films is an incredibly expensive activity that requires significant financial backing. Most films require not only complex technology but also the labor of hundreds of workers with highly specialized skills. One of the factors that allowed the US film industry to dominate internationally starting in the 1920s was a high level of investment not from the studios themselves, but from banks (Bordwell et al. 313–17). Although not every film in a studio's line-up was big-budget, film industries in other countries and independent producers found this level of spending difficult to match. Today, outspending the competition continues to be a strategy used by the major US film studios to maintain their market share.

If there are financial obstacles to making a film outside the Hollywood system—which are challenging but not impossible to overcome—entering the system is also difficult. The studio labor force is organized in a very top-down manner with a clear chain of command, but this does not mean that workers advance along a clear career ladder. Entry-level workers often advance slowly, making lateral career moves rather than moving up to high-profile creative roles like that of the director. Historically, this was the sole option for newcomers wanting to break into the business. It was not until the 1970s that attending film school became a viable path for aspiring filmmakers to hone their skills, but this path does not guarantee success. Along with agents and managers, whose representation is often necessary for creatives to secure work, Hollywood unions also play a role in limiting the entry of newcomers to the industry. By bringing workers together in collective action—including strikes if deemed necessary—unions help set fair wages and enforce safe and humane working conditions. Major film shoots are governed by union agreements. For the most part, only directors, producers, writers, stars, and crew who already belong to the relevant union are able to work on major films. When a new creative team is assembled for each film, there is rarely a formal recruiting process. Personal recommendations weigh very heavily. The importance of personal connections eliminates many opportunities to counter bias related to race, gender, sexuality, and other factors during the hiring process.

Over time, the popularization of 16mm (which is more affordable than the standard 35mm film) and later digital cameras made it cheaper to make independent films. However, arranging distribution and exhibition continue to be the main barriers to these films' success. Although a film's distribution and exhibition can happen only once it is complete, these phases of its lifecycle must be considered from the development phase. Producers must find a company or companies to place their films in theaters at home and abroad. Distributors also negotiate the financial terms that govern how much money from ticket sales goes to the movie theater and how much ultimately goes back to the studio and creative team. The presale of distribution rights is now a key aspect of the development phase and serves as an important source of financing for films. Essentially, this is a cash advance on a film's potential future profits. Distribution deals are difficult to obtain without the backing of an established production company—although film festivals can sometimes help directors land them—and ultimately determine how widely a movie will be shown in theaters. Home viewing on TV, DVD/Blu-ray, or streaming has only become more important in recent years. Yet a theatrical release is still pivotal for raising a film's profile and helping it find an audience among home viewers.

Beyond the role of a theatrical run in generating attention for a film, streaming services do not offer as many possibilities for filmmakers to get their work seen as they might seem to at first. With so much content online, it is difficult for independent films to find interested audiences. In addition, a small number of huge, powerful media companies own the most popular portals for online streaming. These companies can quickly change the rules regarding what kind of content they accept and the terms governing the financial returns that creatives can see from their work. When Amazon Prime Video Direct launched in 2016, anyone could upload a film to the service. If it was accepted, creators would collect a flat fee for every hour customers watched. In early 2021, Amazon announced it would no longer accept unsolicited submissions of documentaries or shorts ([Lindahl and Harris-Bridson](#)). Similarly, in 2018, YouTube made it impossible for users to make videos available for rent or purchase on the platform, though they can still monetize their content in other ways if their videos are sufficiently popular ([“Paid Content”](#)). Other sites like Vimeo still allow creators to sell and rent videos online, but they are less familiar to casual viewers.

When streaming services get into the business of producing films, it can be a double-edged sword for filmmakers. Companies like Netflix, which produced well-received Latinx-cast shows like *One Day at a Time* (2017-2019) and *Gentefied* (2020-2021) do not necessarily have a stronger track record in the area of diversity and inclusion than long-established entertainment companies. In 2018 and 2019, the most recent years for which data is available, only 5.9% of speaking roles in Netflix original series and films made in the United States went to Latinx individuals, who made up an estimated 18.5% of the US population at that time ([Smith et al](#). 11). Nor are these companies necessarily more open than others to unproven talents; rather, they often seek to offer lucrative deals to established creatives. Furthermore, filmmakers have little to no control over whether their film will receive a theatrical release at all. Typically, they receive no financial benefits based on how popular a film proves to be with viewers on the platform or elsewhere. In fact, unlike box office figures or television ratings, streaming services' viewing numbers are usually not revealed to the public and can't be independently verified.

Whether films find an audience is pivotal, not only for recouping the high costs of production but also for its impact on the culture at large. From the perspective of film studies, one can study a movie in isolation, but the full picture does not emerge until one considers how different viewers received it and what proved meaningful for them about the themes, characters, and style. As the academic area of fan studies recognizes, engagement with media may go far beyond viewing and listening to encompass fan fiction, cosplay, and participation in online fan communities. Given the present-day impact of social media, fans can make their opinions known publicly and even pressure studios to include or cut specific characters or storylines.

In making sense of the reception phase of a film's lifecycle, some scholars try to establish general principles of how audiences engage with films based on their basic technical set-up—for example, screening films in a darkened room that isolates viewers from the outside world—or their style. One example is the influential idea of a male gaze in cinema (Mulvey). This refers not solely to shots from male characters' point of view, but rather to all aspects of a film's style that present women as beautiful but passive objects to be looked at. Other film scholars take an ethnographic or historical approach to delve into the reactions of actual audience members. They might use interviews and oral histories with living viewers or historical documents like diaries or film reviews, which represent the opinion of critics but can give some sense of how a film was received. Of particular interest are the reactions of spectators whose perspectives do not align with the film's implicit point of view, which in Hollywood has historically been White, straight, and middle-class. Viewers may suspend their own sense of personal identity and align themselves with a hero who does not resemble them; read a film against the grain (one example would be taking pleasure in a homoerotic subtext, intentional or otherwise, in a film that lacks overt queer themes); or react actively by boycotting or campaigning against a film.

Gaining a fuller understanding of the lifecycle of a film, including the importance of reception, reminds us that while industry barriers may have limited the presence of Latinx individuals in front of and behind the camera, the community has nevertheless exercised considerable agency in its reception of films. Later chapters will explore the history and present of Latinx film and media production through a variety of lenses.

**Rielle Navitski** *is an Associate Professor in the Department of Theatre and Film Studies at the University of Georgia. She is the author of* Public Spectacles of Violence: Sensational Cinema and Journalism in Early Twentieth-Century Mexico and Brazil *(Duke University Press, 2017) and co-editor of* Cosmopolitan Film Cultures in Latin America, 1896-1960 *(Indiana University Press, 2017). Currently she is working on a book manuscript entitled "Transatlantic Cinephilia: Networks of Film Culture Between Latin America and France, 1945-1965" (under contract, University of California Press).*

## BIBLIOGRAPHY

Bordwell, David, et al. *The Classical Hollywood Cinema: Film Style and Mode of Production to 1960*. Columbia UP, 1985.

"Federal Court Terminates Paramount Consent Decrees." *Department of Justice*, 7 Aug. 2020, https://web.archive.org/web/20210415154358/https://www.justice.gov/opa/pr/federal-court-terminates-paramount-consent-decrees. Press release.

*Inequality in 1,300 Popular Films: Examining Portrayals of Gender, Race/Ethnicity, LGBTQ & Disability from 2007 to 2019*. USC Annenberg Inclusion Initiative, Sept. 2020, https://assets.uscannenberg.org/docs/aii-inequality_1300_popular_films_09-08-2020.pdf.

Jones, Nicholas, et al. "2020 Census Illuminates Racial and Ethnic Composition of the Country." *United States Census Bureau*, 12 Aug. 2021, https://www.census.gov/library/stories/2021/08/improved-race-ethnicity-measures-reveal-united-states-population-much-more-multiracial.html.

Lindahl, Chris, and Dana Harris-Bridson. "Amazon Prime Video Direct and the Dystopian Decision to Stop Accepting Documentaries." *IndieWire*, 24 Feb. 2021, https://www.indiewire.com/2021/02/amazon-prime-video-direct-stop-accepting-documentaries-1234617608/

Mulvey, Laura. "Visual Pleasure and Narrative Cinema." *Screen*, vol. 16, no. 3, 1975, pp. 6–18.

"Paid Content Discontinued January 1, 2018." *YouTube Help*, https://support.google.com/youtube/answer/7515570?hl=en. Accessed 1 May 2022.

Smith, Stacy L., et al. *Inclusion in Netflix Original U.S. Scripted Series & Films*. USC Annenberg Inclusion Initiative, 26 Feb. 2021, https://assets.uscannenberg.org/docs/aii-inclusion-netflix-study.pdf.

## FOR FURTHER STUDY

Bordwell, David, and Kristin Thompson. *Film Art: An Introduction*. 9th ed., McGraw Hill, 2010.

---. *Film History: An Introduction*. 4th ed., McGraw Hill, 2019.

Braudy, Leo, and Marshall Cohen. *Film Theory and Criticism: Introductory Readings*. 8th ed., Oxford UP, 2016.

# 2

# Television
Crystal Camargo
(Northwestern University)

**Figure 2.1: Television**
Source: Flickr
Attribution: Esther Vargas
License: CC BY-ND 2.0

Why study television? For starters, television is everywhere. While you probably think of TV primarily in your living room and bedroom, you can also find TV screens in bars, salons, stores, airports, waiting rooms, and many other public places. Moreover, you can access TV content virtually anywhere from your smartphone. In other words, TV undeniably enters people's everyday lives in different spaces, multiple times a day. Today, US adults spend an average of 4.2 hours watching TV each day, with people spending more time watching TV on phones, tablets, and laptops than in front of traditional TV screens ("Nielsen Total Audience Report"). As of 2021, half of US Latinx adults still use traditional cable and satellite services, with more and more Latinx people opting for on-demand streaming platforms like Netflix and Hulu ("Latinx Millennial"). By thinking of television as something that is everywhere in our culture and on different types of screens, we can start to understand how television continues to shift and change, as do its social and cultural impacts.

As a form of mass communication, television is a place where ideas about Latinx people and culture are present. Fictional and nonfictional forms of TV representation—a Latino comedian on a sitcom or a Latina news anchor on the evening news—can reinforce or challenge mainstream notions of what it means to be a Latinx person in the United States. Representation matters to people. Portrayals of Latinxs on television not only affect how others see Latinx people, but it affects how Latinx people see themselves. Across broadcast, cable, and streaming services, on-screen Latinx TV representation makes up less than 6% compared to the 18.5% of Latinx people that make up the US population ("Being Seen on Screen"). The lack of Latinx portrayal on television is discussed on popular culture sites, newspapers, and social media platforms like Twitter. People are often outraged that the TV industry underrepresents Latinx communities compared to other racial and ethnic groups, namely White, non-Latinx Americans. Yet the underrepresentation of Latinx people and culture on television is not a new phenomenon.

The struggle for more Latinx TV representation can be traced back to the late 1960s and early 1970s during the peak of the Chicana/o and Puerto Rican movements. These activists fought for improvements in Latinx representation in both film and TV and the hiring of Latinx talent in various production roles in the media industry (Noriega 24–25). More than six decades later, the National Hispanic Media Coalition and other advocacy organizations address the similar lack of employment and portrayal of Latinx people on and behind the television screen that early Chicana/o and Latinx media activists highlighted in their ongoing struggle for Latinx representation on television (Beltrán, "Latina/os on TV!" 31–32).

The ubiquity of television, the intricate ways it is woven into everyday life, and its complicated relationship with Latinx people and culture can make the study of TV seem challenging to analyze. What follows in this chapter will provide you with new ways to critically think about television and begin to account for its unique relationship with Latinx people and representation. In the next pages, major concepts from the academic study of television will provide a foundation for interrogating four elements of television studies: the historical evolution of TV, TV production, narrative structure, and aesthetics.

**Figure 2.2: A billboard for the hit TV show *Jane the Virgin* (2014–2019) in New York City in 2014.**

Source: Flickr
Attribution: Mike Steele
License: CC BY-ND 2.0

One popular approach to the study of television is the content of TV shows themselves; for example, the aesthetics and visual styles used in a TV text or the representations of race and gender we see on the screen. Another popular approach is the examination of industrial practices and structures that produce such TV shows. For example, one might consider the role of the show's writer-producer or the costs of acquiring the rights to a TV series remake or reboot, such as in the case of the Latinx-led *One Day at a Time* (2017–2020). Studying television audiences, specifically how viewers react and relate to TV texts, is yet another approach to TV analysis. This method might consider if and how Latinx queer people relate to Latinx queer representation in *Love, Victor* (2020–) or *Vida* (2018–2019).

Lastly, you can consider the broader cultural and societal impacts of television itself. TV addresses and comments on ongoing political and societal debates; for example, family separation and deportation. You can see this political issue reflected in fictional and nonfictional TV series that premiered in 2020, such as the remake of *Party of Five* (2020) that was centered on everyday struggles of family separation, and the documentary series *Deportation Nation* (2020) that examines the bureaucracy of US immigration enforcement. Keep in mind that these four approaches to TV analysis are only four of many, and their complexities have been simplified for this explanation.

# BRIEF OVERVIEW OF US TELEVISUAL LANDSCAPE

When the US English-language television industry began in the late 1940s and early 1950s, there were only four major television networks: ABC, CBS, NBC, and the DuMont Television Network (DuMont only lasted for a couple of years). In addition to purchasing their first TV set, Americans only required electricity and an antenna to tune into these three or four channels for free. This was because TV followed a similar business model to radio broadcasting, where television networks covered the cost of programming and distribution by selling commercial airtime to advertisers to promote their products and services. Until the mid-1980s, these three robust networks (ABC, CBS, NBC) controlled the US television's commercial market, creation, and distribution. This period is called the **network era** of television.

As early work on US Latinx television demonstrates, Latinx representation during the network era was limited and marginalized. Despite the television industry's location in Los Angeles—home to the nation's largest Mexican American community—Latinx people did not occupy creative roles in television for decades, except for Cuban Desi Arnaz in *I Love Lucy* (1951–1957; Beltrán, *Latino TV* 13). As the first Latinx person to co-produce, write, and star in their own TV show, Arnaz was not joined by other Latinx producers and writers until the 1970s. These first programs created and produced by Latinxs, predominately Chicanas/os and Puerto Ricans, aired on American publicly funded broadcast television, not on a Big Three network (Beltrán, *Latino TV* 7; Noriega 139–48). Broadcast television did not see another Latinx star in a scripted TV show for another twenty years until Puerto Rican–Hungarian Freddie Prinze starred as a Chicano in East Los Angeles in NBC's *Chico and the Man* (1974–1977).

Due to technological changes impacting the transmission of television, US TV transitioned from a business model controlled by only a few networks into a **post-network era**. In this post-network era, television became multi-channeled with a shift from free broadcast television to paid commercial content. Through the expansion of **cable equipment** in the late 1980s and the development of the **digital video recorder** (DVR) in the early 2000s, television has had multiple iterations of the post-network era, impacting the content available and the timing/airing of such programming. Gone are the days of only having access to three networks and local public television stations. Now viewers have more than fifty national TV networks that air for free, hundreds of TV channels to view with paid cable and satellite services, and nearly two hundred on-demand streaming services.

According to TV scholar Amanda Lotz, who popularized the term "post-network era," television in the twenty-first century is marked by digital technologies and devices, such as the rise of video-on-demand services (e.g., Netflix and Hulu) and mobile telephone/tablet viewing (233–37). With limited options, TV viewers used to watch the same shows at the same times. Now, with thousands of TV shows available, worldwide programming, and video-on-demand content, TV viewers rarely watch the same programs at the same time. Even when you *do* watch the same programs as your friends and family, such as the ten most watched media texts on Netflix, you might view them in different contexts (at home vs. on a plane) and on different devices (TV screen vs. cellphone).

While you may think Netflix, Hulu, Amazon Prime Video, YouTube, and many other streaming services are similar, they all have different business models for monetizing content. For example, **subscription video on demand** (SVOD), such as Netflix, HBO Max, and Disney+, has a flat rate per month, allowing the viewer to determine how much content they want to view each month. On the other hand, **transactional video on demand** (TVOD) is the opposite of monthly subscription video. Here consumers can purchase content on a pay-per-view basis, such as buying a TV series episode or a film. In addition, much like broadcast television, **advertising-based video on demand** (AVOD) is free to consumers if they sit and watch short commercials. An example of AVOD is IMDb Original Videos, through which TV and movies are available for free but include several commercials throughout each episode and film viewing. Whether SVOD, TVOD, or AVOD, all streaming platforms have incorporated a wide range of TV shows and films, transforming how we access both television and film under one viewing location.

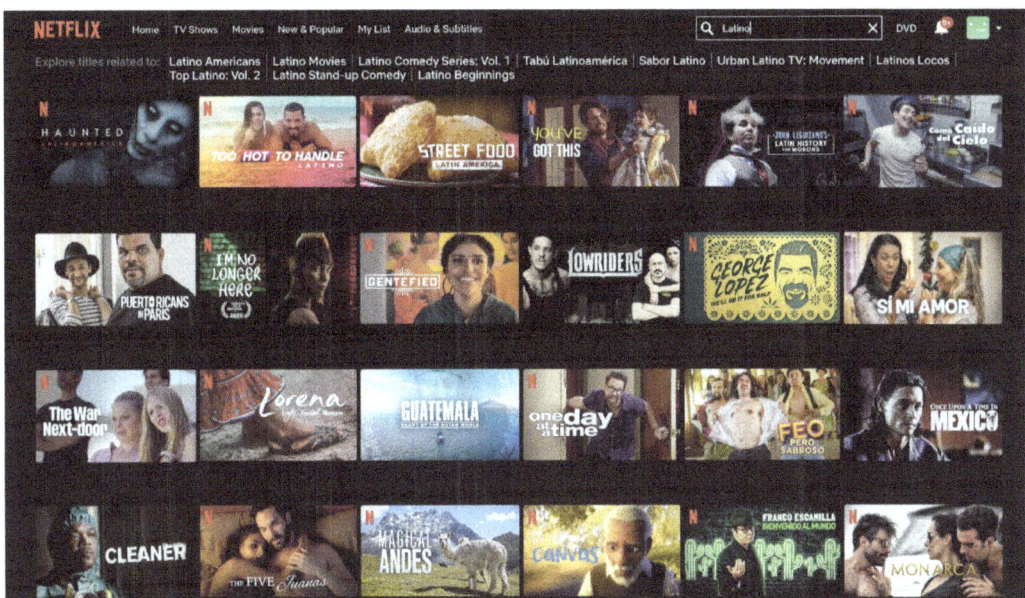

**Figure 2.3: Latinx TV shows and films that appear when searching "Latino" on Netflix.**

Source: Netflix
Attribution: Netflix
License: Fair Use

Unlike the Big Three networks, whose content targeted middle-class White Americans, multi-channels in the post-network era offer programming for niche audiences, which has impacted Latinx representation. A **niche audience** refers to a particular subset of an audience, like women, Latinx, or queer folks. The focus on smaller audiences, such as the Latinx community, has diversified Latinx representation in the last two decades (2000–2020). For example, the early 2000s saw the first nationwide scripted TV shows produced by Latinx people and centered on Latino and Latina lead characters: *George Lopez* (2002–2007) and *Ugly Betty* (2006–2010; Beltrán, *Latino TV* 147–59). While these early shows premiered on network television (NBC, CBS, ABC), the shift to multi-channel and niche audiences transformed the televisual landscape to include diverse, multicultural programming. Due to this shift, the 2010s witnessed a proliferation of Latinx representation on television, amongst other economic reasons. These Latinx-led TV series were produced by the first Latinx, namely Latina, co-producers, showrunners, and writers (Beltrán, *Latino TV* 163). Additionally, with the introduction of digital platforms, in the early 2020s these sites have increasingly become *the* place for Latinx TV representation. For example, *One Day at a Time*, *Gentefied* (2020–2021), and *On My Block* (2019–2021) all premiered on Netflix. Essentially, in the post-network era, television has seen a diversification of programming targeting a wide range of Latinx communities.

## TV PRODUCTION: SHOWRUNNER

Every television show has a creative voice that guides the series from the inception of each episode idea to the finished product we watch. In film, this person is called the director, whereas the TV industry calls this person a showrunner. A **showrunner** is the person who has overall creative authority and management responsibility for a TV program. This person (or persons) are responsible for overseeing all areas of writing and production on a television series, ensuring that each episode is delivered on time and on budget for the production studio that produces the show and the network or platform that airs it. The word showrunner is often used interchangeably with writer-producer or creator of a TV series, but these three terms are different. A **writer-producer** is a person who helps write and produce a TV show. The showrunner is always (or nearly always) a writer-producer of the show; however, a writer-producer is not always a showrunner. Furthermore, each show has multiple executive producers helping with writing, producing, post-production, and managerial roles. Still, they are not necessarily involved with every aspect in the way that a showrunner is. A TV show **creator** is a person or persons who developed the idea for the series but may or may not be the showrunner. The creator is often an executive producer and may be a writer-producer.

Are you confused yet? If so, that is okay. These are complex industrial terms. For example, *One Day at a Time* (*ODAAT*)—a sitcom about a Cuban American single mother raising a teenage daughter and a middle-school-aged son with her Cuban émigré mother in Los Angeles—is a great example of these similar and yet different TV industrial positions. It is also a sitcom based on the 1975 series of the same name created by Norman Lear. In the contemporary version of *ODAAT* that reimagines the original series with a Cuban family instead of a White American family, Norman Lear is an executive producer and original creator, but he is not a showrunner. Instead, Gloria Calderón Kellett and Mike Royce are the showrunners who hold the sitcom's creative authority and management responsibility on each workday. Calderón Kellett and Royce are also writer-producers of the sitcom remake. Lear is still involved with the series, but he is not involved with everyday aspects of the financial, creative, and collaborative nature of running the TV show. He might be involved with specific aspects of the series but does not deal with the budget and production hassles that Calderón Kellett and Royce do.

Overall, showrunners have become central figures in the evolution of television as a medium. Combining managerial and creative roles, showrunners function as television auteurs/directors in complex and rapidly evolving ways, illustrating what it takes to create, write, and run a scripted TV series in today's televisual landscape (Bennett 19–27). For starters, they shape the artistic content and style of TV series. Both Calderón Kellett and Royce shaped the Latinx, queer, and veteran focus of *ODAAT*, adding a new direction that the original 1975 sitcom did not have. Showrunners learn to operate all business aspects of the television industry, even in extreme circumstances. After Netflix canceled *ODAAT,* Calderón Kellett and Royce worked around their Netflix contract that prevented them from airing the series on a broadcast network and found a new home on another on-demand streaming service instead.

Lastly, the work of showrunners has become a platform for discussing larger socio-cultural issues—gender, race and representation, and politics—both in and through television. Calderón Kellett and Royce have received praise for their dedication to diversity in front of and behind the camera. In the second season of *ODAAT*, 50% of writing staff were female and 50% were people of color, higher than the national average, in which women made up 44% of all TV writers while people of color made up only 35% (*WGAW*). Furthermore, Calderón Kellett and Royce lead a team of writers and actors to shed light on issues relating to the LGBTQ community, veterans, and immigration and deportation. For example, Elena (played by Isabella Gomez) is the first Latina character to come out as queer on a sitcom. Calderón Kellett and Royce indirectly made television history by in influencing Latinx representation.

## TV STYLE: NARRATIVE STRUCTURE AND AESTHETICS

Like cinema, television is a story machine where you, too, can analyze visual and acoustic elements, such as mise-en-scène and editing, as described in the previous chapter. However, there are stylistic elements and narrative differences between the television show and the film. In media studies, we refer to these differences as **medium specificity**. Film, television, and digital media allow for different forms of storytelling that are particular to the stylistic and narrative properties of that medium. For example, a feature film can present a situation/circumstance, a disruption of that situation, and then a resolution of that disruption, all within a two-hour frame. While a film can belong to a trilogy or franchise, it always presents some form of narrative conclusion. Television, on the other hand, does not have to obey the rules or restrictions of a film. A twenty-four-episode season, for example, allows for a different type of storytelling; one where character development, conflicts, and resolutions can develop over several episodes or even seasons. This section will discuss key narrative forms and TV aesthetics specific to television itself, illustrating how these television forms are crucial to our understanding of television content.

Two types of narratives forms that contribute to television storytelling are serial and episodic structures. **Serial television** is when a show's story unfolds over multiple episodes, seasons, or even during the duration of an entire series. Serials are a descendant of radio soaps and have been a staple of TV storytelling for over six decades. A television series may reveal parts of plot, conflict, or character developments in each new episode. Sometimes this occurs weekly or daily in a soap opera or **telenovela**, depending on the genre's format. TV serials disclose essential information piece by piece while relying on heavy repetition, allowing viewers to remember information from the previous episodes while making sense of the new clues and information they are receiving.

Latinx-centered shows like *East Los High* (2013–2017); *Jane the Virgin* (2014–2019); *Love, Victor*; *On My Block;* and *Ugly Betty* are all examples of TV serials. In the case of *Jane the Virgin*—a US remake of a Venezuelan telenovela about a devoted Catholic and virgin who gets artificially inseminated due to a mix-up at a clinic—the series relies on a narrator to provide seriality. This off-screen, omniscient narrator recaps essential details from the previous episode, providing heavy repetition while narrating new information through the series' beloved characters, conflict, and resolutions. However, many TV series do not rely on narrators like *Jane the Virgin* and instead provide seriality in different ways. For example, *Love, Victor* is a coming-of-age story about a half-Puerto Rican, half-Colombian American teen struggling with his sexual orientation. Due to the premise of the series, *Love, Victor* explores different aspects of Victor's gay identity, from questioning his identity to coming out to his best friend and parents, all in the first season. In this example, seriality is provided by the coming-of-age/coming-out genre.

**Episodic television** is when a TV show's plot, conflict, and resolution unfold within a single episode in a three-act structure. Episodic is the opposite of seriality. The TV show will reveal all the necessary information to understand the situation or conflict at hand and solve it all in one episode. Unlike **TV anthologies**, such as *Black Mirror* (2011–2019), whose situation, conflict, and resolution also happen in one episode but each with a different set of characters, episodic series showcase the same set of primary characters in the duration of the series. We commonly see this narrative form in sitcoms. Short for situation comedy, a **sitcom** is a distinctive TV genre primarily defined by its structure and the central role of comedy. Each episode is built around a particular situation or problem, often centered on a family or close group of friends. Historically speaking, sitcoms were the first TV fictional genre to openly discuss race, reproductive rights, and wartime conflict. Due to their episodic form, centrality of comedy, and their historical focus on families, sitcoms can introduce a wide range of opinions through various characters on issues that were once taboo.

The sitcom occupies an important place in the construction of **Latinidad** (Latino-ness; discourses and experiences of Latina/o/x identity) in popular culture, as the sitcom was one of the first TV genres to include Latinx representation in the 1950s. Television scholars have examined significant moments in the history of Latinx representation in sitcoms, such as the role of Chicana/o activism in *Chico and the Man* (Noriega 70–71; Beltrán, *Latina/o Stars in U.S. Eyes* 88–91) or the influence of Cuban television in the first bilingual sitcom, *¿Qué Pasa, USA?* (1977–1980; Rivero 97). Latinx comedians, such as Paul Rodriguez, John Leguizamo, George Lopez, Cristela Alonzo, and Gabriel Iglesias, have also transitioned from stand-up comedy to TV sitcoms often starring themselves.

Figure 2.4: The cast of ABC's sitcom *Cristela* (2014) at Disney, starring stand-up comedian Cristela Alonzo (center) as co-creator/executive producer and actress.

Source: Flickr
Attribution: Walt Disney
License: CC BY-ND 2.0

Serial and episodic television allows for two distinct types of storytelling to occur on television. For example, serialization rewards loyal viewers who tune in to each episode, as these series tend to reveal little bits and pieces of the plot and situation over various episodes. On the other hand, episodic provides everything from the main story and conflict to solution in a tight episode due to narrative structure. As a result, viewers are not enticed to watch every episode in order as they are when watching serial television. For example, you could skip an episode from a sitcom or procedural crime show, such as *Law and Order: Special Victims Unit* (1999–), and not miss any crucial information since each episode introduces the plot, situation, and resolution. If you skipped or missed an episode from a serial TV show, however, you might miss out on tidbits to help you further understand the plot or a particular character's persona. To be sure, you can find elements of seriality in episodic television and vice versa. These narrative forms are not fixed or static categories, as the evolution of television is changing how stories are being told. For example, *ODAAT*, a sitcom, serializes Elena's coming-out story arc over the first season instead of having one special episode that focuses on her queer identity.

Aesthetics, such as the use of a close-up on a beloved character's silly face, also enhance the pleasure and emotional engagement of television. The use of visual and sonic aesthetics on television can be thematic or a stylistic choice influenced by a TV genre. For example, sitcoms tend to use a three-camera studio setup and can be filmed in front of a large audience (Dalton and Linder 2). **Three-camera setup**, also known as multiple-camera setup, is a method of TV production commonly used in sports events, news, soap operas, talk and game shows, and most sitcoms. It involves using three simultaneously recording cameras instead of one, taking footage from various angles and maximizing filming time, which is essential when recording shows with a live audience.

A multi-camera show, such as a sitcom, is often accompanied by a live audience or laugh track. The origin of live audiences on television stems from the desire of creating a theatre-like, communal feeling from the comfort of one's couch. A **laugh track** is a pre-recorded soundtrack that contains the laughter of an audience. In some productions, a live audience might be used, while others might opt for artificial laughter. In both cases, a live audience or a laugh track guides your reaction to the performances you see onscreen. The loudness or duration of a laugh indirectly cues how funny a joke or situation is, which scholars have argued can construct biases around race, gender, and sexuality. For example, Alfred Martin, Jr., found that Black-cast sitcoms use more laugh tracks with Black gay characters than Black straight male ones (104–40). Sitcoms can add, subtract, or entirely reconstitute laughter based on the producers' aim or goal in a scene or episode. In the case of a live audience, cue cards are used to encourage the audience to laugh at particular times.

The examples in this chapter have provided a basic understanding of television, highlighting some of the industry barriers and achievements of Latinx professionals. By examining the evolution of the US television industry, the role of a showrunner, and specific TV narrative structures and aesthetics, this chapter has introduced several tools and perspectives to analyze Latinx production and representation. Later chapters will continue to explore Latinx representation, history, and industry politics through various lenses, such as queer identity and US Spanish-language television.

**Crystal Camargo** *is a PhD candidate in the Department of Radio/Television/Film at Northwestern University. Her research explores Latinx representation at the intersections of television studies, language ideologies, and critical race and ethnic studies in US English- and Spanish-language television. She has been published in* Journal for Cinema and Media Studies, Flow, *and* SCMS +. *She received her BA in International Studies, Spanish Language & Literature, and Gender & Women's Studies from the University of Denver and MA in Screen Cultures from Northwestern.*

## BIBLIOGRAPHY

"Being Seen on Screen: Diverse Representation and Inclusion on TV." *The Nielsen Company*, 2 Dec. 2020, https://www.nielsen.com/us/en/insights/report/2020/being-seen-on-screen-diverse-representation-and-inclusion-on-tv/.

Beltrán, Mary. *Latina/o Stars in U.S. Eyes: The Making and Meanings of Film and TV Stardom*. U of Illinois P, 2009.

---. "Latina/os on TV!: A Proud (and Ongoing) Struggle Over Representation and Authorship." *The Routledge Companion to Latina/o Popular Culture*, edited by Frederick Aldama. Routledge, 2016, pp. 39–49.

---. *Latino TV: A History*. NYU Press, 2022.

Bennett, Tara. *Showrunners: The Art of Running a TV Show*. Titan Books, 2014.

Dalton, Mary M., and Laura R. Linder, editors. *The Sitcom Reader: America Viewed and Skewed*. SUNY P, 2005.

"The Latinx Millennial Love Affair with Netflix." *Horowitz Research*, 28 June 2019, https://www.horowitzresearch.com/press/the-latinx-millennial-love-affair-with-netflix-new-horowitz-research/.

Lotz, Amanda D. *The Television Will Be Revolutionized*. 2nd ed., NYU P, 2014.

Martin Jr., Alfred L. *The Generic Closet: Black Gayness and the Black-Cast Sitcom*. Indiana UP, 2021.

"The Nielsen Total Audience Report: August 2020." *The Nielsen Company*, 13 Aug. 2020, https://www.nielsen.com/us/en/insights/report/2020/the-nielsen-total-audience-report-august-2020/.

Noriega, Chon A. *Shot in America: Television, the State, and the Rise of Chicano Cinema*. U of Minnesota P, 2000.

Rivero, Yeidy M. "Interpreting Cubanness, Americanness, and the Sitcom." *Global Television Formats: Understanding Television Across Borders*, edited by Tasha Oren and Sharon Shahaf, Routledge, 2011, pp. 90–108.

*WGAW Inclusion Report*. Writers Guild of America West, 2020.

## FILMOGRAPHY

Aptaker, Isaac, and Elizabeth Berger, creators. *Love, Victor*. Hulu, 2020–present.

Brooker, Charlie, creator. *Black Mirror*. Channel Four and Netflix, 2011–2014 and 2016–2019.

Clusiau, Christina, and Shaul Schwarz, creators. *Deportation Nation*. Netflix, 2020.

Komack, James, creator. *Chico and the Man*. NBC, 1974–1978.

Lear, Norman, Gloria Calderón Kellett, and Mike Royce, creators. *One Day at a Time*. Netflix and Pop, 2017–2020.

Lippman, Amy, and Christopher Keyser, creators. *Party of Five*. Freeform, 2020.

Lungerich, Lauren, Eddie Gonzales, and Jeremy Haft, creators. *On My Block*. Netflix, 2018–2021.

Mendoza, Manny, and Luis Santeiro, creators. *¿Qué Pasa, USA?* PBS, 1977–1980.

Portugal, Carlos, and Kathleen Bedoya, creators. *East Los High*. Population Media Center and Hulu, 2013–2018.

Saracho, Tanya, creator. *Vida*. Starz, 2018–2020.

Urman, Jennie Snyder, creator. *Jane the Virgin*. The CW, 2014–2019.

Urman, Jennie Snyder, Jessica O'Toole, and Amy Rardin, creators. *Charmed*. The CW, 2018–present.

Wolf, Dick, creator. *Law and Order: Special Victims Unit*. NBC, 1999–Present.

## FOR FURTHER STUDY

Alonzo, Cristela, and Kevin Hench, creators. *Cristela*. ABC, 2014–2015.

Báez, Jillian. "Latina/os Audiences as Citizens." *Contemporary Latina/o Media: Production, Circulation, Politics*, edited by Arlene Dávila and Yeidy M. Rivero, NYU P, 2014, pp. 267–84.

---. *In Search of Belonging: Latinas, Media, and Citizenship*. U of Illinois P, 2018.

Ball, Lucille, and Desi Arnaz, creators. *I Love Lucy*. CBS, 1951–1957.

Barrera, Aida. *Looking for Carrascolendas: From a Child's World to Award-winning Television*. U of Texas P, 2001.

Canals, Steven, Ryan Murphy, and Brad Falchuk, creators. Pose. FX, 2018–2021.

Cepeda, María Elena, and Dolores Inés Casillas, editors. *The Routledge Companion to Latina/o Media*. Routledge, 2017.

Chávez, Christopher. *Reinventing the Latino Television Viewer: Language, Ideology, and Practice*. Lexington Books, 2015.

Cherry, Marc, creator. *Desperate Housewives*. ABC, 2004–2012.

---, creator. *Devious Maids*. ABC and Lifetime, 2013–2016.

Dávila, Arlene M., and Yeidy M. Rivero, editors. *Contemporary Latina/o Media: Production, Circulation, Politics*. NYU P, 2014.

Dávila, Arlene. *Latinos, Inc.: The Marketing and Making of a People*. U of California P, 2012.

Georgaris, Dean, creator. *The Baker and the Beauty*. ABC, 2020.

Gifford, Chris, Valerie Walsh Valdes, and Eric Weiner, creators. *Dora the Explorer*. Nickelodeon, 2000–2019.

González, Tanya, and Eliza Rodriguez y Gibson. *Humor and Latina/o Camp in* Ugly Betty*: Funny Looking*. Lexington Books, 2015.

Horta, Silvio, creator. *Ugly Betty*. ABC, 2006–2010.

Iglesias, Gabriel and Kevin Hench, creators. *Mr. Iglesias*. Netflix, 2019–2020.

Kohan, Jenji, creator. *Orange is the New Black*. Netflix, 2013–2019.

Kurland, Seth, and Mario Lopez, creators. *The Expanding Universe of Ashley Garcia*. Netflix, 2020.

Lemus, Marvin, and Linda Yvette Chávez, creators. *Gentefied*. Netflix, 2020–2021.

Lloyd, Christopher and Steven Levitan, creators. *Modern Family*. ABC, 2009–2020.

Lopez, George, Bruce Helford, and Robert Borden, creators. *George Lopez*. ABC, 2002–2007.

MacKenzie, Carina Adly, creator. *Roswell, New Mexico*. The CW, 2019–present.

Mendible, Myra, editor. *From Bananas to Buttocks: The Latina Body in Popular Film and Culture*. U of Texas P, 2007.

Molina-Guzmán, Isabel. *Dangerous Curves: Latina Bodies in the Media*. NYU P, 2010.

---. *Latinas and Latinos on TV: Colorblind Comedy in the Post-racial Network Era*. U of Arizona P, 2018.

Moran, Kristin Clare Engstrand. *Listening to Latina/o Youth: Television Consumption within Families*. Peter Lang, 2011.

Murphy, Ryan, Brad Falchuk, and Ian Brennan, creators. *Glee*. Fox, 2009–2015.

Peacock, Steven, and Jason Jacobs, editors. *Television Aesthetics and Style*. Bloomsbury, 2013.

Rodriguez, Vittoria, and Mary Beltrán. "From the Bronze Screen to the Computer Screen: Latina/o Web Series and Independent Production." *The Routledge Companion to Latina/o Media*, edited by Maria Elena Cepeda and Dolores Inés Casillas. Routledge, 2016, pp. 156–170.

Rojas, Viviana, and Juan Piñón. "Spanish, English or Spanglish? Media Strategies and Corporate Struggles to Reach the Second and Later Generations of Latinos." *International Journal of Hispanic Media*, vol. 7, 2014, pp. 1–15.

Spitzer, Justin, creator. *Superstore*. NBC, 2015–2021.

Thompson, Ethan, and Jason Mittell, editors. *How to Watch Television*. NYU P, 2013.

Valdez, Jeff, Mike Cevallos, and Gibby Cevallos, creators. *The Brothers Garcia*. Nickelodeon, 2000–2004.

Valdivia, Angharad N. *Latina/os in the Media*. Polity, 2010.

Zamora, Moisés, creator. *Selena: The Series*. Netflix, 2020–2021.

# Digital Media
Javier Rivera
(University of Southern California)

In July 1993, *The New Yorker* magazine published the now iconic cartoon by Peter Steiner with the caption "On the Internet, nobody knows you're a dog." The cartoon's image displays a dog seated at a desktop computer vocalizing the caption to a fellow dog who seems fixated by the implication of the statement. The cartoon represents what are now historical narratives of what the Internet and the proliferation of what "the digital" as an emergent media technology would mean for society. The cartoon also reflects popular narratives in the 1990s about the Internet as a space where you can be whoever you want to be without experiencing the social ills of bias and judgment. In line with ideas of a techno-utopian society, rhetoric suggesting that race becomes irrelevant online mimics that of **colorblind ideologies**, or the move to disregard racial and ethnic differences and the realities of discrimination by suggesting we simply need to treat everyone equally (Nakamura and Chow-White). Therefore, much of the early research and public attention at the time was geared toward the idea that simply increasing access to digital technology would amount to a more equitable society. While equal access is imperative, the terrain of digital technologies in the twenty-first century reveals that unequal access is but one of the many areas which require our attention.

Even within the context of the **digital divide**, or the unequal access to new media technologies along ethnoracial and socioeconomic lines, differences among US Latinxs complicate the conversation on what disparities in access look like. Disparities in digital media use exist among US Latinxs along measures of age, language, and immigrant status, where usage is higher for Latinxs under fifty years of age, those that consume English-only content, and those who are born in the United States. While access should be of concern for scholars and policy makers, it should not be ignored that US Latinxs overwhelmingly use the Internet for entertainment, social media, and as a source of news (Retis). With most US Latinx users who consume digital media preferring English-language content, we have seen the spread of sites across platforms which cater to Latinx art, culture, and media, such as Buzzfeed's *Pero Like*, *Mitú*, and *Remezcla*, to name a few.

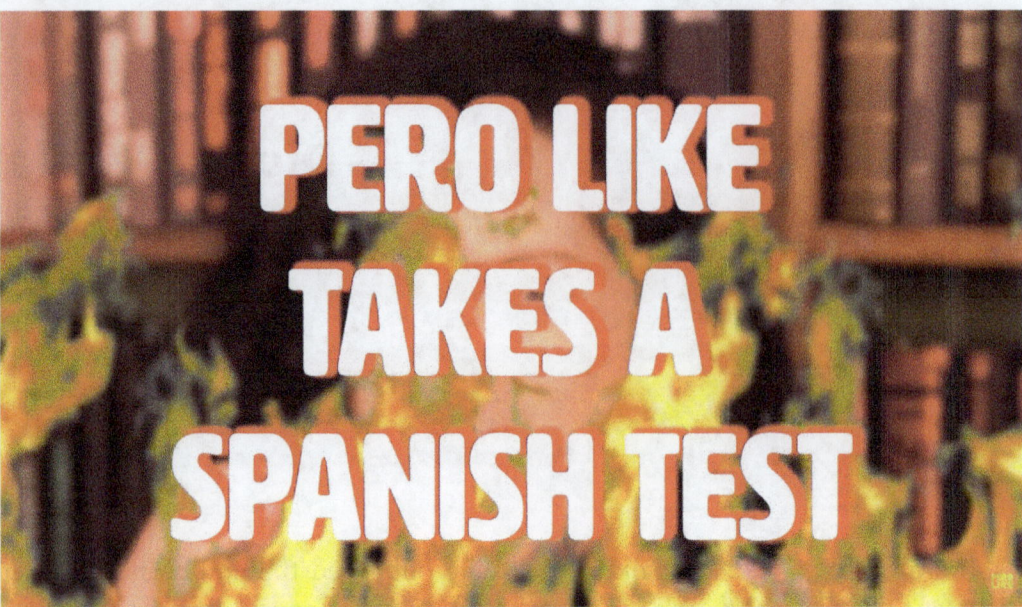

Figure 3.1: Screenshot of *Pero Like's* "Latinos Take a Spanish Test" video.
Source: Pero Like
Attribution: Pero Like
License: Fair Use

Beyond these multimedia projects, Latinx users are overrepresented among online content creators on various social media platforms, such as YouTube, which signals the importance of online media as sites of cultural production and political action (Negrón-Muntaner).

Considering the context of digital media usage for US Latinxs outlined above, this chapter will focus on the field of digital media studies and its contributions. By doing so, a set of tools will be provided to better understand how the proliferation of new technologies influences areas in media, such as the convergence of traditional film and television industries with online streaming platforms, and how the cultural production and social movements of US Latinxs in online space are shaped by **technological affordances**—specific modes of interaction that are made possible or encouraged by networked technologies—and infrastructures.

With shows such as *East Los High* (2013–2017) and *One Day at a Time* (2017–2020) bringing a US Latinx presence to online streaming platforms Hulu and Netflix respectively, it is important to consider both continuing and shifting frames of analysis needed to evaluate post-network Latinx film and television. For example, issues of inclusion in traditional media industries of broadcast and cable television have become increasingly relevant as streaming platforms like Hulu and Netflix have begun to produce their own original content within the last ten years. Online streaming platforms provide access to Latinx producers, whether it be through production companies or social media streaming services like YouTube. Latinx web producers have been found to participate in the practice of "media by any means necessary" (Rodríguez and Beltrán 167). This practice reflects a US Latinidad that is heterogeneous and at times oppositional toward dominant narratives of ethnoracial identity (Rodríguez and Beltrán). With the increasing consideration of online streaming services within film and television studies, technological affordances of production, funding, and what determines a show's cancellation become sites and strategies that require scholarly attention. This includes an expansion of what it means to study representation, production, circulation, and audience reception in a **post-network era**.

An illustrative example of this shifting terrain is the cancellation of the Netflix series *One Day at a Time* (*ODAAT*) in 2019. Based on the 1970s sitcom with the same name, *One Day at a Time* centers on a Cuban American family living in Los Angeles and frequently tackles politically pertinent issues, from immigration to homophobia. However, in March 2019 it was announced that the show would be cancelled after its third season. Soon enough, the hashtag #SaveODAAT began trending on the social media site Twitter. This reaction demonstrates what has now become a regular act of audience response to the cancellation of television series in the social networking landscape of the twenty-first century. The series was brought back for a final season but was cancelled for a second time due to the COVID-19 pandemic. This dynamic landscape of social media visibility and traditional media industries warrants consideration for the ways digital media affects conversations of production, representation, and audience.

## PLATFORMS AS SITES OF SOCIAL CONNECTION

To return to the cartoon that opens this chapter, the idea that "On the Internet, nobody knows you're a dog" refers to an increasingly unpopular notion that social connections in online space somehow lie outside of lived reality. More accurately, online cultures are a product of an interactive relationship between the technological infrastructures that facilitate new and enduring modes of connection and the desire for groups of people to imagine themselves as a part of a larger community. To consider how digital media promotes both new and old forms of social relationships, this section outlines how platforms and their infrastructures can be analyzed to understand the mediation of social ties.

In her study of teenagers' social media use, digital media scholar danah boyd outlines how **networked publics** serve as the ways that people participate in communities that are larger than themselves. boyd describes networked publics as publics which are "simultaneously (1) the space constructed through networked technologies and (2) the imagined community that emerges as a result of the intersection of people, technology, and practice" (8). **Social media**, which is considered broadly to consist of social networking sites such as Twitter and Facebook, blogs, video-sharing sites such as YouTube, and any other online platform that allows users to create their own content and facilitates interaction between groups of people in much the same way as other public spaces have done and continue to do. It is important to consider what technological affordances certain online platforms promote to their users. Affordances of online platforms to consider include persistence, visibility, spreadability, and searchability (boyd). The microblogging social media site Twitter will be used to describe each of these affordances; however, many social media sites shape interactions using these and other affordances. Persistence can be described as the ability for online content to linger. While digital content is notorious for its ephemeral nature, meaning once something is produced online it can be deleted and lost, social media platforms facilitate a persistent nature of content production. For example, Twitter will present to you a timeline of tweets from those you follow, ranging from minutes to hours or longer after they have been produced. Visibility allows for an audience to witness your content. On Twitter, the now popular hashtag is a platform affordance that can allow not only your followers but also those who search the hashtag to see your content, thus increasing its visibility. Spreadability describes how content is encouraged to be shared. This can be in the form of hyperlinks or built-in features on platforms, such as the retweet function on Twitter. Finally, searchability affords an ease to find content and therefore promote interactions among users in ways that were not considered when the content was originally made. For example, users with fan accounts of their favorite artist can scour Twitter through searching the artist's name and connect with fellow fans or, on the contrary, engage in arguments with those that may have less than favorable opinions about their favorite celebrity.

This is by no means an exhaustive list of affordances, and with new platforms emerging, there is a constant consideration of the ways social connections are mediated through networked technologies. For example, relatively recent platforms, such as the video sharing app TikTok and the audio-only app Clubhouse have reminded us how important sound is in the participatory spaces created by networked publics. While TikTok seems to be outlasting Clubhouse in sustained engagement, both platforms showcase how we must go beyond the largely text-based and visual dynamics considered in platform infrastructures.

Platforms should be viewed as sites where publics gather to establish shared relationships. However, online social engagements are highly susceptible to commodification. The Internet is often framed as an unprecedented avenue through which communities that have been excluded from the mainstream public sphere can have a voice and be visible. Yet the politics of visibility are constantly being commodified with the same tools that allow more people to produce media. The commercialization of participatory cultures in online space exists within the culture of Silicon Valley, where the data being collected from users become part of a business model. Therefore, social media is more than just a space where visibility is at stake. Consider these important questions when analyzing platforms as sites of social connection: What are the social behaviors that are encouraged, who is allowed to convene within the space, who is being excluded, and how are such interactions moderated? Finally, what forms of public meaning-making are occurring within networked publics? This last question is the focus of the following section.

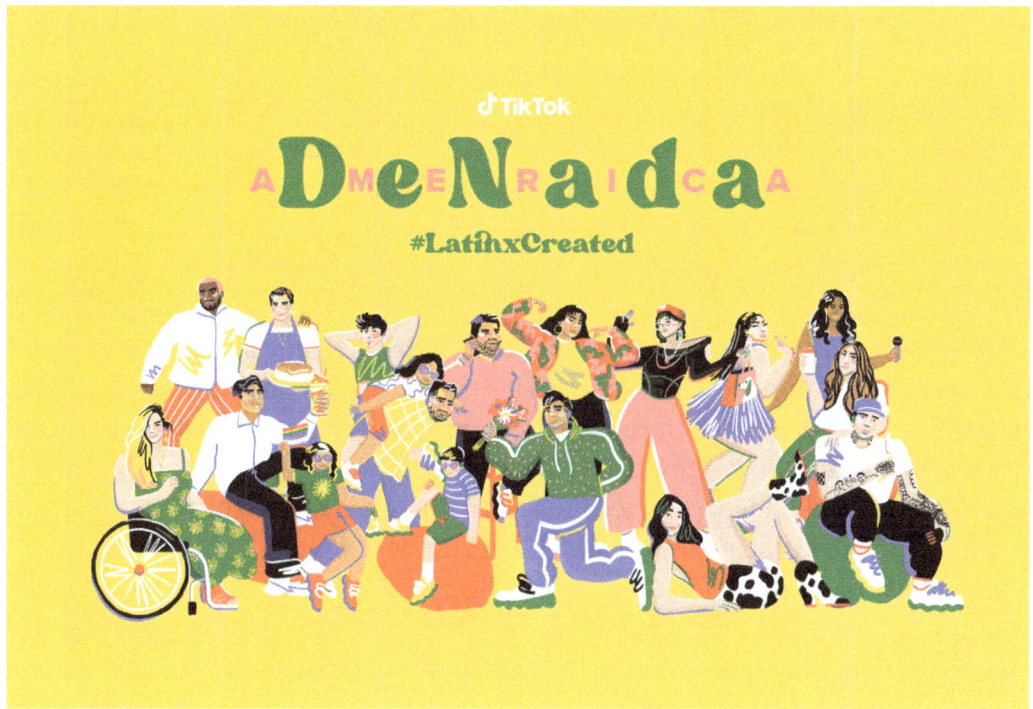

Figure 3.2: TikTok's celebration of Latinx creators during Latinx Heritage Month 2021.
Source: TikTok
Attribution: TikTok
License: Fair Use

## MEANING-MAKING AND DIGITAL MEDIA

Approaching online infrastructures with a critical lens means accepting that they are not neutral terrains. Indeed, platform functionalities carry implicit assumptions about who and how an interface should be engaged with. Here, **interface** is used to describe any online functionality, such as the affordances outlined previously, the layout of a webpage, how a website can be accessed, or any number of structural considerations. Embedded in this analysis of online structures is a consideration of power. Media studies scholar Mel Stanfill defines how power can be understood to operate when interacting with digital technologies. Therefore, it is critical to pay attention to what technology does and does not allow. The power of these possibilities creates norms of engagement with various platforms. It assumes how users will engage with a site, which discounts other possibilities. This assumption structures a user and how they should act rather than how the individual person might otherwise decide. Stanfill uses the lens of discourse to assess the productive power of online structures. The use of the term *discourse* here means how concepts are thought through and made sense of. In other words, it is the process through which we make meaning of things. Analyzing online interfaces as a discourse allows us to consider how dominant cultural ideas about user categories such as ethnoracial and gender identities, language, and other factors may contribute to a user's sense of inclusion and exclusion within an online environment.

Going beyond the interface as a specific source of meaning-making, Black digital studies scholar André Brock outlines a methodological toolkit and conceptual framework he names critical technocultural discourse analysis (CTDA). CTDA is meant to combine analyses of material technology and design (interface analysis), productions of meaning that are driven by certain technological uses, and users of technology within the space of analysis. Brock incorporates interface analysis with an analysis of discourse under the lens of critical race theory. However, the toolkit of analysis is meant to be malleable to any sort of critical and cultural theories, including but not limited to feminist, queer, and/or Latinx studies. Finally, it is important to highlight that CTDA focuses on technological artifacts, practices, and beliefs in its analysis. Therefore, it not only considers what normative use of the technology is being suggested to users, but instead it "reorients technocultural practice to the cultural context in which the artifact is being used" (Brock 1016).

To illustrate an example of how this analysis can be used, we return to TikTok shortly after the 2020 US presidential election. Exit poll results following the election revealed that all US Latinx voters, subdivided by national origin, leaned to varying degrees toward the Democratic nominee Joe Biden—except for the Cuban electorate. This sparked discourse between Latinxs within online spaces about what it means to be "Latina/o/x" and the identity politics of the ethnoracial group. On TikTok, many non-Cuban Latinxs used sounds and built-in augmented reality filters to creatively produce content that spoke to how they believe Latinxs should participate in US electoral politics. Using CTDA as a toolkit to analyze this scenario, TikTok as an artifact would require an examination of the services TikTok provides as well as its protocols. TikTok's interface and how a user is constructed (discursive interface analysis) through a meaning-making process described above would approach the platform as a practice. Finally, the beliefs TikTok mediates would come from content generated by the Latinx users and the engagement of that content. For example, Latinx studies can be used in describing this meaning-making event with concepts such as horizontal hierarchies, defined by Frances Aparicio as "horizontal differences, conflicts, tensions, and affinities between and among Latina/os of diverse national identities" (31). Therefore, the beliefs discussed by TikTok users and the technological interface are accounted for in the analysis of the platform event.

## LATINX VISIBILITY ONLINE

Considering the various ways that networked publics convene through the relationships afforded by platform technologies outlined above, this section will detail examples of how US Latinxs have used digital media to engage in political discourse, online activism, and formation of communities of similar interest. Many scholars and activists alike have long realized the power that social media has in generating social movement organizing and discussions in online spaces.

One example of online organizing that quickly mobilized the potential of social media was that of undocumented Latinx activists in the mid to late 2000s. Circulation of narratives in online space is an important tool that platforms alternative stories often ignored by mainstream media outlets. Through alternative modes of circulation, undocumented activists have been able to tell their own stories by blogging, tweeting, or live streaming their content. Beyond using the visibility provided by online platforms to circulate their stories, undocumented Latinx activists have ignited conversations around a sense of "ideal citizenship" by pointing out the respectability politics involved in DREAM (an acronym derived from the Development, Relief, and Education for Alien Minors Act, a proposal for a law that would have provided a path to citizenship for undocumented individuals brought to the US as children) activist narratives; that is, the way that this group of undocumented immigrants is often presented as hardworking and accomplished and thus "deserving" of the rights associated with the possibility of obtaining US citizenship, whereas other undocumented immigrants are not. This circulation of narratives and counternarratives demonstrates that the spreadability of stories can increase visibility. However, whether this visibility translates into greater access to resources requires further investigation.

Using social media to engage in political mobilization and discourse characterizes what is referred to as hashtag activism. As defined by Jackson et al., **hashtag activism** is "the strategic ways counterpublic groups and their allies on Twitter employ this shortcut to make political contentions about identity politics that advocate for social change, identity redefinition, and political inclusion" (xxviii). From #blacklivesmatter to #metoo, various calls for social change have sought the communicative potential of social media as a space to spark conversation and action.

Figure 3.3: Screenshot of a video promoting TikTok's #familialatina, where users are encouraged to promote their Latinidad in celebration of a "Latinx community."

Source: TikTok
Attribution: TikTok
License: Fair Use

Hashtag activism is a networked activity, meaning not only is the discourse important to consider within such actions, but the relationships formed throughout have demonstrated a potential to move online activism between different media forms and onto the streets.

Another dimension of social movements that has become increasingly visible is the ins and outs of forming coalitions. Returning to the use of networked technology by undocumented activists, many of these activists have used the increased visibility of social networking sites to foreground the lived experiences of being queer and undocumented. Using the term *undocuqueer*, activists have engaged in coalitional politics by organizing collectively around the distinct issues of LGBTQ+ and immigrant rights.

Not all political discourse in online space functions as a moment to build coalitions as just described. Indeed, online spaces such as Twitter or YouTube are far from ideal. In her important analysis of Latinx Twitter, Latinx media scholar Arcelia Gutiérrez examines how online visibility for issues that affect Latinxs often lead to internal fragmentations and anti-Blackness due to what she describes as the "homogenization and the flattening of difference" within Latinx Twitter (8). This characterization of Latinx Twitter allows us to understand how easily certain issues such as media representation are taken as a competition between Black and non-Black Latinx people, a sentiment that erases Black Latinxs from imagined Latinx representation.

Online conversations of ethnoracial identity are ways people can speak back to media industries. An illustrative example of this dynamic was visible with the 2021 release of the musical film *In the Heights*, which was based on the stage musical of the same name. The stage version of the musical was co-created by Lin-Manuel Miranda, who has become a household name due to the success of the Broadway musical *Hamilton*. *In the Heights* takes place in Washington Heights, a neighborhood in New York City known for its large Dominican population. Many Black Latinxs pointed out the lack of dark-skinned cast members, particularly in leading roles for a film that is supposed to take place in a neighborhood like Washington Heights. Discussions of colorism quickly generated a backlash with elements of the anti-Blackness described above. The sense that the increase in representation for dark-skinned Black Latinxs comes at a loss for light-skinned Latinxs showcased the anti-Blackness present in Latinx Twitter discourse. Miranda himself soon issued an apology where he stressed his views on the importance of being seen. This example demonstrates the ways visibility has become not only an issue with who is on the screen but also the conversations that are sparked by the audience and the unprecedented access they and producers of media have with each other.

As alluded to above, visibility is not a neutral field. While social movements have benefited from the ability to mobilize the digital public sphere in a variety of contexts, issues such as content moderation (the review of posts on online platforms to determine if they violate a platform's policies, sometimes leading to their removal), misinformation, censorship, and shadowbanning (the practice of a platform blocking or hiding a user's content without notifying them) complicate the conversations on the politics of visibility in an often unequal terrain.

Studying Latinx media in the digital age involves considering aspects of technology and culture in more ways than can conceivably fit in this chapter. From US Latinx influencers to disinformation campaigns that are culturally specific, this topic area requires a knowledge of scholarly work from Latinx, media, communication, information, and science and technology studies. As we move increasingly into a place where computer technology is used in every aspect of daily life, knowing how Latinxs are seen and see themselves as **data** becomes consequential. Data is socially constructed, and algorithmically driven technological systems are popularly used to make life-altering decisions, from standardized tests to predictive policing (automated systems that attempt to calculate who will commit a crime or re-offend). Therefore, it is vital to understand how data-driven systems reproduce the systemic biases that have long disenfranchised marginalized people.

In this chapter, several tools for analyzing digital media and Latinx cultural productions online were outlined. Recognizing the ways digital technologies and the cultures who use them influence each other approaches a richer understanding of what a networked Latinidad looks like across online spaces. As more attention is paid to this topic and the frame of the digital divide no longer dominates the conversation, the field of Latinx digital media studies will increasingly reflect the complex lives of US Latinxs.

***Javier Rivera*** *is a PhD student in Communication at the University of Southern California's Annenberg School for Communication and Journalism. His research focuses on US Latinx media, ethnoracial performance, and the ways new media and technology shift our understanding of Latinidad.*

## BIBLIOGRAPHY

Aparicio, Frances R. *Negotiating Latinidad: Intralatina/o Lives in Chicago*. U of Illinois P, 2019.

boyd, danah. *It's Complicated: The Social Lives of Networked Teens*. Yale UP, 2014.

Brock, André. "Critical Technocultural Discourse Analysis." *New Media & Society*, vol. 20, no. 3, SAGE Publications, 2018, pp. 1012–30.

Gutiérrez, Arcelia. "Situating Representation as a Form of Erasure: #OscarsSoWhite, Black Twitter, and Latinx Twitter." *Television & New Media*, vol. 23, no. 1, 2022, pp. 100–18.

Jackson, Sarah J., et al. *#Hashtagactivism: Networks of Race and Gender Justice*. MIT P, 2020.

Nakamura, Lisa, and Peter Chow-White, editors. *Race after the Internet*. Routledge, 2012.

Negrón-Muntaner, Frances. *The Latino Media Gap: A Report on the State of Latinos in U.S. Media*. National Association of Latino Independent Producers, Center for the Study of Race and Ethnicity–Columbia University, and National Hispanic Foundation for the Arts, 2014. https://asit-prod-web1.cc.columbia.edu/cser/wp-content/uploads/sites/70/2020/03/Latino-Gap.pdf.

Retis, Jessica. "Hispanic Media Today." *Democracy Fund*, https://democracyfund.org/wp-content/uploads/2020/06/2019_DemocracyFund_HispanicMediaToday.pdf.

Rodríguez, Vittoria, and Mary Beltrán. "From the Bronze Screen to the Computer Screen: Latina/o Web Series and Independent Production." *The Routledge Companion to Latina/o Media*, edited by María Elena Cepeda and Dolores Inés Casillas, Routledge, 2016, pp. 156–70.

Stanfill, Mel. "The Interface as Discourse: The Production of Norms through Web Design." *New Media & Society*, vol. 17, no. 7, 2015, pp. 1059–74.

## FOR FURTHER STUDY

Báez, Jillian M. "Latinx Audiences as Mosaic." *Race and Media: Critical Approaches*, edited by Lori Kido Lopez. NYU P, 2020, pp. 218–29.

Benjamin, Ruha. *Race After Technology: Abolitionist Tools for the New Jim Code*. Polity, 2019.

Gutiérrez, Arcelia. "Pero Like and mitú: Latina Content Creators, Social Media Entertainment, and the Politics of Latinx Millenniality." *Feminist Media Histories*, vol. 7, no. 4, https://doi.org/10.1525/fm.

Jenkins, Henry, et al. *Spreadable Media: Creating Value and Meaning in a Networked Culture*. NYU P, 2013.

Kantayya, Shalini. *Coded Bias*. 7th Empire Media, 2021.

Nakamura, Lisa. *Digitizing Race: Visual Cultures of the Internet*. U of Minnesota P, 2008.

Noble, Safiya Umoja. *Algorithms of Oppression: How Search Engines Reinforce Racism*. NYU P, 2018.

# Part II: Identities

Chapters in the Identities section highlight the diversity within the panethnic category of Hispanic/Latino/a/x as well as the intersections of race, gender, class, sexuality, and other markers of identity that shape the dynamics of inclusion and exclusion within communities and in relation to broader social formations. Chapters in this section also address how different identities and power dynamics have found expression in media representation and production. Chapter 4 offers an overview of how race and ethnicity have been officially defined in the United States versus how race and color are understood in Latin America. Chapter 5 considers Afro-Latinx identity and media, emphasizing that Latinx identity is not a racial category but an ethnic one that can be understood in a relational manner. Chapter 6 examines diasporic Indigenous Latinx identity and media. Not only are Indigenous peoples of Latin America a growing population within the Latinx community, but the diversity of Indigenous populations demands that we recognize the complexities of Latinx identities. Chapter 7 explores some of the ways Latinx feminist perspectives respond to and inform media practices, while Chapter 8 examines films and television shows that have addressed the intersection of Latinx and LGBTQ communities, focusing on the representation and narrative role of Latinx queer characters.

After completing this section, students should be able to do the following:
- Identify the most relevant factors that have shaped definitions and understandings of racial, ethnic, and gender identities for Latinx individuals in the United States.
- Evaluate how the diversity of Latinx identities shape experiences of inclusion and exclusion (or citizenship/belonging) for members of different communities.
- Recognize the diversity within the Latinx community in terms of national origin, race, gender, and sexuality.

# 4 Defining Race and Ethnicity between Latin America and the United States

Rielle Navitski
(University of Georgia)

## DEFINING HISPANIC/LATINO/LATINX: THE US CENSUS

The presence of people of Latin American origin in the United States, whether they have family roots in the region or are recent immigrants, is undeniably significant. According to US census data, in 2020 Hispanic or Latino people numbered over sixty-two million, accounting for an estimated 18.7% of the population, or nearly one in five US residents ([Jones et al.](#)). It has become commonplace in the United States to view individuals of Latin American origin as belonging to a unified population—usually called Hispanic or Latino—in part because the census counts them this way. (Note that the census does not use the gender-neutral term *Latinx* that has gained traction in recent years but is still widely debated. Some view the use of *Latinx* as an important step in moving beyond language that relies on a gender binary and thus excludes non-binary people, while others see the term as an English-language imposition given its departure from the rules of Spanish grammar. The term *latine*, whose ending is a common one in Spanish, is an alternative gender-neutral expression for this idea.)

Even if we set aside these recent, unofficial terms, the seemingly self-explanatory grouping of "Hispanic or Latino" used on the census is not as straightforward as it might seem at first glance. For example, should individuals with family roots in Brazil be considered Latino because that country is part of Latin America, even though their cultural origins are not Hispanic, since Brazil was a Portuguese colony? Should Hispanic/Latino be considered a **race**; that is, a social grouping based on individuals' physical characteristics and ancestry? Should it be considered an **ethnicity**, a category that implies a shared cultural background? The 2020 census form asked respondents to indicate whether they are of "Hispanic, Latino, or Spanish origin" and then choose a racial identity from among the following options: White; Black or African American; American Indian or Alaska Native; one of nine Asian and Pacific Islander nationalities, including Chinese, Japanese, and Vietnamese; or "some other race" ("Decennial Census"). The form specifies that "For this census, Hispanic origins are not races."

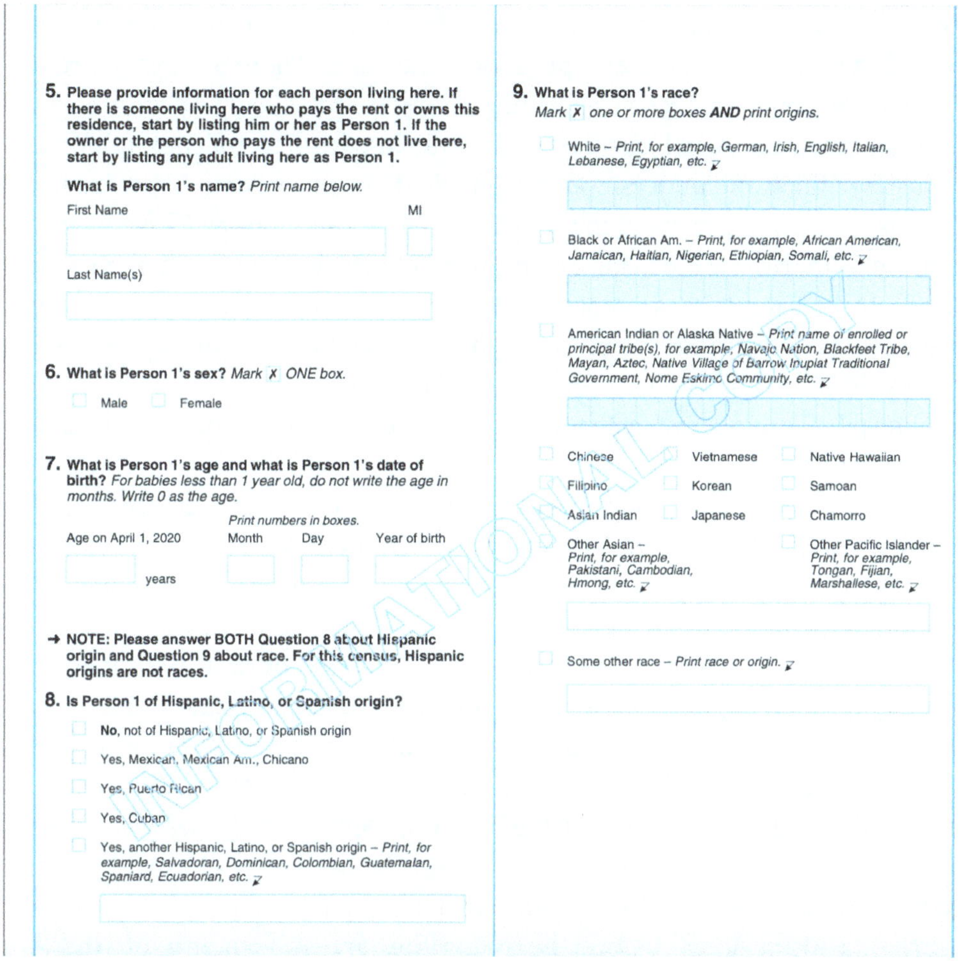

**5.** **Please provide information for each person living here. If there is someone living here who pays the rent or owns this residence, start by listing him or her as Person 1. If the owner or the person who pays the rent does not live here, start by listing any adult living here as Person 1.**

**What is Person 1's name?** *Print name below.*

First Name MI

Last Name(s)

**6.** **What is Person 1's sex?** *Mark ✗ ONE box.*

☐ Male ☐ Female

**7.** **What is Person 1's age and what is Person 1's date of birth?** *For babies less than 1 year old, do not write the age in months. Write 0 as the age.*

*Print numbers in boxes.*

Age on April 1, 2020 ___ years | Month | Day | Year of birth

→ **NOTE: Please answer BOTH Question 8 about Hispanic origin and Question 9 about race. For this census, Hispanic origins are not races.**

**8.** **Is Person 1 of Hispanic, Latino, or Spanish origin?**

☐ No, not of Hispanic, Latino, or Spanish origin
☐ Yes, Mexican, Mexican Am., Chicano
☐ Yes, Puerto Rican
☐ Yes, Cuban
☐ Yes, another Hispanic, Latino, or Spanish origin – *Print, for example, Salvadoran, Dominican, Colombian, Guatemalan, Spaniard, Ecuadorian, etc.*

**9.** **What is Person 1's race?**

*Mark ✗ one or more boxes **AND** print origins.*

☐ White – *Print, for example, German, Irish, English, Italian, Lebanese, Egyptian, etc.*
☐ Black or African Am. – *Print, for example, African American, Jamaican, Haitian, Nigerian, Ethiopian, Somali, etc.*
☐ American Indian or Alaska Native – *Print name of enrolled or principal tribe(s), for example, Navajo Nation, Blackfeet Tribe, Mayan, Aztec, Native Village of Barrow Inupiat Traditional Government, Nome Eskimo Community, etc.*
☐ Chinese ☐ Vietnamese ☐ Native Hawaiian
☐ Filipino ☐ Korean ☐ Samoan
☐ Asian Indian ☐ Japanese ☐ Chamorro
☐ Other Asian – *Print, for example, Pakistani, Cambodian, Hmong, etc.*
☐ Other Pacific Islander – *Print, for example, Tongan, Fijian, Marshallese, etc.*
☐ Some other race – *Print race or origin.*



**Figure 4.1: A sample copy of the 2020 US Census form.**

Source: US Census
Attribution: US government
License: Public Domain

While this might seem to clarify matters, responses to the census questions on Hispanic origin and race suggest a mismatch between official definitions and their own understandings of their identities. In the 2010 census, over a third of individuals who stated that they were Hispanic, Latino, or Spanish checked "some other race" (Navarro A11). This proportion increased significantly in 2020, with over 42% of respondents of Hispanic origin selecting "some other race" (Jones et al.). These respondents might have considered Hispanic or Latino to be a distinct racial identity—one survey suggests that half of US residents with Latin American roots do (Fraga et al. 82)—or simply felt that none of the provided categories were a good fit. Reflecting changes to the design of census questions, as well as understandings of Hispanic/Latino/Latinx identity as rooted in racial mixture (discussed in more detail in this chapter), in 2020 more than five times as many self-identified Hispanics/Latinos chose "two or more races" as their racial identity than they did in 2010 (Jones et al.).

The race options on the census overlap closely but not exactly with the racial categories widely used in the United States. For example, "Asian" is commonly understood as a race, but is not an option on the census. There is an even greater gap between the census categories and how many individuals of Latin American origin understand their racial identity. This is due in part to significant differences in how race is defined and understood in the United States versus in Latin America, which are explored in more detail in the second half of this chapter. This mismatch does not mean that the US census is simply incorrect. Rather, it highlights how racial and ethnic categories are socially constructed (Rodríguez). That is, these categories are a product of a society's widely held ideas about human difference, which can shift over time and vary across social contexts.

The Hispanic/Latino census category is a useful example of the social construction of race and ethnicity, partly because it is so new in historical terms. Despite the fact that it is firmly established in our everyday thinking about race and ethnicity, the category was added only in 1980. Up to that point, individuals who would today be considered Hispanic, Latino, or Latinx were generally counted as White, though they were certainly not always treated as such. The sole exception was the 1930 census, when "Mexican" was added as a racial category. It was removed in 1940 following public outcry from Mexican Americans who objected to being classified with African Americans as "colored," suggesting anti-Black sentiment and fears of losing social privileges and legal rights (Gratton and Klancher Merchant 537, 548). Again, it would be misleading to conclude that the pre-1980 census categories were simply inaccurate or ignoring an obvious reality. Rather, the category of Hispanic/Latino emerged over time in response to changing circumstances.

As Cristina Mora notes, before the 1970s the largest segments of what we now call the Latinx population—namely Mexican Americans, Puerto Ricans, and Cuban Americans—generally viewed themselves as distinct groups. For the most part, they lived in different areas of the country, and their political interests did not necessarily align (2). Several factors converged in the creation of the Hispanic census category—the term *Latino* was added to the relevant question only in 2000 ("Decennial Census")—and the popularization of the idea of Hispanic/Latino as a **pan-ethnic** category that grouped people of different national origins under a single umbrella. As the Mexican American and Puerto Rican social movements of the 1960s gained momentum, organizers realized that there was "strength in numbers." Building a sense of solidarity between different groups of Latin American origin and presenting themselves as a demographic of significant size could boost their political power, even if their priorities differed (Mora 15). Government officials began using the term *Hispanic*, which was all but non-existent in English before the 1970s. *Hispanic* was modeled on the term **hispano**, which had a narrower meaning, referring to individuals with longstanding family roots in what is now the US Southwest (108). These officials advocated for the creation of a census category as a means of tracking a growing population of Latin American origin and more effectively providing them with public services, helping to head off radical demands for social change (14–15).

Alongside these political considerations, advertising, marketing, and media played a key role in popularizing the notion of Hispanic/Latino identity. The rise of Spanish-language TV networks that broadcast from coast to coast, namely Univisión (originally called Spanish International Network) and Telemundo, in the 1970s and 1980s allowed advertisers to target a nationwide market of people of Latin American origin for the first time (Dávila 45–46, Mora 15–16). As Chapter 10 of this book explores in more depth, Spanish-language networks actively promoted the Hispanic census category because cementing the idea of a unified Hispanic/Latino identity benefited them. It allowed them to entice advertisers by promising them access to a sizeable, unified group of potential customers instead of smaller, more localized markets made up of Mexican Americans in the Southwest, Puerto Ricans in the Northeast, and Cuban Americans in Florida. This development was tied to the rapid growth of advertising and marketing agencies targeting the Hispanic/Latino population, which further promoted the notion that individuals from anywhere in Latin America shared an ethnic identity (Dávila 48–49).

Yet despite the many forces that converged to popularize the notion of a shared Hispanic/Latino identity, not all individuals who indicate they are of "Hispanic, Latino, or Spanish origin" on the census identify this way first and foremost. One study found that 90% of Latinos born abroad and over 80% of those born in the United States identified somewhat or very strongly with a specific nationality, such as Mexican, Cuban, or Salvadoran. Yet only about 65% identified somewhat or very strongly as Hispanic or Latino across both groups (Fraga et al. 79–80). Furthermore, the Hispanic/Latino identity category is largely relevant in the United States. Although the idea that former Spanish colonies share some kind of cultural kinship dates back to the early 1800s, when they became independent nations, individuals living in Latin America typically identify with their nationality, not as Latino or Latinx.

The history of the census suggests both the limitations and the advantages of the Hispanic/Latino category. It can help create a sense of solidarity between different national-origin groups and allow for collective political action while also benefiting government and commercial interests. Yet the census category of Hispanic/Latino does not fully account for differences in race or color that decisively shape individuals' everyday experiences and life opportunities. These differences must be acknowledged if we are to grasp not only how the Latinx community as a whole is affected by race-based forms of oppression in the United States, but also to understand race-based forms of oppression *within* this community, including anti-Blackness and anti-Indigenous attitudes. Understanding how notions of race differ in the United States and Latin American nations reminds us of the constructedness of racial categories while shedding light on the different forms of racism that affect the community.

# RACE AND COLOR IN LATIN AMERICA AND THE UNITED STATES

Racial categories have an immense social weight. However, they are not meaningful from the perspective of human biology, according to current scientific consensus. Specific genes do account for differences in physical appearance such as skin and eye color, hair texture, and the shape of one's nose or eyelids. But these physical differences are not linked with the overall degree of genetic variation between populations and cannot be mapped onto other genetic traits with any consistency (Boyd 8). In fact, since humans developed on the African continent and a subset of this population then migrated to other parts of the world, in general non-Africans are more closely related to each other, however distantly, than Africans are. That is, the genetic diversity *within* African populations, whose members are generally considered to be the same race, is much greater than the genetic difference between all non-African populations (Tishkoff and Kidd 522). Keeping this in mind, social scientists use terms such as "racial formation" (Omi and Winant) to stress that racial categories are constructed and are intimately tied to power relations within a society.

Dominant ideas about race in Latin American nations typically stress a history of racial mixture between European colonizers, the Indigenous population, and enslaved people from Africa and suggest that this mixture gave rise to a new racial identity shared by the country's population. Yet often, as in the case of Mexico and the Dominican Republic, the contributions of African-descended people are downplayed (Telles and Paschel 865). Similarly, the significant presence of people of Asian origin in nations like Brazil, Cuba, Mexico, and Peru usually goes unacknowledged in conversations about national identity (Chang 10). The widely held idea that all of a nation's citizens belong to the same race, at least in theory, is implied in the Mexican term *la raza*, which refers not only to a shared racial heritage but also a shared culture and nationality.

This does not mean there are not significant differences of race or color in the population. Typically, in Latin America, an individual's race or color is determined by their appearance rather than the race or color of their parents. When describing themselves, individuals choose from several different terms that describe appearance and/or ancestry, such as *mulato* (meaning of White and Black ancestry), *pardo* (brown or dark), *trigueño* (wheat-colored), or *blanco* (white). Individuals' self-identifications may change over time or in different contexts. By contrast, definitions of racial identity in the United States historically have been more rigid, and racial mixture has been discouraged or widely outlawed. The so-called "**one drop rule**," which meant that an individual with any known or visible African ancestry would be considered Black, was enshrined in law in several states (Murray 22, 39, 90, 164, 237, 358). **Anti-miscegenation laws** made marriage between Whites and Blacks illegal in all but seven US states by the 1940s, and it remained illegal in sixteen states until the Supreme Court declared such laws unconstitutional in 1967 (Kitch).

This does not mean that Latin American nations are necessarily more racially equal than the United States, even if racism takes forms that seem subtle if compared with Jim Crow–era segregation. **Colorism**, or the practice of giving preferential treatment to individuals with lighter skin or more European features, is widespread across the Americas. In many Latin American countries, the term *indio* (indigenous) is used in an insulting manner as a synonym for "ill-mannered" or "lacking in education." Because Indigenous and African ancestry are often stigmatized in daily life, even if they are sometimes celebrated in the abstract, many individuals describe themselves with terms that negate or downplay this ancestry. This seems to be borne out by the results of the 2010 census in the United States. In the absence of a Hispanic/Latino racial category, 53% of those who checked the Hispanic/Latino box identified as White, while only 2.5% identified as Black and 1.4% as American Indian (Almaguer 215). While the 2020 census revealed a drop of more than half in the number of Hispanics/Latinos identifying as White, the number identifying as American Indian more than doubled, while the percentage identifying as Black actually dropped by over 6% ([Jones et al.](#)). Of course, these differences reflect both changes in the population since 2010 and individuals who changed their racial identification when responding in 2020.

Regardless of their own racial self-identification, an individual's physical appearance and family background have a decisive impact on their experiences and life outcomes. In Mexico, on average, the lightest-skinned individuals have more than twice as many years of education as the darkest-skinned, and the darkest-skinned individuals have more than 50% less wealth than the lightest-skinned, even when other variables are accounted for ([Zizumbo-Colunga and Flores Martínez](#) 3–4). While Mexico is the third-most racially unequal country in Latin America and the Caribbean, skin color is correlated with wealth in every nation in the region (3). For comparison, in the United States, Whites are more than twice as likely than Hispanics/Latinos and 1.5 times more likely than Black individuals to have a college degree, while the average income of White households is nearly twice that of Black households and its household wealth (including homes) thirteen times greater ([“On Views of Race”](#)).

Sociologist Eduardo Bonilla-Silva argues that the racial ideology of the United States is no longer defined by a Black/White binary. Rather, following the civil rights movement of the 1960s, it is moving closer to a racial power structure comparable to that of Latin American nations, marked by forms of racial discrimination that are more subtle and less open (3–4). Bonilla-Silva suggests that in this emerging racial order, some non-White individuals, including light-skinned Latinos and some Asian Americans, come to be considered "honorary whites" (4). That is, they share in some of the social and economic benefits that Whites enjoy to a greater degree than other racial groups in the United States and do not necessarily have a sense of solidarity with other individuals who experience a greater degree of race-based discrimination (4, 11).

If the racial power structure of the United States has begun to converge with that of Latin America, both have their roots in shared histories of colonialism whose paths diverged in terms of racial ideology. The colonization of what we now call North and South America by White Europeans in the 1500s proved to be a pivotal moment for the development of notions of race that continue to shape our world today. Europeans were well aware of African, Middle Eastern, and Asian populations who looked physically different from them before their colonization of the Western Hemisphere. However, these groups were not divided into specific races or generally assumed to be inferior to Europeans. Though slavery existed in many societies, being enslaved was not tied to race—many enslaved people were prisoners of war or convicted of crimes—nor was it necessarily permanent (Golash-Boza 7–9). The belief that Whites were superior to Africans and Indigenous people developed over time, in part to justify the genocide of Indigenous people, who died on a mass scale in military conflicts and from Old World diseases to which they had no immunities, and the enslavement of Africans and their descendants, which facilitated the extraction of profit from colonized territories through agriculture and mining of precious metals.

In both British and Spanish colonies, slavery was not initially based on race, but it became a race-based system over time (Smedley and Smedley 97; Cottrol 30). In the United States, Black and White servants—individuals who worked without wages for a set period or indefinitely, typically to pay off a debt or because they were convicts or prisoners of war—initially worked side by side. Yet a series of laws referred to as **slave codes** increasingly assigned Black servants a lower social status than their White counterparts and stripped them of their rights (Smedley and Smedley 101). These incremental changes led to a system of race-based slavery. In Virginia, for example, by 1705, "Negro, mulatto, and Indian" servants were made slaves permanently, and intermarriage between Whites and non-Whites had become illegal (Hening 447–48, 453–54). These changes were motivated in part by the desire to suppress servants' rebellions against their masters by using the logic of "divide and conquer" (Smedley and Smedley 109–10).

Although their histories of colonization are parallel in many ways, the population profile of the British colonies was considerably different from territories occupied by the Spanish and Portuguese, which played a role in the racial ideologies that would later take shape there. Although it is very difficult to estimate the number of Indigenous people that inhabited the Western Hemisphere before European colonization, one estimate suggests that 3.8 million people lived in North America versus 22.8 million in Mexico and Central America, 15.7 million in the Andean region, and 8.6 million in the rest of South America. The Caribbean also had a comparatively smaller Indigenous population of 3 million by this estimate (Denevan 370). Between Columbus's arrival on the island of Hispaniola in 1492 and 1650, the total Indigenous population of the Americas is believed to have dropped by nearly 90% (Denevan 371). Despite this unimaginable devastation, their numbers remained significant in many regions, particularly in the territories occupied by the Mayan, Aztec, and Inca empires. In addition, nearly 95% of enslaved people forcibly brought to the Americas arrived in Latin America: close to 7.3 million, including 5.5 million to Brazil alone ("Trans-Atlantic"). Under half a million enslaved people were brought to what is now the United States ("Trans-Atlantic"). In addition to generating huge amounts of wealth for White elites, Africans and their descendants had a far-reaching cultural and demographic influence in colonized territories.

If slave codes in the British colonies were designed to create an impenetrable social divide between Whites and non-Whites, the barriers separating racial groups in colonial Latin America generally proved much more porous. In addition to interracial sex outside marriage—whether consensual or forced, as was often the case—intermarriage between European, Indigenous, and African-descended people became increasingly common. By 1750 mixed-race individuals made up about 20% of the Mexican population (Seed 24–25). In this period in Mexico, **cuadros de castas** (caste paintings) emerged as a form of visual art that sought to assign clearly defined racial identities to mixed-race individuals, even though class identities were in flux and it became more difficult to judge someone's social status solely by their background (Katzew). The *cuadros de castas* were comprised of images of families that illustrated a complex racial terminology based on the proportions of White, Indigenous, and African ancestry in an individual's family tree. Despite the *cuadro de castas'* efforts to assign each individual a clear place in a social hierarchy, the laws of the Spanish empire sometimes treated race as surprisingly fluid. Provided they had sufficient wealth and status, some mixed-race individuals of African ancestry could actually purchase a royal favor known as a *gracias al sacar* that would allow them to be legally reclassified as White (Twinam).

A clear hierarchy in which Whites occupied the highest position and Blacks the lowest, with mixed race and Indigenous individuals in the middle, had taken shape across the Americas by the 1700s. Yet explicit references to race before this historical moment were uncommon. Modern ideas about race took shape as part of a growing interest in science, a pivotal aspect of the broad cultural movement referred to as the Enlightenment. Yet these new ideas about race, often referred to as **scientific racism**, were not based in methods we would consider rigorously scientific today. Influenced by the racial prejudices of European researchers, they used approaches we now recognize as pseudoscience, such as the belief that measuring the size or shape of a person's head provided useful information about their intelligence and character (Gould). During the 1800s, particularly with the popularization of Charles Darwin's theory of evolution, scientists became deeply interested in attempting to classify variations in the human species and determine which populations were more "evolved" than others. Reflecting these scientists' prejudices, Whites were classified as the most advanced. Disregarding the fact that Darwin's theory applied to changes in species that took shape over millennia, Herbert Spencer's concept of social Darwinism applied the notion of "survival of the fittest" to human societies, suggesting without strong evidence that some racial groups were better equipped than others to thrive under the conditions of modernity.

Figure 4.2: Anonymous *cuadro de castas*, 1700s, from the collection of the Museo del Virreinato in Tepotzlán, Mexico.

Source: New York Public Library
Attribution: Anonymous
License: Public Domain

The flawed principles of scientific racism had a significant impact on public policy in both the United States and Latin America, encouraging anti-miscegenation laws and shaping immigration policy. In the United States, they influenced the Chinese Exclusion Act of 1882, a ban on Chinese immigration that was expanded to all of Asia and parts of the Middle East in 1917, as well as provisions in a 1924 law that limited immigration from Southern Europe in favor of Northern European countries. In Latin America, scientific racism led many government officials and elites to believe that a whiter population would bring benefits, like greater economic productivity. As a result, they encouraged large-scale migration from Europe (Cottrol 91). Argentina, for example, more than doubled its population through immigration between 1880 and 1930 (Cottrol 97). Even today, Argentina styles itself as a White, European nation, often negating Indigenous and African ancestry within its population. Elsewhere in Latin America, given the significant presence of people of Indigenous and African descent, policymakers and academics found themselves obliged to revise core ideas of scientific racism as formulated elsewhere. Many US and European supporters of **eugenics**—the effort to "improve" the human race by careful control of reproduction—argued that mixing between races led to **degeneration**; that is, physical and mental weakness in an individual that contributed to a broader social decline or regression to a more "primitive" state. This idea was unpopular in Latin American societies that were already marked by a high degree of racial mixture. Instead, many scientists and policymakers in the region contended that White ancestry would eventually "win out" over Indigenous and African heritage in their populations because White ancestry was believed to be superior (Telles and Paschel 867–868; Cottrol 96–97). This **ideology of whitening**—which persists today in the notion that having children with a lighter-skinned person is "improving the race" (*mejorar la raza*)—was based on an unfounded belief in White superiority and a basic misunderstanding of how genetics work.

In the early twentieth century, some Latin American thinkers began to argue that racial mixture was not a negative nor simply a necessary step toward the ultimate goal of whitening the nation. Rather, it should be viewed as a positive force that gave nations resilience and cultural richness. Perhaps the most famous example of the ideology of ***mestizaje*** (racial mixture) is José Vasconcelos's concept of ***la raza cósmica***, or the cosmic race. This concept was developed in the wake of the Mexican Revolution, a conflict that overthrew dictator Porfirio Díaz but then devolved into a devastating civil war. The revolution threw light onto deep divides in Mexican society, including between Spanish-speaking populations and Indigenous communities. Vasconcelos predicted that in Latin America, these divides would disappear through a process of racial and cultural fusion, foreshadowing a future cosmic race that would unite all existing races and be superior to them all. These ideas were a clear contrast with the obsession with racial "purity" evident in the United States and the segregation of African American and Indigenous communities. Yet the notion of *la raza cósmica* is not as progressive as it might appear at first glance. Problematically, Vasconcelos championed the disappearance of Indigenous peoples as distinctive groups through their assimilation into the dominant society and suggested that racial mixing would eliminate undesirable African heritage altogether. He also described Asians in derogatory terms while idealizing European ancestry and culture (Manrique). By championing racial mixture, ideologies of race that emerged in Latin America in the early twentieth century have often facilitated efforts to deny the historical and present-day impacts of racial discrimination. These ideologies have been challenged by activists in recent years, who demand the recognition of racial inequality, the persistence of Indigenous peoples, and contributions of Afro-descendants to nations' cultural heritage. In a symbolic but significant change, in 2020 Mexico added a new category which counted people of African descent in the census for the first time.

The racial power structures of the United States and Latin America intersect to shape the daily lives of members of the Latinx community living in the United States. Many non-Latinx people are unaware of the racial complexity of this community. They may read Afro-Latinx individuals as African American while treating light-skinned Latinx individuals as White—or not, depending on their language abilities and accents. As a result, individuals who are grouped together in the Hispanic/Latinx category may experience a wide range of privilege or discrimination. Furthermore, different national-origin groups within the Latinx community may stereotype each other, drawing on beliefs about race forged both in the United States and in Latin America. Tomás Almaguer notes that many Puerto Ricans associated Mexican Americans with stereotypes of the "Indian"—uneducated, unsophisticated, and passive—while many Mexican Americans associated Puerto Ricans with stereotypes associated with Blackness—lazy, violent, and criminal (216–17). Ideologies championing racial mixture may contribute to a sense of pride, unity, and solidarity for Latinx individuals, but by downplaying differences, they can also make it more difficult to confront colorism and anti-Black and anti-Indigenous sentiment within Latinx communities. Understanding the constructed nature of the Hispanic/Latino/Latinx category and the complexities it conceals can prepare us to better confront these inequalities.

**Rielle Navitski** *is an Associate Professor in the Department of Theatre and Film Studies at the University of Georgia. She is the author of* Public Spectacles of Violence: Sensational Cinema and Journalism in Early Twentieth-Century Mexico and Brazil *(Duke University Press, 2017) and co-editor of* Cosmopolitan Film Cultures in Latin America, 1896-1960 *(Indiana University Press, 2017). Currently she is working on a book manuscript entitled "Transatlantic Cinephilia: Networks of Film Culture Between Latin America and France, 1945-1965" (under contract, University of California Press).*

## BIBLIOGRAPHY

Almaguer, Tomás. "Race, Racialization, and Latino Populations in the United States." *The New Latino Studies Reader*, edited by Ramón A. Gutiérrez and Tomás Almaguer. U of California P, 2016, pp. 210–27.

Bonilla-Silva, Eduardo. "We Are All Americans! The Latin Americanization of Racial Stratification in the USA." *Race & Society*, vol. 5, 2002, pp. 3–16.

Boyd, Robert S. "Color's Only Skin Deep." *Racism: A Global Reader*, edited by Kevin Reilly et al. M.E. Sharp, 2003, pp. 8–11.

Chang, Jason Oliver. *Chino: Anti-Chinese Racism in Mexico, 1880-1940*. U of Illinois P, 2017.

Cottrol, Robert J. The *Long, Lingering Shadow: Slavery, Race, and Law in the American Hemisphere*. U of Georgia P, 2013.

Dávila, Arlene. *Latinos, Inc.: The Making and Marketing of a People*. 2nd ed., U of California P, 2012.

"Decennial Census of Population and Housing Questionnaires & Instructions." *United States Census Bureau*, https://www.census.gov/programs-surveys/decennial-census/technical-documentation/questionnaires.Through_the_Decades.html.

Denevan, William M. "The Pristine Myth: The Landscape of the Americas in 1492." *Annals of the Association of American Geographers*, vol. 82, no. 3, 1992, pp. 369–85.

Fraga, Ricardo, et al. *Latinos in the New Millennium: An Almanac of Opinion, Behavior, and Policy Preferences*. Cambridge UP, 2012.

Golash-Boza, Tanya. *Race & Racisms: A Critical Approach*. Oxford UP, 2015.

Gould, Stephen Jay. *The Mismeasure of Man*. Revised and expanded edition, W.W. Norton, 1996.

Grattan, Brian, and Emily Klancher Merchant. "*La Raza*: Mexicans in the United States Census." *Journal of Policy History*, vol. 28, no. 4, 2016, pp. 537–67.

Hening, William Waller. *The Statutes at Large; Being a Collection of All the Laws of Virginia from the First Session of the Legislature, in the Year 1619*. R. & W. & G. Bartow, 1823.

Jones, Nicholas, et al. "2020 Census Illuminates Racial and Ethnic Composition of the Country. *United States Census Bureau*, 12 Aug 2021, https://www.census.gov/library/stories/2021/08/improved-race-ethnicity-measures-reveal-united-states-population-much-more-multiracial.html.

Katzew, Ilona. "Casta Painting: Identity and Social Stratification in Mexico." *New World Orders: Casta Painting and Colonial Latin America*, edited by John A. Farmer and Ilona Katzew. Americas Society Art Gallery, 1996.

Kitch, Sally L. "Anti-Miscegenation Laws." *The Wiley Blackwell Encyclopedia of Gender and Sexuality Studies*, edited by Nancy A. Naples. 1st ed., Wiley-Blackwell, 2016, https://doi.org/10.1002/9781118663219.wbegss617.

Manrique, Linnete. "Dreaming of a Cosmic Race: José Vasconcelos and the Politics of Race in Mexico, 1920s-1930s." *Cogent Arts & Humanities*, vol. 3, no. 1, 2016.

Mora, G. Cristina. *Making Hispanics: How Activists, Bureaucrats, and Media Constructed a New American*. U of Chicago P, 2014.

Murray, Pauli, editor. *States' Laws on Race and Color, and Appendices Containing International Documents, Federal Laws and Regulations, Local Ordinances and Charts*. Women's Division of Christian Service, 1951.

Navarro, Mireya. "For Many Latinos, Racial Identity Is More Culture Than Color." *New York Times*, 14 January 2012, pp. A11–A12.

Omi, Michael, and Howard Winant. *Racial Formation in the United States*. 3rd ed., Routledge, 2014.

"On Views of Race and Inequality, Blacks and Whites are Worlds Apart." *Pew Research Center*, 27 July 2016, https://www.pewresearch.org/social-trends/2016/06/27/1-demographic-trends-and-economic-well-being/.

Rodríguez, Clara E. *Changing Race: Latinos, the Census, and the History of Ethnicity*. NYU P, 2000.

Seed, Patricia. *To Love, Honor, and Obey in Colonial Mexico: Conflicts over Marriage Choice, 1574-1821*. Stanford UP, 1988.

Smedley, Audrey, and Brian D. Smedley. *Race in North America: Origin and Evolution of a Worldview*. 4th ed., Westview P, 2012.

Telles, Edward, and Tianna Paschel. "Who is Black, White, or Mixed Race? How Skin Color, Status, and Nation Shape Racial Classification in Latin America." *American Journal of Sociology*, vol. 120, no. 3, 2014, pp. 864–907.

Tishkoff, Sarah A., and Kenneth R. Kidd. "Implications of Biogeography of Human Populations for 'Race' and Genetics." *Nature Genetics Supplement*, vol. 36, no. 11, 2004, 521–27.

"Trans-Atlantic Slave Trade - Estimates." *Slave Voyages Consortium*, https://www.slavevoyages.org/assessment/estimates. Accessed 27 July 2021.

Twinam, Ann. *Purchasing Whiteness: Pardos, Mulattoes, and the Quest for Social Mobility in the Spanish Indies*. Stanford UP, 2015.

Zizumbo-Colunga, Daniel, and Iván Flores Martínez. "Is Mexico a Post-Racial Country? Inequality and Skin Tone across the Americas." *Latin American Public Opinion Project*, 6 Nov. 2017. https://www.vanderbilt.edu/lapop/insights/ITB031en.pdf.

## FOR FURTHER STUDY

*Afro-Latinx Revolution: Puerto Rico*. Directed by Natasha Alford, 2020.

*The Invisible Color: Black Cubans in Miami*. Directed by Sergio Giral, 2017.

*Invisible Roots: Afro-Mexicans in Southern California*. Directed by Tiffany Walton and Lizz Mullis, 2015.

Telles, Edward. *Pigmentocracies: Ethnicity, Race, and Color in Latin America.* U of North Carolina P, 2014.

Wade, Peter. *Race and Ethnicity in Latin America.* 2nd ed., Palgrave Macmillan, 2010.

*What Are You?* Directed by Anayansi Prado, 2017.

# 5 Afro-Latinx Identity and Media

Keara K. Goin
(University of Virginia)

Hegemonic ideas concerning race in the United States are, quite literally, black and white. Historically, US racialization has been structured in a Black/White binary opposition that designates any person with traceable or observable African descent as Black. (I use the words *traceable* and *observable* as there is a long legacy of racial passing where those of African descent have been perceived as White. These individuals who "passed" did so strategically as a device to combat US racism). Referred to as **hypodescent**, or more colloquially as the "**one-drop rule**," this racial paradigm has its roots in British colonial and early US African enslavement and has continued to shape legal code as well as social understandings of Blackness (Khanna; Davis; Hall). This process of developing "racial formations" in both British and Spanish colonial contexts is covered extensively in Chapter 4 of this book.

Race in the United States has also been marked by process of hegemonic negotiation and incorporation, in which we have seen evolving negotiations involving the construction of Blackness where, in order to reclaim their own racialized identities, African Americans have embraced the hypodescent paradigm (Khanna 99). As such, not only is it the framework for dominant notions of US racialization, but it has been incorporated into self-racialization practices within the African American community. (To clarify my terminology, I use the term *African American* when referring to those whose Blackness is rooted in the US sociohistorical context. The terms *Black* or *African descent* apply to African Americans but also apply to those whose heritage is not exclusive to the United States, i.e., those people who come from one of the dozens of other countries that participated in African enslavement or more recent voluntary immigrants from African countries). Therefore, as a construct, hypodescent permeates all US racial discourses, including individuals whose Blackness originates outside of the country. In application, this means a person "of African descent has little choice but to identify as Black" (Davis 317).

When investigating the influence discourses of hypodescent and Black subjectivity have on those people of African descent who do not fit within the

African American heritage narrative, it is important to note that Blackness in the United States is based on assumptions of the "**essential** Black subject." Long contested, most vigorously by cultural theorist Stuart Hall, it relies on the assumption that there is an essence within Blackness that has an almost spiritual resonance for all those of African descent. In other words, those of African descent, regardless of their individual history, heritage, and experiences, are often thought to share a kind of essentialized notion of what it means to be Black. When dealing with Afro-Latinx racial negotiations, we should avoid the trappings of the essential Black subject and the one-drop rule, which place Afro-Latinas/os as analogous to African Americans, as this could potentially erase the context and specificity of their Blackness. For instance, those that argue that Dominicans suffer from a simple complex of refusing to acknowledge their "true" African descent dehistoricize the Dominican subject. The potential result of this conflation could be the loss of the specific context and plight of Dominicans when they are misappropriated into US Blackness.

However, Blackness itself is constructed in a relational manner. While historically this relation has been positioned in opposition to whiteness, it nonetheless is a fluid category that can and does bend. Reflecting on the work of Stuart Hall, who argues that race is not a fixed and essentialized category but instead a floating signifier, potential emerges not for Afro-Latinx inclusion in constructions of Blackness but also for the inclusion of Black bodies in constructions of Latina/o/x that have categorically excluded them. As such, the room for—more accurately, the demand for—negotiation becomes evident when Afro-Latinas/os in the United States are forced to make sense of their racialization in a system that categorizes them within discourses of Blackness. As a result, Latinx African descent is not necessarily denied, but it is qualified in relation to the Blackness of African Americans and various notions of Latinidad.

## LATINIDAD AND BLACKNESS

Among the most salient concepts of identity, Latinidad has emerged as a framework articulating Latinx subjectivity in the United States. Deriving from an identification with the term *Latino* and its variants, **Latinidad** can be conceptualized as the "processes where Latino/a identities and cultural practices are contested and created in media, discourse, and public space" (Guidotti-Hernandez 212). In application, Latinidad becomes a flexible and ambivalent association with Latinx identity, culture, and community on a **pan-ethnic** level. Yet there is not a singular or monolithic Latinidad. Therefore, the more nuanced articulation of *Latinidades* better acknowledges the diversity and hybridity among those commonly identified as Latina/o/x. Frances R. Aparicio and Susana Chávez-Silverman assert that Latinidad is not an all-encompassing category including all things related to Latin America but a far more complex notion that is "contestatory and contested, fluid, and relational" (15). It is through US homogenizing pan-ethnic discourses that all those who would be categorized as Hispanic/Latino become consolidated into one identity category: an identity category that fundamentally ignores and erases ethnoracial, national, and cultural specificity. Consequently, there is not one singular umbrella Latinidad, but rather multiple Latinidades.

While Latinidad by its very nature challenges racialized binary thinking in the United States, Afro-Latinidad problematizes this thinking even further by complicating what becomes acceptably included within the boundaries of Latinidad, Blackness, and/or whiteness. Ultimately, what this speaks to is the contentious relationship between Blackness and Afro-Latinidad that is rooted in colonialist history and a complicated relationship with African descent.

## AFRO-LATINIDAD

Popularly imagined as a homogenous "Brown" race with a mixed Indigenous and Spanish ethnoracial heritage, the extreme diversity within the Latinx population is systematically flattened, ignored, and erased. Furthermore, regardless of the significant presence of African ancestry among Latin American and Caribbean populations, Blackness is obscured in multiple ways. A common phenomenon in the Spanish Caribbean is the suggestion that non-European features and heritage are not of African descent, but Indigenous. Examples include the ***mestizaje***-based nationalistic discourse of ***la gran familia puertorriquena*** in Puerto Rico and how ***antihaitianismo*** manifests in the Dominican Republic through those of African descent being referred to as *indio* (Rivero 13–15; Candelario 2; Sagás 35). In many countries of Central and South America, Blackness tends to be rendered invisible through lack of acknowledgment altogether or the suggestion that any population of African descent in these countries originate from Caribbean immigrants. Others, like Brazil or Cuba for instance, are politically celebratory of their African heritage, but in practice their claims of racelessness or racial democracy cover up the reality of anti-Black discrimination. Such heritages of anti-Blackness do not disappear within a US context but merely enter into a dialogue with one another.

The result of internalization of US racial ideology is a collective distancing among those in the pan-Latinx community from connections to Blackness (Cruz-Janzen; Román and Flores). In application this means the Latinx community, and those who represent it, often implicitly reinforce anti-Black racism through their hesitance to acknowledge the Afro-Latinas/os that make up part of their community. According to Marta I. Cruz-Janzen, "the more Latinos become immersed in the racial ideology of the United States, . . . the more powerful is their need and desire to free themselves of any and all vestiges of African ancestry" (286). Without explicit acknowledgment and inclusion of Afro-Latinas/os within the Latinx community, it is no surprise that, as standard political and representational practice in the United States, Latinas/os are consolidated under the label "Latino" and their heterogeneity masked by a generic representation. Pan-ethnic Latinidad, though beneficial in terms of alliance politics and solidarity, privileges certain experiences, representations, and identifications over others. Certainly, many Afro-Latinas/os claim a Hispanic/Latino identification; however, this identification is more appropriative or assimilationist than organic. Their association with this identity category is more nuanced than current articulations of "Latino" allow for and results in a desire to qualify where they fit within this pan-ethnic conglomeration.

One particular manifestation of the complex relationship between Latinidad and Blackness is the prevalence of **colorism**. The various expressions of this in Latin America and the United States is fully nuanced in Chapter 4. In practice this means that the lighter one's skin, the more legitimate the claim to Latinidad. The manifold impact of colorism among Latinas/os is the abjection and marginalization of dark-skinned Afro-Latinas/os. Yet, Afro-Latinidad is much more palatable, both within and outside the Latinx community, if it is subtle (e.g., an ambiguous brown skin tone, curly hair that has been relaxed or straightened, more "European" facial features, etc.). Furthermore, colorism swings the other way as well. Afro-Latinas/os often have their Blackness put into question among other groups of African descent (African Americans, Continental Africans, **West Indians**). For these groups, Afro-Latinas/os are often not Black enough. They are seen as culturally distinct and, therefore, are marginalized among Black communities as well.

Even in the face of these multiple and contradictory approaches to minimizing Latinx Blackness, there are many who have immersed themselves in US Black politics and culture. Alliances between African Americans and Afro-Latinas/os have a legacy dating back to the Haitian Revolution in 1791, and many enslaved Africans worked on Caribbean plantations before they were sold in the United States. Afro-Latinas/os have played key roles in some of the most significant periods of Black cultural influence; for example, Arturo Schomburg during the Harlem Renaissance of the 1920s and jazz virtuoso Dizzy Gillespie. Some have collaborated with African American civil rights leaders, and others were key members of the alliance-based movements that emerged in the 1960s and 1970s, such as the feminist Third World Women's Alliance. It was the cultural collaboration of Puerto Ricans and African Americans in the 1970s that created hip-hop culture and music, a subject that has been studied extensively by sociologist Raquel Rivera.

Regardless of varied and hegemonic processes of symbolic annihilation, contestation, and acceptance of African descent, Afro-Latinidad not only exists but is thriving. Movements celebrating and promoting the various articulations of Afro-Latinidades can be found in almost every part of the Americas. Afro-Latinidad, like Latinidad and Latinidades, is about articulating identity and subjectivity. It is a way of both distinguishing and centering Blackness within the Latinx imaginary. Its continued visibility actively works against the contradictions within amorphous constructs of "Latino" (Román and Flores 2). Influenced by the identity politics of Black Power and Afrocentrism, Afro-Latinas/os have become increasingly vocal about and attentive to their African descent. Activists, scholars, artists, musicians, and everyday people are finding empowerment in not just acknowledging their Blackness but in understanding it as a weapon for post-colonial identification. For example, in his discussion of (Afro-)*Antillanismo,* Juan Flores contends that what separates *caribeños* (those that situate their identities within the Spanish Caribbean) from Latinx pan-ethnicity is Blackness and an Afro-Atlantic imaginary. His analysis suggests that people from the major Spanish Caribbean countries (Puerto Rico, Cuba, and the Dominican Republic) engage with US notions of Blackness, nationally constructed racial ideologies, and constructions of race articulated through pan-Caribbean/Antillean discourses. Afro-Latina/o conferences, festivals, research institutes, websites, student groups, social media hashtags, etc. have become productive spaces to establish and enrich the "foundational historical and cultural connection to Africa, an affirmation that simultaneously defies the Eurocentric ideologies that have characterized Latin America and the Caribbean" (Román and Flores 2). While these phenomena are encouraging, they are not reflected in media representation.

## AFRO-LATINAS/OS IN THE MEDIA

With such a complex ethnoracial terrain to contend with, it should be a surprise to no one that inclusion, acknowledgment, and adequate representation of Afro-Latinas/os and Afro-Latinidad in media is at best negligible. The politics of media representation has made one thing quite clear: "as far as the mainstream media are concerned, Latin@s are not black and Blacks are not Latin@" (Román and Flores 10). Due to a legacy of Blackness "tainting" anything it mixes with, Afro-Latinidad is rendered invisible, even as Afro-Latinas/os have long participated in the industry.

In a visual medium, the way actors look is not only important but significantly influences the frameworks within which audiences interpret the characters they portray. And in a society where race matters, ethnoracial categorization is assigned based on what an actor *appears* to be. As Blackness is not included within the parameters of the mediated "**Latin look**," Afro-Latinas/os rarely appear Latina/o to mainstream audiences. Even for audiences familiar with a star's Afro-Latina/o background, their Latinidad is made marginal in the presence of Blackness. This not only limits Afro-Latinas/os to roles already signified with Blackness but often prohibits them from portraying Latina/o characters all together. Actors like Christina Milian and Zoe Saldana have dark enough skin tones that casting them as African American seems appropriate, if not the only option. (Milian is of Afro-Cuban descent and Zoe Saldana is Dominican-Puerto Rican). Michelle Rodriguez, who better embodies a typical Latina look, can easily play a **Chicana** (Mexican American) although she is of partial Dominican descent. Casting agents therefore rely on dominant conceptions of racialization to construct a racial understanding of racially "ambiguous" actors (Warner 49). What becomes important is not how the actor self-identifies but how a mainstream audience would racialize them playing a given character. Essentially, do they have the "right look?"

Furthermore, the various US English media avenues and industries mis- and under-represent Afro-Latinas/os in a way that marginalizes their identities and shapes the way mainstream US society reads their racialization. Representations of Afro-Latinas/os are extremely rare in US mass media and are regularly limited to certain narrative locations (New York City, for example). In Spanish-language media, such representations, while sustaining a more visible presence, are secondary, limited, and "negative," usually seen in their positioning as background characters or domestics in **telenovelas**, the trivializing of Spanish Caribbean interests in news coverage, and an almost total lack of cultural representation based in Afro-Latinidades (Román and Flores 10–11).

The phenomenon of invisible Afro-Latinidad in media is a historical and contemporary one. To demonstrate this, I will examine three Afro-Latina/o actors—Juano Hernández, Gina Torres, and Rosario Dawson—and the ways in which they have navigated a media industry that sees Black and Latina/o as mutually exclusive.

## JUANO HERNÁNDEZ

Figure 5.1: Juano Hernández as Wesley in *The Breaking Point* (1950).
Source: DVD of *The Breaking Point*
Attribution: Michael Curtiz
License: Fair Use

Born in Puerto Rico, Juano Hernández was a boxer, circus acrobat, vaudeville performer, script writer, theater actor, and radio performer before 1949, when he was cast as Lucas Beauchamp in the major Hollywood film *Intruder in the Dust*

(1949), a role that would earn him a Golden Globe nomination and BAFTA win. Hernández was among the first actors of African descent to be cast in a leading role along with big-name White Hollywood stars, including Kirk Douglas, Steve McQueen, and Doris Day (Alexander). Along with actors like Sidney Poitier and Harry Belafonte, the lesser-remembered Hernández took part in a period of Hollywood history that dealt with changing racial politics by including "dignified" and "respectable" African American characters (Bastién; A. Vargas). In addition to a couple earlier 1930s "race films" (independent films starring African Americans that catered to Black audiences), Hernández also appeared in a handful of Black-cast films in the 1950s and '60s with actors like Nat King Cole, Pearl Bailey, Sidney Poitier, Ruby Dee, and Eartha Kitt (Alexander).

Everyone knew Hernández was from Puerto Rico, but the ways in which his Blackness was represented never affirmed his Afro-Latinidad. Instead, he was hailed as a great "Negro" actor. Brian Eugenio Herrera uses the term "Stealth Latinos" to refer to Latina/o actors whose Latinidad was not denied but also not reflected in the roles they played in film and television. While this usually manifested in the ability to play White characters, Hernández was almost exclusively cast as either African American or African (Rodriguez; Herrera). Shortly before the release of *The Breaking Point* (1950), a piece in *Ebony* magazine said of Hernández's success: "It is a symbol of the changing pattern of race relations in motion pictures since in every role Hernandez has played a dignified, understanding Negro character" ("Hollywood's 'Hottest'"). The fact that Hernández was so often written about in *Ebony*, a publication explicitly rooted in the African American experience and dedicated to a mission of Black racial uplift, is quite telling. It reveals just how extensive is the reach of hypodescent, as well as a hesitation to distinguish one form of Blackness from another. In the same piece from *Ebony*, the film's director, Michael Curtiz, is quoted as saying, "Hernandez is the 'new Negro' in our movies. No longer do we have the janitors and shoe shine boys. Now we have a dignified, intelligent, big man" ("Hollywood's 'Hottest'"). Yet important to note for this film in particular is the fact that the character Hernández played, Wesley Park, was not originally written as a Black character (both in the source material of Hemingway's *To Have and Have Not* and the original film script). As such, it is an apt media text to discuss a little further.

*The Breaking Point* is a film noir-style production that focuses on the moral challenges its protagonist, Harry Morgan (John Garfield), must navigate in order to support his business and family. Harry is a boat captain, and Hernández's Wesley is his firstmate. Wesley is the moral compass Harry turns to as he starts to head down a path of illegal activities and human smuggling. When things go wrong, Wesley is killed, to the horror of Harry. While the film shows a level of Black and White coexistence that was relatively anomalous for a film made in segregated America, it is nonetheless "emblematic of a recurring motif in liberal white films, which often recruited black partners to help white protagonists learn more about themselves" (Civille 9). The film ends in the bleak and tragic vein so common of film noir, with most of the main characters dead and hope destroyed. Poignantly, the last scene of the film shows Wesley's son waiting on a pier for a father that will never return, completely unaware that his father has been killed and dumped in the ocean—a suitable metaphor for the devaluing of Black lives as well as the lack of cultural memory of an early and well-respected Afro-Latino actor.

## GINA TORRES

**Figure 5.2: Gina Torres at a press conference promoting the television show *The Catch* (2016–2017).**

Source: Flickr
Attribution: Walt Disney
License: CC BY-ND 2.0

Finding more success in television than film, Gina Torres's career exemplifies the contemporary invisibility of Afro-Latinidad within US media. Afro-Cuban Torres has been very candid about her experience as an Afro-Latina who is only cast as Black/African American characters. In the Mun2 (now NBC Universo) network's short documentary *Black and Latino* (2012), Torres says, "When I became an actress, I quickly realized that the world liked their Latinas to look Italian, not like me. And so I wasn't going up for Latina parts, I was going up for African American parts." Torres's Blackness has affected her career the most in terms of role opportunities. In fact, many audiences are completely unaware of her Cuban heritage, even considering her Latinx surname. In many ways a cult star, Torres has starred in or been featured in many science-fiction and fantasy television shows. Known best for her roles in *Cleopatra 2525* (2000–2001), *Firefly* (2002–2003), *Serenity* (2005), and the last two installments of *The Matrix* trilogy in 2003, she also appeared in reoccurring roles in *Hercules: The Legendary Journeys* (1995–1999), *Angel* (1999–2004), *24* (2001–2010), *Alias* (2001–2006), and *Suits* (2011–2019).

While her career has been mostly on television, she has been cast in a handful of African American cinema films. Torres has played a Black/African American character in films like the Mo'Nique vehicle *Hair Show* (2004) and the Black-cast film *Fair Game* (2005). In the film *I Think I Love My Wife* (2007), directed by and starring Chris Rock, Torres plays Brenda Cooper, wife of Richard Cooper (Rock), who is caught between staying loyal to his wife and family and pursuing his seductive former crush Nikki (Kerry Washington). While not a film necessarily targeted toward the African American audience, race is far from invisible and the film does retain a watered-down version of Rock's racial comedy sensibility. Brenda discusses a desire to find an African American "mocha mothers" support group, and the narrative trades in discourses of middle-class African American politics of respectability. (The politics of respectability emerged during racial segregation within the African American community as a way to improve their social situation and emphasized acting "respectable" [Higginbotham]).

Torres's casting does not raise any eyebrows, and her Afro-Latinidad is rendered invisible in the process. When asked how she feels about playing African American characters, Torres told *Latina* magazine "I don't feel like I'm living a lie, because the fact is the world sees me as an African American woman unless they ask the question. Therefore my experience in the world, outside of my family, is that of an African American woman" (Trivino). Not much has changed since the time of Juano Hernández. Appearance of Blackness is enough to preclude any meaningful inclusion in representational Latinidad.

## ROSARIO DAWSON

Figure 5.3: Rosario Dawson at the Streamy Awards in 2009.
Source: Flickr
Attribution: Bui Brothers/Streamy Awards
License: CC BY-ND 2.0

Among the three actors discussed in this chapter, Rosario Dawson has found the most mainstream success. She is probably also the most racially ambiguous. Having Puerto Rican, Afro-Cuban, Irish, and Native American heritages, Dawson's racialization is often ambiguous and even flexible (Beltrán, *Latina/o Stars*; Hensley). Her mixed heritage is frequently credited for her good looks and is something she is asked repeatedly to comment on during interviews. Consequently, in the majority of her films and television shows, race must be implied by various markers, including darkness of skin, presence of accent, language spoken, location of character origin, fashion and styling, and the ethnic quality of the character's name (Beltrán, "Hollywood Latina"; Valdivia). Audiences' ethnoracial readings of Dawson are highly context/narrative specific and, at times, reflect ideological challenges to normative racial thinking in the United States.

Unlike Hernández and Torres, Dawson's career is marked by more casting flexibility; the characters she portrays are often racialized as *either* African American *or* Latina (Beltrán, *Latina/o Stars*). As an example, in *The Adventures of Pluto Nash* (2002), Dawson seems to be racialized as vaguely Black in relation to Eddie Murphy's unquestioned racialization as African American. Beyond the pairing of Dawson with an African American leading man, a strategy that harkens back to the discomfort toward miscegenation for a US audience, she is depicted as an R&B singer, a designation that, in turn, potentially races her as African American. Similarly, in *Josie and the Pussycats* (2001), Dawson portrays Valerie Brown, the African American band member of the Pussycats, based on the Archie Comics animated series character from the 1970s. As a continuation of a previously racialized character, her "café au lait" skin tone is read as light-skinned African American. Furthermore, the character's non-ethnic name distances Dawson from an alternative Latina reading. She is, additionally, regularly represented in this film with hairstyles that are associated with an African American aesthetic, such as afro puffs, braids, and salon-styled tight curls. Both these films represent Dawson as African American in a way that would rule out a connection to a Latina identity.

However, this racialization as African American is not as common in her other films. As the character of Mimi in the film *Rent* (2005), one of her most famous roles, Dawson is the epitome of the New York City Latina. She has a **Nuyorican** (New York Puerto Rican) accent, a darker skin tone, long dark hair with some texture, and she works as a stripper. In any other location outside of New York City, her racialization would be difficult to read; however, in the context of the city, she is unmistakably Latina of Caribbean heritage. Similarly, in the film *Side Streets* (1998), a story that is meant to reflect the ethnic and racial diversity of the individual boroughs of New York City, the audience is presented with two couples of arguable Caribbean origin: one West Indian and one Puerto Rican. The West Indian couple in Brooklyn are of clear primary African descent and are therefore Black. However, the Latinx couple, Marisol (Dawson) and Ramon (John Ortiz), are generically depicted as Latinx. Here we see an overt depiction of a conceptualization of Spanish-speaking Caribbeans as not Black in comparison with more explicitly Black West Indians. In fact, Dawson's African descent is downplayed in her character by placing her within a family of lighter-skinned Latinas (her mother and sister), which helps negate a connection to African descent within her character. Moreover, the sub-narrative of the Bronx utilizes spoken Spanish to further mark Dawson as primarily Latina while the exclusively English-language dialogue within the sub-narrative of Brooklyn suggests that the couple's origin is from an island that was colonized by the British and therefore rules out any possible connection to the Spanish Caribbean. Admittedly, there might be an unspoken understanding that Puerto Ricans have varying degrees of African descent, yet the juxtaposition of Dawson's character to those uncritically racialized as Black prevents a mainstream reading of her character from being anything but Latinx in general and maybe, more specifically, Puerto Rican for those who are familiar with the specific Latinx populations in New York City.

## RE-CENTERING BLACKNESS WITHIN LATINIDAD

One clear result of Latinx pan-ethnicity is the marginalizing of Blackness within a system of representation that gives preference to Latinx whiteness. This is a representational cycle that must be broken, and not just by lighter-skinned and more ambiguous Afro-Latinas/os like Rosario Dawson. While Afro-Latina/o actors are occasionally represented as Latina/o, that Latinidad is a marginalized and contextualized one. Significantly, each actor's public acknowledgment of their African descent negates the polarity of US media racialization that attempts to place characters in an either/or construction, in this case either African American or Latinx. Afro-Latinidad threatens to deconstruct long-held racial ideologies, in both the United States and Latin America.

One might ask if this dearth of representation is on the verge of a revolution. Of note is the award buzz around the Afro-Latina Ariana DeBose, who plays the role of Anita in Steven Spielberg's *West Side Story* (2021). Yet when seen in relation to the claims of colorism for the film *In the Heights* (2021)—which is discussed in more detail in Chapter 3 of this book—it is too early to tell. Regardless, Latinx African descent is not an outlier; it is just as central to Latinidad as Spanish and Indigenous heritages. Consequently, a re-centering of Blackness demonstrates the potential of Afro-Latina/o subjectivity to blur the boundaries of racial binary as well as pan-ethnic Latinidad.

## BIBLIOGRAPHY

Alexander, Otis. "Juano Hernández (1896-1970)." *BlackPast*, 8 Sept. 2009, https://www.blackpast.org/african-american-history/hernandez-juano-1896-1970/.

Aparicio, Frances R., and Suzanne Chávez-Silverman. *Tropicalizations: Transcultural Representations of Latinidad*. UP of New England, 1997.

Bastién, Angelica Jade. "Juano Hernández Should Have Been the First Afro–Puerto Rican Screen Legend." *Vulture*, 7 Jan. 2020, https://www.vulture.com/2020/01/juano-hernandez-should-have-been-a-hollywood-legend.html.

Beltrán, Mary. *Latina/o Stars in U.S. Eyes: The Making and Meanings of Film and TV Stardom*. U of Illinois P, 2009.

---."The Hollywood Latina Body as Site of Social Struggle: Media Constructions of Stardom and Jennifer Lopez's 'Cross-over Butt.'" *Quarterly Review of Film & Video*, vol. 19, no. 1, 2002, pp. 71–86.

*Black and Latino*. Produced by Mun2.tv, 2012.

Candelario, Ginetta E.B. *Black Behind the Ears: Dominican Racial Identity From Museums to Beauty Shops*. Duke UP, 2007.

Civille, Michael. "'Ain't Got No Chance':The Case of The Breaking Point." *Cinema Journal* vol. 56, no. 1, 2016, pp. 1–2.

Cruz-Janzen, Marta I. "Latinegras: Desired Women—Undesirable Mothers, Daughters, Sisters, and Wives." *The Afro-Latin@ Reader: History and Culture in the United States*, edited by Miriam Jiménez Román and Juan Flores. Duke UP, 2010, pp. 282–95.

Davis, Angela. "Interview with Lisa Lowe, Angela Davis: Reflections on Race, Class, and Gender in the USA." *The Politics of Culture in the Shadow of Capital*, edited by Lisa Lowe and David Lloyd, Duke UP, 1997, pp. 303–23.

Flores, Juan. *The Diaspora Strikes Back: Caribeño Tales of Learning and Turning.* Routledge, 2009.

Guidotti-Hernández, Nicole M. "Dora The Explorer, Constructing 'LATINIDADES' and The Politics of Global Citizenship." *Latino Studies*, vol. 5, no. 2, 2007, pp. 209–32.

Hall, Stuart. *Race, the Floating Signifier Featuring Stuart Hall.* Produced by Sut Jhally, Media Education Foundation, 1997.

Hensley, Dennis. "Rosario Dawson: From Tenement to Tinseltown." *Marie Claire*, 31 Oct. 2005, https://www.marieclaire.com/celebrity/a151/rosario-dawson/.

Herrera, Brian Eugenio. *Latin Numbers: Playing Latino in Twentieth-Century US Popular Performance.* U of Michigan P, 2015.

Higginbotham, Evelyn Brooks. *Righteous Discontent: The Women's Movement in the Black Baptist Church, 1880–1920.* Harvard UP, 1994.

"Hollywood's 'Hottest' Negro Actor: Dynamic Juano Hernández Gets His Fourth Important Role in Single Year in 'The Breaking Point'." *Ebony* Aug. 1950, pp. 20–26.

Khanna, Nikki. "'If You're Half Black, You're Just Black': Reflected Appraisals and the Persistence of the One-Drop Rule." *Sociological Quarterly*, vol. 51, 2010, pp. 96–121.

Rivero, Yeidy M. *Tuning Out Blackness: Race and Nation in the History of Puerto Rican Television.* Duke UP, 2005.

Rodriguez, Clara E. *Heroes, Lovers, and Others: The Story of Latinos in Hollywood.* Smithsonian Books, 2004.

Román, Miriam Jiménez, and Juan Flores. "Introduction." *The Afro-Latin@ Reader: History and Culture in the United States*, edited by Miriam Jiménez Román and Juan Flores. Duke UP, 2010, pp. 1–18.

Sagás, Ernesto. *Race and Politics in the Dominican Republic.* UP of Florida, 2000.

Trivino, J. "Gina Torres Talks About Being Afro-latina in Hollywood." *Latina*, April 2013.

Valdivia, Angharad N. "Is Penelope to J. Lo as Culture is to Nature? Eurocentric Approaches to 'Latin' Beauties." *From Bananas to Buttocks: The Latina Body in Popular Film and Culture*, edited by Myra Mendible. U of Texas P, 2007, pp. 129–48.

Vargas, Andrew S. "A Look Back at the Films of Juano Hernández, Hollywood's Very First Afro-Latino Movie Star." *Remezcla*, 5 Feb. 2015, https://remezcla.com/lists/film/tbt-look-back-films-juano-hernandez-hollywoods-first-afro-latino-movie-star/.

Warner, Kristen. *Colorblind TV: Primetime Politics of Race in Television Casting.* 2010. U of Texas, PhD dissertation.

## FILMOGRAPHY

*Adventures of Pluto Nash*. Directed by Ron Underwood, performances by Eddie Murphy, Rosario Dawson, Randy Quad, and Jay Mhor, Warner Brothers, 2002.

*The Breaking Point*. Directed by Michael Curtiz, performances by John Garfield, Patricia Neal, Phyllis Thaxter, and Juano Hernandez, Warner Brothers, 1950.

*I Think I Love My Wife*. Directed by Chris Rock, performances by Chris Rock, Gina Torres, Kerry Washington, and Steve Buscemi, Fox Searchlight, 2007.

*Intruder in the Dust*. Directed by Clarence Brown, performances by David Brian, Claude Jarman Jr., Juano Hernandez, and Porter Hall, MGM Studios, 1949.

*Josie and the Pussy Cats*. Directed by Harry Elfont and Deborah Kaplan, performances by Rachael Leigh Cook, Tara Reid, and Rosario Dawson, Universal Pictures, 2001.

*Rent*. Directed by Chris Columbus, performances by Tay Diggs, Wilson Jermaine Heredia, Rosario Dawson, Anthony Rapp, Adam Pascal, Jesse L. Martin, Idina Menzel, and Tracie Thoms, Columbia Pictures, 2005.

*Side Streets*. Directed by Tony Gerber, performances by Valeria Golino, Rosario Dawson, Shabana Azmi, Jennifer Esposito, Shashi Kapoor, Miho Nikaido, David Vadim, Art Malik, Leon, Merchant Ivory, 1998.

## FOR FURTHER STUDY

Hall, Stuart. "What Is This 'Black' in Black Popular Culture?" *Social Justice/Global Options*, special issue of *Social Justice*, vol. 20, no. 1/2, 1993, pp. 104–14.

---. "New Ethnicities." *Stuart Hall: Critical Dialogues in Cultural Studies*, edited by David Morley and Kuan-Hsing Chen. Routledge, 1996, pp. 442–51.

*In the Heights*. Directed by Jon M. Chu, performances by Anthony Ramos, Corey Hawkins, Leslie Grace, Melissa Barrera, Olga Merediz, Jimmy Smits, Stephanie Beatriz, and Dascha Polanco, Warner Brothers, 2021.

Ovalle, Priscilla Peña. "Framing Jennifer Lopez: Mobilizing Race from the Wide Shot to the Close-Up." *The Persistence of Whiteness: Race and Contemporary Hollywood Cinema*, edited by Daniel Bernardi. Routledge, 2007, pp. 165–84.

Rivera, Raquel Z. *New York Ricans From the Hip Hop Zone*. Palgrave MacMillan, 2003.

Smith, Carol A. "Myths, Intellectuals, and Race/Class/Gender Distinctions in the Formation of Latin American Nations." *Journal of Latin American Anthropology* vol. 2, 1996, pp. 148–69.

Vargas, Lucila. *Latina Teens, Migration, and Popular Culture*. Peter Lang, 2009.

*West Side Story*. Directed by Steven Spielberg, performances by Ansel Elgort, Rachel Zegler, Ariana DeBose, David Alvarez, Rita Moreno, and Mike Faist, 20th Century Studios, 2021.

# Diasporic Indigenous Latinx Identity and Media

Argelia González Hurtado
(St. Mary's College of Maryland)

Like other Indigenous communities around the world, Indigenous Latinx creators put to use diverse forms of media, including video and film, to create and disseminate their own cultural, historical, and political viewpoints, signaling the growing place of Indigenous-led voices in twenty-first-century media production. In this chapter, you will discover individual Indigenous Latinx media-makers and their practices, identify some general characteristics of Indigenous Latinx audiovisual practices, and interpret the ways Indigenous creators understand their **indigeneity**, particularly in a **diasporic** context (that is, a context where individuals are living outside their original homelands due to migration or forced relocation). You will also consider the ways Indigenous Latinx media-makers challenge rigid and reductionist understandings of both **Latinidad** and indigeneity in their works. First, you will briefly review the cultural context of the diversity of Indigenous peoples in Latin America. Next, you will become equipped to assess the problematic and stereotypical representations of Indigenous communities by dominant cinemas in both Latin America and the United States, contextualizing the challenges Indigenous creators must overcome in depicting their own communities. Finally, you will reflect on two critical case studies of Indigenous Latinx filmmakers and explore strategies and practices of Indigenous self-representation in cinema.

## INDIGENOUS PEOPLES IN LATIN AMERICA

Indigenous cultures and peoples do not belong to a single shared identity category as there are great historical, cultural, and linguistic differences among Indigenous communities within Latin American regions. For example, in Mexico there are around seventy Indigenous groups and approximately sixty-eight Indigenous languages (Sistema de Información Cultural; "Indigenous Peoples in Mexico"). Guatemala is home to twenty-four ethnic groups and around twenty-two Indigenous languages, with descendant groups of the Mayans in the majority ("Indigenous Peoples in Guatemala"). When referring to Indigenous communities, the reality of multiple indigeneities and the specifics of history, language, and culture in shaping identity must always be considered.

What Latin American Indigenous groups all have in common, however, is a shared history of colonization that has continued to perpetuate systemic racism and marginalization in national contexts. Following the period of independence from European colonial authority (predominantly Spanish and Portuguese) beginning around 1820, the inclusion of Indigenous societies in emerging understandings of Latin American nationhood was seen as problematic. Indigenous communities presented a puzzle for the nation-building process, which sought political, economic, and cultural unification. In order to forge a "unified" nation, countries chose to adopt an ideological state project of **mestizaje**—the process of racial, ethnic, and cultural mixing. Through different periods, political and intellectual elites of Latin American and Caribbean states have promoted different versions of *mestizaje* as a model of the nation. Underlying the concept of *mestizaje* has been the validation of a series of assimilationist policies that undermine and suppress unique Indigenous identities in favor of a national identity where the **mestizo** (mixed descent) person is the ideal citizen.

Indigenous peoples of Latin America are a growing population within the US Latinx community. An Indigenous Latinx diaspora has been precipitated by economic crises and political violence in places of origin. For instance, the number of Indigenous migrants (of Mayan, Garifuna, or Xinca descent) fleeing Guatemala has increased since the 1980s due to the systematic genocide perpetuated by dictatorships and civil war. When Indigenous Latinx people migrate to the United States, they must contend with the ethnic and racial conceptions of a new social context. For example, in the United States, Indigenous individuals are marginalized, much like those from other non-White, non-Anglo racial and ethnic groups. Despite the growing number of Indigenous Latinx people located within the United States, the population has remained less visible in American society as it is incorporated into more generalized identity categories such as Mexican, Guatemalan, Hispanic, and Latino. In reality, complex Indigenous cultural, historical, and linguistic backgrounds do not necessarily conform to such reductive identity categories. For example, the term *Hispanic* refers to a Spanish heritage of Latin America, while *Latino* alludes to the geographical origins of people from Latin America. Both of these identity categories are the most used in the United States to classify people of diverse background or origin from Latin America. However, neither category fully acknowledges the wide variety of peoples of Indigenous and/or African descent that make up Latin America. Indigenous Latinx, therefore, is a more representative way to refer to the population since it better recognizes the complexities of ethnic identity and is also a gender-neutral term.

# RECURRING STEREOTYPES OF INDIGENOUS PEOPLES IN FILM

The dominant cinemas in both Latin America and the United States historically developed stereotypical representations of Indigenous people. In North America, Indigenous characters have been depicted within a narrow range of tropes: savage, warrior, medicine man/woman, stoic Indian, or beautiful maiden. Further, Indigenous societies have been represented as vanishing cultures, unable or unwilling to adapt to modernity. Michelle H. Raheja explains that since the beginning of the North American film industry, there has been a persistent fascination with the image of the American Indian. Although Native Americans are hypervisible in films produced during the twentieth century, they are simultaneously "rendered invisible" through plotlines that "reinforce the trope of Indigenous people as vanishing or inconsequential" (Raheja). Such films influence non-Indigenous audiences, shaping their perceptions of indigeneity through stereotypes that ignore Indigenous societies in modern contexts.

Indigenous Latinx communities have faced similar misrepresentations in the national cinemas of Latin American countries. In the case of Latin America, there have generally been few cinematic stories about Indigenous people. In Mexico, however, between the 1940s and 1950s, a series of films were produced with stories about Indigenous characters, yet the films showed an idealized version of a "whitened Indian." The actors who portrayed Indigenous characters were always *mestizos* or White.

Figure 6.1: In *María Candelaría* (1943) non-Indigenous actors like Dolores del Río (pictured) perform the main Indigenous characters.

Source: DVD of *María Candelaría*
Attribution: Emilio Fernández
License: Fair Use

Even after these films became dated, several generations of audiences have still been exposed to the productions due to constant re-airings by Spanish-language television networks in Mexico (Televisa, Azteca) and in the United States (Univisión, Azteca América, Telemundo), thereby perpetuating problematic cultural representations.

Indigenous Latinx communities that migrate to the United States must also deal with the broader stereotypes of Mexicans and other Latin American ethnicities by **mainstream** Hollywood cinema. The tropes used by Hollywood to represent Mexicans and Latin Americans in general include "*el bandido* [the bandit], the harlot, the male buffoon, the female clown, the Latin lover, and the dark lady" (Ramírez Berg 66). Such stereotypes can be traced back to the silent era of Hollywood cinema (1910–l920) and its consolidation during the Golden Age of Hollywood (1920–1960), where the Mexican bandit was a recurring character, mostly in Western dramas. In more contemporary films, the figure of the immigrant (particularly undocumented ones) as well as the maid or housekeeper have also emerged as common tropes. As Ramírez Berg further explains, in such film representations, "Mexicans and Mexican Americans may be stereotypically believed to be lazy, dirty, dishonest, unmoral, and with low regard toward life. These traits are then applied to actual Mexicans encountered in lived experience" (39). In both North American and Latin American contexts, then, Indigenous populations have been strongly stereotyped on film. The cinematic misrepresentation of Indigenous peoples is due to many factors, including a dominant ideology of social and cultural assimilation, but also the fact that such audiovisual representations have been made by non-Indigenous people.

## INDIGENOUS SELF-REPRESENTATION IN FILM

Among global Indigenous communities, there is a growing movement of using audiovisual media to undo the negative effects of colonialism that have denied and excluded Indigenous realities, histories, stories, and knowledges (Mignolo; Smith). By creating their own content through processes of self-representation, Indigenous creators look to subvert dominate narratives that marginalize Indigenous lived experience and instead show the myriad of realities in which contemporary Indigenous communities are immersed.

In the case of diasporic Indigenous Latinx media creators, they also reveal and represent the complexity of what it means to be Indigenous within the migrant experience. In their works, they embark on social, political, and cultural quests to make visible aspects of Indigenous identity and culture, such as traditions, languages, belief systems, and knowledges, that render a more nuanced depiction of reality. In other words, diasporic Indigenous Latinx creators emphasize ethnic and cultural expressions to distinguish their specific communities from more general categories such as Guatemalan, Mexican, Hispanic, Latino, and/or immigrant. Further, many of these media-makers undertake a dialogue with such generalized identity categories within both the United States and communities of origin, questioning what it means to be Indigenous and hold other identity markers, such as those based on ability, age, class, gender, religion, and/or sexual orientation. Moreover, diasporic Indigenous Latinx media-makers show the way Indigenous migrants renegotiate and build **transnational** identities as a result of the process of understanding their relationship with their communities of origin and the wider US society. In doing so, they show how this dialogue also shapes the way they assume their indigeneity and sense of identity in a diasporic context.

## INDIGENOUS LATINX MEDIA-MAKERS

In the Latinx media landscape, there has been an increase in the number of filmmakers and media-creators that self-identify as Indigenous. For example, the database Latinx Directors shows twelve film directors in the Indigenous Latinx category, many who highlight their Indigenous background in their biographies. For instance, Cristina Kotz Cornejo's biography mentions that she is a descendant of the Indigenous Huarpe people of the Cuyo region of Argentina; Peter Bratt's biography emphasizes his Quechua heritage and the fact he was raised by a strong, Indigenous, single mother from Peru; and Yolanda Cruz describes herself as a Chatina who films in Oaxaca and the United States. The Latinx Directors database only provides a small glimpse of the panorama of Indigenous creators who are currently developing a body of work in the film industry. However, we must also take into account the existence of media creators in the form of collectives and collaborative groups focused on producing media by and for their communities, and that draw on local, translocal, or non-local stories.

It is important to note that if a filmmaker identifies as Indigenous Latinx, it does not necessarily mean that their work always revolves around their identity or that their narrative themes are related to Latinidad, indigeneity, or immigration. However, this chapter highlights filmmakers who, in addition to identifying as Indigenous Latinx, develop their work taking these characteristics into account. It is also relevant to understand that even when some filmmakers identify themselves as Indigenous Latinx, they must continuously negotiate identity labels. In an interview by Moi Santos for Sundance Institute with Aurora Guerrero and Yolanda Cruz, both filmmakers explain what the term *Latinx* means to them. (Guerrero's directorial debut was the acclaimed narrative film *Mosquita y Mari* [2012]; Cruz has distinguished herself with documentaries related to immigration issues.) Questioned about whether they identify as Latinx or another term, Guerrero mentions that while she uses the term *Latinx* because it is genderless and inclusive, she also identifies as Xicana because it "puts the Indigenous over the European." Cruz also mentions the inclusivity of Latinx but nevertheless recognizes the importance of intersecting identities: "Yes, I am identified as a Latinx; I am also Indigenous and Chatina." It is clear that while identity may shift depending on a number of situational contexts, for these filmmakers it is important that their indigeneity be recognized as an aspect of their identity formation that in turn influences the content that they create.

Although each Indigenous Latinx filmmaker develops their own particular style, those with a more prominent ethnic consciousness may present certain characteristics in their films, such as a connection with their place of origin—an especially common practice among immigrant filmmakers. Hamid Naficy explains in his seminal work about the filmmaking practices of exiled, diasporic, or immigrant filmmakers that such practices are distinguished by an ethnic consciousness and distinctiveness that the filmmakers maintain over time and that gives them a horizontal and **multi-sited** consciousness involving both homeland and compatriot communities elsewhere. For these reasons, we can find in their works a blend of topics or techniques. For instance, some of the filmmakers integrate different linguistic codes in their films, such as English, Spanish, and Indigenous languages, or even a mishmash of different languages, such as Spanglish. For others, in order to reveal their diverse geographical and life experiences, they utilize a combination of fiction, documentary, and experimental forms. Still others choose to prominently integrate Indigenous knowledge and cultural expressions like rituals, dances, songs, and storytelling into their works.

Diasporic Indigenous Latinx media-makers also depict what Lynn Stephen has conceptualized as the "transborder" experience, best characterized in the migration of Mexican Indigenous peoples to the United States. Stephen argues that Indigenous migrants not only cross a physical, national border but also a number of other metaphorical borders or frontiers (such as ethnic, gendered, generational, regional, or linguistic) that shape their experience and identity (24–25). Similar to other diasporic communities, Indigenous Latinx must build bridges between their communities of origin and their new communities in the United States. Diasporic Indigenous Latinx filmmakers, when seeking to connect with their communities of origin, use media as a way of extending cultural networks while telling current stories about their communities. Some of these filmmakers use their media practices to provide support to their communities or nation of origin and seek to explore deeper political and cultural issues faced by their communities through actively engaging in forms of activism. Activism is gaining an increasingly central role and theme in the media practice of diasporic Indigenous Latinx filmmakers, addressing issues of dual citizenship and cultural rights, among other concerns. In addition, some of the Indigenous Latinx creators inquire about the historical, political, and cultural marginalization in which Indigenous peoples have been immersed since the period of colonization.

In the next section, you will explore two case studies that illustrate how diasporic Indigenous Latinx creators shape their films to reflect perspectives and agendas that are informed by their indigeneity and their status as migrants. In the first case study, you will be introduced to the documentary works of the Chatina filmmaker Yolanda Cruz. In the second case study, you will learn about the Taraspanglish Migrant Video Project, a binational collaborative and community project that focuses on the Purépecha Indigenous migrant community. The Taraspanglish Migrant Video Project is an example of media production made by the community and for the community, both in their region of origin and in the United States.

## YOLANDA CRUZ

Yolanda Cruz reflects the transborder experience of Indigenous Latinx immigrants since her personal story shows the multiple frontiers of her journey as a Mexican and Chatina filmmaker. Cruz is originally from Cieneguilla, a small Chatino town in Oaxaca, Mexico. She moved first to the state capital, Oaxaca City, and later emigrated to the United States. Her training as a filmmaker was obtained through a master's degree in directing from the School of Theater, Film and Television at the University of California, Los Angeles (UCLA). When asked about her identity and the way in which she perceives herself, Cruz outlines the categories that she has incorporated into her sense of identity, which is both dynamic and situational. For example, as Cruz is Chatina, she is considered Indigenous in Mexico, but when she moved to the United States, she became Latina or Mexican. Although Cruz embraces all the labels that tell part of her personal journey, she considers herself more than anything an Indigenous and Chatina filmmaker (Chávez-García, 2011). In this sense, Cruz shows the fluidity of her Indigenous identity that incorporates other identity categories as her reality changes, deconstructing the notion of a fixed Indigenous identity.

Cruz's documentaries conceptualize identity as based on acts of self-definition—an active and constant process of choice and positioning that is shaped by migration experiences. In particular, her documentaries *Guenati'zá: Los que vienen de visita* (*Guenati'zá: The Ones Who Come to Visit* [2004]), and *Sueños binacionales* (*Binational Dreams* [2005]), explore the diaspora of Indigenous peoples of Oaxaca and the formation of transnational networks. The sixteen-minute documentary *Guenati'zá* narrates the return of immigrant Ulises García and his family to Mexico for the celebration of the Christmas holidays in his native town of Analco in Oaxaca. García is a Zapotec who works as a gardener in Los Angeles, California. In the documentary, Cruz shows glimpses of the interactions that migrants have with their community of origin when they temporarily return for local festivities, intertwining the voices of migrants, locals, young people, old people, women, and the filmmaker. The film reveals how identity is not always imposed by others but can be actively created and shaped by migration experiences and the act of leaving and returning.

*Guenati'zá* begins with a close-up of the face of a man who says to the interviewer in Spanish: "Look, I'm *Oaxacaliforniano*, but I'm from Oaxaca."

Figure 6.2: Zapotec Ulises García describes himself as *Oaxacaliforniano* in *Guenati'zá* (2004).

Source: DVD of *Guenati'zá*
Attribution: Yolanda Cruz
License: Fair Use

Then, a narration by Yolanda Cruz states "García is Zapotec, one of the largest Indigenous groups in Oaxaca, México. Ulises came to Los Angeles in 1982 when he was eighteen. He has been a gardener and a community organizer." This commentary accompanies a sequence of medium-long shots and close-ups that depict Ulises in his activities as a gardener. Ulises establishes from the first moment his identity recreated by his migrant situation when he states that he sees himself as a *Oaxacalifornian*, integrating two spatial realities that, in his opinion, define him. The elements that shape Ulises's identity are in this case dictated by the geography in which he moves, each location carrying a particular historical and symbolic load within their national contexts. More than sixteen Indigenous groups inhabit the state of Oaxaca, each with distinctive identities, languages, and traditions. California, a former Mexican territory, is one of the states with the highest gross domestic product in the United States, thanks to the diversification of economic activities in the areas of agriculture, tourism, technology, and information technology. This makes the state an attractive point for migrants (both domestic and foreign) seeking to improve their living conditions. As Cruz mentions in her narration, "Los Angeles has become a home away from home." For Ulises, both regions give him a sense of identity, but it is his connection of origin that continues to occupy a primary place when he emphasizes, "but I'm from Oaxaca."

Another documentary by Cruz offers a closer look at the way in which two diasporic Indigenous groups from Oaxaca establish ties with their communities of origin. *Binational Dreams* is a thirty-minute documentary that deals with the migration of Mixtecs and Chatinos to the United States. The structure of this documentary is divided into two parts. The first part narrates the experiences of the Mixtecs, who since the 1970s have moved to harvest the fields of California. During this time, they have been able to establish a network of communication, and political and economic organization with their community in Oaxaca through the creation of the *Frente Indígena de Organizaciones Binacionales* (Indigenous Front of Binational Organizations; FIOB). The second part of the documentary refers to the Chatino population, to which Cruz belongs. The Chatino community, unlike the Mixtecs, began to migrate to the United States in the 1990s and, therefore, do not have a solid organization to help both those who have emigrated and those who have remained in their place of origin. The documentary presents the more difficult context and future that this Chatino community must face due to the lack of social organization.

The element that Cruz focuses on in this documentary is the political and cultural activism carried out by the Mixtecs. This work is introduced when Rufino, one of the interviewees, explains that one of the first programs of the FIOB was a project that involved Indigenous peoples and California Rural Legal Assistance to guide and educate migrant workers about their labor rights under California law in their own languages such as Mixtec: "We speak a language that is not Spanish and it is not English. There are many organizations that defend human rights, migrant rights, but we are the only ones who speak the language."

One of the most interesting parts in the film, and which gives its name to the documentary, is the idea of a hybrid identity that Rufino outlines. Both he and his colleagues who live in the United States are proudly Mixtec: "We, the leaders, must be Indigenous, feel pride in being Indigenous. Understand that our culture must prevail, and feel that our identity is all we have in the world." However, he points out that they are conceived as binational by living and working in the United States. In fact, the organization to which they belong highlights binationality in its name. Thus, considering oneself as binational is a reflection that occurs in the diaspora, a condition that is characterized by the insistence of individuals not only to affirm their identity of origin but also to ratify the identity acquired in the diaspora.

Figure 6.3: The Mixtec group gets organized in California in *Binational Dreams* (2005).
Source: DVD of *Binational Dreams*
Attribution: Yolanda Cruz
License: Fair Use

## TARASPANGLISH MEDIA PROJECT

The series of videos that make up *Cortos Taraspanglish* (*Tarasplanglish Shorts*) addresses different sides of the experience of migration and the cultural continuity/discontinuity forged by the Purépecha communities that have migrated to Madera, California from Michoacán, Mexico. The shorts were produced for the Taraspanglish Migrant Video Project (2002), an initiative formed by Javier Sámano Chong and the Purépechas Juana Soto Sosa and Aureliano Soto Rita. The project trained migrants in the production of video as a space for reflection and as a tool to inform their communities (in Madera as well as Michoacán) about their rights, obligations, and requirements as Mexican citizens and immigrants in the United States. The main themes addressed by *Taraspanglish Shorts* include the preservation of customs and traditions, political organization, living conditions of the migrants, and ties with members of their communities of origin. The videomakers in the Taraspanglish project also consider the uses of language in migrant contexts, and the combination of three languages (Purépecha or Tarasco, Spanish, and English) is reflected in the name of the project. Shorts produced by the project include: *Danza de la identidad (Dance of Identity), Así son mis días (These Are My Days), La salida (The Way Out), Pues ya ves lo que pasó con ellos (Well, You See What Happened to Them), Si la migra te detiene (If Immigration Stops You), Good bye acuerdo migratorio (Good Bye Immigration Agreement), Mexicanos vs mexicanos,* and *What is Taraspanglish?* One of the points of interest of the Taraspanglish project is the use of a variety of strategies that integrate multiple artistic elements and representational techniques that oscillate between fiction and nonfiction, including elements such as docudrama, video recording in studio (*Mexicanos vs mexicanos*), fiction, video-letters, music video style (*These Are My Days*), sketch comedy (*What is Taraspanglish?*), parody, and performance (*Dance of Identity*).

A universal aspect of the migrant experience is longing for the place of origin, which can often be encapsulated as a sense of loss. The short *Dance of Identity* represents this struggle, showing the multiple layers of meaning in diasporic identity by exploring the ways nostalgia for the homeland and local traditions are experienced at a distance. *Dance of Identity* is an intimate portrait of the nostalgia of a Purépecha migrant who longs for the traditional dance of his hometown. The title of this segment appears with other titles that read "Kúrpiti: Danza Celeste/ Hip Hop ¡Cielos que danza!" The next shot presents the black and white image of a young man sitting on the floor and talking directly to the camera, which is also on the same low level.

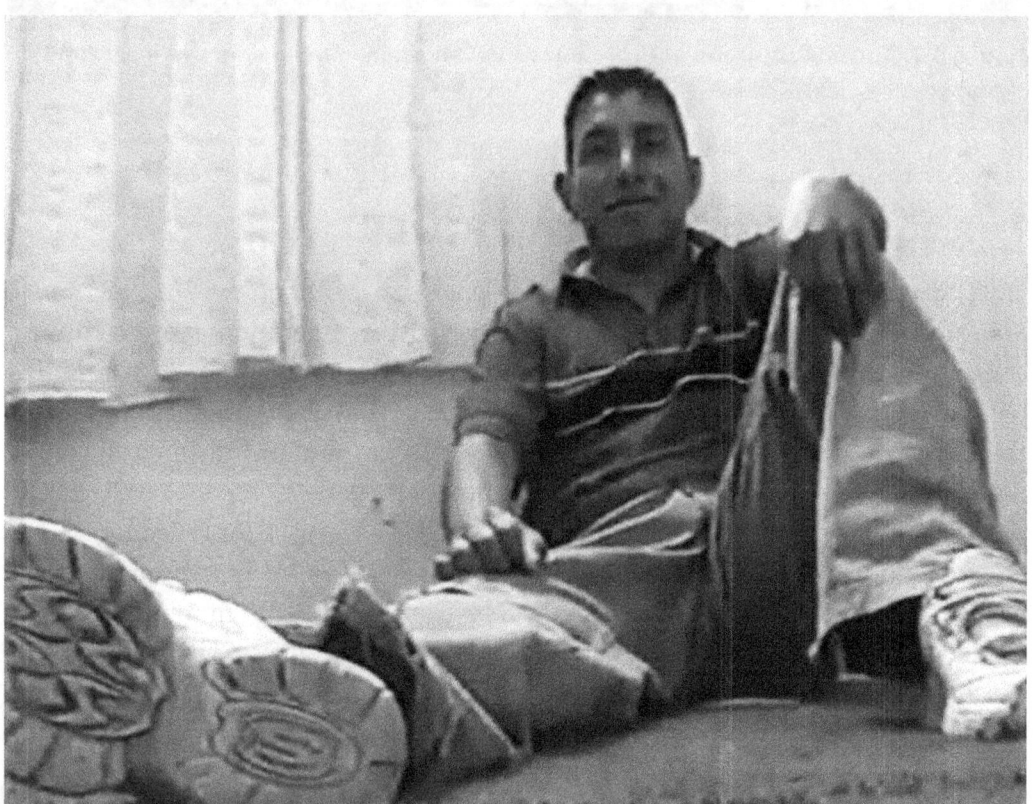

Figure 6.4: A young Purépecha longs to perform a traditional dance once again in *Dance of Identity* (2002).

Source: DVD of *Dance of Identity*
Attribution: Taraspanglish Project
License: Fair Use

This builds a moment of intimacy between the viewer and the subject while the migrant states: "*Extraño mucho la danza. Ya quiero ir a bailar otra vez ahí, para que vean que todavía puedo* (I miss dancing. Now I want to dance again there for them to see that I can still dance)." Feelings of nostalgia in the confession are accentuated by black and white aesthetics; meanwhile, the framing seems to imprison the man. Thus, themes of sadness and loneliness, revealed through sad and lonely characters, are recurrent in films made by diasporic or immigrant filmmakers because, as Naficy points out, "loneliness is an inevitable outcome of transnationality" (55). A diasporic nostalgia involves the idealization of the homeland and the past; consequently, these videos evoke landscape, music, family, monuments, history, and traditions as part of the work of remembrance.

The image following the confession changes from black and white to color. In a studio with a white background we see a music player on the floor; a man enters the frame and turns it on. The individual begins to dance, and although the steps performed seem to be a traditional folk dance, the music that is heard is "¿Comprendes, Mendes?" by the Mexican group Control Machete.

Figure 6.5: Two generations perform a traditional dance in a diasporic context in *Dance of Identity*.

Source: DVD of *Dance of Identity*
Attribution: Taraspanglish Project
License: Fair Use

In the following sequence, hip hop is replaced by traditional Purépecha music. This combination comments on the negotiation between the local and the global. In this association of ideas, the directors show how through embodied practices such as dance it is possible to transmit important cultural aspects like traditions and values, as well as make connections between original communities and new ones. By relating hip hop and traditional folk dance, the videomakers suggest that it is impossible to escape the influence of the diasporic environments in which they are now living. The choice of hip hop music is meaningful since some of the main qualities of this musical style are its political commitment and its search for social justice and empowerment, as well as respect for the cultural differences that coexist in the musical mix. Hip hop is a musical form that sometimes calls for community renewal and can be associated with projects of civil resistance. Within the framework of the quest for Indigenous autonomy, hip hop is presented as a creative tool that can bring about the cultural and political changes demanded by Indigenous peoples.

Overall, the segments of this project compiled by the videomakers form a repertoire on the subject of migration that is revealed through the everyday experiences of migrants and their families. The variety of styles of these shorts also gives us an idea of the way the Taraspanglish videomakers conceive their migrant identities: mobile, **performative** (i.e., the way their identity is enacted), and dynamic. Diasporic Indigenous videomakers have found a vehicle to express their cultural activism by showing how cultural heritage can be adapted in new and changing ways within the everyday life of migrants, challenging the idea that traditions practiced by Indigenous peoples are pure, static, or dying. The Taraspanglish videomakers express through the medium of film that while the culture they live in and the identities that they assume must be situational and fluid, they are also distinct.

In this chapter, you have hopefully come to appreciate the importance of the use of film as a way for Indigenous Latinx creators to review identity categories in the context of migration, on both a discursive and aesthetic level. Many creators have taken on the task of elaborating the meanings of changing identities assumed through the migratory experience. In their media productions, creators make use of the expressive, technical, and conceptual resources learned in their new context while at the same time reflect on the subjectivities of such experiences. Currently, diasporic Indigenous Latinx media creators are an emerging group within the United States. It is important that scholars continue to explore their productions and the thematic and aesthetic approaches they utilize in order to better understand identity formation in migrant contexts.

**Argelia González Hurtado** *is an Assistant Professor of Spanish and Latin American Studies at St. Mary´s College of Maryland. She holds a PhD in Spanish & Latin American Studies from the University of Alberta. Her academic interests include Latin American Cinema and Indigenous Media. She has published in several journals such as* Decolonization: Indigeneity, Education & Society; *and* Latin American Perspectives. *She contributed chapters to the books* Adjusting the Lens: Community and Collaborative Video in Mexico, *edited by Freya Schiwy and Byrt Wammack Weber; and* Politics of Children in Latin America Cinema, *edited by María Paz-MacKay and Omar Rodríguez.*

## BIBLIOGRAPHY

Chávez-García, Miroslava. "Interview with Yolanda Cruz." *Boom*, vol. 1, no. 3, 2011, pp. 57–61. https://doi.org/10.1525/boom.2011.1.3.57.

"Indigenous Peoples in Guatemala." *IWGIA*, https://iwgia.org/en/guatemala.html.

"Indigenous Peoples in Mexico." *IWGIA*, https://iwgia.org/en/mexico.html?start=6.

Mignolo, Walter. *Local Histories/Global Designs. Coloniality, Subaltern Knowledge and Border Thinking*. Princeton UP, 2000.

Naficy, Hamid. *An Accented Cinema: Exilic and Diasporic Filmmaking*. Princeton UP, 2001.

Raheja, Michelle H. "Reading Nanook's Smile: Visual Sovereignty, Indigenous Revisions of Ethnography, and *Atanarjuat (The Fast Runner)*." *American Quarterly*, vol. 59, no. 4, 2007, pp. 1159–85.

Ramírez Berg, Charles. *Latino Images in Film: Stereotypes, Subversion, and Resistance*. U of Texas P, 2002.

Santos, Moi. "Perspectives: Aurora Guerrero and Yolanda Are Redefining Notions of Latinidad One Film at a Time." *Sundance Institute*, 6 Oct. 2021, https://www.sundance.org/blogs/perspectives-aurora-guerrero-and-yolanda-cruz-are-redefining-notions-of-latinidad-one-film-at-a-time/?fbclid=IwAR15LiYAGIfIWjP8NpQ4QHWbdN-rRcntpLNAYHenBJbWGjL81UabAkPbxqs.

Sistema de Información Cultural México. "Pueblos indígenas por estado." *Gobierno de México*, https://sic.cultura.gob.mx/lista.php?table=grupo_etnico&disciplina=&estado_id.

Smith, Linda Tuhiwai. *Decolonizing Methodologies: Research and Indigenous Peoples*. Zed Books, 1999.

Stephen, Lynn. *Transborder Lives: Indigenous Oaxacans in Mexico, California, and Oregon*. Duke UP, 2007.

## FILMOGRAPHY

*Cortos Taraspanglish / Taraspanglish Shorts*. Directed by Javiér Sámano Chong, Juana Soto Sosa, and Aureliano Soto Rita, Taraspanglish Migrants Video Project, 2002.

*Guenati'zá (The Ones Who Come to Visit)*. Directed by Yolanda Cruz, Petate Productions, 2004.

*María Candelaria*. Directed by Emilio Fernández, performances by Dolores del Río, Pedro Armendaríz, Alberto Galán, Miguel Inclán, Films Mundiales S.A., 1943.

*Sueños binacionales (Binational Dreams)*. Directed by Yolanda Cruz, performances by Rosa Cruz, Rogelio Cruz, Rufino Dominguez, and Centolia Maldonado, Petate Productions, 2005.

## FOR FURTHER STUDY

*2501 Migrants: A Journey*. Directed by Yolanda Cruz, Petate Productions, 2010.

Aldama, Frederick Luis, editor. *Latinx Ciné in the Twenty-First Century*. U of Arizona P, 2019.

*Chuj Boys of Summer*. Directed by Max Walker-Silverman, performances by Yack Alux, Juan Marcos Gémez, Felipe Jorge, and Pedro Lucas, Cow Hop Films, 2020.

*El Norte*. Directed by Gregory Nava, performances by Zaide Silvia Gutiérrez, David Villalpando, and Ernesto Gómez Cruz, Frontera Films, 1983.

García Blizzard, Mónica. *The White Indians of Mexican Cinema: Racial Masquerade Throughout the Golden Age*. SUNY P, 2022.

Gleghorn, Charlotte. "Indigenous Filmmaking in Latin America." *A Companion to Latin American Cinema*, edited by Maria M. Delgado, Stephen Hart, and Randal Johnson, Wiley-Blackwell, 2017, pp. 167–86.

González Hurtado, Argelia. "Narrating the Diaspora: Taraspanglish Video Project." *Adjusting the Lens: Community and Collaborative Video in Mexico*, edited by Freya Schiwy and Byrt Wammack Weber, U of Pittsburgh P, 2017, pp. 90–118.

Kummels, Ingrid. *Transborder Media Spaces: Ayuujk Videomaking Between Mexico and the US*. Berghahn, 2017.

Smith, Laurel C. "Decolonizing Hybridity: Indigenous Video, Knowledge, and Diffraction." *Cultural Geographies*, vol. 19, no. 3, July 2012, pp. 329–48.

Wilson, Pamela and Michelle Stewart. "Indigeneity and Indigenous Media on the Global Stage." *Global Indigenous Media: Cultures, Poetics, and Politics*, edited by Wilson and Stewart, Duke UP, 2008, pp. 1–35.

# Feminist Perspectives in Latinx Media

Myra Mendible
(Florida Gulf Coast University)

A range of ancestries, dialects, cultural histories, and circumstances shape Latinx identities in the United States and inform their perspectives as media producers and consumers. This chapter explores this diverse landscape through the lens of gender, first offering a glimpse at the theoretical roots of this approach, then suggesting some of the ways that Latinx feminist perspectives respond to and inform media practices. Given the global reach of contemporary digital platforms, the ubiquity and endurance of certain stereotypes and tropes in Hollywood films, and the profit-driven consolidation of media industries, the cultural politics of representation serves as a useful organizing framework for investigating multiple Latinx feminist perspectives. Indeed, representation is a site of contention and resistance, an intersection where the dynamics of class, gender, race, and sexuality converge. It offers a unique vantage point from which to explore feminist perspectives in Latinx media.

Representation is always mediated through power, as those who create or control images and stories inform public attitudes, opinions, and even policies. Practices of representation (both visual and textual) produce forms of knowledge and ways of seeing the world and interpreting one's place in it. Representational perspectives in media theory and practice interrogate the ways that ideology operates through visual and textual images to "normalize" ethnic, racial, gender, or other inequalities. Latina feminist theories focus on the politics of representation and help complicate, subvert, or revise how popular notions about "Latin women" and **Latinidad** are articulated or internalized in Latinas' own formulations of group and self-identification. As media producers, Latinx feminists may challenge enduring stereotypes, not merely to replace these with uplifting, positive images, but to expand a repertoire of themes, messages, and perspectives. Latinx feminist practices, in all their multiplicity, aim to empower Latinas as media subjects, producers, and consumers.

## FEMINISM: WHO SPEAKS, AND FOR WHOM?

Before considering specific examples of contemporary Latinx feminist theory and practice, let us address a question you may be asking: Why the need for a *Latina* feminism? Doesn't feminism advocate on behalf of all women? While the **second-wave feminist movement** of the late 1960s and '70s launched significant challenges against patriarchal economic and social structures, it also sidelined issues of vital importance to many women of color. Universalizing "woman" as White, middle-class, and heterosexual, the movement's leaders tended to overlook critical distinctions among women that further complicated their roles in society, their access to educational and economic opportunities, and their relationship to the state and its institutions. What this universalizing tendency obscures is that women face inequalities and discriminatory policies based not only on gender but also race, class, ethnicity, sexuality, and other markers of identity subject to distinct forms of social control. Issues related to citizenship status, cultural differences, language usage, labor practices, and policing, for example, which impacted Latinx communities and shaped Latina feminist perspectives, scarcely informed the movement's priorities. As White feminist scholar Rachel Blau Duplessis later wrote, "we thought all women were us, and we were all women" (106).

Latina feminisms grew out of these disparities and omissions, first inspired by Black and Chicanx liberation movements, later spreading into wider Latinx constituencies. Latina feminist activists also looked inward, challenging intragroup sexism, homophobia, racism, and colorism. They developed an **intersectional** lens through which to explore, for instance, the subordinated status of Afro-Latinas and the heteronormative roots of machismo within Latino social or political groups. They organized to dismantle sexism from within the ranks of **Chicano**, **Boricua**, and other Latino movements (e.g., **Young Lords, Brown Berets, La Raza Unida**), where women were frequently relegated to menial tasks or secondary roles. As a result of these and other challenges, Latinx feminist media scholarship, as well as Latinx creative expression, cultural production, and political agency, was irrevocably enriched.

## CROSSING BORDERS: THE EMERGENCE OF LATINX FEMINIST THEORY

These tensions, power dynamics, and changing landscapes found expression in formative Latinx feminist theories and practices. By the 1980s, the rise of Spanish-language television networks, Univision and Telemundo, brought Latinx-centered stories and news broadcasts into American living rooms (see Chapter 10 for a detailed discussion of this development). This decade also saw the emergence of independent US Latinx film, the "discovery" of US Latinos as a viable niche market (Valdivia), and the slow integration of Latinx scholarship and visual media into university media studies courses (Cepeda). But it was the pioneering work of Latinx scholar-activists during this period that helped a new generation of Latina feminists confront "the many-headed demon of oppression" (Alarcón 289). Gloria Anzaldúa and Cherríe Moraga's anthology *This Bridge Called My Back: Writings by Radical Women of Color,* first published in 1981 and now in its fourth reissue, showcased "the complex confluence of identities—race, class, gender, and sexuality—systemic to women of color oppression and liberation" (xix). The publication of Anzaldúa's *Borderlands/La Frontera: The New Mestiza* further contributed new ways of thinking about borders as symbolic, psychological, linguistic, and sexual constructs. Anzaldúa formulated the notion of identity defined by **mestizaje** as a borderland, a site where two or more cultures or ways of being collide, blend, and coexist. "*Mestiza* consciousness" represented the erosion of rigid boundaries and mutually exclusive categories such as Indigenous/European, Spanish/English, Black/White. A pivotal figure in Chicana feminist, queer, and Indigenous activism, Moraga's continuing work as an award-winning playwright and director highlights Chicanx cultural history and experiences, offering perspectives that erode rigid linguistic and social boundaries. Still building bridges of solidarity, she recently founded, in collaboration with Chicana artist Celia Herrera Rodríguez, [Las Maestras Center for Xicana(x) Indigenous Thought, Art and Social Praxis](#), a collaborative site for Chicanx creative expression and scholarship.

Many other Latina feminist writers, activists, and organizers contributed to emergent Latinx feminist theory and praxis, including writer-activist Martha Cotera, who responded to sexism within the Chicano nationalist movement by cofounding the *Mujeres de La Raza Unida* (Women of the Raza Unida) women's caucus in 1973. Cotera's book, *Diosa y Hembra: The History and Heritage of Chicanas in the US*, offered a seminal history of Chicanas' feminist activism in social justice movements, a perspective excluded from school curricula and public memory. Cotera and Linda Garcia Merchant later founded the [Chicana por mi Raza Digital Memory Collective](#) to ensure preservation of civil rights era Chicanx and Latinx oral histories and personal archives. Latinx feminists have worked tirelessly to dismantle or expand Eurocentric frameworks, redefining traditional notions of ethnic identity, "Americanness," or citizenship. Feminist community organizer and writer Elizabeth "Betita" Martinez, Swarthmore College's first Latina graduate (1946), for example, cofounded the influential newspaper *El Grito del Norte* in 1968. While focused primarily on exposing social injustice against Chicanx communities, the paper also had an anti-imperialist bent, challenging power at the local level while aligning Latinx feminisms with broader international human rights struggles. In 1997, Martinez founded the Institute for Multiracial Justice, fostering coalitions on behalf of women's rights, LGBTQ rights, racial justice, and immigrant rights.

In her efforts to bridge differences and build coalitional movements, noted scholar-activist Chela Sandoval introduced methods gleaned from Third World feminism to help confront postmodern forms of oppression. In her essay "US Third World Feminism: The Theory and Method of Oppositional Consciousness in the Postmodern World" and later in the groundbreaking book *Methodology of the Oppressed*, Sandoval proposes strategies for accommodating women's varying positionalities and building a decolonizing "**coalitional** consciousness" (*Methodology* 78). Grounded in well-defined identity politics, her approach entails the flexibility to "shift gears" and adapt perspectives as needed to forge strategic alliances "between and among" various kinds of oppositional ideologies and political strategies (Sandoval, "US Third World Feminism" 13–14). Sandoval's methods situated Latinx feminism at the forefront of US postmodern feminist theory and practice.

These foundational texts and movements confronted a range of issues related to racism, violence, the exploitation and also empowerment of women; they highlighted Latinas as speaking subjects rather than objects of a dominant "White" gaze. Latinx feminist scholar-activists initiated modes of self-representation and intervention capable of negotiating and traversing a complex postmodern media landscape. In so doing, their collective efforts inspired the transnational, intersectional approaches that inform contemporary Latinx feminist media theory and praxis.

## REPRESENTING LATINX FEMINIST PERSPECTIVES ONSCREEN AND ONSTAGE

Some *feminista* approaches draw on a political definition of representation, that is, on methods for advocating on behalf of others or in processes that "give voice" to diverse constituencies. Others see representation as a tool for reconstituting or reimagining (re-imaging) Latinx identities through aesthetic and visual media production. For example, Anna Nieto-Gomez, the first female president of the Movimiento Estudiantil Chicano de Aztlán (**Chicano Student Movement of Aztlán**; MEChA) and cofounder of **Hijas de Cuauhtémoc**, a Latinx feminist-centered publication, used visual media to counter images of Mexican women as domesticated, passive victims of machismo. Her screenplay for the groundbreaking film *Chicana,* produced in 1979, traced a long history of contributions by women of Mexican- and Indigenous-descent as workers, activists, organizers, educators, and leaders. A notable figure in Latinx media, the film's director, Sylvia Morales, followed up with a sequel in 2009, *A Crushing Love: Chicanas, Motherhood and Activism,* honoring the legacies of five Latinx activists in the United States: Dolores Huerta, Elizabeth "Betita" Martinez, Cherríe Moraga, Alicia Escalante, and Martha Cotera. Similarly, Aurora Levins Morales used poetry, essays, and scriptwriting to focus attention on Puerto Rican women's experiences and contributions to the radical US Puerto Rican women's movement. She also participated in the Chicago Women's Liberation Union, performed with La Peña Cultural Productions Group, and produced radio programs.

Filmmakers, screenwriters, and playwrights also set the stage for contemporary Latinx creative talents, showcasing viewpoints mostly absent from mainstream productions. US Chicana filmmaker, director, and producer Lourdes Portillo explains that she "was drawn to filmmaking because I never saw people like me—and stories like mine—on the screen" (Portillo). She launched her filmmaking career with *Después del terremoto (After the Earthquake)* (1979), which focuses on the struggles of a Nicaraguan woman living in San Francisco. Portillo's internationally renowned documentary, *Las Madres: The Mothers of Plaza de Mayo*, features mothers whose sons and daughters were "disappeared" by the Argentine dictatorship during the "Dirty War" (1976–1983). These women turned grief into action, risking their lives by organizing and staging ongoing demonstrations demanding government accountability. The film was nominated for an Emmy and an Academy Award for Best Documentary Feature in 1986. Portillo is the subject of an anthology, *Lourdes Portillo:* The Devil Never Sleeps *and Other Films,* edited by Rosa Linda Fregoso. (Additional information on Portillo's career can be found in the Key Creatives section of this book).

A new generation of independent Latinx feminist filmmakers, such as Frances Negrón-Muntaner, expanded this legacy further, examining homophobia, racism, colonization, and Puerto Rican identities on the island and US mainland. Influenced by late 1960s and early 1970s Chicanx and Puerto Rican feminist filmmakers, Negrón-Muntaner's first film (with Peter Biella) in 1989, *AIDS in the Barrio,* examines the devastating impact of the disease on Puerto Rican communities in north Philadelphia. Her award-winning 1994 film, *Brincando el Charco: Portrait of a Puerto Rican,* highlights the difficulties of navigating diverse aspects of identity—as a lesbian, a Puerto Rican living in the United States, and a light-skinned Latinx female. Alberto Sandoval-Sánchez calls the film "a foundational text" in giving visibility to Puerto Rican lesbians and gays striving to articulate their "relationships with the father, the family, the home, the nation, the burial place, and even with the myth of the eternal return" (160). In addition to several films, monographs, edited collections and articles, Negrón-Muntaner has generated research data that broadly informs current media scholarship, including *The Latino Disconnect: Latinos in the Age of Media Mergers* and *The Latino Media Gap: A Report on the State of Latinos in US Media*, both of which document Latinx underrepresentation in US broadcasting and film industries.

Latinx feminist playwrights such as María Irene Fornés, Milcha Sanchez-Scott, Coco Fusco, and Josefina López also helped set the stage, literally and figuratively, for emergent twenty-first-century talents such as Alexis Scheer, Melinda Lopez, Hilary Bettis, Tanya Saracho, and Caridad Svich, whose plays are expanding the repertoire of Latinx characters and themes today. Blending aesthetic and cultural influences, resisting linear plot structures and other "realist" devices, they disrupt dominant discourses about Latinx cultures and suggest possibilities for ever-evolving feminist poetics. For example, Dolores Prida (*Beautiful Señoritas*), parodies dominant images of Latina bodies, while Milcha Sánchez-Scott (*Latina*) portrays the challenges of "Brown"-bodied actresses in a White-dominant theater world. Sánchez-Scott's bilingual play, *The Cuban Swimmer*, captures the ambivalent and sometimes discordant aspirations shaping immigrant family dynamics; it also challenges generic and geographical borders, moving between realism and magical realism and among different spatial realities. These Latinx feminists, along with many others too numerous to list here, are agents of social change. They inform and vitalize transnational, anti-essentialist modes of apprehension and representation, chipping away at racialized, sexist paradigms and binary models of cultural difference that have worked to erase, displace, or devalue Latina subjectivities and creative expression.

Figure 7.1: Claudia (Frances Negrón-Muntaner) reflects on race and identity in while reflecting on her privilege as a light-skinned Latina in *Brincando el Charco: Portrait of a Puerto Rican*.

Source: DVD of *Brincando el Charco: Portrait of a Puerto Rican*
Attribution: Frances Negrón-Muntaner
License: Fair Use

## THE LATINA BODY AS A CONTESTED SITE OF REPRESENTATION

The Latina body has long represented an ambivalent, troublesome presence in the US national imaginary. Assumptions about US Latinas as perpetual foreigners, racial hybrids (typified as neither White nor Black), or hypersexual and hyperemotional Others form the basis of tropes promoted in popular film, magazine, news, and television images. As a site of knowledge production, Anzaldúa reminds us, "The body is the ground of thought. The body is text" (Anzaldúa, *Light in the*

*Dark* 5). Latinx feminist media perspectives play a critical role in decolonizing representations of the Latinx body, carving out interstitial spaces for bicultural, bilingual, or hybrid subjects to tell their own stories.

The commercial success of "crossover" Latina film stars—those who achieve success within the Latinx market then successfully expand their reach to a broader "mainstream" audience—and the increasing participation of Latinas behind the camera play a crucial role in this process. As Mary Beltrán argues, "stardom operates on a national and increasingly global scale as a powerful social force. Stars—or the lack of stars from particular social groups in a society—'teach' notions of identity and leadership to citizens from all walks of life, including lessons regarding the meaning of gender, class, race, and ethnicity in a particular time and place" (5). Latina star power is significant not only in terms of visibility and access but also for its role in facilitating Latinas' participation as producers, directors, and screenwriters. US Latina film directors such as Patricia Cardoso and actresses-turned-producers like Salma Hayek help expand the kinds of roles available to US Latina actresses. Hayek founded her own production company, Ventanarosa, produced *In the Time of the Butterflies* (2001), and directed *The Maldonado Miracle* (2003) for the Showtime cable channel. She was the also first Latina actress nominated for a Best Actress Academy Award (for *Frida*, in 2003). A Mexican American international star, Hayek convinced ABC to pick up the TV series *Ugly Betty* (2006–2010), starring America Ferrera, which went on to win a Peabody Award and run for four seasons.

In 2007, Ferrera made history as the first Latina to win an Outstanding Lead Actress Emmy for her role. The series was one of the first English-language shows to offer a positive fictional representation of an "illegal alien," as Betty's father, Ignacio, is an undocumented immigrant; it was also the first to show an interracial, same-sex adolescent kiss on primetime TV (Gonzalez and Rodriguez y Gibson). The "dramedy's" hybridity captures its Latin American roots (it was adapted from a Colombian **telenovela**), its protagonist's ambiguous place within a US professional workspace, and the permeability of generic borders between melodrama, comedy, and the telenovela. Betty is also a self-identified feminist with a strong career drive and aspirations, whose humor often subverts notions about "authentic" Latinidad, beauty myths, or the American Dream. Ferrera's success helped her bring other more complex Latinx images to the small screen. She produced a digital series that grew into *Gentefied* (2020–2021), a bilingual dramedy on Netflix. The series premiered in 2020, with award-winning Xicana screenwriter/producer Linda Yvette Chávez as co-executive producer and lead writer of the show.

Sundance Audience Award–winner *Real Women Have Curves* (2002), directed by Colombian Patricia Cardoso and also starring Ferrera, was based on a play by Mexican American Josefina López, who also cowrote the screenplay. The film rejects beauty myths that privilege thin, blonde, White women's bodies, celebrating the full-figured bodies of its Latina cast; it also foregrounds working-class Latinas, calling attention to the exploitation and disregard many of these workers face. Now an international star, Ferrera is a vocal activist for Latinas/os in the United States, serving as spokesperson for Voto Latino, active supporter of **DREAM**ers, and participant in the #MeToo campaign; she is also a founding member of the Time's Up Legal Defense Fund to help victims of sexual violence. In 2016, Ferrera won the Feminist Majority Foundation's Eleanor Roosevelt Award for her many contributions to Latinx human rights activism.

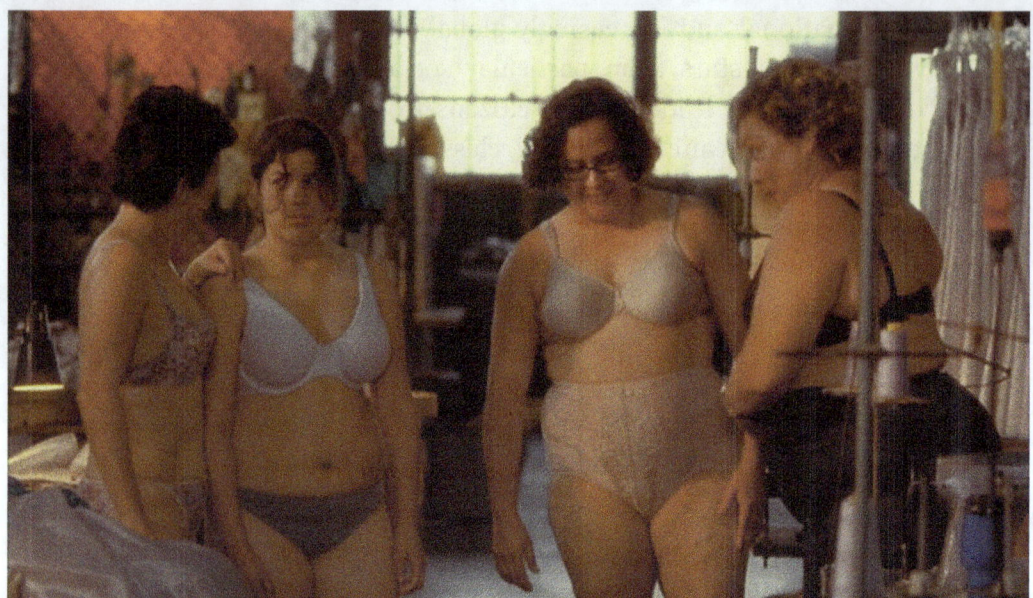

Figure 7.2: Ana (America Ferrera) and her coworkers in her sister's sweatshop strip to their underwear in an effort to cool down, rejecting the body-shaming comments of Ana's mother (Lupe Ontiveros) in *Real Women Have Curves* (2002).
Source: DVD of *Real Women Have Curves*
Attribution: Patricia Cardoso
License: Fair Use

Mexican-born film director/producer Patricia Riggen is also a rare breed: one of the most prominent Latina directors working in Hollywood today, Riggen's debut feature film, *Under the Same Moon* (2007) starring Kate del Castillo and America Ferrera, won an American Latino Media Arts (ALMA) Award and a Young Artist Award, among others. (The film is discussed in detail in Chapter 11). Riggen is part of a nonprofit production company, We Do It Together, which produces and finances films, TV shows, and other media dedicated to the empowerment of women. Actress/producer Eva Longoria, who has a master's degree in Chicanx studies, has also used her fame to open doors for other women. An avowed feminist, she founded the Eva Longoria Foundation to empower Latinas in education and entrepreneurship. Speaking at the Women's March in 2018, she called for "systematic change to the experience of women and girls in America. A change from fear and intimidation to respect. From pain and humiliation to safety and dignity. From marginalization to equal pay and representation."

Afro-Latina actresses such as Gina Torres, Zoe Saldana, Gina Rodriguez, Rosie Perez, Lauren Vélez, Rosario Dawson, and Michelle Rodriguez overcame not only gender discrimination but also racial discrimination to achieve stardom. (See Chapter 5 for a detailed discussion of the careers of Torres and Dawson and Afro-Latinx identity more broadly). Yet they still face challenges in a casting system that functions within a narrowly prescribed set of binaries and assumptions. As Afro-Cuban actress Torres explains in a *Vibe* interview, "They didn't care about the Latina part of me at all because I didn't look like the Spanish, Eurocentric standard of what Latina women were supposed to look like" (Reichard). Torres is the first Afro-Latina to create, produce, and star in her own show, *Pearson* (2019), on the USA Network. "I finally got into a position of power, and said, 'We're going to write this character as Afro-Latina. I'm going to use my Spanish as often as possible" (Reichard). After working with a Telemundo affiliate and as an on-camera host for public television, Kim Haas also became aware of the lack of Afro-Latinx representations, even in Spanish-language media: "We all know the power of television to create stereotypes, certain images, and people's perceptions about other people. I wanted to be part of a change." She started a blog, *Los Afro-Latinos*, and now hosts a PBS travel series, *Afro-Latino Travels with Kim Haas*, where she highlights contributions by Africans and people of African descent in the Americas ([Estevez](Estevez)). Afro-Latinas Jeanette Dilone (*Rizo*, 2020) and Janicza Bravo (*Zola*, 2020) also give us a view of subjects and experiences rarely seen onscreen.

Today's Latinx feminist activists are crossing spatial, linguistic, and representational borders using technologies not available to earlier *feministas*. Most have access to social media and other digital platforms that broaden their audiences and extend their transnational reach. Diverse Latinx feminist voices are now heard in podcasts such as *Latina Theory* and the shows featured on the Latina Podcasters Network; via Latinx Twitter, where Latinas build networks and connections (Gutiérrez); through blogs such as *Los Afro-Latinos* and *We All Grow Latina*; and in Instagram accounts such as Latina Rebels ([@latinarebels](@latinarebels)). These expansive discursive and representational spaces empower a new wave of *Latinidades feministas,* many inspired, informed, and nourished by a rich heritage of Latinx activism and bridge-building.

**Myra Mendible** *is Professor, founding faculty, and Fellow with the Center for Critical Race and Ethnic Studies at Florida Gulf Coast University. Her interdisciplinary scholarship explores links between national politics, cultural identity, and conflict. She is editor of* From Bananas to Buttocks: The Latina Body in Popular Film and Culture *(University of Texas Press, 2007);* Race 2008: Critical Reflections on an Historic Campaign *(BrownWalker Press, 2012); and* American Shame: Stigma and the Body Politic *(Indiana University Press, 2016). Her most recent book,* American War Stories: Veteran-Writers and the Politics of Memoir *was published by the University of Massachusetts Press in 2021.*

# BIBLIOGRAPHY

Alarcón, Norma. "The Theoretical Subject(s) of *This Bridge Called My Back* and Anglo-American Feminism." *The Second Wave. A Reader in Feminist Theory*, edited by L. Nicholson, Routledge, 1997, pp. 288–99.

Anzaldúa, Gloria. *Borderlands/La Frontera: The New Mestiza*. 4th ed., Aunt Lute, 2012.

---. *Light in the Dark /Luz en lo oscuro: Rewriting Identity, Spirituality, Reality*, edited by Ana Louise Keating, Duke UP, 2015.

Beltrán, Mary C. *Latina/o Stars in U.S. Eyes: The Making and Meanings of Film and TV Stardom*. U of Illinois P, 2009.

Cepeda, María Elena. "Beyond 'Filling in the Gap': The State and Status of Latina/o Feminist Media Studies." *Feminist Media Studies*, vol. 16, no. 2, 2016, pp. 344–60.

Cotera, Martha. *Diosa y Hembra: The History and Heritage of Chicanas in the US*. Austin: Information Systems Development, 1976.

DuPlessis, Rachel Blau. "Reader, I Married Me: A Polygamous Memoir." *Changing Subjects: The Making of Feminist Literary Criticism*, edited by Gayle Greene and Coppelia Kahn, Routledge, 1993.

Estevez, Marjua. "TV Host Kim Haas Is Tracing the African Link in Latin America." *Condé Nast Traveler,* 9 Oct. 2020, https://www.cntraveler.com/story/afro-latino-travels-with-kim-haas.

Fregoso, Rosa-Linda, editor. *Lourdes Portillo*: The Devil Never Sleeps *and Other Films*. U of Texas P, 2001.

Gonzalez, Tanya, and Eliza Rodriguez y Gibson. *Humor and Latina/o Camp in* Ugly Betty*: Funny Looking*. Lexington, 2015.

Gutiérrez, Arcelia. "Situating Representation As a Form of Erasure: #OscarsSoWhite, Black Twitter, and Latinx Twitter." *Television & New Media*, vol. 23, no. 1, 2022, pp. 100–18.

Moraga, Cherríe, and Gloria Anzaldúa, editors. *This Bridge Called My Back: Writings by Radical Women of Color*. 4th ed., SUNY P, 2015.

Negrón-Muntaner, Frances. *The Latino Media Gap: A Report on the State of Latinos in U.S. Media*. National Association of Latino Independent Producers, Center for the Study of Race and Ethnicity–Columbia University, and National Hispanic Foundation for the Arts, 2014. https://www.latinodonorcollaborative.org/original-research/latino-media-gap-report-2014.

Negrón-Muntaner, Frances, and Chelsea Abbas. *The Latino Disconnect: Latinos in the Age of Media Mergers*. Center for the Study of Race and Ethnicity–Columbia University and National Hispanic Foundation for the Arts, 2016. https://asit-prod-web1.cc.columbia.edu/cser/wp-content/uploads/sites/70/2020/03/The-Latino-Disconnect.pdf.

Portillo, Lourdes. *Lourdes Portillo*. https://www.lourdesportillo.com/.

Reichard, Raquel. "For Gina Torres, The Mission Is Afro-Latina Excellence In Her New Series *Pearson*." *Vibe*, 16 July 2019, http://www.vibe.com/features/viva/gina-torres-afro-latina-excellence-interview-656966/.

Sandoval, Chela. *Methodology of the Oppressed*. U of Minnesota P, 2000.

---. "US Third World Feminism: The Theory and Method of Oppositional Consciousness in the Postmodern World." *Genders*, vol. 10, 1991, pp. 1–24.

Sandoval-Sánchez, Alberto. "Imagining Puerto Rican Queer Citizenship: Frances Negrón-Muntaner's *Brincando el charco: Portrait of a Puerto Rican*." *None of the Above: Puerto Ricans in the Global Era*, edited by Frances Negrón-Muntaner, Palgrave Macmillan, 2007.

Valdivia, Angharad. "Latina/o Communication and Media Studies Today: An Introduction." *The Communication Review*, vol. 7, 2004, pp. 107–12.

## FILMOGRAPHY

*Afro-Latino Travels with Kim Haas*. Created by Kim Haas, PBS, 2020.

*Después del terremoto* (*After the Earthquake*). Directed by Lourdes Portillo and Nina Serrano, performances by Vilma Coronado and Agnelo Guzmán, 1979.

*AIDS in the Barrio: Eso no me pasa a mí*. Directed by Peter Biella and Frances Negrón-Muntaner, AIDS Film Initiative, 1989.

*Brincando el Charco: Portrait of a Puerto Rican*. Directed by Frances Negrón-Muntaner, performances by Frances Negrón-Muntaner, Agnes Lugo-Ortiz, Moisés Agosto, Toni Cade Bambara, ITVS International, 1994.

*Chicana*. Directed by Sylvia Morales, UCLA School of Film and Television, 1979.

*A Crushing Love: Chicanas, Motherhood and Activism*. Directed by Sylvia Morales, 2009.

*Frida*. Directed by Julie Taymor, performances by Salma Hayek, Alfred Molina, Geoffrey Rush, Lionsgate, 2002.

*Gentefied*. Created by Marvin Lemus and Linda Yvette Chávez, Netflix, 2020–2021.

Horta, Silvio, creator. *Ugly Betty*. ABC, 2006-2010.

*In the Time of the Butterflies*. Directed by Mariano Barroso, performances by Salma Hayek, Edward James Olmos, Marc Anthony, Showtime, 2001.

Korsh, Aaron and Daniel Arkin, creators. *Pearson*. USA Network, 2019.

*Las Madres: The Mothers of Plaza de Mayo*. Directed by Lourdes Portillo and Susana Muñoz, 1986.

*The Maldonado Miracle*. Directed by Salma Hayek, performances by Eddy Martin, Peter Fonda, Mare Winningham, Showtime, 2003.

*Real Women Have Curves*. Directed by Patricia Cardoso, performances by América Ferrera, Lupe Ontiveros, and Ingrid Oliu, HBO Films, 2002.

*Rizo*. Directed by Jeannette Dilone, performances by Laura Guzmán and Jeannette Dilone, 2020.

*Under the Same Moon*. Directed by Patricia Riggen, performances by Adrián Alonso, Kate del Castillo, Eugenio Derbez, Maya Zapata, Carmen Salinas, María Rojo, Mario Armada, America Ferrera, and Los Tigres del Norte, Fox Searchlight Pictures and The Weinstein Company, 2007.

*Zola*. Directed by Janicza Bravo, performances by Taylour Paige, Riley Keough, Nicholas Braun, Killer Films/Ramona Films/Gigi Films, 2020.

## FOR FURTHER STUDY

Fregoso, Rosa Linda. *The Bronze Screen: Chicana and Chicano Film Culture*. U of Minnesota P, 1993.

Mendible, Myra, editor. *From Bananas to Buttocks: The Latina Body in Popular Film and Culture*. U of Texas P, 2007.

Molina-Guzmán, Isabel. *Dangerous Curves: Latina Bodies in the Media*. NYU P, 2010.

Ruiz, Vicki L., and Ellen Carol DuBois. *Unequal Sisters: A Multicultural Reader in US Women's History*. Routledge, 1994.

# Latina/o/x LGBTQ Identities

Gilberto M. Blasini
(University of Wisconsin, Milwaukee)

Cultural theorist Stuart Hall explains that "identity is not only a story, a narrative which we tell ourselves about ourselves, it is stories which change with historical circumstances. And identity shifts with the way we think and hear [those stories about ourselves] and experience them" (8). The role that media plays in contemporary society makes it vital for us to think about the versions of identity that films and TV shows create about the different groups that comprise the United States as a nation. This is particularly significant for those groups that have historically had more limited opportunities to tell their own stories within the larger arena of media culture, for example Latinas/os and LGBTQ people. In this chapter, I will examine films and TV shows that have addressed the intersection of Latina/o and LGBTQ people, focusing on their representation and narrative role. The examples that I have selected are not meant to be exhaustive. They represent a point of departure for further exploration into these communities and their mediated versions. All the texts analyzed in this chapter also involve the social institution of the family. As Cherríe Moraga explains, "the Latino family, what happens in families, *punto*, is the heart of everything. The family is this private place, so everything is allowed to happen there, any kind of power exchanges, any kind of control. . . . It's the first place where you learn to suffer and also the first place where you learn to love" (Umpierre 58).

## UNDERSTANDING QUEERNESS

During the late 1980s and early 1990s, LGBTQ activist groups like ACT UP and Queer Nation reappropriated the derogatory term *queer*, which had mostly been used to demean gay men, and turned it into a self-affirming word as part of their fight against their discrimination in the United States. The government's lack of action to curb the HIV/AIDS pandemic propelled these groups to demonstrate on the streets and demand changes in our society. During this same period, feminist scholars in disciplines like philosophy, English, and media studies started to develop what is now known as queer theory. These writings questioned what our society has edified as normative roles and behaviors in terms of gender and sexuality, specifically as they relate to understanding identity as an essence—i.e., the idea that people are or behave in certain ways because they were born into a particular sex and not another. Examples of this essentialism would be that women are more emotional than men or that men are more rational than women.

Queerness shifted the focus of gender and sexuality from biological determinism into notions of social constructionism and **performativity**, that is, the idea that although behaviors associated with a particular gender or other identity category might appear natural, people learn to behave in those ways. The development of studies of queerness went beyond pointing out the hegemony of heterosexuality and its rigid division of gender into male and female to include criticisms of what became the dominant forms of "gay" and "lesbian" identities (White, bourgeois positions that looked for acceptance from and assimilation to heterosexual society). These studies also included other forms of gender and sexual expression that have often been disregarded, misunderstood, or historically marked as deviant: bisexuality, transgenderism, sadomasochism, pornography, sex work, etc. These studies sought to expand and complicate not only what gender and sexuality have meant in our society but also the functions they have played in broader discourses about power and identity formation. Scholars, activists, and artists such as Tomás Almaguer, Lawrence La Fountain-Stokes, José Esteban Muñoz, Ray Navarro, Frances Negrón-Muntaner, Yeidy M. Rivero, and Richard T. Rodríguez have examined the different ways in which queerness intersects with Latinidad in general as well as with the identities of national-origin groups like Mexican Americans, Cuban Americans, and Puerto Ricans. Their writings explain the ways in which particular cultural discourses related to desire, colonialism, racism, Christianity/Catholicism, and machismo provide further specificity to the ways in which Latina/o/x queer subjects articulate versions of themselves.

## THE NEW QUEER CINEMA OF THE 1990S

The emergence of discourses about queerness also found articulation in the arts. Many film- and videomakers started to use media to engage with issues in their communities, especially the devastating effects of the AIDS pandemic for LGBTQ people as well as BIPOC communities. These works ranged from documentaries, educational videos, and experimental shorts to feature films. In 1992, B. Ruby Rich coined the term **New Queer Cinema** to characterize a "flock of films that were doing something new, renegotiating subjectivities, annexing whole genres, revising histories in their image" (164). Rich's short history of new queer films included works by Derek Jarman, Christopher Münch, Tom Kalin, Gregg Araki, Laurie Lynd, Sadie Benning, and Jennie Livingston, whose *Paris Is Burning* (1990) became central not only to the theorizing of performativity that queer theory proposed but also to other projects such as the TV show *Pose* (2018–2021), which will be discussed later in the chapter. While acknowledging the importance of their work, Rich laments that most of the critical attention and distribution deals were given to (mostly White) gay male directors even when lesbians were creating relevant and innovative films and videos. To address in part this lack, I would like to highlight three films released in 1994 that were directed by Latinas and focused on issues related to queerness.

*Go Fish* was directed and cowritten by Rose Troche, an openly lesbian Puerto Rican filmmaker. The film won the Teddy Award for Best Feature Film at the Berlin International Film Festival. The Teddy Award is the festival's official queer award, which was first given in 1987 to Pedro Almodóvar's *La ley del deseo* (*Law of Desire*). *Go Fish* revolves around a group of lesbian friends in the Chicago neighborhood of Wicker Park. As Troche explains, "Wicker Park was mainly a Latino area with artists, gays and lesbians moving in, as well as unwelcome yuppies who were attracted by the low real estate costs" (Turner and Troche 17). Although the main storyline focuses on the constitution of the romantic couple of Max (Guinevere Turner) and Ely (V.S. Brodie), the film also provides insights into the lives of the other three lesbian characters. One of them is Evy (Migdalia Melendez), a young Puerto Rican nurse who is in a committed relationship with Kia (T. Wendy McMillan), a women's studies college professor. Evy is divorced from a man called Junior (Alfredo D. Troche) and lives with her mother (Betty Jeannie Pejko), who doesn't know her daughter is a lesbian. *Go Fish* addresses this situation in a scene where Evy's mother confronts her daughter about her sexuality after Junior has outed Evy.

During a tense confrontation, Evy's mother asks, "Oh my God, is that how I brought you up? Is that what I taught you, to become a *pata*? *Ay, no me digas.* No wonder Junior left you." The mother uses the Puerto Rican colloquial term **pata**, a derogatory word for lesbian, as an accusation against her daughter. She further adds, "Listen, so what do you want? You sleep with women? You kiss women? What do you think you are—a man?" Evy's lack of a clear and direct response to these recriminations leads her mother to voice an ultimatum: "As long as you live in my house, you are going to go by my rules! . . . If you leave now, forget it." Evy leaves after yelling, "I'm getting out of here," and goes to Kia's apartment. Once there, Max, Kia's roommate, lets her in and attempts to help Evy figure out her situation. At one point Evy says, "Max, listen, I've just gotten kicked out of the house. My mom thinks I'm going to hell. I don't have a place to live." Max earnestly responds, "Evy, you know you can live with us. We can be your new family." With Evy's affirmative response, "Fine," the film redefines the concept of family as one that is chosen instead of given through birth. As John D'Emilio explains, gay men and lesbians "have had to create, for [their] survival, networks of support that do not depend on the bonds of blood or the license of the state, but are freely chosen and nurtured" (14).

Figure 8.1: Evy (Migdalia Melendez) is confronted about being a lesbian by her mother (Betty Jeannie Pejko) and ex-husband (Alfredo D. Troche) in *Go Fish* (1994).

Source: DVD of *Go Fish*
Attribution: Rose Troche
License: Fair Use

Through Evy's outing and expulsion from her home, *Go Fish* addresses the regrettable reality of discrimination that many LGBTQ people have lived, including from blood relatives. The film connects these painful experiences to unfair expectations of women in general and prejudices against lesbians that exist in our society and, consequently, in Latina/o/x culture. Through the use of voice-over narration, *Go Fish* reveals how these expectations populate the psyche of two characters, Max and Evy. Before the scene where Evy fights with her mother, we see a sequence that starts with Max writing in her journal. Through a voice-over, we hear Max's thoughts about how life would've been had she not become a lesbian and had she followed the normative path of getting married to a man and having children. Her ideas are filmically illustrated through phantasmagoric images of six women (including herself) playing the role of bride by getting dressed and undressed in a white bridal gown. A different voice-over in Spanish is heard after Evy leaves her mother's house and is en route to Kia's apartment. The voice-over includes the voices of a young girl and a woman, implying that they belong to young Evy and her mother. The dialogue reveals the girl's aspirations for the future, including becoming a teacher. The mother asks the girl if she would like to have a husband—one like her papá. The girl says no and instead responds that she would like to live in a house with her best female friend. Since the voice-over is not subtitled, only Spanish-speaking audiences would understand the exchange. The stylistic choice of using Spanish for this voice-over gives cultural specificity to the character of Evy and her experience as a Latina who is inculcated from an early age the normative script of the importance of (heterosexual) marriage.

Frances Negrón-Muntaner, an openly lesbian Puerto Rican filmmaker and scholar, directed, wrote, and starred in *Brincando el Charco: Portrait of a Puerto Rican*. The film's main character is Claudia, a woman who, just like Evy in *Go Fish*, suffers family rejection due to homophobia after an unexpected outing. The traumatic scene, however, takes place in the past and in Puerto Rico. In the film's present, Claudia resides in Philadelphia, where she moved in pursuit of personal growth and professional development. Although the United States might represent new possibilities for her, Claudia faces new challenges stemming from her positionality as a Puerto Rican lesbian. She is forced to deal with questions related to a newly found racial identity as well as the impact that the legacies of centuries of colonialism—both from Spain and the United States—might have had in the formation of her desire and sexual identity.

*Carmelita Tropicana: Your Kunst Is Your Waffen* also made its debut in 1994, and won the Teddy Award for Best Short Film that year. Cuban American filmmaker Ela Troyano directed the film and cowrote it with her sister, Alina Troyano, who is an openly lesbian performance artist whose artistic persona is Carmelita Tropicana. The short provides a fictionalized version of Carmelita's life in New York City's Lower East Side, specifically of a day when Carmelita's activism lands her in jail along with her best friend Orchidia (Livia Daza-Paris) and her sister Sophia (Sophia Ramos). The film reconfigures the Latina family in two different ways. First, Carmelita's family involves three siblings from different racial categories. Younger brother Pepito is Chinese and Sophia is "a dark-skinned Latina yuppie wanna-be" (Troyano 145). At one point, a store cashier mistakes Sophia for African American. In response, Sophia asserts, "Latinas come in all different colors!" (Troyano 148). The other reconfiguration is through the character of Dee (Anne Iobst), an HIV+ White woman who is in the same cell with Carmelita, Orchidia, and Sophia. At one point, Dee speaks in Spanish, a language she learned in prison after becoming a member of the *Sandungueras*, a Puerto Rican prison gang that adopted her after she defended one of their members against another gang. Dee explains that "in prison, your family picks you. I was one of the six hermanas. María was mom. Josefa papá. She taught me salsa and merengue. Leticia was abuela, the peacemaker. You get adopted, you do better. It's good" (Troyano 161). It is important to notice how in prison the structure of the nuclear family is adapted to create protective and affective relationships that subvert who could step into a particular role—e.g., a woman as the father. Dee's insistence through the statement, "I am a *Sandunguera*" asserts not only her pride in belonging to the Puerto Rican gang/family that adopted her but also that a sense of Puerto Ricanness informs the way in which she understands herself.

By the end of the 1990s, New Queer Cinema had lost its original momentum. Studios recognized the profitability of LGBTQ moviegoers as a niche audience and started producing more mainstream films like *In & Out* (1997) and *Chasing Amy* (1997). During this period, network TV in sitcoms like *Will & Grace* (1998–2006, 2017–2020) and *The Ellen Show* (2001–2002) started to feature LGBTQ individuals as leading characters. The centrality of these characters became possible after Ellen DeGeneres came out as a lesbian in 1997, both in real life and on her sitcom *Ellen* (1994–1998).

## QUEERNESS ON NETWORK TV

US network television (currently represented by ABC, NBC, CBS, Fox, and The CW) followed radio's economic organization as an advertiser-supported system. Nick Browne claims, "Advertising regulates the exchange between general processes of production and consumption of TV shows. In fact, any TV show must provide a suitable 'environment' for the commercial message" (72). The idea of TV shows as "suitable environments" for ads explains why network TV's representations of sexuality in general and queer sexuality in particular are tamer than those in film, cable TV (particularly premium channels), and streaming services that produce their own original programming. For the purposes of this section, we should also notice that Latina/o/x queerness has been explored through secondary characters.

In 2006, *Ugly Betty* premiered on ABC and ran for four seasons. Silvio Horta, an openly gay Cuban American screenwriter and TV producer, adapted the wildly successful Colombian telenovela entitled *Yo soy Betty, la fea* (1999) into an hour-long dramedy set in New York during the new millennium. The series focuses on Betty Suarez (America Ferrera) and her family: her father Ignacio (Tony Plana), her sister Hilda (Ana Ortiz), and her teenage nephew Justin (Mark Indelicato). Betty is a smart Mexican American woman who, despite not being a fashionista, gets a job at a well-known fashion magazine. The series has several LGBTQ characters, including Justin. For the first seasons, *Ugly Betty* codifies Justin's gayness through cultural markers that have stereotypically been associated with gay men. Justin is gentle mannered, is obsessed with impeccable grooming, has vast knowledge of fashion, and loves musical theater. The character, however, is never a stereotype. Importantly, his immediate family always shows love and support for him, including when they find out he is gay.

The series' final season explores Justin's sexual identity by providing him with a romantic interest, Austin (Ryan McGinnis). In the series' penultimate episode, "The Past Presents the Future," Justin comes out. He mostly does it because his mother's fiancé, Bobby (Adam Rodriguez), sees him and Austin kissing. However, Justin chooses to confide in Marc (Michael Urie), Betty's openly gay coworker, instead of his family. Marc reassures Justin that his family will not turn its back on him. When the Suarez family finds out, they are ready to throw Justin a surprise coming-out party, but Marc convinces them to let Justin do things on his own terms. Justin finally comes out to his family at his mother's wedding reception. During the newlywed couple's first dance, Justin asks Austin to dance with him in front of everyone.

Figure 8.2: Justin (Mark Indelicato) comes out by dancing with his boyfriend Austin (Ryan McGinnis) in *Ugly Betty* (2006–2010).

Source: DVD of *Ugly Betty*
Attribution: Silvio Horta
License: Fair Use

While the teenagers dance, we see the facial expressions of every single family member. They are all tenderly smiling in support of Justin and his decision to come out. Afterward, while Justin dances with his mom, Hilda seeks complicity with her son and declares, "That Austin is a cutie!" Justin ignores the comment and coyly replies, "Mom!"

Fox's *Glee* (2009–2015) features a Latina character, Santana Lopez (Naya Rivera), who explores her sexual identity until deciding that women are the objects of her love and desire. Santana is originally presented as a mean girl, mostly through her sarcasm and quick wit. These attributes could have made the character into a stereotypical Latina spitfire. However, Naya Rivera's immense talent imbues Santana with depth and made the character a fan favorite, especially with LGBTQ audiences. In the season 3 episode "I Kissed a Girl," Santana suffers a painful outing as well as her grandmother Alma's rejection on the grounds that lesbianism is a sin. By the sixth and final season, Alma (Ivonne Coll) comes around and attends Santana's wedding to the love of her life, Brittany (Heather Morris). The episode titled "A Wedding" also includes Santana's mother, Maribel (Gloria Estefan), who never had a problem with her daughter's love for women.

For eleven seasons, Dr. Callie Torres (Sara Ramírez) was a regular character on ABC's *Grey's Anatomy* as a successful orthopedic surgeon. Between seasons

2 and 12, this Latina character had romantic and sexual relations with both men and women. From season 5 until the character's departure, all of Callie's love interests were women, including Dr. Arizona Robbins (Jessica Capshaw), whom she married in season 7. After Callie decided she was a lesbian, she encountered some resistance from her father Carlos (Héctor Elizondo). Yet, contrary to teenage characters like Justin and Santana, Callie dealt with the situation in a different way. The character's professional standing, financial stability, and strong group of supportive friends allowed her to come out on her own terms. Sara Ramírez, the Mexican American actor who played Callie, came out as bisexual in 2016 and as nonbinary in 2020.

## QUEERNESS IN TV'S POST-NETWORK ERA

Television in the United States has dramatically changed from the domination of a few networks to what is known as the current **post-network era**. This era was ushered in through the expansion of cable channels, the development of new technologies that allow viewers to record and watch shows outside of traditional scheduled airings (e.g., DVR), and the rise of streaming services that gather all sorts of content, from old TV shows to new original programming. (See Chapter 2 for additional information on this shift). TV audiences have become further fragmented, which has allowed for more niche programming to emerge, be it in the form of shows or even entire channels for specific intended audiences (e.g., Logo TV, El Rey Network). Well-established producers like Shonda Rhimes (*Grey's Anatomy*) and Ryan Murphy (*Glee*) have been lured away from network TV and basic cable through lucrative deals with Netflix and other streaming services to create new series where they have even more control over their projects than they ever had before.

The constant need for new and specialized content has led up to the creation of shows that were previously deemed unsuitable and unprofitable for network television. Consequently, the televisual landscape now counts with a more expansive—albeit still incomplete—representation of the social groups that comprise our nation. Steven Canals, co-creator of FX's *Pose*, is one of the creative talents that has expanded new voices to the post-network arena. Canals, who identifies as a queer Afro-Puerto Rican man, wrote the show's first draft while studying screenwriting at UCLA. Canals explains that "exhausted by the erasure of my experience, *Pose* was conceived as way to fill a gap that has long existed. A love letter to New York City and the miraculous queer and trans, black and brown souls who managed to create community in the face of a plague, violence, and familial rejection." With the backing of established TV **writers-producers** Ryan Murphy and Brad Falchuk, Canals was able to get *Pose* on the air in 2018.

Taking partial inspiration from the subjects of Jennie Livingston's *Paris Is Burning*, *Pose* provides a fictionalized version of the lives of Black and Brown queer characters in New York City between the late 1980s and the mid-1990s.

The series highlights these queer characters' relationships to ball culture, i.e., the underground drag competitions that include posing, dancing, and voguing, where participants battle in different categories that require performing as specific types/personas/identities such as Butch Queen, Femme Queen, Successful Businessman, Rich Woman, etc. Ball participants often belong to a "house" or drag family (e.g., House of LaBeija, House of Xtravaganza) that provides support inside and outside competitions. One of the series' two main characters is Blanca Evangelista (Michaela Jaé Rodriguez), an HIV+ trans Afro-Latina woman who becomes the show's emotional center. Upon being diagnosed HIV+, Blanca creates and becomes the leader of her own drag family under the name of House of Evangelista. As the Mother, she looks after three children, Angel (Indya Moore), Damon Richards (Ryan Jamaal Swain), and Lil Papi (Angel Bismark Curiel), and helps them succeed in the ball scene as well as in everyday life. In the final season, Blanca pursues a career as a nurse who specializes in treating HIV and AIDS, drawing upon her experiences and gift of helping others. She also turns into an ACT UP activist once she realizes that patients of color were not being included in HIV experimental treatments. In 2021, Michaela Jaé Rodriguez, who plays Blanca, became the first transgender performer to be nominated for an Emmy for Outstanding Lead Actress in a Drama.

Tanya Saracho, a Mexican-born artist who identifies as queer and Latinx, created Starz's *Vida* (2018–2020). The show focuses on two sisters, Emma (Mishel Prada) and Lyn (Melissa Barrera), who return to their childhood home in Boyle Heights, Los Angeles, upon their mother's sudden death. Once there, they discover that their mother Vidalia "Vida" (Rose Portillo), had been married for two years to a woman, Eddy (Ser Anzoategui). News of the marriage is particularly shocking to Emma since Vida had sent Emma away to live with her grandmother in Texas when she was eleven as punishment for having been found expressing her desire for other girls. *Vida* exposes how Mexican American/Chicanx/Latinx women are relentlessly at odds with patriarchy, whiteness, and normative (hetero)sexuality in the United States. For example, character Mari Sanchez (Chelsea Rendon) is a fierce community activist who fights against her neighborhood's gentrification with gusto. Yet when she's at home, she must abide by her father's rules without complaining. Eddy's gay bashing at a neighborhood bar where she is called a **marimacha** (a pejorative colloquial term for lesbian) exemplifies the perils that butch women and nonbinary people encounter in the United States for not following normative gender standards of self-presentation. Emma's decision to take over her mother's bar at the end of season 1 partly arises from realizing the importance of having a secure gathering space for queer people like Eddy and herself in Boyle Heights. As Cruz (Maria-Elena Laas) says to Emma in the episode 6, Vida's bar "is the only place in the neighborhood where *mujeres* (women) like me, girls like us, can go. . . . I know when I walk into your mom's bar, I feel safe."

All the examples that I have provided come from fiction films and TV shows. It is also important to consider how entertainment genres like reality television have helped to enhance the representation of LGBTQ Latinas/os in US popular culture. One of the most prominent examples comes from the MTV reality show *The Real World: San Francisco* (1994), which introduced the whole nation to Pedro Zamora, an openly gay, HIV+ Cuban American activist and educator. He became the televisual face for many queer Latina/o/x youth in the United States. The heartfelt candidness with which Pedro spoke about his gayness and HIV+ status broke ground in the depiction of Latinos and gay men in general. Since 2009, *RuPaul's Drag Race* has become the preeminent TV series to showcase queer Latinas/os as well as African Americans, Asian Americans, and other racial and ethnic minority groups extant in our nation. Contestants like Nina Flowers, Adore Delano, Alexis Mateo, Vanessa Vanjie Mateo, Olivia Lux, and Kandy Muse have discussed serious issues such as homophobia, poverty, sexism, racism, and domestic violence in the Latino community, as well as in US society at large. They have also highlighted the significant contributions of Latina and Latin American artists such as Selena, Frida Kahlo, and Walter Mercado, among others, expanding their influence into contemporary world culture.

The examples in this chapter have mostly emphasized issues related to the representation and narrative function of Latina/o/x LGBTQ characters in films and TV shows. Rather than thinking about if these representations were "fair," "authentic," or "positive," we should pay attention to how these texts create versions of race, ethnicity, gender, and sexuality, among other axes of identity, to apprehend the stories US media privileges when it comes to Latina/o/x LGBTQ communities. More work could be done in terms of the production of these texts (e.g., is it important who the makers of these films/TV shows are? What kind of imprint do different artistic talent—an actor vs. a writer, a director vs. a producer—leave in these representations?) as well as their reception (e.g., do Latina/o/x audiences enjoy these films/TV shows? Is their response different if they identify as LGBTQ?).

**Gilberto M. Blasini** *is Associate Professor of English and Film Studies at the University of Wisconsin, Milwaukee. His research and teaching focuses on Latin American and Caribbean cinemas; colonial and postcolonial cinemas; queerness in cinema, television, and performance art; and film genres, especially road movies and post-1960 horror cinema.*

## BIBLIOGRAPHY

Browne, Nick. "The Political Economy of Television's (Super)Text." *American Television: New Directions in History and Theory*, edited by Nick Browne, Harwood Academic Publishers, 1994, pp. 69–79.

Canals, Steven. "FX's 'Pose' Creator on His Difficult Journey Bringing the Groundbreaking Trans Series to TV." *The Daily Beast*, 3 Apr. 2019, https://www.thedailybeast.com/fxs-pose-creator-on-his-difficult-journey-bringing-the-groundbreaking-trans-series-to-tv.

D'Emilio, John. *Making Trouble: Essays on Gay History, Politics, and the University*. Routledge, 1992, pp. 3–16.

Hall, Stuart. "Negotiating Caribbean Identities." *New Left Review*, vol. 209, 1995, pp. 3–14.

Rich, B. Ruby. "Homo Pomo: The New Queer Cinema." *Women and Film: A Sight and Sound Reader*, edited by Pam Cook and Philip Dodd, Temple UP, 1993, pp. 164–74.

Troyano, Alina. *I, Carmelita Tropicana: Performing Between Cultures*, edited by Chon A. Noriega, Beacon P, 2000.

Turner, Guinevere, and Rose Troche. *Go Fish: The Full Original Screenplay*. The Overlook P, 1995.

Umpierre, Luz María. "Interview with Cherríe Moraga." *The Americas Review*, vol. 14, no. 2, 1986, pp. 54–67.

## FILMOGRAPHY

*Brincando el Charco: Portrait of a Puerto Rican*. Directed by Frances Negrón-Muntaner, performances by Frances Negrón-Muntaner, Agnes Lugo-Ortiz, Moisés Agosto, Toni Cade Bambara, ITVS International, 1994.

Canals, Steven, Ryan Murphy, and Brad Falchuk, creators. *Pose*. FX, 2018–2021.

*Carmelita Tropicana: Your Kunst Is Your Waffen*. Directed by Ela Troyano, performances by Alina Troyano, Sophia Ramos, Livia Daza-Paris, Annie Lobst, First Run Features, 1994.

*Go Fish*. Directed by Rose Troche, performances by V.S. Brodie, Guinevere Turner, T. Wendy McMillan, Migdalia Melendez, and Anastasia Sharp, Samuel Goldwyn, 1994.

Horta, Silvio, and Fernando Gaitán, creators. *Ugly Betty*. ABC, 2006–2010.

Murphy, Ryan, Ian Brennan, and Brad Falchuk, creators. *Glee*. Fox, 2009–2015.

Rhimes, Shonda, creator. *Grey's Anatomy*. ABC, 2005–present.

Saracho, Tanya, creator. *Vida*. Starz, 2018–2020.

## FOR FURTHER STUDY

Almaguer, Tomás. "Chicano Men: A Cartography of Homosexual Identity and Behavior." *The Lesbian and Gay Studies Reader*, edited by Henry Abelove, Michèle Aina Barale, and David M. Halperin, Routledge, 1993, pp. 255–73.

Hames-García, Michael, and Ernesto Javier Martínez, editors. *Gay Latino Studies: A Critical Reader*. Duke UP, 2011.

La Fountain-Stokes, Lawrence. *Translocas: The Politics of Puerto Rican Drag and Trans Performance*. U of Michigan P, 2021.

*Latin Boys Go to Hell*. Directed by Ela Troyano, performances by Irwin Ossa, John Bryant, and Mike Ruiz, Strand Releasing, 1997.

Lear, Norman, Gloria Calderón Kellett, and Mike Royce, creators. *One Day at a Time.* Netflix and Pop, 2017–2020.

*Mosquita y Mari.* Directed by Aurora Guerrero, performances by Fenessa Pineda, Venecia Troncoso, Maya Entertainment, 2012.

Muñoz, José Esteban. *The Sense of Brown.* Duke UP, 2020.

Navarro, Ray. "Eso, me está pasando." *Queer Looks: Perspectives on Lesbian and Gay Film and Video,* edited by Martha Gever, John Grewyson, and Pratibha Parmar, Routledge, 1993, pp. 38–40.

Negrón-Muntaner, Frances. *Boricua Pop: Puerto Ricans and the Latinization of American Culture.* NYU P, 2004.

*Paris Is Burning.* Directed by Jenny Livingston, performances by Blanca Xtravaganza, Willi Ninja, Octavia St. Laureant, Pepper LaBeija, Prestige Pictures, 1990.

Rivero, Yeidy M. "Diasporic and Marginal Crossroads: The Films of Frances Negrón-Muntaner." *Latino Studies,* vol. 7, no. 3, 2009, pp. 336–56.

Rodríguez, Richard T. "Making Queer Familia." *The Routledge Queer Studies Reader,* edited by Donald E. Hall and Annamarie Jagose, Routledge, 2012, pp. 324–32.

# Part III: Histories

Chapters in the Histories section provide a brief overview of distinct Latinx national-origin communities' historical experiences in the United States and trace the various ways these experiences have been mediated onscreen. Chapter 9 offers an overview of how representations of people of Latin American origin shifted over time from the introduction of cinema in the late nineteenth century to the 1950s and charts viewers' responses to these representations. Chapter 10 examines Spanish-language television and the concept of pan-Latinidad, noting how media have contributed to shaping the common notion of a unified "Latin" population living in the United States. Chapter 11 considers the Mexican American experience in film and provides three case studies of Mexican American representation onscreen. Chapter 12 provides an introduction to Puerto Rican media in the latter half of the twentieth century to the present, exploring media-making on the island, in the United States, and in between. Chapter 13 provides a historic overview of the Cuban American experience onscreen from the late nineteenth century to the present. Chapter 14 discusses the cinematic images of Dominican Americans that have emerged in recent decades, countering the invisibility of Dominicans in United States and offering complex portraits of this community. Chapter 15 discusses Central American experiences onscreen and calls attention to the ways media (mis)represent this diverse population.

After completing this section, students should be able to do the following:
- Identify and describe artistic traditions and approaches linked to specific Latinx national-origin communities.
- Identify key moments in the history of people of Latin American origin in the United States and describe how these histories are represented in film and visual culture.
- Identify the driving forces of migration from Latin America to the United States (or, in the case of Puerto Rico, from the island to the mainland) and evaluate the role of US government policies in this phenomenon.

# Latino Images and Audiences to 1960

Laura Isabel Serna
(University of Southern California)

Chicano poet Tino Villanueva begins his book-length poem *Scene from the Movie GIANT* like this: "What I have from 1956 is one instant at the Holiday/Theater, where a small dimension of a film, as in/A dream, became the feature of the whole" (1). The "small dimension of a film" he is referring to in this line is a scene at the end of the 1956 film *Giant*. That film, which starred famous Hollywood stars Elizabeth Taylor, Rock Hudson, and James Dean, is an epic Western that tells the story of a wealthy Texas family and the changes they face as cattle ranchers confront the new wealth generated by the discovery of oil. Toward the end of the film, the family stops at a diner, where the racist owner insults the family's Mexican American daughter-in-law and grandson and refuses to serve a Mexican family. This causes a violent confrontation between the family patriarch and the diner's owner. In the film, this sequence represents the beginning of a new chapter for the now racially mixed family, but the scene of anti-Mexican racism stayed in Villanueva's mind, stirring up feelings of exclusion from onscreen representation.

Villanueva's poem sums up the predicament that many audience members who in the 1950s might have identified as Latin American, Spanish-speaking, or simply Mexican, Puerto Rican, or Cuban, as the case might have been, found themselves in during the first half of the twentieth century. They were hungry for images of themselves onscreen but frequently found that those images represented communities with origins in Latin America stereotypically, rarely allowed them to be the main characters, or protagonists, and often framed their very existence as a social problem that needed to be solved. This chapter surveys how representations of the groups we gather today under the umbrella of terms such as Latino (which existed in the period under discussion) or Latinx (which did not) shifted over time from the introduction of cinema in the late nineteenth century to the 1950s, and how viewers responded to those representations.

## STEREOTYPES IN THE SILENT ERA

The first Latinos (as we might use that term today) to appear onscreen were two members of Buffalo Bill's Wild West show, a traveling live show that recreated scenes audiences associated with the western United States. Pedro Esquivel and Dionicio Gonzalez performed their act *Mexican Knife Duel* (1894) in front of Thomas Edison's early film camera. This lost film, which was between thirty and sixty seconds long, would likely have confirmed preexisting conceptions audiences had about Mexicans formed by interacting with other forms of popular culture such as dime novels, political cartoons, and plays: Mexicans were violent, unsophisticated, and cruel. This early film established the norms that would govern the depiction of Latino characters, with slight variations, through the late 1920s. The majority of the over one hundred films made before 1930 set in Mexico or the US–Mexico borderlands portrayed Mexican or other Latino characters in ways that conformed to what scholar Charles Ramírez Berg identifies as six basic **stereotypes**, widely held but simplified images of a person or group: "the harlot, the male buffoon, the female clown, the Latin lover, and the dark lady" (66).

Figure 9.1: A production still from *Broncho Billy and the Greaser*, published in *Motography*, October 3, 1914, 754.

Source: Media History Digital Library
Attribution: *Motography*
License: Public Domain

Early silent films, usually about fifteen minutes long (the length of one reel of film) depicted Mexicans, male or female, as untrustworthy if not criminal. A **film cycle** (a group of films made around the same time that share thematic concerns) of **"greaser" films** made between 1908–1914 exemplify how Mexican characters were portrayed as "a sexual threat to the European American home and public sphere" (Noriega 5). An instructive example is the **single reel film** *Broncho Billy and the Greaser* (1914), which tells the story of a "half-breed" or mixed-race character, the "greaser" of the title, who harasses a White woman in the post office where the mail is being delivered by Broncho Billy, the cowboy character developed by Gilbert M. Anderson. After Billy defends the woman, the "half-breed" plots revenge, a plan that is foiled by the girl who brings help in the nick of time. This short film conforms to a narrative structure that positioned Anglo-Americans as heroic defenders of their communities and families against racially inferior individuals or groups.

## FROM THE BORDER TO THE HACIENDA

In 1910, at the height of the greaser films' popularity, the Mexican Revolution, a civil conflict between various factions that sought to end the dictatorship of Porfirio Díaz, erupted. Many residents of the United States were deeply interested in this conflict that was taking place just across the southern border, in part because many wealthy Americans had extensive financial investments in agriculture and mining in Mexico. US film studios capitalized on this fascination by highlighting the revolution in **newsreels** (weekly compilations of footage of current events) and creating fiction films that made the revolution part of their story line or included characters who resembled the conflict's most visible protagonists. Perhaps the most often mentioned of the numerous films that made the revolution a central theme was the now lost film *The Life of General Villa* (1914) that combined a fictional account of Villa's life, including an ending in which he becomes the president of Mexico, with documentary-type footage of soldiers and battles. This film was part of a contract between Villa and the Mutual Film Corp. that exchanged media access to Villa and his troops for a percentage of any profits. While by all accounts this portrayal of Villa was sympathetic—the United States briefly supported his movement—the line between revolutionary and bandit was blurry. Most of these films perpetuated the image of Mexico as a chaotic, barbarous land and Mexicans as incapable of organizing and running their own government.

In the mid-nineteen-tens, the US film industry moved westward from its early base on the East Coast. The history of the industry's new home as first Spanish and then Mexican territory became the backdrop for numerous feature films with titles such as *Mission Bells: A Romance of San Juan Capistrano* (1913), *Rose of the Rancho* (1914), and *A Yoke of Gold* or *In the Days of the Missions* (1916). These films offered a romantic vision of California's past, representing life in "Old California" as colorful, decadent, and exotic. One prominent and extensively studied example of films that romanticized life in California under Spanish and then Mexican rule is *Ramona,* a 1910 film directed by D.W. Griffith. Based on a novel of the same title by Helen Hunt Jackson, the film tells the story of an orphaned girl, the Ramona of the title (played by the popular actress Mary Pickford), who is taken in by the wealthy **hispano** (a person descended from Spanish settlers in the Southwest before it became part of the United States) owners of a ranch. There she meets and falls in love with an Indigenous laborer named Alessandro, whom the mistress of the ranch sends away to thwart their romance. When Ramona discovers she also has Indigenous heritage, the girl flees to be with Alessandro. The couple are unable to find peace as White settlers drive them away from the places they try to settle. Ultimately, Alessandro dies and Ramona is rescued by the son of the rancho family, Felipe, who is also in love with her. While Hunt Jackson wrote the novel as a means of drawing attention to the mistreatment of Indians in the United States, many readers were captivated by her description of the novel's setting in California just after the Mexican-American War (1846–1848). This was an aspect of the film that audiences also found intriguing. Reviewers emphasized that the film had been shot on location at a former rancho and its supposedly authentic costuming and portrayal of rancho life. So intriguing was the story that several additional film adaptations were made after Griffith's, including one in 1928 starring Mexican actress Dolores del Río.

Throughout the 1920s, the border continued to furnish a backdrop for romance and adventure. Films with titles like *Rio Grande* (1920), *A California Romance* (1922), and *Border Intrigue* (1925) set their stories in cantinas, on ranches, and in border towns. Though these narratives sometimes portrayed Mexican characters, especially those with one White parent, sympathetically, they typically focused on their White protagonists. Mexican characters played villains in the form of bandits, revolutionaries, or cattle rustlers. In broad strokes, audiences were attracted to scenes of fiestas or fandangos, vaguely Spanish costumes, or the rough-and-tumble ambiance of the border. These films allowed audiences to visit the Spanish or Mexican past and the border region without having to think about present-day discrimination against ethnic Mexican communities made up of long-time residents and new immigrants.

Ironically, film producers in the United States had worked hard to cultivate Latin American audiences, and film exhibition had become a lucrative endeavor in immigrant communities across the southwestern United States. Since, for example, ethnic Mexican patrons might be excluded from motion-picture theaters that served White audiences, entrepreneurs both from the community and from outside established local theaters specifically for Spanish-speaking audiences. By the mid-1920s, a vibrant film culture emerged in immigrant communities. While the films they showed might not be different from those shown in other theaters, these motion-picture venues advertised in Spanish-language newspapers, provided meeting space for community events, and featured entertainment before or between films by community members or by performers who formed part of a Spanish-language theater and musical performance circuit. These practices created a welcoming environment that spoke to the experiences and concerns of local audiences, characterized by shared experiences of immigration and language (Serna 180-214; Gunckel, *Mexico on Main Street*).

**Figure 9.2: A publicity photograph of Dolores del Río published in *Motion Picture Magazine*, March 1926, 18.**

Source: Media History Digital Library
Attribution: *Motion Picture Magazine*
License: Public Domain

Those audiences were just as fascinated by the idea of Hollywood stardom as other motion-picture goers. However, when they saw themselves onscreen, it was typically in stereotypical roles or as extras who appeared in the background of Westerns and other films set on the border or in Latin American settings. Major roles, even of Latino or Latin American characters, were frequently played by White actors in brownface makeup or simply in costumes and makeup that signaled a racialized identity. A small handful of successful Latino actors in Hollywood provided immigrant communities in the United States and Latin America with stars that they felt connected to by language or national origin. Ramon Novarro and Dolores del Río were from well-off Mexican families, and though press coverage emphasized their exotic good looks, they both conformed to the European beauty standards that reigned in the industry. Del Río publicly committed herself to only playing dignified roles, while Novarro was known for supporting charitable causes in the immigrant community (Rodriguez; López; Chávez). In fact, though she continued to be cast in Hollywood after the introduction of sound, del Río opted to return to Mexico in the 1940s, where the thriving film industry gave her the opportunity to play more artistically complex roles. Lupe Vélez's short career offers a counterpoint to their star personae. She came to Hollywood from the world of theater in Mexico City and worked in both silent and sound film, appearing alongside stars such as Douglas Fairbanks Jr. Her characters, especially the *Mexican Spitfire* character she played in a series of films in the 1940s, were volatile and hot-tempered, characterizations that were supported by press coverage that referred to her as "the hot tamale" and focused on her tumultuous personal life. Although she successfully made the transition from silent to sound films, Vélez's **star persona** (the combination of her onscreen roles and the way she was represented in the press) seemed to affirm stereotypes about Latinas (Sturtevant).

## EARLY SPANISH-LANGUAGE PRODUCTIONS

In the late 1920s, just as Vélez was beginning her career in Hollywood, the introduction of sound technology changed the industry in significant ways. Major American studios had relied on the relative ease with which silent films could be translated for non-English speaking audiences. **Intertitles**, slides inserted at specific points in the film that conveyed narrative information or dialogue, could, with a small amount of effort, be translated into other languages. In fact, studios had set up foreign departments that handled the translation of intertitles and publicity material and shipped those film prints to distribution offices across the globe. Introducing sound and specifically spoken dialogue presented a challenge to this system. Initially, because setting up theaters to screen sound films required significant investments in technology, Hollywood studios continued to produce silent films for a time. But soon they began to grapple with how they were going to keep the attention of non-English-speaking audiences around the globe. Films that focused on musical performances were one solution, but the major studios soon began to experiment with making films in multiple languages.

Studios began to make the same film with different casts speaking the dialogue in different languages. Although they made films in German, French, Italian, and other languages, **Spanish-language film production** became the most extensive and the most long-lasting of these experiments (Jarvinen 8). One often cited example of Hollywood's Spanish-language production and its possibilities and challenges is the 1931 Universal film *Drácula* directed by George Melford. The Spanish-language version starring Carlos Villarías and Lupita Tovar was shot at night on the same set used by the English-language cast and even used the same costumes. Some believe that the Spanish-language version was superior to the "original." But that was not always the case. Spanish-speaking audiences in the United States and across Latin America were hopeful that these films would reflect their experiences, but they were often disappointed. These productions were made with smaller budgets and thus were often of significantly lower quality. Even more importantly, audiences had become attached to Hollywood stars and resented films full of unknown talent. Although audiences were ambivalent about Hollywood's Spanish-language productions, their production created more opportunities for Latino talent. Spanish-language production led to an influx of Spanish-speaking talent who sought work not only as performers but also as screenwriters, dialogue coaches, and consultants. Newcomers to Hollywood and those that had been working for a long time in Los Angeles's vibrant Spanish-language theater scene jockeyed for opportunities, while producers tried to determine what regional or national dialect of Spanish was most appropriate (Gunckel, "War of the Accents").

Figure 9.3: A publicity image for the Spanish-language version of *Drácula*, featuring Lupita Tovar and Carlos Villarías, published in *Cine-Mundial*, January 1931, 21.

Source: Media History Digital Library
License: Public Domain

The introduction of sound also created opportunities for film producers in Latin America. Companies sprang up in Argentina, Mexico, and Cuba, eager to fill Latin American and Latino audiences' desire for films that more accurately reflected their historical and contemporary realities. These film industries benefited from the experience of creative and technical staff who had worked in Hollywood's Spanish-language production. For example, Mexico's first sound film, *Santa* (1931), was the second film adaptation of a late-nineteenth-century novel that told the story of a country girl corrupted by the city. It was directed by Spaniard Antonio Moreno, who had become a major Hollywood star, and featured Lupita Tovar and Donald Reed (born Ernesto Guillen). Significantly, the film made use of a sound-on-film technique developed by two brothers, Roberto and Joselito Rodríguez, who had worked in Hollywood.

## LATIN AMERICAN FILMS IN THE UNITED STATES

By the late 1930s, the films made by increasingly stable and productive film industries in Latin America found receptive audiences in the Spanish-speaking enclaves across the United States where they shared screen time with Hollywood films. In movie theaters in Los Angeles, New York, San Antonio, and Denver, these films solidified immigrants' ties to their homelands and reinforced audiences' attachment to two film traditions: Hollywood and popular Latin American cinema. Before 1960, over one thousand unique Spanish-language films were shown in Los Angeles alone (Gunckel et al. 18). As this figure suggests, the United States became the Mexican film industry's largest foreign market, and profits from distribution in the United States were key to the industry's financial health (Fein). Los Angeles became a particularly important site for the exhibition of Latin American film in general and Mexican cinema in particular. Premieres, especially at the first run Teatro California, were sometimes attended by stars such as Tito Guízar and José Mojica (Gunckel, *Mexico on Main Street* 185).

Even as Latin America's major film producers became part of the cultural imaginary of Latino immigrants in the United States, Hollywood continued to make films set in Latin American locales featuring Latino performers. The **Good Neighbor Policy**, a program designed to improve US–Latin American relations and draw Latin American countries into the United States' sphere of influence, used film as a key way to spread the message of hemispheric solidarity (Woll; Adams). In collaboration with the federal government, consultants were brought in to ensure that the industry's representations of Latin Americans and Latin America were sympathetic, stars were briefly sent to Latin America as goodwill ambassadors, and studios were encouraged to make more films with Latin American characters and locations. The films produced included many musicals, which capitalized on the growing popularity of Latin music and provided opportunities for new talent, such as Brazilian singer and dancer Carmen Miranda and Mexican-born Ricardo Montalbán. Among the notable films produced during this period is the Walt Disney film *Los Tres Caballeros* (*The Three Caballeros* [1944]), in which Donald Duck visits various Latin American countries, a trip that is punctuated by catchy musical numbers and visuals, animated and live action, that by mobilizing what some scholars have referred to as a tourist or ethnographic gaze, emphasized Latin America's landscape and picturesque local traditions.

Another set of films made during this period and into the 1950s focused on Latino social issues. These films were part of a larger post–World War II film cycle that focused on social problems such as racism, assimilation, and inequality. Films that focused on Mexican Americans included *A Medal for Benny* (1945), *Border Incident* (1949), and *The Ring* (1952). Perhaps the most impactful **social problem film** that focused on Mexican American communities is *Salt of the Earth* (1954), directed by Herbert J. Biberman, who had been pushed out of Hollywood because of his political beliefs. The film featured a substantial number of nonprofessional actors and focused on the story of a successful real-life strike by Mexican American miners who wanted better working and living conditions. It is unusual in its positioning of Mexican Americans as capable of producing change in their own life circumstances. Although technically not a social problem film, the Western drama *Giant* (1956), which had such a powerful impact on young Tino Villanueva, had elements of the social problem film, as it highlighted discrimination and segregation in Texas.

Figure 9.4: The female relatives of striking miners take their places on the picket line, using a legal loophole to circumvent a legal challenge to the strike in *Salt of the Earth* (1954).

Source: DVD of *Salt of the Earth*
License: Fair Use

For the first six decades of the twentieth century, Latino audiences at home and abroad faced the dilemma of being wooed by Hollywood as ticket buyers and fans while simultaneously only seeing themselves onscreen in stereotypical roles. Opportunities for Latino performers in the Hollywood film industry were limited, though there were notable exceptions such as the success of Novarro, del Río, and Vélez during the silent period. Performers whose careers began in the 1940s and '50s often found themselves forced to de-emphasize their Latino identity publicly even if they privately supported campaigns for social justice in Latino communities. Some like Rita Moreno, who began her career in the 1950s, had to fight being typecast.

Even as audiences eagerly participated in the fan culture that grew up around both Hollywood and eventually Latin American popular cinema, they were critical consumers of motion pictures. From the nineteen-tens onward, the Spanish-language press served as an outlet for criticism of both onscreen representation and the offscreen discrimination that characterized Hollywood's hiring practices. Though infrequent, immigrants wrote letters to their consulates, noting the way that stereotypes affected their everyday lives. In the early 1920s, these types of letters, in combination with consular reports, led the Mexican government to ban the products of certain US film companies. Concerned that Mexico's stance would spill over into other Latin American markets, US film companies tried, sometimes halfheartedly, to ensure that their film would not offend Mexican viewers (Serna 163–74). What is more, the Spanish-language press regularly offered criticism of not only individual films but also the film industry and what the circulation of Spanish-language films made in Mexico, Argentina, or Cuba meant for Spanish-speaking audiences. Even as second and third generations thought of themselves as more American in the 1940s and 1950s, audiences comprised of long-term residents, more recent immigrants, and their children embraced alternatives to Hollywood's representations of Latin Americans and Latinos, alternatives that celebrated the culture of their home countries and drew them into a community of moviegoers that exceeded national borders. Some, like Tino Villanueva, sought to represent themselves. He did this through poetry, but others picked up cameras themselves.

**Laura Isabel Serna** *is Associate Professor of History and Cinema and Media Studies at the University of Southern California. She is the author of* Making Cinelandia: American Films and Mexican Film Culture before the Golden Age *(Duke University Press, 2014) and has published on issues of race and media in film in journals such as* Aztlán: A Journal of Chicano Studies *and* Americas: A Journal of Cultural History.

## BIBLIOGRAPHY

Adams, Dale. "*Saludos Amigos*: Hollywood and FDR's Good Neighbor Policy." *Quarterly Review of Film and Video*, vol. 24, no. 3, 2007, pp. 289–95.

Chávez, Ernesto. "'Ramon is not one of these': Race and Sexuality in the Construction of Silent Film Actor Ramón Novarro's Star Image." *Journal of the History of Sexuality*, vol. 20, no. 3, 2011, pp. 520–44.

Fein, Seth. "Hollywood and United States-Mexico Relations in the Golden Age of Mexican Cinema." 1996. U of Texas at Austin, PhD dissertation.

Gunckel, Colin. *Mexico on Main Street: Transnational Film Culture in Los Angeles Before World War II*. Rutgers UP, 2015.

---. "The War of the Accents: Spanish Language Hollywood Films in Mexican Los Angeles." *Film History,* vol. 20, no. 3, 2008, pp. 325–43.

Gunckel, Colin, Chris Horak, and Lisa Jarvinen, editors. *Cinema between Latin America and Los Angeles: Origins to 1960*. Rutgers UP, 2019.

Jarvinen, Lisa. *The Rise of Spanish-Language Filmmaking: Out from Hollywood's Shadow, 1929-1939*. Routledge, 2012.

López, Ana M. "From Hollywood and Back: Dolores Del Rio, a Trans(national) Star." *Studies in Latin American Popular Culture*, vol. 17, no. 5, 1998, pp. 5–32.

Noriega, Chon A. "The Western's 'Forgotten People'." *Aztlán: A Journal of Chicano Studies*, vol. 34, no. 1, 2009, pp. 1–9.

Ramírez Berg, Charles. *Latino Images in Film: Stereotypes, Subversion, and Resistance*. U of Texas P, 2002.

Serna, Laura Isabel. *Making Cinelandia: American Films and Mexican Film Culture before the Golden Age*. Duke UP, 2014.

Sturtevant, Victoria. "Spitfire: Lupe Vélez and the Ambivalent Pleasures of Ethnic Masquerade." *Velvet Light Trap*, vol. 55, no. 1, 2005, pp. 19–32.

Villanueva, Tino. *Scene from the Movie GIANT*. Curbstone Press, 1993.

Woll, Allen. "Hollywood's Good Neighbor Policy: The Latin Image in American Film 1939-1946." *Journal of Popular Film*, vol. 3, no. 4, 1974, pp. 278–93.

## FILMOGRAPHY

*Border Incident*. Directed by Anthony Mann, performances by Ricardo Montalban, George Murphy, and Howard Da Silva, Metro-Goldwyn-Mayer, 1949.

*Broncho Billy and the Greaser*. Directed by Gilbert M. "Broncho Billy" Anderson, performances by Gilbert M. "Broncho Billy" Anderson, Lee Williams, and Marguerite Clayton, The Essanay Film Manufacturing Company, 1914.

*Drácula*. Directed by George Melford, performances by Carlos Villarias, Lupita Tovar, and Barry Norton, Universal Pictures Corporation, 1931.

*Giant*. Directed by George Stevens, performances by Rock Hudson, James Dean, Elizabeth Taylor, and Dennis Hopper, Warner Bros., 1956.

*A Medal for Benny*. Directed by Irving Pichel, performances by Dorothy Lamour, Arturo de Córdova, J. Carrol Naish, Paramount, 1945.

*Ramona*. Directed by D.W. Griffith, performances by Mary Pickford, Henry B. Walthall, Francis J. Grandon, and Kate Bruce, Biograph, 1910.

*The Ring*. Directed by Kurt Neumann, performances by Gerald Mohr, Rita Moreno, and Lalo Ríos, King Bros. Productions, 1952.

*Salt of the Earth*. Directed by Herbert J. Biberman, performances by Rosaura Revueltas, Will Greer, Juan Chacón, and David Bauer, Independent Productions, 1954.

*Santa*. Directed by Antonio Moreno, performances by Lupita Tovar, Donald Reed, and Carlos Orellana, Compañía Nacional Productora de Películas, 1932.

*Los Tres Caballeros*. Directed by Norman Ferguson, voice performances by Clarence Nash, José do Patrocínio Oliveira and Joaquin Garay, Walt Disney Productions, 1944.

## FOR FURTHER STUDY

Brégent-Heald, Dominique. *Borderlands Films: American Cinema, Mexico, and Canada during the Progressive Era*. U of Nebraska Press, 2015.

*The Bronze Screen: 100 Years of the Latino Image in Hollywood*. Directed by Susan Racho, Nancy de los Santos, and Alberto Domínguez, Bronze Screen Productions/Latino Media Entertainment Institute, 2002.

de Orellana, Margarita. *Filming Pancho: How Hollywood Shaped the Mexican Revolution*. Verso, 2009.

Rodríguez-Estrada, Alicia I. "Dolores del Rio and Lupe Vélez: Images on and off the Screen, 1935-1944." *Writing the Range: Race, Class, and Culture in the Women's West*, edited by Elizabeth Jameson and Susan Armitage, U of Oklahoma P, 1997, pp. 475–92.

Lopez, Ana M. "Are All Latins from Manhattan? Hollywood, Ethnography, and Cultural Colonialism." *Ethnicity and American Cinema*, edited by Lester Friedman, U of Illinois P, 1991, pp. 404–24.

Meléndez, A. Gabriel. *Hidden Chicano Cinema: Film Dramas in the Borderlands*. Rutgers UP, 2013.

Rodriguez, Clara. *Heroes, Lovers, and Others: The Story of Latinos in Hollywood*. Oxford UP, 2004.

Serna, Laura Isabel. "Latinos in Film." *Oxford Research Encyclopedia of American History*, 2017, https://oxfordre.com/americanhistory/view/10.1093/acrefore/9780199329175.001.0001/acrefore-9780199329175-e-363.

# 10 Spanish-Language Television and Pan-Latinidad

Craig Allen
(Arizona State University)

Spanish-language television is well known as the largest component of Spanish-language mass media in the United States. The two chief providers of Spanish-language television, the broadcast/online networks Univision and Telemundo, are foremost US media institutions. Delivering news broadcasts, sports events, and signature entertainment programs, the two networks at peak hours together have reached upwards of one-half of the nation's 75 million Latinx residents (Conlon). They perhaps are best identified for instituting a television program genre that defines Latinx media. **Telenovelas**, continuing episodic dramas similar to soap operas, generate more Latinx participation than any other mass media form.

While familiar, big, and abounding in superlatives, Spanish-language television is said to have brought about something still bigger, a so-called US **pan-Latinidad**. Many believe that, largely because of Spanish-language television, Latinos living in the United States consider themselves part of a single Latinx community. The idea was popularized by scholar and author América Rodríguez. In a 1999 study, she proposed that the main effect of Spanish-language television was the "creation of an American 'Hispanic' population" (557–59). Today, common Latinx behaviors—from lifestyle choices to everyday shopping decisions—are traced to messages and symbols that Spanish-language television uniquely conveys to Latinx viewers regardless of their backgrounds or where they live.

As was discussed in Chapter 4, there is in fact no objectively defined Hispanic/Latinx/Latino population. Individuals living in the United States who are of Latin American descent tend to identify with their ancestral nationality. They often refer to themselves, for example, as Mexican, Cuban, Guatemalan, or Colombian instead of or in addition to Hispanic, Latino, or Latinx. The majority of Latinx media outlets are newspapers, radio stations, and websites that typically reach localized segments of the Latinx population, catering to one of the many national-origin groups. That's why this textbook covers Mexican, Puerto Rican, Cuban, Central American, and Dominican media.

Yet as Chapter 4 goes on to emphasize, a dynamic process driven by social movements in the 1960s, and which was heeded by the US government's breakout of "Hispanic" as a category in the 1980 census, helped build what Cristina Mora terms a "sense of solidarity" between different groups of Latin American origin (14–15). Spanish-language television galvanized and drove the process. Unlike Latinx newspapers and radio stations, it grew from the expectation it would reach the entire Latinx population. Univision and Telemundo broadcast to all fifty states. It remains essential they encourage Latinx viewers to dismiss national origins and amalgamate into a homogeneous "American" constituency.

The effect is both demonstrated and criticized. Not only is Spanish-language television, namely Univision and Telemundo, among the very few US institutions capable of cutting across nationalities and massing the entirety of the Latinx population—it was invented to do just that. Programming, entertainers, and presenters do not communicate to separate Latinx nationalities. News is not reported from one country's perspective. Telenovelas are often synonymous with pan-Latinidad. They are devoid of dialects, performed in "standard Spanish," and frequently feature generic plots filmed in unidentified locations. While many credit Spanish-language television for creating one "American" Latinx population, critics maintain that Latinos' distinct national identities are lost.

## THE MEXICAN ORIGINS OF US SPANISH-LANGUAGE TELEVISION

This account of the development of Spanish-language television draws on my book *Univision, Telemundo, and the Rise of Spanish-Language Television in the United States*. Spanish-language television developed much in the manner of its English-language counterpart. It is a **commercial broadcasting** enterprise supported by advertising. It formed from the model that had incubated national radio, that of generating profits as an entertainment provider. It was first seen shortly after World War II in a small number of cities on local stations. Not long after the founders of English-language television hastened the joining of local stations into the national networks ABC, CBS, and NBC, their counterparts in Spanish-language television also initiated national broadcasting in the United States.

A seminal event was the launch in 1961 of the Spanish International Network (SIN), which exists today as the modern network Univision. Its debut was noteworthy. Initiated barely a decade after ABC, CBS, and NBC, SIN was the nation's fourth television network. Over the next fifty years, SIN/Univision was the dominant Spanish-language mass medium. It was a trend-setter, and among its advances, discussed ahead, was its creation of a "Latino market." A bulwark of telenovelas, SIN defined Spanish-language programming. Not long after SIN's rechristening as Univision in 1986, the network's programs in Spanish were so popular that they often exceeded ABC, CBS, NBC, and other English-language networks in TV's daily and nightly Nielsen ratings. In 2013, Univision achieved a milestone when its audience exceeded that of all other TV providers in a seasonal

**ratings sweep** (De La Fuente). Thus, frequently, Univision has been America's No. 1 source of mass communication in any language.

The genesis of Univision also was significant for having identified the founders of US Spanish-language television. Notably, they were not Americans. Instead, they were members of a rich and powerful Mexican family that Mexicans refer to as the Azcárraga dynasty. The founding parent of US Spanish-language television was Don Emilio Azcárraga Vidaurreta. One of Mexico's most renowned historical figures, the first Azcárraga brought radio to all of Mexico, a poor country, in the 1930s. His radio network, XEW, was heard throughout Latin America. In the 1940s, his empire enlarged with his acquisition of Mexico's film studios. With his launch of XEW-TV in 1951, he pioneered Mexican television. He was assisted by his son and heir, Emilio Azcárraga Milmo. By the mid-1950s, the Azcárragas had established Mexico City as the Spanish-language "Hollywood." The world's best Spanish-language actors, performers, and entertainers converged on Mexico City for opportunities to star in the Azcárragas' movies and TV shows.

**Figure 10.1: Portraits of Emilio Azcárraga Vidaurreta and his son Emilio Azcárraga Milmo in the 1950s.** *Broadcasting-Telecasting*, **June 15, 1953, 82. Don Emilio Azcárraga Vidaurreta was the patriarch of Mexican radio and television and principal founder of Univision. He launched the US Spanish International Network, Univision's predecessor, in 1961.**

Source: Media History Digital Library
Attribution: *Broadcasting-Telecasting*
License: Public Domain

Grasping the global appeal of their then-new TV productions, the Azcárragas took a bold step. To facilitate foreign sales, they sped a process of de-Mexifying content. They refined a "standard" Spanish without Mexican dialect. They filmed programs with generic settings and themes. The Azcárragas concentrated de-Mexification on their signal invention, the telenovela. A soap-opera-like drama of a fixed three- or six-month duration, the first telenovela, *Ángeles de la calle*, was seen on XEW-TV in 1951. The Azcárragas quickly thrived on foreign sales. Regardless of nationality, viewers throughout Latin America as well as in Spain and the Philippines flocked to programs the Azcárragas mass produced. By 1960, their firm, Telesistema Méxicano, was an international powerhouse.

The seeds of US Spanish-language television were sown when in 1958 Azcárraga Vidaurreta partnered with Hollywood film mogul Frank Fouce in a venture to broadcast Telesistema's programs in the United States. Huge advertising revenues beckoned. However, aware the nation's English-language networks would not broadcast Spanish-language content, they formed their own network, which became SIN. The Federal Communications Commission (FCC) had opened channels on TV's ultra-high frequency (UHF) band. Azcárraga began acquisition of UHF stations in cities across the United States. Upon acquiring KCOR-TV, a UHF station in San Antonio in 1961, Azcárraga shipped programs to the Texas city. SIN commenced when programs received and telecast by KCOR were distributed to stations along the US–Mexican border.

SIN struggled for several years. Latinos living in the United States numbered fewer than ten million. There were no Spanish-language Nielsen ratings. Without data to confirm that SIN reached viewers, businesses refused to advertise. While UHF TV channels could be acquired in all two hundred US markets, most 1960s TV sets were not equipped to receive them.

Yet abundant were hints of the pervasiveness and impact of Spanish-language television. Immigration and high birth rates promised a growing Latinx population. Azcárraga's choice as head of SIN, Rene Anselmo, was a forceful if eccentric figure adept at winning favors from the FCC. The network's fortunes gelled in 1962 when Anselmo launched KMEX in Los Angeles, the largest Latinx market. Broadcasting to Southern California's one million Latinos, KMEX became the Spanish-language media's first profit center.

## TOWARD PAN-LATINIDAD

Pan-Latinidad refers to a widely known amalgamation of Spanish-speaking individuals in which distinctive national identities are subsumed by, and may give way to, the perception of belonging to a single Latinx population. Not only is Spanish-language television considered a driving force behind pan-Latinidad; it was an invention mothered by necessity.

The founders had no doubt their audience must include all US Latinos. Concentrating on the largest national group, Mexican Americans, who comprised 60% of the Latinx population, would have meant sacrificing 40% of the audience. One challenge became a vital concern: geography. Latinos of various nationalities resided in different parts of the United States; while those of Mexican origin were concentrated in the US Southwest, Puerto Ricans and many from Caribbean countries resided in the Northeast, notably in New York. Cubans and many from South American countries resided on the southern East Coast, notably in south Florida in and around Miami. Breakthroughs in two early tests of national Spanish-language television demonstrated that pan-Latinidad was possible.

A turning point in the rise of SIN was its entry into New York. Seven years after its founding, the network had been comprised of stations in California, Arizona, and Texas. In 1968, with the launch of its New York station WXTV, SIN extended to the US East Coast. Anselmo engaged in debates on whether SIN's variety of programs designed to appeal to Mexican Americans would succeed in New York, where Puerto Ricans comprised the largest Spanish-speaking group. Assistant Carole Bird, who had grown up in Caribbean and South American countries, proposed a solution. She recalled the immense popularity of the Azcárragas' generically produced telenovelas in every Spanish-speaking country. Anselmo vetoed SIN's schedule of Mexican-oriented content. He had the Azcárragas ship to New York a collection of telenovelas that had driven audiences when distributed internationally. On WXTV, he broadcast the telenovelas back to back throughout prime time.

Figure 10.2: Television's role in pan-Latinidad was heralded when globally popular Mexican telenovelas were first broadcast to diverse Latinx audiences in the United States. A turning point was the 1968 broadcast of *La Leona* on New York City's WXTV. Although produced in Mexico, it attracted New York's large Puerto Rican audiences. Because of their multinational appeal, telenovelas became a defining feature of Spanish-language television as it expanded to other communities across the United States.

Source: YouTube
License: Fair Use

It was a path-clearing innovation. Against predictions of failure, WXTV's premiere was a triumph. As had happened internationally, New York's predominantly non-Mexican audience embraced the generically themed telenovelas the Mexicans produced. WXTV toppled an existing and popular Spanish-language station, WNJU, in the first Spanish-language audience ratings. Within a year, SIN scrapped its existing schedule of varied programs in favor of a prime-time lineup comprised entirely of telenovelas. Because telenovelas guaranteed multinational viewership, the exclusive scheduling of telenovelas in peak prime-time hours became a defining feature of Spanish-language television.

The second stride occurred three years later in 1971. That year, upon Anselmo's acquisition of WLTV, SIN entered Miami. The Azcárragas strongly opposed Anselmo's move. Miami was a hotbed of anti-Castro sentiment. The Azcárragas insisted that a Mexican presence in Miami would be opposed, perhaps violently, because Mexico backed the Castro regime. In a confrontation, the son, Emilio Azcárraga Milmo, fired Anselmo when Anselmo argued that a true US network could never emerge if Miami was cut out. Anselmo was allowed to return to make good on his claim that with telenovelas that did not identify Mexico, and with other generic programs including the first World Cup telecasts, Cuban Americans would not detect a Mexican presence. They and the numerous Colombians, Venezuelans, Peruvians, and others who populated Miami rushed to view SIN's shows.

Spanish-language television's capability for joining US Latinos was cemented when in 1976 SIN became the first US broadcaster to relay programs coast to coast by **satellite**. SIN's technological coup was envisioned and directed by Emilio Azcárraga Milmo. Upon the passing of his father in 1972, the younger Azcárraga reorganized the family firm into a technology-rich conglomerate he named Television Via Satellite or "Televisa." Employing Televisa's technology, SIN dramatically enlarged its reach. By the early 1980s, its twenty-four-hour schedule was broadcast on stations in one hundred markets. It and a sister network Galavisión were available nationally on cable TV. With the 1981 premiere of *Noticiero SIN*, the first Spanish-language national newscast, an audience that comprised nearly one-half of US Latinos was informed by US-produced news. Its content did not concentrate on any particular non-US nation or nationality.

## EXPANSION OF UNIVISION, TELEMUNDO, AND PAN-NATIONALIZATION

It was in the 1980s and 1990s that observers first noted pan-Latinidad. Interest precipitated from census reports that headlined a "Latino boom." The 1990 census had shown a doubling of the US Latinx population to forty million during the preceding ten years. The Census Bureau itself contributed to emerging recognition of pan-Latinidad. Beginning in 1980, rather than distinguishing Latinos by nationality, the Bureau lumped them together into a single group, officially designating them as "Hispanics."

Yet the concept of pan-Latinidad did not congeal from observers' fascination with the census. Nor was there conclusive evidence of the effect on audiences that tuned in to Univision, which swelled in the 1990s, or of the premiere of a second Spanish-language network, Telemundo, in 1987. That which sealed understanding of pan-Latinidad was an extremely visible development that grew out of Spanish-language television: the networks' manufacture of a so-called "Latino market."

Figure 10.3: A US "Latino market" was galvanized in the 1990s when Latinx viewers flocked to Univision's *María* trilogy. Starring Thalía, the 1996 novela *María la del barrio* was seen by 85% of Latinos in the US. It remains one of the most watched programs in US television history.

Source: DVD of *María*
Attribution: Mario Rodríguez
License: Fair Use

At Univision and the new Telemundo, no tasks had greater priority than those directed at establishing and promoting a Latinx market. The networks' prospects depended on persuading large corporations to spend money on advertising. Big business was aware that growing numbers of Latinos resided in the United States. However, large companies could not sell products by appealing separately to multiple Latinx groups Accustomed to a single and homogeneous market delivered by English-language TV, businesses demanded the same in Spanish-language television. Univision and Telemundo complied with ceaseless measures that finally convinced big business, and more directly its advertising directors and creators on Madison Avenue, that a single Latinx market did exist.

A key measure was a 1980 research project commissioned by SIN. It culminated in a series of books titled *Spanish USA*. For many years, the *Spanish USA* project was considered the most authoritative source of information on Latinos' lifestyles, attitudes, and behaviors. Assembled by acclaimed social scientist Daniel Yankelovich, researchers who spanned the country emphasized findings consistent with a theory called "acculturation." The theory proposed that, regardless of nationality, Latinos absorbed American culture in the course of adapting to life in the United States. Acculturation was unmistakable, they maintained, and was most fostered by Latinos' extensive use of television. In succeeding volumes, *Spanish USA* reiterated that the viewing of Spanish-language television accomplished "a blurring of differences in the way Hispanics of varying nationalities feel about each other" (Yankelovich et al. 15–28).

Six years after the publication of *Spanish USA*, the event that resulted in SIN's rechristening as Univision brought urgency to moves aimed at recognizing a single US Latinx community. In 1986, the FCC banished Emilio Azcárraga Milmo and Televisa for violations of US laws prohibiting foreign ownership. Under pressure to "Americanize" the network and further promote the concept of a single Latinx market, new owner Hallmark Cards adopted the name Univision. It meant "one vision." Hallmark consolidated Univision's network personnel at a newly built headquarters-studio in Miami. From there, Hallmark coordinated a national campaign called "Vision of America" that instilled among Latinos a perception that, guided by Univision, they no longer hailed from a foreign country. Instead, they formed a single and rising US Latinx citizenry. Efforts not only to reinforce Latinos' sense of US identity but to promote their personal opportunities as consumers of television-advertised products and services—strategies that helped convince advertisers that Latinos had ever-increasing buying power—expanded still further when US television mogul Jerry Perenchio acquired Univision in 1992.

While Univision boomed, the second network, Telemundo, struggled. Upon its launch by financier Saul Steinberg in 1987, Telemundo countered Univision with programs that targeted largely Puerto Rican, Cuban, and South American–identified viewers on the East Coast. A tailspin of low ratings forced Telemundo's bankruptcy in 1993. Reorganized, Telemundo shifted toward emulating Univision's multinational strategy. Telemundo partnered with Televisa's Mexican rival, TV Azteca, which had perfected telenovelas comparable to Televisa's productions, those long known for their high quality and universal storylines not specific to any country or nationality. Telemundo followed by pioneering "domestic production." Occasioned by a series of US-themed telenovelas produced at Telemundo's studios in Miami in 1993, the second network used promotional messages and public affairs programs to press the idea that Spanish-speaking individuals were "American," not individuals transplanted from another country.

An iconic Univision program called *Sábado gigante* perhaps had done the most to galvanize scholars' and observers' concept of pan-nationalization. Launched in 1962 on Chile's Canal Trece, host Mario Kreutzberger, better known by his stage name Don Francisco, moved the program to Univision's Miami studios in 1986. Broadcast on Univision for three hours every Saturday night, the combination talk-quiz-skit-comedy show, while generic in terms of nationality, nevertheless showcased identification of the numerous nationalities brought by the program's performers and studio audiences. Frequently the No. 1 Spanish-language television program in the United States, *Sábado gigante* affirmed its pan-national appeal from its success when syndicated in virtually every Spanish-speaking country. Kreutzberger retired in 2015 after hosting the broadcast for fifty-three years. In the *Guinness World Records* books, *Sábado gigante* is distinguished as the world's longest running and most viewed television show ("Interview").

Figure 10.4: Pan-Latinidad was driven by Univision's immensely popular three-hour Saturday night spectacular *Sábado gigante* (1962–2015). Mario Kreutzberger hosted Sábado gigante for fifty-three years. Seen here is a segment from his farewell program in 2015.

Source: DVD of *Sábado gigante*
Attribution: Mario Rodríguez
License: Fair Use

As they had nearly from the beginning of Spanish-language television, telenovelas defined the character and social impact of the endeavor. In Mexico, Televisa passed to Emilio Azcárraga Jean in 1997. Under the third Azcárraga, Televisa rose further as the worldwide epicenter of telenovela production. During the 1990s, a trilogy of Televisa telenovelas shown on Univision and which were capped by the blockbuster *Maria del la barrio* were seen by 75% of all US Latinos. More ratings records were set with Univision's broadcast of Televisa's *El privilegio de amar* in the early 2000s.

# THE UNCERTAIN FUTURE OF SPANISH-LANGUAGE TELEVISION

Yet the millennium's turn had ushered in uncertainty. The 2000s began auspiciously. Telemundo's breakout came in 2000 with its telecast of a Colombian telenovela called *Yo soy Betty, la fea*. Relating the comedic travails of an unattractive teenage girl, *Yo soy Betty, la fea* generated huge ratings and rose to iconic stature. As Crystal Camargo observes in Chapter 2, the Colombian telenovela that spurred Telemundo in 2000 inspired an English-language series in 2006. Under the name *Ugly Betty*, the English-language version became a hit series on the US English-language network ABC. In 2001, NBC's purchase of Telemundo opened a floodgate of finance that at last made the second network competitive. Money poured into co-production agreements with studios in Mexico, Colombia, and Venezuela. The agreements propelled a new generation of hip, contemporary telenovelas. They contrasted with the traditional, fantasy telenovelas that Televisa produced and which continued to dominate Univision's programming. Telemundo's ratings soared.

Figure 10.5: Telemundo's 2000 premiere of *Yo soy Betty, la fea* changed the direction of Spanish-language television. For the first time, telenovelas departed from traditional storybook story lines and introduced unconventional characters involved in contemporary plots and themes. The program starred Colombian actress Ana María Orozco.

Source: DVD of *Yo soy Betty, la fea*
Attribution: Mario Rodríguez
License: Fair Use

Nevertheless, two developments challenged Spanish-language television. First, broadcast television was in decline. The introduction of the Internet, online streaming, and social media fragmented broadcast audiences. By the 2020s, Univision's average audience, once in the tens of millions, had shrunk to five million.

Second, accumulating evidence suggested a decline in use of the Spanish language in the United States. After long tracking expansion of the language, demographers reading the 2010 census issued revised predictions. The 2010 census showed more expansion: US Latinos had come to number 75 million. Yet notably, two-thirds were under the age of thirty-five. This meant that growth of the Latinx population was no longer driven by immigration but by expanding birth rates among Latinx families already settled in the United States.

During the 2010s, amid evidence that confirmed years of speculation that younger Latinx viewers would change the nature of the Latinx market—and that a "generation gap" would divide and distinguish Latinos' media consumption habits, scholars and market researchers concentrated on the mass of Latinos in the young adult and teenage age groups. Recurrently, upwards of 95% of younger Latinos said they did not routinely speak Spanish but favored English. They were born and raised in the United States, attended English-language schools, made friends who spoke English, took jobs in English-language workplaces, and used English in posting on social media (Carter). Older Latinos, many having immigrated, were weaned on Spanish. But because larger numbers of younger English-speaking Latinos would replace diminishing older Spanish-speaking Latinos, questions about the future of Spanish in the United States multiplied. Surveys showed that fewer than 15% of younger Latinos viewed Spanish-language television (*State of the Hispanic American Consumer*).

Another development also stung Spanish-language television: the first instance of extensive criticism of its politics. Conservative groups published evidence alleging that news broadcasts on Univision and Telemundo were biased and devoted to persuading Latinx viewers to support liberal causes. In 2007, Republican California Governor Arnold Schwarzenegger urged Latinos to "turn off the Spanish TV." Then-President Donald Trump was vehement in complaining that Spanish-language television spread divisions in US society. Confronted by Univision news anchor Jorge Ramos at a news conference in 2015, Trump called security guards and had Ramos removed.

Criticism reached beyond the political arena. Public review of Spanish-language television that brought increasing awareness of pan-Latinidad fomented concerns. Influenced by Arlene Dávila's 2001 exposé *Latinos, Inc.* (181–215), scholars and opinion leaders joined in criticizing Univision and Telemundo for their years of "Americanizing" Latinx viewers while undermining their distinct national identities. Héctor Amaya (130) and Christopher Chávez (9–10) concurred that the networks' quest for a "Latino market," and the billions of dollars they extracted from it, had unfairly encouraged Latinx individuals to dismiss their past national identities in order to perceive themselves as members of a questionably-concocted homogeneous US Latinx population. In a 2019 forum, researcher Miguel Salazar warned observers of "problems with Latinidad."

Gradually, Univision and Telemundo reacted. Both shifted priorities from broadcasting to online streaming. In 2021, Univision announced the then largest-ever venture in Spanish-language television, a Netflix-scale streaming service that combined both its and Televisa's troves of programming (Harrup and Pérez).

Yet looking ahead, little was clear. The shift from mass-unifying broadcast channels to infinitely programmed and audienced streaming services tended to sound the death knell of "big" Spanish-language television and the pan-Latinidad that accompanied it. The future will determine whether the experience of Spanish-language television has lasting meaning—or is meaningful only as history of an iridescent era in Latinx affairs.

**Craig Allen** *is Associate Professor at the Walter Cronkite School of Journalism and Mass Communication at Arizona State University. He has written extensively on mass media history, international mass communication, political media, and presidential communication. His books include* Univision, Telemundo and the Rise of Spanish-Language Television in the United States *(University of Florida Press, 2020),* News Is People: The Rise of Local TV News and the Fall of News from New York *(University of Iowa Press, 2001), and* Eisenhower and the Mass Media: Peace, Prosperity, and Prime-Time TV *(University of North Carolina Press, 1993).*

## BIBLIOGRAPHY

Allen, Craig. *Univision, Telemundo, and the Rise of Spanish-Language Television in the United States*. UP of Florida, 2020.

Amaya, Héctor. *Citizenship Excess: Latino/as, Media, and the Nation*. NYU P, 2013.

Carter, Philip M. "A Linguist Explains How the Three Generation Pattern Could Wipe Out Spanish in the US." *Quartz*, 2018, https://qz.com/1195658/spanish-to-english-us-is-increasingly-monolingual-despite-latino-immigration/.

Chávez, Christopher. *Reinventing the Latino Television Viewer: Language, Ideology, and Practice*. Lexington, 2015.

Conlon, Ginger. "Univision vs. Telemundo: A Fierce Battle for US Hispanic Audiences and Ad Dollars." *The Drum*, 2019, https://www.thedrum.com/news/2019/05/10/univision-vs-telemundo-fierce-battle-us-hispanic-audiences-and-ad-dollars.

Dávila, Arlene. *Latinos, Inc.: The Marketing and Making of a People*. U of California P, 2001.

De La Fuente, Anna Marie. "Univision Hits Ratings Milestone with July Sweeps Win." *Variety*, 22 July 2013, https://variety.com/2013/tv/news/nivision-to-end-july-sweeps-in-top-spot-1200566685/.

Harrup, Anthony, and Santiago Pérez. "Mexico's Televisa to Merge Content Business with Univision." *Wall Street Journal*, 2021, https://www.wsj.com/articles/mexico-s-televisa-to-merge-content-business-with-univision-11618353691.

"Interview with Mario Kreutzberger." *Television Academy Foundation*, 20 Jul 2011, https://interviews.televisionacademy.com/interviews/mario-kreutzberger.

Mora, G. Cristina. *Making Hispanics: How Activists, Bureaucrats, and Media Constructed a New American*. U of Chicago P, 2014.

Rodríguez, América. "Creating an Audience and Remapping a Nation: A Brief History of Spanish Language Broadcasting 1930-1980." *Quarterly Review of Film and Video*, vol. 16, 1999, pp. 357–74.

Salazar, Miguel. "The Problem with Latinidad." *The Nation*, 16 Dec. 2019, https://www.thenation.com/article/archive/hispanic-heritage-month-latinidad/.

*The State of the Hispanic-American Consumer*. Simmons Research, 2018, http://hispanicad.com/sites/default/files/simmons_2018_state_of_the_hispanic_american_consumer.pdf.

Yankelovich, Daniel, et al. *Spanish USA: A Study of the Hispanic Market in the United States*. SIN Television Network, 1981.

## FILMOGRAPHY

*Ángeles de la calle*. Telesistema Méxicano, XEW, 1952 (motion picture rendition).

"Emilio Azcárraga." *Gigantes de México*, season 1, episode 1, History Channel, 2017.

*Maria del la barrio*. Televisa, 1995.

*Sábado gigante 50 años*, Univision, WLTV, 2012.

*Yo soy Betty, la fea*. RCN Televisión, 2000.

## FOR FURTHER STUDY

Casillas, Dolores Inés. *¡Sounds of Belonging!*. NYU P, 2014.

*Emilio Nicolás, Sr. Pioneer of Spanish Language Television*, SINTV41, April 2006, https://www.youtube.com/watch?v=dAmTzG6HLfA.

Fernández, Claudia, and Andrew Paxman. *El Tigre: Emilio Azcárraga y Su Imperio Televisa*. Raya en el Agua-Grijalbo, 2000.

Gutiérrez, Félix F. "More Than 200 Years of Latino Media in the United States." *American Latinos and the Making of the United States: A Theme Study*, National Park Service, 2012, pp. 99–121.

Pew Hispanic Center. "Latinos' Choices in News Media are Shaping Their Views of Their Communities, The Nation, and The World." April 2004. *The Pew Charitable Trusts*, https://www.pewtrusts.org/en/about/news-room/press-releases-and-statements/2004/04/19/latinos-choices-in-news-media-are-shaping-their-views-of-their-communities-the-nation-and-the-world.

Ramos, Jorge. *No Borders*. HarperCollins, 2002.

Salinas, Maria Elena. *I Am My Father's Daughter*. HarperCollins, 2006.

Wilkinson, Kenton Todd. *Spanish-Language Television in the United States: Fifty Years of Development*. Routledge, 2015.

# 11

# The Mexican American Experience Onscreen

Libia Jiménez Chávez
(University of Georgia)

This chapter will provide a brief history of the Mexican American community, followed by an overview of Chicanx cinema's stylistic elements and cultural influences, and will conclude with three case studies—*Stand and Deliver* (1988), *Selena* (1997), and *Under the Same Moon* (2007)—calling attention to the influence of Mexican culture on American history, media, and identity.

A unique link exists between the Mexican community and the United States, one which differs from the history of many other groups. Mexico has shared a border with the United States since its independence from Spain in 1821, and today they coincide at one of the world's busiest borders ("Border Facts"). For centuries, the two nations have shared important elements of culture, commerce, and migration, among others, and their relationship has been inextricably tied by their shared "multicultural, multiracial, and multilingual history" (Newman 67).

Despite the connection and cooperation between the United States and Mexico, the Mexican community residing within the United States has endured state-sanctioned discrimination and a status of second-class citizenship. Its presence has been continuously contested by public opinion. For instance, California Superior Judge Gerald S. Chargin has referred to Mexicans as "lower than animals . . . miserable, lousy, rotten people" (Salazar). More recently, former President Donald Trump referred to Mexicans as "criminals and rapists." Ruben Salazar, a Juárez-born journalist and activist writing in the 1960s, wrote that the word *Mexican* has been "vilified" and "dragged through the mud of racism since the Anglos arrived in the Southwest." He further wrote, "all this, and more, has contributed to the psychological crippling of the Mexican-American when it comes to the word Mexican. He is unconsciously ashamed of it" (Salazar).

The term *Mexican American* is also challenged within the community. Like all identifiers, its definition is as limited or expansive as one chooses. It has been used to describe US-born Americans of Mexican heritage, whether their ancestors lived in the Mexican states of the Southwest prior to their annexation into the United States or they arrived in later centuries. (For simplicity, *American* is used in this context to describe individuals born and/or living within the United States of America). Likewise, the term may also be used by Mexican-born individuals who have resided in the United States (independent of residency status) and/or have become naturalized citizens. Furthermore, beginning in the 1960s, *Mexican American* became increasingly rejected by activist youth who associated the term with assimilation into Anglo culture. Instead, **Chicano** became popularized among the young politically active and socially conscious. (*Chicano* will be replaced by the gender-neutral term *Chicanx* unless the term is used in a quote, title, or to avoid historical anachronism.)

Ruben Salazar famously asked, "Who is a Chicano?" He answered, "A Chicano is a Mexican-American with a non-Anglo image of himself" (Salazar). The roots of the term are contested, and the word itself has been associated with descendants of Aztlán, a region believed to be the ancestral home of the Mexica (known as Aztecs in western historiography) and located in the US Southwest.

## A BRIEF HISTORY OF THE MEXICAN AMERICAN PEOPLE

In spite of this inflammatory commentary about Mexican Americans, the community has greatly and positively contributed to the history of the United States. Decades before Manifest Destiny became a dominant political ideology in the United States, Mexicans and Native people were living in the states of Texas, New Mexico, California, and others. Westward expansion and the prominence of Manifest Destiny prompted the United States to instigate a war with Mexico. The Mexican-American War (1846–1848) concluded with the Treaty of Guadalupe Hidalgo, which demanded the Mexican cession of California, New Mexico, Arizona, Utah, Nevada, and Colorado, and parts of Oklahoma, Kansas, and Wyoming ("Mexican-American War"). The Mexican people living in these territories were subject to the agreements of the treaty and were extended US citizenship and a promise that their culture, property, and language would be respected. Through time, however, Mexican landowners were forced to renounce their property to White settlers, and during the Great Depression of the 1930s, an estimated 600,000 US citizens of Mexican descent were pressured or forced to relocate to Mexico by officials ("America's Forgotten History").

Shortly after this so-called Mexican Repatriation campaign, World War II erupted. The conflict caused a labor shortage in the United States, which was resolved through the Bracero Program (1942–1964), a bilateral agreement that extended approximately 4.6 million seasonal visas to Mexican agricultural workers. To date, it is the largest US contract labor program (Bracero History Archive). While the governments of Mexico and the United States worked in partnership to resolve the economic and labor concerns of the mid-twentieth century, tension between youth of color and White servicemen were at an all-time high. During this period, **zoot suits**—characterized by a roomy cut that defied the rationing of cloth in a period of wartime scarcity—were popular among Mexican men as a form of self-expression and cultural pride. However, popular media represented the suits as gang-affiliated, leading to a negative perception among the public (Library of Congress, "1942"). During the Los Angeles summer of 1943, racially motivated violence erupted between Mexican youth and White servicemen, dubbed the "Zoot Suit Riots," resulted in injuries and arrests.

In 1946, a brave Mexican American family defied school segregation in the state of California and helped pave the way for the desegregation of schools nationwide following the Supreme Court's 1954 landmark decision in *Brown v. Board of Education of Topeka*. Three short years after the Zoot Suit Riots of Los Angeles, the US Court of Appeals ruled that forcible segregation based on Mexican ancestry, skin color, and the Spanish language was unconstitutional and unlawful. The historic case *Mendez v. Westminster* was brought by the Mendez family, who sued several California school districts for denying children entry based on their ancestry and physical appearance ("Background").

The 1960s was an exciting and revolutionary decade for many Americans, including racially marginalized groups, women, and LGBTQI+. The Mexican American community, principally through the Chicano Movement (also known as *La Lucha*, *La Causa*, and *El Movimiento*), made important contributions to the changing social and political landscape. The community established grassroots organizations such as the **United Farm Workers** (UFW), **Brown Berets**, and the **League of United Latin American Citizens** (LULAC). César Chávez and Dolores Huerta, founders of the UFW, led nonviolent protests that demanded higher wages and improved labor standards for domestic agricultural workers. Their organizing efforts extended across the nation and established one of the country's most effective agricultural labor campaigns.

The Brown Berets were established in 1967 in Los Angeles and were modeled after Oakland's Black Panther Party. They fought against police brutality and racism, demanding better conditions for Mexican Americans. While they began in California, they later expanded to other states such as Texas and Michigan (Estrada).

LULAC has served as a champion for the rights of Mexican Americans and Hispanic people since its founding in Corpus Christi, Texas, in 1929. As the country's largest and oldest Hispanic organization, LULAC has influenced landmark legislation and lawsuits in favor of the Hispanic community. The organization was an important legal ally of the Mendez family during the *Mendez v. Westminster* case ("LULAC Education Issues").

The 1968 East LA Walkouts, one of the largest student protests in the history of the United States, united over fifteen thousand Mexican American students, their families, and community organizers, in protest of the unequal, discriminatory, and subpar educational resources available to the city's Mexican American youth (Library of Congress, "1968").

The fight for greater civil, political, and economic rights continued into the 1970s. The Chicano Moratorium of August 29, 1970, was a mass broad-based coalition in opposition to the Vietnam War and the disproportionately high deaths of men of color in the conflict. The legacy of the Chicano Movement continues to impact the community today. The Mexican American and Latinx communities carry on fighting for the rights of the collective, as demonstrated by the 2006 immigration marches and the founding of new Latinx organizations such as the Georgia Association of Latino Elected Officials (GALEO) and the Latino Community Fund (LCF).

The decades that followed the 1980s witnessed consistent surges in the country's Latinx population. Arguably, political and economic policies—such as the militarization of the Southwest border, the 1986 Immigration Reform & Control Act that granted amnesty to undocumented immigrants, and the 1994 North American Free Trade Agreement that strengthened economic ties between the United States, Mexico, and Canada—played a role in the demographic transformations of the 1980s, 1990s, and present day.

## CHICANX CINEMA

The social movements of the 1960s and 1970s left a profound and lasting impact on American civil rights legislation and society. Importantly, they also impacted the artistic expression of a generation and gave rise to the "Decade of the Hispanic," which was marked by growing visibility of Latinos and Latinas with the U.S. population. The 1980s witnessed a surge in the representation and recognition of Chicanx and Latinx actors (Noriega, *Chicanos and Film* xvii). The ideologies of Chicanx leaders crept into art and music and influenced such films as *Zoot Suit* (1981), *Born in East L.A.* (1987), *Chicano Park* (1988), and *Stand and Deliver*. According to Kathleen Newman, these and other similar films were an attempt by Chicanx filmmakers to reorient the "anglocentric US film industry" (68). A short list of notable Chicanx actors includes Emmy and Golden Globe winner Edward James Olmos and comedian Cheech Marin (although Marin's work was initially dismissed by Chicanx activists due to its negative portrayal of the Chicanx community) (Tatum 111–12). Chicanx directors include Sylvia Morales, one of the first Chicana filmmakers, Luis Valdez, popularly known for his work on *Zoot Suit* and *La Bamba* (1987), and Gregory Nava, who directed *El Norte* (1983) and *Selena* (Tatum 89).

However, the construction of Chicanx cinema surfaced earlier and in parallel to the Chicanx civil rights movement, including works like Valdez's *I am Joaquín* (1969), based on a poem by youth activist Rodolfo "Corky" Gonzales (Noriega, *Chicanos and Film* xviii). While its definition has been a subject of debate among filmmakers, Chon Noriega defines the genre as "films (or videos) by and about Chicanos" that center Chicanx production, participation, and signification (*Chicanos and Film* xviii). Noriega further proposes a conceptual framework for analyzing Chicanx thought and artistic expression. The framework utilizes three Chicanx cultural elements introduced in *Arte Chicano: Annotated Bibliography of Chicano Art, 1965-1981*: resistance, maintenance, and affirmation of Chicanx culture within a society governed by Anglo norms (Noriega, "Between a Weapon and a Formula" 168). According to Noriega, these "culture-based concepts" operate within a larger strategy of Chicanx pride, or *Chicanismo,* that respond to "political, economic, legal, and social oppression" (168). The elements overlap, work in unison, and construct the Chicanx cultural identity. Noriega's framework includes a fourth element of **mestizaje** (cultural mixing) that "incorporates or engages rather than resists or denies the dominant culture" (169).

However, this analysis is incomplete without the four cinematic practices of production, exhibition, signification, and reception (Noriega, "Between a Weapon and a Formula" 170). According to Noriega, we must identify if and how cultural elements interact with cinematic practices. Firstly, in their interpretation of Chicanx films, critics should consider the financial and ideological limitations often present during the production of Chicanx films, as well as the *movidas* (innovative coping strategies) employed by filmmakers under these constraints (170). The exhibition of a film refers to its distribution and audience, where it will air (film festivals, theaters, community centers, etc.) and who it will reach (American, Chicanx, and/or Latin American audiences). The goal of Chicanx filmmakers is to reach greater audiences and to "put Chicano film into discourse" (171). By signification, Noriega proposes a reclaiming of the Chicanx past through narrative cinema (as opposed to documentary) that offers a "counter-image" to the often distorted and racialized Chicanx image popular among mainstream cinema (171). Noriega's fourth cinematic element of reception reminds filmmakers and critics of the diversity within the Chicanx community. The community is diverse in its identifiers (Hispanic, Chicanx, Tejano) and in its critical reception of a film (174). Importantly, he notes the need for "a more complex conceptualization of the Chicano spectator and of Chicano culture, and to avoid to a certain extent the essentialism that pervades scholarship on cultural and sexual differences" (174). Finally, to the conceptualization of Chicanx cinema, Noriega highlights its "bicultural and bilingual" context that should be recognized as a formal element, a style unto itself, or a substructure for a counter-narrative (172–73).

## REPRESENTATION OF MEXICAN AMERICANS IN FILM

The 1980s, 1990s, and 2000s witnessed a surge in films for and by Mexican Americans that contest false clichés, assert the community's belonging within American society, and humanize the immigration narrative.

### *Stand and Deliver* (1988)

*Stand and Deliver,* directed and co-written by Cuban American filmmaker Ramón Menéndez, recounts the true story of Bolivian-born mathematician and educator Jaime Escalante (played by award-winning Chicanx actor Edward James

Olmos), who accepts a teaching position at under-resourced Garfield High School in East Los Angeles and successfully guides a group of Mexican American students to pass the AP Calculus exam and obtain college credit. The *mise-en-scène* of the film's early scenes portrays Mr. Escalante driving through the colorful and Chicanx mural-dominated streets of East LA. Inside the school, he encounters a predominately Mexican American student population; the scene is characterized by young men dressed as **pachucos** and Spanish written across the board and shouted across the classroom. While other teachers may have seen a rambunctious group of students, he saw untapped potential.

The movie develops inside East LA's private and public spaces, areas where Mr. Escalante and his students negotiate their culture and homelife against the constraints of a White-dominated educational system. For instance, in a meeting with the math department, the department's chair states, "You cannot teach logarithms to illiterates," to which Mr. Escalante replies, "Students will rise to the level of expectations," and that all they need is *ganas* (desire, motivation). Through his philosophy of *ganas*, he challenged negative stereotypes surrounding students of color and empowered his pupils to believe in themselves.

*Stand and Deliver* is also astute in discussing the racial and ethnic discrimination faced by the Mexican American community of East LA. For example, after successfully passing the AP Calculus exam, the Educational Testing Service launches an investigation against the students, thus questioning their belonging within academic spaces. As Mr. Escalante perfectly notes, "Those scores would have never been questioned if my kids did not have Spanish surnames and come from *barrio* schools." Similar to Chicanx leaders, Mr. Escalante understands that structural inequalities and prejudices, not a student's heritage or class in themselves, damage educational outcomes. After retaking the exam, the students once again prove that *barrio* students are worthy and capable of taking up space in academic arenas.

Based on true events, *Stand and Deliver* attempts to "reclaim a forgotten past" and build a "culture-based alternative form of history" (Noriega, "Between a Weapon and a Formula" 171). The film employs culturally relevant content to establish a connection with its audience, including historical references (the Mayan concept of zero), the use of Spanish, and the adoption of popular Mexican words (*órale, chale, burro*). Furthermore, the film serves as a historical reflection of the inequalities and discrimination experienced by the Mexican American community and its enduring struggle for cultural recognition and validation.

Figure 11.1: Jaime Escalante (Edward James Olmos) confronts ETS administrators for discriminating against his students in *Stand and Deliver* (1988).

Source: DVD of *Stand and Deliver*
License: Fair Use

## *Selena* (1997)

*Selena*, like *Stand and Deliver*, is a narrative feature film based on historical events. The movie fuses Mexican and American cultures and is a remembrance of the life of Selena Quintanilla Pérez, *la Reina de la Música Tejana*, through her childhood, rise to stardom, and tragic death. The film can be described as the beginning of *Selenidad*, a concept coined by Deborah Paredez, which she describes as "the creative endeavors that constituted the dynamic and vibrant afterlife of the Latina superstar" (xii). The film was directed by Gregory Nava and produced two years after the artist's heartbreaking death. *Selena* starred **Boricua** actress Jennifer Lopez as Selena and Edward James Olmos as the patriarch of the Quintanilla family. Through her story, the film captures the duality of growing up Mexican American in the Southwestern United States. The complexity of her identity—gender and ethnicity—were central to her persona on and off stage.

The film begins backstage moments before Selena greets a sold-out Houston Astrodome in February 1995. She is greeted by screaming fans, many of whom are dressed in sparkling bustiers, and across the stadium, her fans carry signs labeled "La Reina." She opens the concert with an English-language disco medley before singing in Spanish. It is the film's first example of Noriega's bicultural and bilingual elements (Noriega, "Between a Weapon and a Formula" 172–73). The Quintanillas' bilingual and bicultural experience is the film's most salient theme, and the tension between the Mexican and American cultures a recurring drama. In the earliest scenes of the movie, a young Abraham Quintanilla and his band, *Los Dinos*, are refused by Anglo and Chicano clubs; *Los Dinos* were considered too Mexican for an Anglo club and too Americanized for the Chicano audience. However, this roadblock does not deter Mr. Quintanilla, and he eventually forms the family band, Selena y Los Dinos.

Selena encounters the cultural tension and begins exploring her identity the moment her father asks her to sing in Spanish, to which she replies, "I don't know how to sing in Spanish," and, "I don't like music in Spanish. I like Donna Summer." Her father explains that while she is American, she is also Mexican. In this moment she understands that she does not have to choose between two parts of herself. The influence of both cultures follows her throughout her music career; on stage, she sings and dances *cumbia* while mimicking the fashion of Madonna and Janet Jackson.

Figure 11.2: A young Selena (Jennifer Lopez) bonds with her father as he introduces the concept of biculturalism in *Selena* (1997).

Source: DVD of *Selena*
License: Fair Use

The path to forming a sense of belonging within seemingly opposing cultures can be an arduous process for bicultural individuals. Mr. Quintanilla's script perfectly captures the pain of this process while discussing a tour to Monterrey, Mexico, when he describes being Mexican American as "tough." According to Mr. Quintanilla, their family had been in the United States for centuries but continues to be treated "as if we just swam across the Rio Grande." Mexican Americans have to be "twice as perfect as anybody else" and "know about John Wayne *and* Pedro Infante." He continues, "We gotta be more Mexican than the Mexicans and more American than the Americans, both at the same time. It's exhausting! Nobody knows how tough it is to be a Mexican American." As the idiom states, "*No somos ni de aquí, ni de allá*" ("We're from neither here nor there").

The film also evidences the balance between the Mexican and American identities through the dynamics of the Chicanx family. It stereotypes the Quintanilla family as a unit highly dependent on the will of the patriarch. However, Mr. Quintanilla's demands are challenged by Selena, who marries her band's drummer, Chris Pérez, against her father's wishes. She also refuses to censor her body and sexuality, to the delight of an admiring male gaze. Throughout the film, her choice of bright and colorful bustiers is contested by her father, who feels she is showing too much skin. As a Mexican American woman with strong family values, she is torn between seemingly traditional Mexican customs and more liberal American practices. She is also caught between the wishes of her family's patriarchy and her blossoming sexuality. In the end, her eye for fashion leads her to design many of her own outfits, launch her own clothing line, and open a chain of boutiques.

The stress between seemingly opposing cultures is resolved through Selena, her image and music. She was a *revolucionaria* who epitomized what Guillermo Gómez-Peña calls a "border culture" (Noriega, "Between a Weapon and a Formula" 169). As the Queen of Tejano Music, she was the first woman to break into the male-dominated genre and the first Mexican American to bring *música tejana* to the top of US music charts (Tatum 30). Selena's *mestizaje*, her embodiment of the two cultures, brought visibility and a sense of belonging to the community; she taught Latinx and Mexican American people across the country how to navigate the intricacies of hyphenated identities and to refuse contracted definitions of self.

The film *Selena* captured the spirit of the late artist and her profound impact on the hearts of Mexican Americans and Latinx communities. Her career and unfortunate death "reveal how, through the collective expression of grief, Latinas/os assembled themselves as a political and cultural constituency in the United States at the close of the twentieth century" (Paredez xiii). Thanks to Selena, the Mexican American community felt seen and valued, and she reminded them that you can proudly be *Mexicana* and *Americana* and that biculturalism deserves to be celebrated.

## *Under the Same Moon* (2007)

In the early 1990s, the attitudes and policies toward immigrants began to shift, particularly as the United States experienced a growth in the populations of Mexican immigrants and immigrants overall ("Countries of Birth"). California's 1994 Proposition 187 sought to limit undocumented immigrants' access to public services. While unsuccessful, Proposition 187 was accompanied by a powerful campaign that ultimately influenced public attitudes toward undocumented immigrants (Kil XVI). Alongside changing public attitudes, the Southwest border became progressively militarized. The implementation of border control policies, such as El Paso's 1993 Operation Hold the Line and San Diego's 1994 Operation Gate Keeper, closed safer, urban crossing paths and forced migrants into the dangerous Sonoran Desert (Kil XIV). As crossing became increasingly dangerous,

**circular migration** patterns decreased and individuals began to lay down roots north of the US–Mexico divide (Massey et al. 1588).

*Under the Same Moon* offers a counter-narrative to the criminalizing and dehumanizing discourses surrounding Mexican immigration during this period. The film, directed by Mexican director Patricia Riggen, tells the story of Carlitos (Mexican actor Adrián Alonso Barona), a young boy who risks his life crossing the Southwest border to reunite with his mother, Rosario (Kate del Castillo). The film, whose dialogue is in Spanish with a few exceptions, features a long list of renowned Mexican actors; Eugenio Derbez, America Ferrera (Honduran American), and Carmen Salinas play noteworthy roles in Carlito's odyssey to reach Los Angeles.

The relationship between Carlitos and his mother highlights the issues of family separation, the trauma of the migration journey, and the hardships of undocumented life in America. Each Sunday, Rosario calls Carlitos from a payphone in LA. He tells her about school, his birthday, and how much he misses her. As he pleads for her return, tears roll down her face. While she desperately misses him, she must remain in the United States to work and send money home. Her return is indefinite.

**Figure 11.3: Rosario (Kate del Castillo) speaks with Carlitos (Adrián Alonso Barona) every Sunday in *Under the Same Moon* (2007).**

Source: DVD of *Under the Same Moon*
License: Fair Use

Through montage, their stories unfold in parallel; as Carlitos encounters the perilous experience of border crossing, his mother endures the abusive labor conditions common among undocumented workers in the United States. To cross the border, Carlitos has no choice but to trust his life to inexperienced coyotes. He travels through the scorching desert underneath the seats of their van, which lacks air conditioning. Once he is across the frontier, he makes his way to a bus terminal, where he unfortunately meets an addict who later sells him for drugs. Luckily, he is saved by a kind woman who introduces him to a group of undocumented agricultural workers. An iconic scene follows when Immigration and Customs Enforcement (ICE) arrests the men in a workplace raid. Carlitos and Enrique (Derbez) escape but are left stranded. Meanwhile, Rosario desperately confronts a sudden job loss and limited employment opportunities when her White employer dismisses her without cause, notice, or pay, threatening Rosario with deportation if she reports the abuse. This scene is a sharp critique of the pervasive exploitation of undocumented workers.

After escaping *la migra* (INS), Enrique and Carlitos are picked up by a musical group. While the musicians are not named, the group is likely identifiable to the Mexican community. They are Los Tigres del Norte, the popular folk band who sing "*Por Amor*." The lyrics of this **corrido** (folk ballad) salute the love and courage behind the act of migration; they sing, "*a mí no me asusta el peligro, la vida sin riesgo no es vida/* I don't fear danger, life without risk is not a life" and "*y por amor es que voy a cruzar la frontera sin miedo/* I will cross the border for love and without fear" (Los Tigres del Norte). The inclusion of cultural elements such as the *corrido* is a common technique among Chicanx filmmakers aiming to connect with the audience through the construction of a "minority cultural identity" (Noriega, "Between a Weapon and a Formula" 168). It is also employed as a form of resistance and to "affirm a political stance on both historical and allegorical levels" (168).

When they finally reach Los Angeles, Carlitos and Enrique explore the colorful and Chicanx mural scene of East LA, a *mise-en-scène* comparable to the scenery of *Stand and Deliver*. It is depicted as an immigrant neighborhood containing crucial services such as laundromats and Latinx grocery stores. Near the climax of the film, moments before Carlitos reunites with his mom, Enrique is arrested by law enforcement and presumably deported. The movie's bittersweet ending, like migration, is beautiful and painful. In conclusion, by telling the courageous stories of immigrant mothers and children, the film affirms the humanity of immigrants and counters xenophobic narratives.

The Mexican American community is one of the country's largest and most historic. While White supremacy ideologies and colonial-settler practices have attempted, and momentarily succeeded, to erase and disguise its contributions, they are irrefutable. Moving forward, American leadership must recognize the economic, political, and cultural contributions of Mexican and Chicanx people and stand up to anti-**BIPOC** discourses. Likewise, community leaders and educators must incorporate Mexican American history, and the history of other racialized groups, into the K-12 and higher education curricula. A greater understanding of shared histories will result in great equality for all.

*Libia Jiménez Chávez is Mexicana-Colombiana. She graduated from the University of Rochester with a double bachelor's degree in Political Science and Philosophy. She holds a master's degree in Human Rights from University*

*College London in addition to professional and graduate certifications in the areas of project management, development policy, fundraising, and Latin American studies. She is currently a History PhD student at the University of Georgia in Athens. Her research interests include Latinx studies, Latin American and transnational histories, as well as Decolonial and Borderland studies. She has extensive experience in the nonprofit and higher education sectors working alongside Latinx youth. In her free time, she enjoys eating her favorite foods, mole and arepas; cycling; and spending time with her family and chihuahua, Pouky.*

## BIBLIOGRAPHY

"1942: People v. Zamora (sic) 1943: Zoot Suit Riots." *Library of Congress*, 12 July 2021, http://guides.loc.gov/latinx-civil-rights/people-v-zamorra.

"1968: East Los Angeles Walkouts." *Library of Congress*, 12 July 2021, http://guides.loc.gov/latinx-civil-rights/east-la-walkouts.

"America's Forgotten History of Mexican-American 'Repatriation.'" *National Public Radio*, 13 July 2021, www.npr.org/2015/09/10/439114563/americas-forgotten-history-of-mexican-american-repatriation.

"Background – Mendez v Westminster Re-Enactment." *United States Courts*, 10 July 2021, http://www.uscourts.gov/educational-resources/educational-activities/background-mendez-v-westminster-re-enactment.

"Border Facts." *Southern Border Communities Coalitions*, 13 July 2021. www.southernborder.org/border-facts.

*Bracero History Archive*. 13 July 2021, http://www.braceroarchive.org/about.

"Countries of Birth for US Immigrants, 1960-Present." *Migration Policy Institute*, 4 July 2021, http://www.migrationpolicy.org/programs/data-hub/charts/immigrants-countries-birth-over-time?width=900&height=850&iframe=true.

Estrada, Josue. "Mapping American Social Movements." *University of Washington*, 1 July 2021, http://depts.washington.edu/moves/brown_beret_map.shtml.

Goldman, Shifra M., and Tomás Ybarra-Frausto. *Arte Chicano: A Comprehensive Annotated Bibliography of Chicano Art, 1965-1981*. Chicano Studies Library Publications Unit, U of California, 1985.

Kil, Sang Hea. *Covering the Border War. How the News Media Creates Crime, Race, Nation, and the USA-Mexico Divide*. Rowman & Littlefield, 2020.

Los Tigres del Norte. "Por Amor." *Por Amor,* Fonovisa, 2008.

"LULAC Education Issues." *The League of United Latin American Citizens*, 1 July 2021, http://lulac.org/advocacy/issues/education/

"LULAC History – All for One and One for All." *The League of United Latin American Citizens*, 1 July 2021, http://www.lulac.org/about/history/

Massey, Douglas S., Jorge Durand, and Karen A. Pren. "Why Border Enforcement Backfired." *American Journal of Sociology*, vol. 121, no. 5, pp. 1557–1600.

"The Mexican-American War in a Nutshell." *The National Constitution Center*, 4 July 2021, http://constitutioncenter.org/blog/the-mexican-american-war-in-a-nutshell.

Newman, Kathleen. "Latino Sacrifice in the Discourse of Citizenship: Acting Against the 'Mainstream,' 1985-1988." *Chicanos and Film: Essays on Chicano Representation and Resistance,* edited by Chon Noriega. Garland Publishing, 1992, pp. 67–82.

Noriega, Chon A. "Between a Weapon and a Formula: Chicano Cinema and Its Contexts." *Chicanos and Film: Essays on Chicano Representation and Resistance,* edited by Chon Noriega. Garland Publishing, 1992, pp. 159–204.

---. *Chicanos and Film: Essays on Chicano Representation and Resistance*. Garland Publishing, 1992.

Paredez, Deborah. *Selenidad: Selena, Latinos, and the Performance of Memory*. Duke University Press, 2009.

Salazar, Ruben. "Ruben Salazar, A Selection of Columns Reprinted from the Los Angeles Times." *University of California San Diego Library*, 1 July 2021, http://library.ucsd.edu/dc/object/bb4096888h/_1.pdf.

Tatum, Charles M. *Chicano Popular Culture: Que Hable El Pueblo*. U of Arizona P, 2001.

## FILMOGRAPHY

*Selena*. Directed by Gregory Nava, performances by Jennifer López, Edward James Olmos, Jon Seda, Constance Marie, Jacob Vargas, Lupe Ontiveros, and Jackie Guerra, Warner Bros. Entertainment Inc, 1997.

*Stand and Deliver*. Directed by Ramón Menéndez, performances by Edward James Olmos, Lou Diamond Phillips, Rosanna DeSoto, and Andy García, Warner Bros. Entertainment Inc, 1988.

*Under the Same Moon*. Directed by Patricia Riggen, performances by Adrián Alonso, Kate del Castillo, Eugenio Derbez, Maya Zapata, Carmen Salinas, María Rojo, Mario Armada, America Ferrera, and Los Tigres del Norte, Fox Searchlight Pictures and The Weinstein Company, 2007.

## FOR FURTHER STUDY

*Alambrista!* Directed by Robert M. Young, performances by Domingo Ambriz, Trinidad Silva, and Linda Gillen, Filmhaus, 1977.

*American Me*. Directed by Edward James Olmos, performances by Edward James Olmos, William Forsythe, and Sal López, Universal Pictures, 1992.

*The Ballad of Gregorio Cortez*. Directed by Robert M. Young, performances by Edward James Olmos, James Gammon, and Tom Bower, American Playhouse, Corporation for Public Broadcasting, National Council of La Raza, and The National Endowment for the Humanities, 1982.

Barrueto, Jorge J. *The Hispanic Image in Hollywood: A Postcolonial Approach*. Peter Lang, 2014.

*Born in East L.A.* Directed by Cheech Marin, performances by Cheech Marin, Daniel Stern, Paul Rodríguez, Universal Pictures, 1987.

*Chicana*. Directed by Sylvia Morales, performances by Carmen Zapata, Alicia Escalante, and Francisca Flores, UCLA School of Film and Television, 1979.

*A Day without a Mexican*. Directed by Sergio Arau, performances by Caroline Aaron, Tony Abatemarco, and Melinda Allen, Plural Entertainment, 2004.

Fregoso, Rosa Linda. *The Bronze Screen: Chicana and Chicano Film Culture*. U of Minnesota P, 1993.

*I am Joaquín*. Directed by Luis Valdez, El Centro Campesino Cultural, 1969.

*La Bamba*. Directed by Luis Valdez, performances by Lou Diamond Phillips, Esai Morales, Rosanna DeSoto, Columbia Pictures, 1987.

*Mi Familia*. Directed by Gregory Nava, performances by Jimmy Smits, Esai Morales, and Edward James Olmos, New Line Cinema, 1995.

*Please, Don't Bury Me Alive!* Directed by Efraín Gutiérrez, performances by Efraín Gutiérrez, José Armando, and Margarita Armando de Hoyas, Chicano Arts Film Enterprises, 1976.

*Real Women Have Curves*. Directed by Patricia Cardoso, performances by America Ferrera, Lupe Ontiveros, and Ingrid Oliu, HBO Films, 2002.

*Zoot Suit*. Directed by Luis Valdez, performances by Daniel Valdez, Edward James Olmos, and Charles Aidman, Universal Pictures, 1981.

# 12 The Puerto Rican Experience Onscreen

Dalina A. Perdomo Álvarez
(Eli and Edythe Broad Art Museum) and
Pedro Noel Doreste
(University of Chicago)

Puerto Rican film history is often studied in the context of its political relationship to the United States and its effects on Puerto Ricans' already complicated cultural identity, both on the island and its diaspora. Puerto Ricans had been emigrating to the United States even during Spanish rule, with a surge occurring after the Spanish-American War in 1898 and another when Puerto Ricans became US citizens in 1917 after the passing of the **Jones-Shafroth Act**, which further facilitated Puerto Ricans' mobility between the two countries. A larger surge in the 1950s, known as the **Great Migration**, was brought on by the advent of air travel and a precarious economic situation on the island. Since then, Puerto Ricans often engage in **circular migration**, moving back and forth between the archipelago and the United States, settling primarily in urban centers along the East Coast. These unique migratory flows also contribute to the ambivalent cultural identity Puerto Ricans hold, which at the moment could be considered to be simultaneously Latin American and Latinx. Although there was sporadic filmmaking on the island since the medium's infancy, cinema in Puerto Rico would take a more defined shape as film production—or cultural production more broadly—became institutionalized in 1949 following the election of Luis Muñoz Marín, the first democratically elected governor of Puerto Rican descent in the island's history and also known as the figure responsible for ratifying the archipelago's current status as a US territory. This imposed political status, along with its attendant unsettling of cultural identity, informs the majority of artistic practice on the island. This chapter will provide an introduction to Puerto Rican media from the advent of sound film to the present moment, focusing largely on cinema and related media, and exploring media-making on the island, in the United States, and in between.

## EARLY PUERTO RICAN CINEMA

The history of Puerto Rican cinema has experienced several upheavals in recent years. In 2017, the first feature-length sound film made on the island was located after being lost for eighty years. *Romance tropical* (1934), directed by Juan Emilio Viguié Cajas, is currently the earliest Puerto Rican film known to be extant, and its rediscovery has opened up new possibilities for the study of Puerto Rican media history. The discovery and restoration of *Romance tropical* is an invaluable addition to the ongoing discourse surrounding Puerto Rico's national cinema, or lack thereof. Yet it also raises questions of ownership due to the complicated geopolitical relationship between Puerto Rico and the United States, as it remains housed at the UCLA Film & Television Archive and there are no imminent plans for its repatriation ([Horak](#)).

In terms of content, the film perpetuates certain imperialist and racist ideologies typically associated with the Unites States' treatment of its unincorporated territories (including Puerto Rico): a relationship of occupation, discrimination, and othering. It allows a suspiciously White Puerto Rico to cast itself as metropolis, with its inhabitants invading and plundering a different island populated by a Black and Indigenous people who are portrayed as uncivilized. What is remarkable about *Romance tropical*'s narrative is the potential reading of Puerto Rico reimagined as a colonial power in the context of the tumultuous thirties, a time when its citizens were confronting the idea of a Puerto Rican identity as doubly colonized, with the centuries-long legacy of Spanish governance suddenly interrupted by continued US occupation.

**Figure 12.1:** *Bomba* **sequence from** *Romance Tropical* **(1934).**

Source: DVD of *Romance Tropical*
License: Fair Use

Although the narrative never explicitly identifies Puerto Rico as the film's setting, certain cultural markers reveal themselves in *Romance tropical*'s score and screenplay. The choice of music in particular may help place the listener in Puerto Rico, as both the score and the musical performances were originally composed by Rafael Muñoz, a prolific and well-known bandleader. There is clear inspiration from *danza*, a creolized ballroom dance genre, as well as *bomba*, a call-and-response genre born from the Afro-diaspora that functions as a percussive conversation between drummer and dancer. The differing ways these two musical styles are presented and utilized in the narrative further exemplify the anti-Black nature of the production. The *danza* style is presented as belonging to a high-class, "civilized" society and provided more space in the film, with two musical numbers performed by its leads to express their romantic emotions. The *bomba* style, in turn, is only utilized when the White lead sails out and arrives at an island belonging to a Black and presumably indigenous population, using negative ethnographic stereotypes to suggest this society is "uncivilized." Moreover, the script was written by Luis Palés Matos, considered a pioneer of Afro-Antillean poetry though he wrote as an outside observer of the Black community in Puerto Rico, as he was a White Puerto Rican himself. On the page, Palés Matos's skillful rhythmic verses can be appreciated in their original format as experiments in poetic form, complete with a dose of regionalisms, latent musicality, and onomatopoeic flourishes, which is how his work has traditionally been performed. Onscreen, however, *Romance tropical* provides the spectator a full visual and sonic expression of the screenwriter's flattening conception of both Blackness and indigeneity. Discussions about the exploitation or outright fabrication of Afro–Puerto Rican culture have long accompanied Palés Matos's literary work. Yet what the film belatedly provides is an opportunity to pair an intellectual care for cultural specificity with concomitant attention paid to the specificity of film as a medium. Such a discussion about White supremacy in Puerto Rico and the politics of film preservation has not taken place in the eighty years during which *Romance tropical* was lost, but the film has since been a flashpoint in recent debates about Puerto Rican identity, cultural nationalism, and the limits of **mestizaje**. The intersections of race, class, empire, and culture—especially music—are crucial themes to keep in mind when studying Puerto Rico's film heritage.

## THE DIVISION OF COMMUNITY EDUCATION (DIVISIÓN DE EDUCACIÓN DE LA COMUNIDAD; DIVEDCO)

Local film production made in Puerto Rico by Puerto Ricans, such as in the case of *Romance tropical,* was sparse during the first half of the twentieth century, but the midcentury period saw a rise in both public and private filmmaking ventures. Under the Muñoz Marín administration, the Popular Democratic Party (PPD) would begin instituting a series of reforms that shifted the island toward New

Deal–style public investment while simultaneously allowing the United States to gesture toward decolonization on the international stage. The most notorious of these reforms, named **Operation Bootstrap** (*Operación Manos a la Obra* in Spanish), was an initiative between the local and the US federal government to transform the island's economy from an agrarian system into an industrial one (Dávila 33–34). The creation of high-skilled jobs in urban manufacturing did not offset the sudden contraction of the agricultural sector, which triggered mass unemployment and led to another wave of economic migration to the United States in the 1950s and '60s. To ameliorate the effects of rural displacement and the rapid shocks to the island's economy, the administration set their sights on combating underdevelopment through a new cultural pedagogy project. The **Division of Community Education** (**División de Educación de la Comunidad; DIVEDCO**) was formed in an attempt to educate the local populace on the topics of public health, economic self-sufficiency, the perils of consumerism, and the benefits of participation in liberal democracy, among other outreach to the poor and disenfranchised. As the cultural courier of the modernizing effort, the DIVEDCO's mission became to cultivate—or rather, to consolidate—a cultural nationalism which rested on the idea of the Puerto Rican *jíbaro* (peasant worker) as an idealized figure, to be seen in the factory just as in the fields.

After a change in Puerto Rico's status to an ***estado libre asociado*** **(commonwealth)** in 1952, the DIVEDCO became the cultural and educational front of this colossal political project, bringing in artists, writers, and general expertise from the mainland first to train the next generation of artists. Foreign-born artists such as Edwin Rosskam, Jack Delano, Irene Delano, Benjamin Doniger, and Willard Van Dyke, all of whom had experience with New Deal cultural programs, were brought in to oversee the formation of the DIVEDCO's graphic, literature, and, ultimately, film departments. Jack Delano's *Los peloteros* (*The Ballplayers* [1951]) is the first feature-length film produced by the DIVEDCO. Shot on location with a mostly nonprofessional cast, the film borrows its style from both Italian neorealism and Depression-era social documentaries to show how a group of young boys do odd jobs around their neighborhood to raise funds to buy uniforms for their baseball team, and how one man's avarice threatens to undermine their collective action. Following in the tradition of films before it, Delano cast famous comedian Ramón Rivero (affectionately known as Diplo on the island), not as a hedge against the talent of the child actors but instead as a way to showcase his considerable skill as a comedian and musician. Delano, a photographer by trade, found in film a way to combine the ambitious, transdisciplinary artistic aims of the DIVEDCO by blending in other aspects of Puerto Rican culture—from scenes highlighting folk music and vernacular theater to images of stilt houses in the *campo* (countryside) and, yes, even baseball!

*Los peloteros*'s formula of representing local culture and customs while couching social critique—in this case, nurturing a sense of solidarity within a community in the face of rampant poverty—within a fictionalized narrative became a blueprint for the DIVEDCO's ensuing filmography, which would soon settle on the **docudrama** as its preferred mode. Artists such as Amílcar Tirado, Luis Maisonet, Marcos Betancourt, Ángel Rivera, and Dominican Oscar Torres, to name a few, continued the DIVEDCO's commitment to this social-democratic ethos by directing a series of films that addressed most aspects of the experience of living on the island during this time, from preparing for a hurricane to participating in elections. Although Puerto Rico had become a hub for filmmaking in the Caribbean during the 1950s and '60s, in large part due to DIVEDCO, the cultural sector was subject to budget cuts and was deprioritized as policy following the electoral victory of the New Progressive Party in 1968. Running on a pro-statehood platform, the artists who comprised the DIVEDCO were seen as political opponents, their work considered a thinly veiled platform for the Puerto Rican independence movement. While its graphic and theater divisions would remain, film production by DIVEDCO petered out in the ensuing decade before its film department was shuttered. Regardless, the catalog of social films produced by the DIVEDCO in the period between 1949 and 1968—many of which are readily accessible on the [Institute of Puerto Rican Culture's YouTube channel](#)—remains unmatched in both breadth and quality, and to this day is considered the foundation of Puerto Rico's national cinema.

## THE EMERGENCE OF A TRANSNATIONAL, INDEPENDENT CINEMA

Beginning in the early 1960s—roughly coinciding with the rise of the New Progressive Party—the rate of publicly funded film production dwindled in Puerto Rico while competition from private studios and independent filmmaking collectives began to emerge. At the same time, the archipelago graduated from the dictums of developmentalism necessitated by the midcentury push toward industrialization and instead focused on incentivizing North American capital to invest in the island via federal tax incentives and subsidies. The promise of a modern Puerto Rico had arrived, culminating in an economic boom, which peaked in the 1970s and is colloquially known as *La edad de oro*, the Puerto Rican "golden age." With it, dreams of upward mobility into an idyllic upper-middle class began to materialize on the screen as Puerto Rico became a destination for film professionals from all corners of the hemisphere.

Foreign filmmakers, such as the Mexicans Juan Orol, Ramón Pereda, Gilberto Martínez Solares, and Julián Soler; Argentinians Oscar Orzábal Quintana, Orestes Trucco, and Leopoldo Torre Nilsson; and Spaniards Juan Fortuny and José Díaz Morales, joined homegrown talents such as Amílcar Tirado, Tony Felton, Jacobo Morales, Jerónimo Mitchell Meléndez, and Glauco del Mar in directing comedies, crime films, domestic melodramas, and other genre features during this period, whose fuzzy boundaries overlap with the height of DIVEDCO productions in the late '50s and end with scattershot production in the late '80s and early '90s. Orol, known for his long career as a marginal figure of the Mexican Golden Age of the mid-1930s to early 1950s, directed a series of gangster films and comedies in Puerto Rico shortly before ending his filmmaking career in the United States. Similarly, the emergent independent film industry in San Juan solicited the expertise of the Argentinian Orzábal Quintana, who produced films for the successful commercial ventures of Probo Films, the company that started this cycle of filmmaking on the back of the successes of *Maruja* (1959), *El otro camino* (*The Other Road* [1959]), and *Ayer amargo* (*Bitter Yesterday* [1960]). Former DIVEDCO film professionals attempted to finance their independent ventures through a filmmakers' cooperative or found work on the sets of emerging directorial talents such as Jerónimo Mitchell Meléndez, who leveraged a successful acting career abroad to become one of the most prolific Puerto Rican filmmakers of the 1960s. These features privileged the escapism and levity of Hollywood films, their main competitor, but they also signal a turn away from the nation-building, pedagogical project of DIVEDCO, despite much of its talent successfully making the transition from the public agency to independent filmmaking. The turn to a style of filmmaking that proved successful at the box office while keeping hints of a distinctly local flavor is a reflection of the newfound freedom of leisure afforded to the rising middle class that developed during the economic boom of the period. The development of independent cinema within the bounds of the archipelago nevertheless failed to address a side effect of the "miracle" in Puerto Rico that facilitated the growth of a local film industry in the first place: namely, a third wave of out-migration to US urban centers as a result of a drastically contracted agricultural sector, which emptied the country of dignified employment in rural areas. This latest exodus, in turn, spawned its own generation of grassroots and independent filmmaking chiefly in the *barrios* of New York City, one organized against the threats of gentrification, discrimination, and state violence in the metropolis.

In the late 1960s and '70s, the members of this wave of the diaspora came of age in a country racked by mass objection to an unpopular war in Vietnam and a crescendo in the long struggle for Black civil rights. As such, this generation of **Nuyoricans**, as Puerto Ricans who have resettled in New York are typically called, repudiated the static politics of their predecessors and resisted calls for assimilation in the face of blatant discrimination in health, housing, and education. The Nuyorican Movement, a collective of New York–based Puerto Rican artists, emerged out of poetry workshops and music clubs to address these deepening fractures in Puerto Rican identity and to cultivate an uneasy sense of belonging for the **Boricua** community living in the metropolis. During this time, the **Young Lords** chapter in New York City quickly took a more confrontational approach, affiliating with established organizations in New York City but also adopting a decidedly more militant stance toward the manifestations of US imperialism of the time, namely the US military incursions in Vietnam as well as the crushing of nationalist and independence movements in unincorporated territories like Puerto Rico. The Young Lords adopted guerrilla filmmaking as one front of their media operations, producing newsreels on Puerto Rican history as well as the contemporary struggles of the Nuyorican community, many of which were broadcast on regional public television or were compiled into long-form documentaries later, such as in the case of Iris Morales's ¡Pa'lante, siempre pa'lante! (1996). At the same time, a popular groundswell had developed at Hunter College at the City University of New York to found and foster a Puerto Rican Studies Center, and documentary film became an important tool through which students were able to garner support for their cause. While the films of this period were rudimentary in technique and appearance—a limitation imposed by a lack of access to financial and technological resources in the *barrios*—together they functioned to "assert that Puerto Ricans should occupy the center of cinematic discourse in order to reflect the variety of implicit and explicit responses to oppression" (Jiménez). For example, Ana María García's *La operación* (*The Operation* [1982]), Edin Vélez's video work from 1978 to 1989, Diego Echevarría's *A Colony the American Way* (1981) and *Los Sures* (1984), and Frances Negrón-Muntaner's *Brincando el Charco: Portrait of a Puerto Rican* (1994) are standout films in this style, each treating the particularities of Puerto Ricanness through the lens of liberation. With their demands now in part institutionalized, organizations like the Nuyorican Movement, the Young Lords, the Puerto Rican Student Union, and other anti-imperialist and pro-independence groups laid the foundation for a thriving contingent of documentary filmmakers to emerge in the 1980s, one less concerned with taking their fight to the streets than giving voice to them.

**Figure 12.2: Screen capture from *¡Pa'lante, Siempre Pa'lante!* (1996).**
Source: DVD of *¡Pa'lante, Siempre Pa'lante!*
License: Fair Use

## BREAKTHROUGH AND THE CONTEMPORARY MEDIA LANDSCAPE

An opposite tendency was underway on the island during the 1980s and 1990s with the domestic melodramas of directors such as Marcos Zurinaga and Jacobo Morales. The latter's film *Lo que le pasó a Santiago* (*What Happened to Santiago* [1989]) was nominated for Best Foreign Language Film—renamed Best International Feature Film in 2020 ("Academy")—at the 62nd Annual Academy Awards in 1990, becoming the first and only Puerto Rican film to ever be nominated. The film follows Santiago, a grumpy, widowed, and recently retired accountant living in San Juan, bored of his uneventful life and frustrated with his children's overly complicated lives—one a single mother going through a divorce, and one being treated for clinical depression. Nostalgic for the days before major tax incentives led to mass manufacturing and tourism on the island, he yearns for a slow life in the *campo*—it is no longer the Puerto Rico of the DIVEDCO films. Ultimately, the narrative expresses an affinity for an upper-class sensibility for Puerto Ricans of White Spanish descent—Afro–Puerto Ricans are notably missing from the story and the screen—whose families owned *haciendas* (estates) that typically run as plantations. The main character's implicit rejection of the Americanization of the island exemplifies the lingering tension between empires and the lasting effects of the Spanish-American War, and subsequently the disparity in how this colonial entanglement affects different social classes and racial identities in the archipelago.

Figure 12.3: Final scene from Jacobo Morales' *Lo que le pasó a Santiago* (1989).

Source: DVD of *Lo que le pasó a Santiago*
License: Fair Use

After the film's loss at the Academy Awards, concerns circulated amongst disgruntled fans of Puerto Rican cinema that the island's status as a United States' possession automatically placed it at a disadvantage as not domestic or foreign enough to compete fairly in any category. Previously, Zuringa had unsuccessfully submitted two of his works for consideration, and several filmmakers tried their luck after the *Lo que le pasó a Santiago* fluke to no avail. Yet it was not until 2011, with the disqualified submission of the film *América* (2011) by Sonia Fritz, that the Academy formally announced that it would not be considering US territories for the Best Foreign Language Film category, confirming long-standing suspicions of a competitive disadvantage ("Puerto Rico"). Morales, whose fantasies of a Puerto Rican landed gentry made him the most prolific and commercially successful director of the 1980s and 1990s, made films with the style and substance of Douglas Sirk's melodrama to wide critical acclaim, yet even his magnum opus could not pierce the boundary that separates Puerto Rican artists at the margin from the Academy's movers and shakers at the center. This perceived slight on the part of the Academy, while a disappointment to the film's producers, would have come as no surprise to their Nuyorican contemporaries. The incompatibility was no longer strictly about preserving a sense of national identity across a splintering nation but about a divergent class consciousness in the filmmaking of this period.

In recent years, it is not uncommon to hear that Puerto Rico is experiencing another golden age in cinema. Films like *Broche de oro* (*The Gold Brooch* [2012]), *Las vacas con gafas* (*Cows Wearing Glasses* [2014]), *Antes que cante el gallo* (*Before the Rooster Crows* [2016]), and *Perfume de gardenias* (*Scent of Gardenias* [2021]), to name just a few, certainly support that hypothesis. However, it would be insufficient to say that Puerto Rican media-making has thrived in the previous decade solely on the back of prestige, feature-length filmmaking. A wave of scathing social documentaries, often produced by activist-filmmakers, has emerged in response to three major events of the past decade. The first of these was the enactment of a US federal law (PROMESA) in response to the economic collapse caused by the withdrawal of tax incentives for corporations between 1996 and 2006. PROMESA further undermined local autonomy and deployed a wave of austerity measures to ensure repayment of the island's debt to bondholders. The second was the manifold failures of US federal aid to Puerto Rico after Hurricane Maria in 2017, and the third was the popular uprising that resulted in governor Ricky Rosselló's ouster in the summer of 2019 following the release of text messages where Rosselló mocked victims of Hurricane María and made misogynistic and homophobic remarks. Films such as *Seva Vive* (*Seva Lives* [2008]), *Las Carpetas* (*The Files* [2011]), *The Last Colony* (2015), *Filiberto* (2017), and *Landfall* (2020) all tackle various aspects of Puerto Rico's colonial history and present, criticizing the vestiges of Operation Bootstrap–style philosophies on the island and pulling no punches when it comes to denouncing forms of oppression from within and without. Lastly, screen media today is in the throes of a creative deregulation, whereby artists may move seamlessly between producing feature-length pictures, reggaeton music videos, and streaming shows, to name a few venues where one may find Puerto Rican cinema in the present moment.

Film in Puerto Rico and its diasporas has evolved beyond discourse of national cinema, revealing in its wake the inadequacy of both of those terms when applied to the case of Puerto Rico, a stateless nation without a robust cinematic tradition. Throughout the twentieth and twenty-first centuries, media-making in Puerto Rico has been both supported by US-based resources while also conducted in opposition to American film culture, but only as a byproduct of layered fiscal, political, and environmental crises has it attained its contemporary thematic coherence against the colonial imposition. The history of cinema in the Puerto Rican archipelago remains one of fits and starts, failed ventures, censorship, scarcity, marginalization, and wishful thinking. What recent events—such as the commitment to a cinema of denunciation or the archival misadventures of a film such as *Romance tropical*—ultimately reveal is that even if one forgoes the construction of a national cinematic canon as an ideal, cinema nevertheless remains the most incisive medium through which one may interrogate not only Puerto Rican history but also broader histories of US imperialism and its consequent disorientations and dislocations in moving images.

**Dalina A. Perdomo Álvarez** *(she/her) is a Puerto Rican curator and writer, currently Curatorial Assistant at the MSU Broad Art Museum. In 2021, she was selected as the inaugural curatorial fellow for the Chicago Underground Film Festival. Previously, she was the 2018–2020 curatorial fellow at the Museum of Contemporary Photography, and she has also worked at the Video Data Bank and the National Museum of Puerto Rican Arts & Culture. She received her MA in Film Studies from The University of Iowa in 2018 and her BA from the University of Puerto Rico–Mayagüez.*

**Pedro Noel Doreste Rodríguez** *is a doctoral candidate in Cinema and Media Studies at the University of Chicago. His research surveys transnational and minor cinemas of the Caribbean, with a particular focus on the islands of the Hispanic Caribbean. His work is interested in media archaeologies of underdevelopment, film and modernity in the circum-Caribbean, archival studies, and the intersections of cultural production and/under coloniality in its many configurations. He loves his dogs, Congrí and Ossie.*

## BIBLIOGRAPHY

"Academy Announces Rules for 92nd Oscars." *Oscars*, 23 April 2019, https://www.oscars.org/news/academy-announces-rules-92nd-oscars.

Dávila, Arlene M. *Sponsored Identities: Cultural Politics in Puerto Rico*. Temple UP, 1997.

Horak, Jan-Christopher. "How to Find a Lost Film." *UCLA Film & Television Archive*, 10 November 2017, https://www.cinema.ucla.edu/blogs/archival-spaces/2017/11/10/romance-tropical-how-to-find-lost-film.

Jiménez, Lillian. "Moving from the Margin to the Center: Puerto Rican Cinema in New York." *Jump Cut*, vol. 38, June 1993, pp. 60–66.

"Puerto Rico queda excluido de la carrera por el Oscar." *El Nuevo Día*, 5 October 2011, https://www.elnuevodia.com/entretenimiento/peliculas-series/notas/puerto-rico-queda-excluido-de-la-carrera-por-el-oscar/.

## FILMOGRAPHY

*Romance tropical*. Directed by Juan Emilio Viguié Cajas, performances by Jorge Rodríguez, Ernestina Canino, and Raquel Canino, Latin Artists Pictures Corp., 1934.

*Los peloteros*. Directed by Jack Delano, performances by Ramón Rivero and Miriam Colón., DIVEDCO, 1951.

*Pa'lante, siempre pa'lante*. Directed by Iris Morales, 1996.

*Lo que le pasó a Santiago*. Directed by Jacobo Morales, performances by Tommy Muñiz, Gladys Rodríguez, and Johanna Rosaly, Dios Los Cría Inc., 1989.

## FOR FURTHER STUDY

Álvarez Curbelo, Silvia. "Vidas prestadas: El cine y la puertorriqueñidad." *Revista de Crítica Literaria Latinoamericana*, vol. 45, 1997, pp. 395–410.

*América*. Directed by Sonia Fritz, Isla Films, 2011.

*Antes que cante el gallo* (*Before the Rooster Crows*). Directed by Arí Maniel Cruz, performances by Cordelia González, Miranda Purcell, and Kisha Tikina Burgos, Deluz, 2016.

*Ayer amargo* (*Bitter Yesterday*). Directed by Amílcar Tirado, performances by Marta Romero and Arturo Correa, Mitchell Productions Inc., 1960.

*Brincando el Charco: Portrait of a Puerto Rican*. Directed by Frances Negrón-Muntaner, performances by Frances Negrón-Muntaner, Agnes Lugo-Ortiz, Moisés Agosto, Toni Cade Bambara, ITVS International, 1994.

*Broche de oro* (*The Gold Brooch*). Directed by Raúl Marchand Sánchez, performances by Jacobo Morales, Adrian Garcia, and Diego de la Texera, Puerto Rico Film Corporation, 2012.

*Las Carpetas* (*The Files*). Directed by Maite Rivera Carbonell, 2011.

*A Colony the American Way*, Diego Echevarría, Terra, 1981.

*Filiberto*. Directed by Freddie Marrero, 2017.

García-Crespo, Naida. *Early Puerto Rican Cinema and Nation Building: National Sentiments, Transnational Realities, 1897-1940*. Bucknell UP, 2019.

Kennerley, Catherine Marsh. *Negociaciones culturales: los intelectuales y el proyecto pedagógico del estado muñocista*. Ediciones Callejón, 2009.

*Landfall*. Directed by Cecilia Aldarondo, Blackscrackle Film, 2020.

*The Last Colony*. Directed by Juan Agustín Márquez, 2015.

*Maruja*. Directed by Orzabal Quintana, performances by Marta Romero, Roberto Rivera Negrón, and Mario Pabón, Probo Films, 1958.

*La operación*. Directed by Ana María García, Latin American Film Project, 1982.

Ortiz Jiménez, Juan. *Nacimiento del cine puertorriqueño*. Editorial Tiempo Nuevo, 2007.

*El otro camino* (*The Other Path*). Directed by Oscar Orzábal Quintana, performances by Axel Anderson, Rosaura Andreu, Víctor Arrillaga, Probo Films, 1959.

*Perfume de gardenias* (*Scent of Gardenias*). Directed by Gisela Rosario, performances by Georgina Borri, Magali Carrasquillo, and Flor Joglar, 3 Gardenias, 2021.

Ramos Perea, Roberto. *Cinelibre: Historia desconocida y manifiesto por un cine puertorriqueño independiente y libre*. Editions Le Provincial, 2008.

*Seva Vive* (*Seva Lives*). Directed by Francisco Serrano, 2008.

*Los Sures*. Directed by Diego Echevarría, distributed by UnionDocs, 1984.

*Las vacas con gafas* (*Cows with Glasses*). Directed by Alex Santiago Pérez, performances by Daniel Lugo, Cristina Soler, and Jaime Bello, Cozy Light Pictures, 2014.

# 13

# The Cuban American Experience Onscreen

Ana M. López
(Tulane University)

For as long as there has been media, as we use the term today to refer primarily to audiovisual productions, Cubans have been present in it and been part of its imaginary. The first such audiovisual medium was the cinema, and Cuba played an integral role in its growth since 1895, year of the "birth" of cinema and especially since 1898, the year of the Spanish-American War, in which the United States intervened in Cuba's long-standing struggles for independence from Spain (since 1868).

## HISTORY OF US–CUBAN RELATIONS AND IMMIGRATION

The United States and Cuba have always had relations, given the island's proximity (about ninety miles from Key West, Florida). There has always been traffic between the countries, especially given that Cuba was the center point of global trade in the colonial period, triangulated between Spain, Britain, and the United States. After the Louisiana Purchase of 1803 and the Florida Purchase of 1819, there was much traveling and immigration. That immigration became more significant after 1868, during the first Cuban wars of independence from Spain, when many tobacco growers settled in Key West and Tampa and established the latter's tobacco industry. Later, many who were involved in the struggles for independence also moved to the United States to gain support, most notably José Martí. Throughout the first half of the twentieth century, there was significant travel between the two countries and some immigration, dependent on economic factors and Cuban politics. Cuban immigration to the United States became a full-scale exodus only after the Cuban Revolution ending in 1959, especially after Fidel Castro's government aligned itself with the Soviet Union and introduced communism to the country, which led the United States to break off diplomatic relations with the island and put in place a crippling trade embargo in 1961, engage in the Bay of Pigs invasion the same year, and invest in other measures to destabilize the Cuban government.

There have been several waves of immigration to the United States from Cuba since then. During the first wave, moneyed elites and allies of the deposed dictator Fulgencio Batista followed their interests. Then, parents frightened about the state's expanding powers over all citizens collaborated in **Operation Peter Pan**, in which more than fourteen thousand unaccompanied minors were sent to the United States and resettled first in Miami and subsequently all over the country in orphanages and foster homes. Many of these children's White, upper/middle-class families also managed to immigrate through third countries or **Freedom Flights**, twice-daily flights operated though an agreement between the United States and Cuban governments that brought about 300,000 refugees to the United States between 1965 and 1973. The best known exodus, however, was the one that occurred through the Port of Mariel in 1980, known as the **Mariel Boatlift**. Approximately 125,000 Cubans reached the United States in privately chartered boats that sailed from Florida, where refugees settled in camps. Many remained in the Miami areas and became known as Marielitos. The Marielitos were noticeably different from the prior Cuban exiles: they were less educated, less affluent, and less "White," more were male and homosexual, and many had prior criminal and/or mental health backgrounds. This was because many were leaving Cuba due to extreme poverty rather than ideological differences and because Castro expelled many people considered undesirable during the temporary lifting of the ban on leaving Cuba without government permission. The term *Marielito* became a term of opprobrium and was eventually linked to the growth of the drug trade in the region in the 1990s. Subsequent exoduses, such as the 1994 **balsero crisis**, triggered by the collapse of Cuba's economy in the wake of the fall of the Soviet Union, the island's main trading partner, were somewhat less impactful. The crisis did lead to the United States implementing the **wet foot, dry foot policy** that granted Cuban immigrants the right to stay if they made it to US soil. If they were intercepted at sea, they would be turned back. Although it placed limitations on the **Cuban Adjustment Act**, a 1966 law that granted permanent residency to any Cuban who had lived in the United States for a year or more, the wet foot, dry foot policy, which remained in place until 2017, gave Cubans a privileged status in comparison to other immigrants from Latin America. In total, more than 1.3 million Cubans have immigrated to the United States (the population of the island is roughly eleven million).

On December 17, 2014, US President Barack Obama, with President Raul Castro in Cuba, announced the start of a process of normalizing relations between the two nations, which led to unprecedented exchanges, including the establishment of embassies in Havana and DC and Obama's own visit to the island in 2016. In 2017 and beyond, President Donald Trump reversed all of the Obama's administrations overtures toward Cuba and even imposed greater restrictions on economic and cultural relations between the two countries.

## CUBA AND US MEDIA

The earliest images of Cubans generated by US cameramen were of the Spanish-American War of 1898. The Library of Congress has preserved and made available a rich repository of the work of these amazing cameramen who braved sea travel and perilous conditions to bring images of the ongoing struggle to their audiences back in the United States, barely three years after the introduction of the medium as a mass spectacle ("Spanish-American War"). Granted, as has been outlined in the literature about these images, a good number of them were what we would now call "fake news": battle scenes were staged in bathtubs with toy ships and tobacco smoke. But there was also much legitimate footage of the fighting and its aftermath, like the Battle of San Juan Hill, and of Cubans surviving in unimaginable conditions, including the opponents of Spanish rule who had been sequestered in concentration camps.

Figure 13.1: A still from the film *Pack mules with Ammunition on the Santiago Trail, Cuba*, shot by William Daly Paley for the Edison Company, 1898.

Source: Library of Congress
License: Public Domain

These are not only the first motion picture images of a war but are also the first motion picture images of Cuba and Cubans to enter the US imaginary. Alongside these motion pictures, photographers for the major US newspapers (and the sensationalistic "yellow press") also captured thousands of pictures of the island

and its freedom fighters before and during the war. These widely circulated images played a major role in drumming up popular sentiment for the US intervention and its subsequent protectorate over the island.

Cuba did not feature very prominently in Hollywood cinema in the silent period, although many Americans became very familiar with Cuba during Prohibition (1920–1933). After the **Volstead Act** banned the manufacture, transportation, and sale of alcohol, US distillers, bar owners, bartenders, customers, and smugglers flocked to the island, especially to Havana, which quickly became a mecca for tourists looking for fun. *Havana Widows* (1933), for example, features two burlesque dancers who flee to Cuba's capital to find millionaires to fleece for money. With the fascination with "exotic" musical rhythms that followed the popularization of sound film (1927–1929), "fun" in Cuba was often featured in Hollywood musicals like *Week-End in Havana* (1941), in which a Macy's shopgirl achieves her dream of a Cuban holiday, and *Holiday in Havana* (1949), which features Desi Arnaz as a hotel busboy who dreams of becoming a musician.

### *I Love Lucy* (1951–1957)

Desi Arnaz was, in fact, the first and most successful Cuban American star of the era. He had been the leader of a very successful band in New York City, with which he introduced conga line dancing, and had already appeared in several Hollywood musicals when he and his wife, actress Lucille Ball, established Desilu Productions in 1950 and secured a deal with CBS for a television sitcom. *I Love Lucy*, which premiered in October 1951, was a pioneering TV program: it was the first to be filmed in front of live audiences, use multiple camera set-ups, and film in 35mm to allow stations around the country to offer high-quality broadcasts. It was also the first television program to feature a successful Cuban American (or any Latino, for that matter) and, above all, one happily married to a White American woman (redheaded to boot). The norm in Hollywood cinema was, basically, that the Latino man never got to remain with the White girl. Yet here we had a successful Cuban American musician who always managed to outwit his wife's slapstick antics and come out "right." He was, after all, the "I" of *I Love Lucy*.

The huge cultural impact of Arnaz's Ricky Ricardo persona was evidenced in Oscar Hijuelos's Pulitzer Prize–winning novel *The Mambo Kings Play Songs of Love* (1989) that evokes Ricky Ricardo, *I Love Lucy*, and Desi Arnaz himself (Desi Arnaz, Jr. plays Ricky Ricardo in the film version of the novel) as *the* central cultural icons of New York's Latino community in the first half of the 1950s. The novel's recreation of an actual episode of *I Love Lucy*—in which the Castillo brothers appear on the program as Ricky's Cuban cousins—restructures the program's ethnic and gender relationships in a revealing way. The episode makes use of the Cubanness of the Castillo brothers and their relationship with Ricky (defined through their shared ethnicity and musicality) to displace Lucy's antics, making it impossible for her to undermine what has been understood as Ricky's ethnic power. Framed by an iconic television screen from the 1950s, the clips of the program are a hit with the "real" Latino community gathered in the living room to watch the show together. This audience, like the one in the studio, laughs at the jokes but takes delight when the Castillo brothers repeatedly say, "No hablamos inglés" ("We don't speak English"). What is even more significant is how *Mambo Kings* places *I Love Lucy* at the dramatic climax of the novel's nostalgic and historically imperfect narration of the origins of the construction of Cuban American identity. In so doing, the novel and film affirm and confirm the power of televised images and stories in the construction of the history of our ethnic past.

## AFTER THE 1959 REVOLUTION

After the mass exodus from the island motivated by the Cuban Revolution of 1959, mediated Cuban Americanness began to shift away from rhythm, dancing, and comedy and toward politics and the immigrant experience. The media at large was filled with images of the arrival of exiles in the 1960s, all coded as political exiles, not immigrants. In fact, many were indeed involved in the failed US-backed **Bay of Pigs** invasion that took place on April 17, 1961. After the Cuban Missile Crisis in October–November 1962, sparked when the Soviet Union placed missiles in Cuba that were pointed at the United States, also failed to motivate the United States to invade the island or to intervene militarily in Cuban affairs, a steady exodus continued though the 1960s and '70s, especially through the Freedom Flights.

### *El Super* (1979)

On a frigid New York City morning during the notoriously snowy winter of 1978, the protagonist of *El Super*, Roberto, harshly awakens in his basement apartment to the sound of the pipes clanging and tenants clamoring for the boiler to be turned on. Roberto (Raimundo Hidalgo-Gato) is the Cuban exile superintendent ("el super") of a building in Washington Heights, where he lives with wife Aurelia (soap-opera star Zully Montero) and teenage daughter Aurelita (Elizabeth Peña in her first film role). After ten years in exile, Roberto has trouble believing in the possibility of a mythical return to the island and even more difficulty dealing with the dreariness of the tenants' unending demands and the harshness of winter. His wife, Aurelia, is still psychologically in Cuba, while daughter Aurelita has moved away from the "Cuban way" and seems to be fully embracing the American teen life of late 1970s New York (marijuana, sex, and disco dancing).

Produced on a shoestring budget of twenty thousand dollars, with a mostly volunteer cast and crew, Leon Ichaso and Orlando Jiménez's *El Super* remains, more than forty years after its release in 1979, the most poignant filmic articulation of the Cuban exile life as it became a permanent state. Stylistically as deceptively simple as the Cuban American lives it chronicles, *El Super* deploys a transparent style of editing but evidences a tremendous visual sensibility via its careful use of framing, a realistic but symbolically charged mise-en-scène (the close-ups of the flaming boiler, the calendar with the *Virgen de la Caridad* on the wall, and the small altar to Santa Bárbara, for example) and its measured cinematography. After the claustrophobia and humor of the action set in the basement apartment, Roberto's forays into the frigid streets of New York, replete with plowed snowbanks at every corner and mounds of garbage in front of every building, are carefully framed and filmed. Rather than represent moments of openness or freedom, the figure of Roberto in his tightly buttoned heavy coat and ear-flapped cap, surrounded by snow and oppressively gray skies, remains visually as downtrodden as when he is inside.

Figure 13.2: Roberto (Raimundo Hidalgo-Gato) and Aurelia (Zully Montero) in their basement apartment kitchen, reminiscing about Cuba as the Americanized Aurelita (Elizabeth Peña) looks on in *El Super* (1979).

Source: DVD of *El Super*
License: Fair Use

What makes *El Super* unusual is how it frames the Cuban exile experience. Most of the films produced by first-generation Cuban exile filmmakers such as Orlando Jiménez Leal (*La otra Cuba/The Other Cuba* [1983]) and Néstor Almendros (*Conducta impropia/Improper Conduct* [co-directed with Jiménez Leal, 1984]) were documentaries that mythologized prerevolutionary Cuba in order to differentiate it from the revolutionary present of the island and make sense of their exile. Although *El Super* precedes these documentaries, it explicitly avoids their self-justificatory work of denunciation. It is a film of exile, longing, and displacement. In the years spent "cleaning stairs, picking up garbage, and shoveling snow," Roberto has come to recognize that the reality of exile is far more tragic than the simple act of leaving to escape an allegedly impossible and frustrating situation and/or to make a political statement. Leaving means losing a way of life and one's moorings and passions, and the exile's life is one of loss and anxiety. No matter how hard he tries to invoke Cuba, Roberto's home is now the dreary basement, the grim reality of a blustery New York winter, and his increasingly Americanized daughter who blasts the radio even though he "can't stand English first thing in the morning." The genius of *El Super*, however, is that it presents this pathos without melodramatic grandiosity. Rather, its gently humorous rendering of Cuban exile angst operates to demystify a community that all too often had been characterized exclusively by its sociopolitical positions.

Figure 13.3: Roberto surrounded by grayness and snow in *El Super*.
Source: DVD of *El Super*
License: Fair Use

## FROM EXILES TO CUBAN AMERICANS

Almost at the same time as *El Super*, *¿Qué Pasa, USA?* (1977–1980), the first bilingual sitcom on US television, began to air on PBS stations around the country (produced by WPBT, the Miami-South Florida Public Broadcasting Service, the show had aired in Florida since 1975). *¿Qué Pasa, USA?* shifted registers: rather than exiles, we are presented with a truly Cuban American family. The show explores the challenges faced by the three generations of the Cuban American Peña family as they deal with their new lives in the Little Havana neighborhood of Miami, in a new country and in a new language. It was originally imagined as an avenue to help Cuban American teenagers navigate their Cubanness and Americanness. The program was funded by the US Office of Education's Emergency School Assistance Act-Television Program (ESAA-TV), whose goal was to promote educational television programming to encourage positive racial attitudes in children, and their programs were designed to attract specific ethnic groups. It was in place from 1972 to 1982 (Rivero). The show had very high production values and eventually reached a much broader heterogeneous national audience (Rivero). The working-class, bilingual Peña family included the teenagers Joe (born in Cuba) and Carmen (born in Miami); their Cuban parents, Pepe and Juana; and their grandparents, Adela and Antonio. As fitting for the situation comedy genre, each episode featured order, confusion, and the restoration of order, for the most part associated with Joe and Carmen's negotiations between their Cuban and American identities, Pepe and Juana's efforts to balance their home environment between Cubanness and US educational values, and Adela and Antonio's inability to find a space in their new foreign and English-based environment. In its five-year run, the show broached a variety of significant themes that included but also exceeded the concerns of the Cuban American experience, such as racial and ethnic prejudices, homophobia and feminism, and the then-new equal opportunity programs.

Figure 13.4: Opening credits for ¿Qué Pasa USA? (1977–1980).
Source: PBS Streaming of ¿Qué Pasa USA?
License: Fair Use

Not unlike *El Super*, *¿Qué Pasa, USA?* also challenged the discourse of the exile community as upper-middle class, strongly politicized, and Cuba-centric. The Peñas are resolutely working class, uninterested in Cuban politics, and doing their best to gracefully assimilate into the US mainstream. The show also demystified the dream of a return to Cuba (i.e., the overthrow of the Castro government): in the universe of *¿Qué Pasa, USA?*, Cuba is only the remembered nostalgic homeland (especially invoked by the grandparents), but the United States is the present and the Peñas' new home. However, unlike *El Super*, which featured all Spanish dialogues and was subtitled for its release, *¿Qué Pasa, USA?* was completely bilingual (approx. 60% English–40% Spanish) and without subtitles, which led to some interesting audience reactions. English monolingual audiences could understand the narrative and main points but would miss the jokes (often delivered in Spanish by the grandparents) that triggered the laughter of the bilingual live in-studio audience. *¿Qué Pasa, USA?* was an early and successful example of diasporic mass media that addressed the objective of transforming Cuban exiles into US immigrants. And it was the media representation of what has come to be called the 1.5 generation, in between Cubanness and Americanness, as theorized by Gustavo Pérez Firmat in his books *The Cuban Condition* and *Life on the Hyphen*.

## MARIEL AND BEYOND

The two significant exoduses of the 1980s and 1990s—the Mariel Boatlift of 1980 and the balsero crisis of 1994—changed the face of Cuban exiles and Americans in the media through the 1990s. Mainstream media constantly circulated images and videos of desperate immigrants hanging off the sides of extraordinarily overcrowded vessels as they made their way across the Florida Straits, followed by another barrage of audio-visual material about the "tent cities" and relocation centers that were created in Miami and, later, elsewhere (Arkansas, Pennsylvania, Wisconsin, and Puerto Rico) to accommodate the refugees for processing. The latter were reserved primarily for "hard to sponsor" refugees who had criminal records and/or mental health issues. After some well-documented riots in the tent cities and relocation centers, the perception and popular belief was that the Marielitos were spreading crime and moral turpitude (many were openly homosexual and fleeing anti-LGBTQ policies in Cuba), especially throughout South Florida. The Mariel migration, highly stigmatized and vilified, challenged the image of Cuban American success in the US national imaginary.

Brian De Palma's *Scarface* (1983), a remake of Howard Hawks's gangster classic of 1932, picked up on this popular perception and substituted Marielitos for the Italian gangsters of the original. Starring Al Pacino as the penniless Marielito Tony Montana, who eventually becomes a powerful drug lord in Miami, the film was initially criticized for its explicit violence and drug usage, but has gone on to become a cult classic and has been considered among the best gangster movies ever made. Nevertheless, its depiction of Marielitos contributed to a national moral panic about these Cuban immigrants, irrespective of social and demographic status.

By 1995, the tone had shifted to comedy. In Mira Nair's *The Perez Family* (1995), a male and female who happen to share the common last name Pérez are assumed to be a family unit by an immigration official upon their arrival at Mariel. Juan Raúl Pérez is a former aristocrat who was thrown into jail for burning his cane fields rather than handing them over to the government. Fresh from prison, all he wants is to reunite with his wife Carmela, who has been in Miami for the past twenty years. Two decades younger than Juan, Dottie Pérez is a farm worker and occasional prostitute who dreams of rock and roll and wants to sleep with John Wayne. When she discovers that it is easier to find American sponsors as a family than as singles, she convinces Juan to go along with the farce since he is so eager to reunite with Carmela. Ultimately, the film is much more about the vagaries (and humor) of immigration than it is about the Cuban American experience per se, undoubtedly also a result of the casting of non-Cubans/non-Latinos in all the principal roles.

## SELF-REPRESENTATIONS

In the 1980s and through the 1990s, we also begin to see Cuban Americans engaging more pointedly with media to represent their own experiences, particularly in the realms of experimental cinema and performance art (López). Miñuca Villaverde, for example, developed a small but significant body of experimental films that were at once formally innovative, in dialogue with the filmic avant-garde, and very much inflected by her Cubanness and migration. Villaverde had already been involved in filmmaking in Cuba (alongside her husband Fernando Villaverde, who briefly worked for the Cuban Film Institute (*Instituto Cubano del Arte e Industrias Cinematográficas* [ICAIC]) but became involved with the New York avant-garde scene in the 1970s. Beyond her experimental short films of the 1970s, Villaverde also produced one of the most incisive and formally interesting documentaries about the Mariel exodus: *La ciudad de las carpas* (*Tent City* [1980]). Filmed with an old 16mm hand-cranked Bolex camera and with sound captured with a nonsynchronous Nagra recorder, Villaverde's film is the fruit of her immersion in the world of a tent city under the I-95 interstate in the heart of Miami that had been quickly erected for the refugees waiting to be processed. Because of her technical limitations, there is no synchronous sound in the film, but the juxtaposition of still images and recorded testimonies and songs are staggering in their simplicity and affectivity. The dislocation of sounds and images affords the characters and their daily lives a sense of privacy and dignity that is very unusual in the realm of documentaries about a poor, marginalized, and at-risk community.

Also in an avant-garde tradition, the work of Alina Troyano as the lesbian spitfire Carmelita Tropicana spans performance art, theater, and film. With her sister Ela Troyano directing, her *Carmelita Tropicana: Your Kunst is Your Waffen* (1994) introduced Tropicana as a Lower East Side, New York political activist by day and nightclub performer by night, who straddles Latinidades. Although Tropicana is very Cuban, she is also very Latinx, and the film tackles stereotypes across the ethnic paradigm and genres like the musical and the telenovela with brilliant ease. But her work does point to an interesting phenomenon: the gradual blending of Cuban Americanness with other Latinx ethnicities.

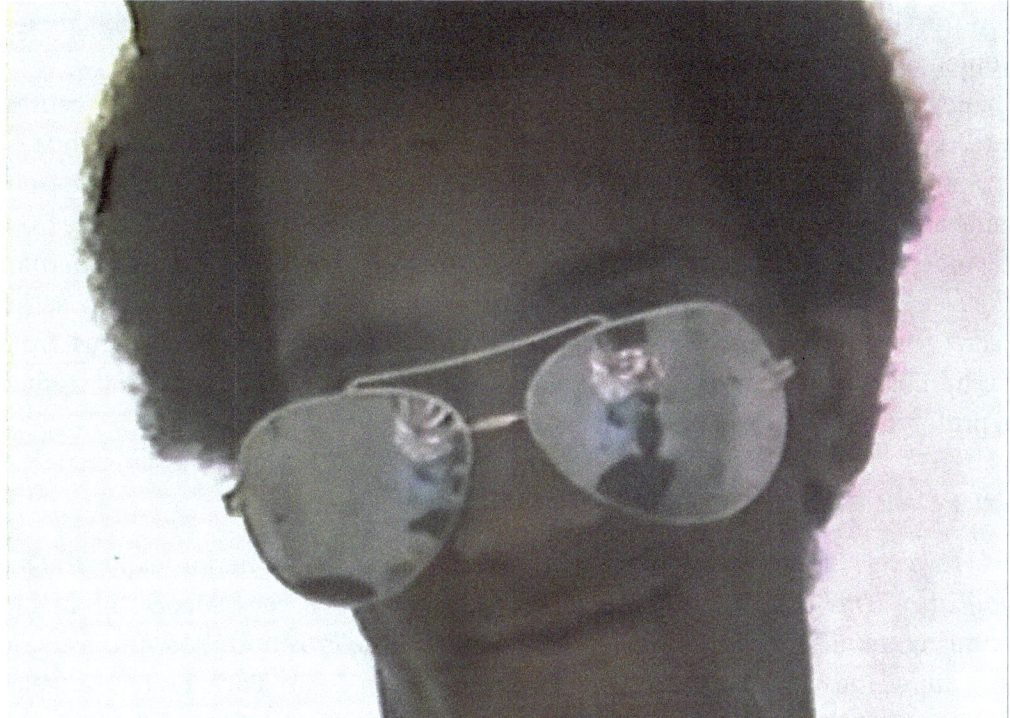

Figure 13.5: One of the witnesses in Miñuca Villaverde's *Tent City* (1980).
Source: DVD of *Tent City*
License: Fair Use

## THE TWENTY-FIRST CENTURY: NOSTALGIA, MUSIC, RETURNS AND ASSIMILATIONS

Wim Wenders's documentary *Buena Vista Social Club* (1999) ushered in a nostalgia that became the norm for the representation of Cuba and Cubans and a defining characteristic of Cuban Americanness in the twenty-first century. First there was the 1997 album produced by Ry Cooder featuring a group of veteran Afro-Cuban musicians devoted to preserving the music of pre-Revolutionary Cuba (*boleros*, *danzones*, and *sones*), which became an international bestseller. Wim Wenders's film ostensibly "documents" (after the fact) how Ry Cooder, his longtime friend, organized the musicians and arranged for their trip abroad and the recording of the album and the group's two subsequent shows in Amsterdam and New York's Carnegie City Hall. There were a lot of misconceptions involved in the framing of the *Buena Vista* narrative for international consumption. In fact, these musicians were far from forgotten (several were simply retired; others, like Omara Portuondo, had never stopped performing) and these popular rhythms had never stopped being played and happily consumed by Cuban audiences. Through Wenders's exquisite cinematography, however, the image of a city in ruins yet peopled by extraordinarily attractive and talented older citizens became the leitmotif of US representations of Cuba ever since. The metaphor of a country frozen in time and the extraordinary beauty of Havana's ruins have taken over how the United States thinks of Cuba today: just think old cars, sexy dark-skinned women, beaches, and ruined structures.

Beyond the centrality of ruins, music and nostalgia continue to be central threads for how media portrays Cubans and Cuban Americans. The ethos to recapture what must surely have been a glorious past and to wallow in its present ruin has been a constant in many US media representations of Cuba that range from the independent—for example, *Habana: El arte nuevo de hacer ruinas* (*Havana: The New Art of Making Ruins* [2006])—to the mainstream, like the Netflix series *Celia* (2015–2016), which chronicles the life of the talented singer Celia Cruz, from her humble beginnings in Cuba to super stardom in the United States, all framed in prototypical melodramatic biopic style.

## *One Day at a Time* (2017–2020)

However, the representation of Cuban Americans took a major leap with *One Day at a Time* (*ODAAT*). A remake of Norman Lear's very successful sitcom featuring an all-White cast that aired on CBS in the '70s and '80s, this version is centered on a Cuban American family living in Echo Park in Los Angeles and negotiating contemporary social and political issues—sexuality, consent, queerness, racism, mental health, and the struggles of veterans. With oversight from Lear himself, executive producers Gloria Calderón Kellett (herself Cuban American) and Mike Royce put together a stellar cast that included Rita Moreno (*West Side Story*) as Lydia, a sassy grandmother; Justina Machado as Penelope, a newly divorced former military nurse and mother; Isabella Gomez as Elena, the teenage daughter; and Marcel Ruiz as Alex, the tween son. The role of Schneider, their friend and landlord, is a carryover from the original show and played by Todd Grinnell. Like the original, the show was shot with multiple cameras in front of a live audience, which enhances its nostalgic feel, yet *ODAAT* is resolutely a twenty-first century media artifact, with story lines that continue throughout the seasons to shape the serial as a coherent narrative. Thus, for example, the first season follows the preparations for Elena's *quinceañera*, during which she must contend with her own desires and sexuality and her mother and grandmother's cultural expectations. Furthermore, although the *ODAAT* is bilingual, it is subtitled/dubbed as is typical of Netflix shows, thus eliminating the zones of incomprehension of a program like *¿Qué Pasa, USA?*. Finally, the show's initial production and distribution by Netflix—which relies on building its subscriber base, rather than selling advertising as is typical of network television—enabled the producers and writers to take unusual steps for their representation of the Latinx family. Although this is a Latinx family and there is a certain reliance on typical Latinx media stereotypes, it is very much a Cuban American one with an unusual level of cultural and historical specificity that producer Calderón Kellett hoped would "resonate" with Latinx and other audiences in general (Del Río and Moran 8).

One of the most striking aspects of *ODAAT* is its focus on sexuality in season 1. Latinx women have historically always been represented as overly sexualized, often pitting the hypersexual young woman against an asexual maternal figure, but *ODAAT* develops a complex multi-generational array of sexualities that shatters that narrative device. All the three principal female characters are in a process of transition: Grandmother Lydia is recently widowed, Penelope is recently divorced, and Elena is discovering her sexuality. However, each of the three characters sits ambiguously on the stereotype: Lydia, a former entertainer in Cuba, is very sexualized, but as the grandmother her sexuality is normalized through her memories of her deceased husband and serves as a moral signpost for her family; Penelope is "sexy" but reluctant to date and struggling as a single mother; finally, Elena is an active feminist engaged in an exploration of her sexuality and sexual identity that leads her to come out as queer in season 1. Thus, the show spreads out the complexities of sexual identity among the characters and establishes multiple points of identification.

The show's treatment of immigration is similarly complex and polyvocal. Lydia's immigration to the United States from Cuba frames the family's identity and points to the challenges of sustaining Cuban Americanness across generations. But it also allows the show to speak to immigration more generally as it stages multiple immigration stories (that of Elena's friend Carmen, a Mexican immigrant, and that of Schneider, a Canadian, for example) and highlights the inconsistencies of US immigration policy (see season 1, episode 5).

Figure 13.6: Penelope (Justina Machado) learns from her daughter Elena (Isabella Gomez) that her friend Carmen's parents have been deported and Carmen has no place to go in *One Day at a Time* (2017–2020).

Source: DVD of *One Day at a Time*
License: Fair Use

Simultaneously Latinx and Cuban American, *ODAAT* highlights a process of assimilation that is decades long and that continues to mark the Cuban American experience and its representation in the media without losing or magnifying the specificity of Cuban American experiences.

The most recent socio-political conflicts in the island, including massive popular protests on July 11, 2021 that led to extreme governmental repression, have produced a barrage of representations of Cubans in and out of the island unlike anything we had experienced since the Mariel exodus. Social media in general (Facebook, Instagram, Twitter, etc.) have been overwhelmed by posts from both sides of the Florida Straits, establishing often acrimonious political debates. It is only a matter of time before we see these new developments emerge in both documentary and fictional forms across mainstream media.

**Ana M. López** *is a Professor and Chair of the Department of Communication, Associate Provost for Faculty Affairs, and Director of the Cuban and Caribbean Studies Institute at Tulane University. Her research is focused on Latin American and Latino film and cultural studies. She is coeditor of* The Routledge Companion to Latin American Cinema *(2017) and the editor of the journal* Studies in Spanish and Latin American Cinemas. *She is also the author of* Hollywood, Nuestra América y los Latinos *(2012), coeditor of three collections on Latin American cinema, and has published more than three dozen essays and book chapters.*

## BIBLIOGRAPHY

Del Río, Esteban, and Moran, Kristin C. "Remaking Television: *One Day at a Time*'s Digital Delivery and Latina/o Cultural Specificity." *Journal of Communication Inquiry*, vol. 44, no. 1, 2020, pp. 5–25.

López, Ana M. "The 'Other' Island: Exiled Cuban Cinema." *Jump Cut,* no. 38, 1993, pp. 7–15, http://www.ejumpcut.org/archive/onlinessays/JC38folder/ExileCubanCinema.html

Pérez Firmat, Gustavo. *The Cuban Condition*. Cambridge UP, 1989.

---. *Life on the Hyphen: The Cuban-American Way*. U of Texas P, 1994.

"The Spanish-American War in Motion Pictures." *Library of Congress,* https://www.loc.gov/collections/spanish-american-war-in-motion-pictures/about-this-collection/

Rivero, Yeidy. "Interpreting Cubanness, Americanness, and the Sitcom: WPBT-PBS's *¿Que Pasa USA?* (1975-1980)." *Global Television Formats: Understanding Television Across Borders*, edited by Tasha Oren and Sharon Shahaf, Routledge, 2012, pp. 90–108.

## FILMOGRAPHY

*Buena Vista Social Club*, directed by Wim Wenders, Road Movies Filmproduktion, 1999.

*Carmelita Tropicana: Your Kunst Is Your Waffen*. Directed by Ela Troyano, performances by Alina Troyano, Sophia Ramos, Livia Daza-Paris, Annie Lobst, First Run Features, 1994.

*La ciudad de las carpas* (*Tent City*). Directed by Miñuca Villaverde, 1980.

*Conducta impropia* (*Improper Conduct*). Directed by Néstor Almendros and Orlando Jiménez Leal, Antenne 2 and Films du Losange, 1984.

*Havana – Arte nuevo de hacer ruinas* (*The New Art of Making Ruins*). Directed by Florian Borchmeyer, Raros Media, 2006.

*Havana Widows*. Directed by Ray Enright, performances by Joan Blondell, Glenda Farrell, Guy Kibbee, First National Pictures, 1933.

*Holiday in Havana*. Directed by Jean Yarbrough, performances by Desi Arnaz, Mary Hatcher, Ann Doran, Columbia Pictures, 1949.

*I Love Lucy*. Created by Lucille Ball and Desi Arnaz, CBS, 1951–1957.

Lear, Norman, Gloria Calderón Kellet, and Mike Royce, creators. *One Day at a Time*. Netflix and Pop, 2017–2020.

Mendoza, Manny and Luis Santeiro, creators. *¿Qué Pasa, USA?* PBS, 1977–1980.

*El otro Cuba* (*The Other Cuba*). Directed by Orlando Jiménez Leal, Radiotelevisione Italiana, 1984.

*The Perez Family*. Directed by Mira Nair, performances by Marisa Tomei, Alfred Molina, Anjelica Huston, Samuel Goldwyn, 1995.

*Scarface*. Directed by Brian De Palma, performances by Al Pacino, Steven Bauer, Michelle Pfeiffer, Universal Pictures, 1983.

*El Super*. Directed by Leon Ichaso and Orlando Jiménez Leal, performances by Raymundo Hidalgo-Gato, Zully Montero, and Elizabeth Peña, 1979.

*Weekend in Havana*. Directed by Walter Lang, performances by Alice Faye, Carmen Miranda, John Payne, Twentieth-Century Fox, 1941.

## FOR FURTHER STUDY

*Azúcar amarga* (*Bitter Sugar*). Directed by Leon Ichaso, performances by René Laván, Mayte Vilán, Pelayo García, Azúcar Films, 1996.

*Crossover Dreams*. Directed by Leon Ichaso, performances by Rubén Blades and Elizabeth Peña, Max Mambru Films, 1985.

Eckstein, Susan Eva. *Cuban Privilege: The Making of Immigrant Inequality in America*. Cambridge UP, 2022.

Fojas, Camilla. *Islands of Empire: Pop Culture and US Power*. U of Texas P, 2014.

Rubio, Raúl. "Framing the Cuban Diaspora: Representation and Dialogue in Recent Filmic Productions." *Cuba: Idea of a Nation Displaced*, edited by Andrea O'Reilly Herrera, SUNY P, 2007, pp. 314–27.

Zarza, Zaira. "From Exilic to Diasporic: New Cuban Cinemas in the United States." In *The Cinema of Cuba: Contemporary Film and the Legacy of Revolution*, edited by Guy Baron, Ann Marie Stock, and Antonio Álvarez Pitaluga. I.B. Tauris, 2017, pp. 287-308.

# 14 The Dominican American Experience Onscreen

Sharina Maillo-Pozo
(University of Georgia)

The development of Dominican film in the United States is intricately tied to the mass migration of Dominicans in the late 1960s and throughout the 1970s and 1980s as a result of the political climate in the island-nation. The culmination of the thirty-one-year dictatorship of Rafael Leónidas Trujillo (1930–1961) opened up the possibility of democracy and freedom for Dominicans to the extent that democratic elections were held in 1962. Juan Bosch, a social-democrat leader and strong opponent of Trujillo's autocratic regime who had spent most of the dictatorship in exile, won the election. This significant political shift in Dominican politics was short-lived, and after the overthrow of Bosch in 1963—only seven months into his term as president—the prospect of political stability and transition to democracy was compromised. Political chaos and social unrest ensued over the course of the next few years. Among the many insurrections, perhaps the most significant was that of April 24, 1965, when civilian men and women, supported by a liberal wing of the armed forces, took to the streets to demand the legal and constitutional reinstitution of Juan Bosch to power. Four days later, President Lyndon B. Johnson sent US troops to the Dominican nation, which culminated in the second US invasion of the island-nation (the first invasion took place from 1916–1924). This interference in domestic politics resulted in one of the most renowned ideologues of the Trujillo regime, Joaquín Balaguer, becoming president for twelve years (1966–1978). As noted by Ramona Hernández and Silvio Torres-Saillant in *The Dominican Americans*, Balaguer's economic policies, the violent persecution of revolutionaries and political dissidents, and the promulgation in the United States of the **1965 Immigration Act**, which allowed authorized immigrants to sponsor close family members for visas to come to the United States, were key factors that "propel[led] a massive, growing, and continuous exodus of Dominicans from their native land" (30–31). As such, the emigration of Dominicans to the United States post-1965 also reveals the role of US politics in shaping migratory movements from Latin America and the Caribbean.

The invisibility of Dominicans' contributions to US cultural expression does not correspond with the abovementioned historical relationship between these two countries. In addition, it does not correspond with the dynamic, prolific, and active cultural production of "the fifth-largest population of Hispanic origin living in the United States, accounting for 4% of the US Hispanic population in 2017" (Bustamante et al.). We can trace cultural activity by Dominicans as early as the beginning of the twentieth century in fields such as music, literature, and film. In the area of film, although there was not actual Dominican cinematic production in the United States by and about Dominicans/Dominican Americans prior to the late eighties, the popularity of María Montez, commonly known as The Queen of Technicolor, is indicative of Dominican presence in US cultural consciousness even before the great exodus of the 1970s.

Over the last four decades, there has been a slow yet meaningful increase in filmmaking that captures diverse Dominican narratives of migration to the United States, spanning the experiences of under/undocumented migrants to the challenges of growing up Dominican in the United States and the quotidian struggles and challenges in pursuing the American Dream of multiple generations in the Dominican enclave of Washington Heights. Thus, film is a key artform for countering the invisibility of Dominicans in the US collective consciousness and a pivotal means of creating fluid portraits of this ethnic community.

## MIGRATION TO THE UNITED STATES (1980S–1990S)

In the 1980s and 1990s, two films by Dominican-based directors Agliberto Meléndez and Ángel Muñiz focused on the tribulations of Dominican men who, in search of a better life, leave the island, or try to, in order to migrate to the United States. These audiovisual stories capture the economic pressures that affect underprivileged sectors of Dominican society and the extreme measures taken to seek better opportunities abroad. Both directors develop narratives that capture the experiences of Dominican men who flee the Dominican Republic illegally by ship and plane. These cinematic depictions of migration serve as critiques of flawed economical structures that increased poverty in the Dominican Republic. Further, they examine the fluid borders between the island-nation and the United States.

*Un pasaje de ida* (*One Way Ticket* [1988]), directed by Agliberto Meléndez, is the first feature film that captures the experience of Dominican migration to the United States. The objective of this cinematic piece could be seen as twofold. On one hand, it denounces the structural corruption behind the enterprise of underground illegal trips. On the other hand, it highlights the struggles of Dominican migrants who are desperate to leave the island for economic reasons. The film is based on true events that took place in 1980 twenty-two out of thirty-four Dominican men lost their lives suffocating while stowed away in the containers of the cargo ship, Regina Express. In this sense, *One Way Ticket* can be situated within the paradigm of **Third World cinema** since it offers a realistic depiction of a social event that impacted the Dominican nation and its diaspora in the United States (Lora 58).

While *One Way Ticket* depicts the failed and tragic journey of thirty-four Dominican men to the United States, **Nueba Yol** (Dominican slang for "New York," 1995), focuses on the journey, arrival, and failed process of adaptation of Balbuena (Luisito Martí), a Dominican migrant who, with the help of his Puerto Rican friend, Fellito (Raúl Carbonell), manages to obtain a tourist visa to enter the United States. In his debut film as director, Ángel Muñiz offers a social critique of the dire economic reasons that motivate Dominican emigration to the United States through the comedy film. In it, there is an attempt to demystify the American Dream through the experiences of Balbuena even before his arrival to New York City. In the opening scene, while Balbuena is reflecting upon the socio-economic circumstances of life in the Dominican Republic on the grave of his late wife, Natalia, he sees his friend Fellito, who assisted with the funeral for a Dominican who died in New York City under questionable circumstances that seem to indicate he was involved in drug dealing. A few days later, Fellito shows up in Balbuena's house and tells him that he could get him a legal visa if he pays him five thousand dollars, which Balbuena ends up doing to pursue the dream of a better life. Prior to encountering his family at JFK airport in Queens, New York, he and his friend Fellito bump into "El Flaco," a Dominican man who has achieved success and prosperity in America through illicit means.

Figure 14.1: Fellito (Raúl Carbonell), tries to convince Balbuena (Luisito Martí), to pursue a visa to travel to New York in *Nueba Yol* (1995).

Source: DVD of *Nueba Yol*
License: Fair Use

The film presents an ambivalent perspective on Dominican transnational subjects. The image of Balbuena, a hardworking, naive, and kind migrant who is very much attached to his cultural roots (García-Crespo 160), is juxtaposed with Americanized Dominican migrants who either lack family and moral values or who would resort to any means to attain the American Dream. Said juxtaposition becomes quite evident immediately upon Balbuena's arrival to New York City. While staying in the living room of his cousins' two-bedroom apartment in the Dominican enclave of Washington Heights where there are already six tenants, he encounters decaying family values in a household where the three children do not respect their elders, prefer American food, and mock his Dominican ways. In the streets of New York City, his experiences are similar: he struggles to find a job, and his dreams of prosperity begin to fade shortly after his arrival to Manhattan. Nonetheless, he never engages in the illicit drug trade, which his fellow Dominicans pursue as a means to economic success. In the end, Balbuena returns home after being shot in New York City. With the return to the Dominican Republic, on the surface, *Nueba Yol* "debunks the notion of the American dream and suggests that Dominicans would be better served by struggling for a better life at home" (Goldman 183). As such, the film still holds a romanticized view of the homeland in spite of the economic difficulties Dominican subjects may face there.

## COMING OF AGE DOMINICAN IN THE UNITED STATES (2000S)

Whereas Dominican/Dominican American cinema of the 1990s focused more on the experience of first-generation migrants and their journeys and processes of adaptation to life in the United States, in the 2000s there is an increase of coming-of-age audiovisual narratives of the first US-born generation of Dominicans in the New York City area, created by directors of non-Dominican ethnic backgrounds. Four films depict the diverse experiences of young Dominicans growing up in various neighborhoods of NYC: *My American Girls: A Dominican Story* (2001), directed by Aaron Matthews; *Washington Heights* (2002), directed by Alfredo Rodríguez de Villa; *Raising Víctor Vargas* (2002), directed by Peter Sollett; and *Mad Hot Ballroom* (2005), directed by Marilyn Agrelo. The two fiction films, *Washington Heights* and *Raising Victor Vargas*, take place in Washington Heights in upper Manhattan and the East Village, respectively. Both offer insight into the struggles, challenges, and quotidian lives of the first US-born generation of Dominicans as they are caught between their aspirations and those of their immigrant families. In *Washington Heights*, Carlos Ramírez, a comic book illustrator who works in the East Village, is caught between family responsibility and the pursuit of his dream to leave the *barrio* and become a successful comic book artist. Throughout the film, he discovers that these two aspects of his life do not have to be at odds, and that in order to be successful, he must infuse the soul of his neighborhood into his artistic creations. On the other hand, *Raising Victor Vargas* offers an intimate depiction of Latinx families from the Spanish-speaking Caribbean—Dominicans and Puerto Ricans. The film's portrayal of Victor Vargas as he navigates his journey from adolescence through adulthood in the streets of the East Village is a meditation on the impact of family and social factors in shaping gender roles.

In the same vein, the nonfiction documentary films *Mad Hot Ballroom* and *My American Girls. A Dominican Story* highlight the experiences of prepubescent girls and boys and three sisters, respectively. *Mad Hot Ballroom* documents the experiences of young girls and boys from Public School 115 in Washington Heights as they compete in the yearly ballroom dance competition sponsored by New York's public school system alongside youngsters from more financially stable school districts in the Bensonhurst neighborhood of Brooklyn and Tribeca in lower Manhattan. The documentary shows how the dance competition awakens the kids' class and gender consciousness as well as how ballroom dance becomes a way to cross borders between three communities that would have otherwise remained isolated from each other.

Moreover, the documentary *My American Girls: A Dominican Story* is a window into the lives of a Dominican family in Brooklyn and the ways in which daughters and parents negotiate their intergenerational tensions. Directed by award-winning documentary filmmaker Aaron Matthews, *My American Girls* offers an intimate portrayal of a Dominican family composed of two immigrant parents and their US-born daughters. Although some of the experiences captured by the documentary are specific to Dominicans, you will notice that many of the underlying issues depicted are relatable to Latinx communities at large and immigrant communities from other ethnic groups. Such is the case of the intergenerational clashes between immigrant parents and their children as the former are fighting to preserve their cultural roots and yearn to return to the homeland whereas the latter become more Americanized and see life in the United States as their only option. Yet the film also shows how the process of Americanization is different for each of the daughters, presenting in this way diverse experiences of Dominican Americanness within the same family unit.

Throughout the film, it is evident that hard work is equated to different kinds of success. In the case of Sandra Ortiz and Juan Bautista Ortiz, mother and father of Mónica (twenty-one), Aida (sixteen), and Mayra (thirteen), success means to provide a better life for their daughters, help their families back home, and build a house where they will retire in their rural homeland. Although the price of accomplishing these goals is spending their days working two jobs away from their children most of the time, they are willing to pay it in pursuit of better opportunities. In one of the scenes, Sandra says that she can't wait to go to her country, but she can't do so until she saves more money to finish building their house back home and until the last two of her three children graduate from high school.

Figure 14.2: Mónica prepares to attend her undergraduate graduation at Columbia University in *My American Girls: A Dominican Story* (2001).
Source: DVD of *My American Girls: A Dominican Story*
License: Fair Use

For the eldest of the daughters, Mónica, success means doing the best with the opportunities her parents have provided to her. On her shoulders rest the fact that she is the first one in the family to graduate from college. While the other two sisters remain in the three-story house they share with extended family in the Sunset Park neighborhood of Brooklyn, upon her graduation from Columbia University, Mónica moves to the Upper East Side and continues to uproot herself geographically and emotionally from her family and their traditions to become, in the words of her mother, "a real American girl." Aida, the middle sister, seeks success by slowly breaking away from family expectations by pursuing a job at McDonald's while she is still a junior in high school and by informing her mother that she is not going back with her to the Dominican Republic to go to college. Although both Mónica and Aida yearn to remove themselves from family traditions and expectations, respectively, in the film they both express how proud and grateful they feel toward their mother for all the sacrifices she made on their behalf. In this sense, the film goes beyond merely presenting the intergenerational shift of values to also show the appreciation of the first US-born generation of Dominican children for their immigrant parents. This is even more evident in the case of the youngest sister, Mayra, the most defiant of the sisters, who does worst in school and often rebels against her mother. During the trip to the family's rural homeland, she expresses how much she appreciates the communal values of the family and friends in the town. Although it is clear that she wants to stay in the United States, toward the end of the film she exclaims, "I always miss this place when I leave," referring to the rural homeland of her parents. In other words, she longs for the birthplace of her mother, creating in this way an emotional connection to the land, the people, and the memories that keep her mother's hope of return alive.

Noteworthy is the fact that *My American Girls: A Dominican Story* begins and ends with two celebrations: a wedding and a baby shower. Both events celebrate family in their particular ways. The documentary is just that: a celebration of life, unity, and love in spite of the many contradictions of immigrant life depicted in the film.

## WOMEN FILMMAKERS OF THE DOMINICAN DIASPORA IN NEW YORK CITY (2010S)

Until the second decade of the 2000s, Dominican American cinema was mostly dominated by male filmmakers, with a few exceptions, such as *Mad Hot Ballroom*, the documentary film directed by Cuban American filmmaker Marilyn Agrelo, mentioned in the previous section. The latter half of the 2010s saw an increase in films directed by Dominican American women based in New York City—a significant change from previous decades. Such is the case with the short documentaries *Mami y Yo y mi Gallito* (*Mom and Me and My Little Rooster* [2015]), directed by Arisleyda Dilone; *Buhoneros* (*Street Vendors* [2016]) and *Layers of a Baker* (2019), directed by Carla Franchesca; and the feature film *De lo mío* (meaning "my thing" or "of my people," 2019), directed by Diana Peralta. These young women directors gear their attention to matters related to gender and sexuality, the struggles of first-generation immigrants to survive in the United States, and the return to the island of US-born Dominican women. They narrate intimate tales of Dominican migration in a sublime yet poignant way. In *Street Vendors* and *Layers of a Baker*, Franchesca, the director and founder of Rayoelú Films, records the stories of two first-generation immigrants of Ecuadorian and Dominican descent to show the struggles of women and men trying to prosper economically in the United States. In *Street Vendors*, Franchesca takes to the streets of upper Manhattan to follow "the daily life and challenges faced by several of New York City's 20,000 street vendors, most of whom are immigrants and people of color" ("BMCC Alumna"). Similarly, in *Layers of a Baker*, she examines these aforementioned struggles and challenges through the story of a Dominican small business owner.

In her directorial debut documentary film *Mami y Yo y mi Gallito,* Dominican American, queer **intersex** filmmaker Arilseyda Dilone takes the audience on a journey through her story as an intersex person and her relationship to womanhood. (The term *intersex* refers to a condition experienced by an estimated 1-2% of the population in which an individual's genetic material and anatomy do not follow the common XX/female or XY/male patterns.) This emotionally charged, intimate sixteen-minute documentary film examines the ways in which a Dominican migrant family navigates issues of gender and sexuality. Through conversations, confrontations, and constant interrogation of the intentional silence about her intersex body in the family narrative, Dilone tries to find a path to healing intergenerational traumas caused by lack of communication and acknowledgment of her being a woman in an intersex body.

Figure 14.3: Dilone and her mother have a conversation about Dilone's gender identity and sexuality in *Mami y Yo y mi Gallito* (2015).

Source: DVD of *Mami y Yo y mi Gallito*
License: Fair Use

Whereas Franchesca and Dilone use the camera to document real-life experiences of diasporic Dominican subjectivities, Afro-**Dominicanyork** writer and director Diana Peralta creates a fictional narrative of growing up between the borderlands of New York City and the Dominican Republic in her debut feature film *De lo mío*. The film explores universal themes of longing, separation, death, loss, and family dynamics through the story of three siblings who are dealing with the demons of their pasts, the loss of their father and grandparents, and the imminent demolition of the family house and all the memories it holds in their native Santiago Province in the Dominican Republic. Throughout the runtime of the film, one can appreciate the complicated relationship of US-born Dominicans with the homeland as they are perceived both as foreigners and natives by their Dominican counterparts on the island-nation. When the two US-born sisters Rita (Sasha Merci) and Carolina (Darlene Demorizi), who lived with their father in New York until his death, arrive in the Dominican Republic to meet their brother Dante (Héctor Aníbal), who was born and raised on the island by their grandparents, their sibling welcomes them with a *Presidente* beer and exclaims, "Welcome home!" Yet in other instances, he treats them as outsiders who do not know the social norms of the island. The scene where Carolina leaves the door of the house open and burglars ransack it instantiates Dante's view of his sisters as tourists. When Dante pulls out a gun to inspect the house, Rita yells at him and questions his choice to carry a gun and naively says, "We could have called the cops." Dante responds, "First of all, you guys are tourists. You don't know how shit works over here." This fluctuating sense of acceptance and rejection of Carolina and Rita as Dominicans is further exacerbated by the constant changes in the sisters' attitudes toward a home-island that is equally packed with ancestral memories, the resentment of a brother who begrudges them for having better opportunities in the United States than he has on the island, and their constant exoticization by fellow islanders.

**Figure 14.4:** Tension between the siblings about Dante's (Héctor Aníbal) choice to carry a gun for protection in *De lo mío* (2019).
Source: DVD of *De lo mío*
License: Fair Use

The film presents a complicated yet realistic picture of what it means to be second-generation Dominicans. Although some of the dialogues where the sisters either romanticize or fetishize the island may seem reductionist, there is an intention there to dig into the open wounds of migration stories. By depicting the constant changes in attitudes toward the sisters, the island, the United States, the deceased father, and the soon-to-be demolished house, Peralta creates a nuanced and humanized Dominican American story.

## FINAL CONSIDERATIONS

Since its beginnings in the late 1980s, Dominican American cinema has taken various directions and has become a useful archive to explore the intricacies of borderland Dominican identity. The last two decades have seen a thematic shift as well as a wider array of experiences related to the Dominican/Dominican American community. Further approaches to Dominican cinema could include the sequel to *Nueba Yol* titled *Nueba Yol 3: bajo la nueva ley* (*Nueba Yol 3: Under the New Law*

[1997]), which takes a critical stance toward US immigration policies. The film *La Soga* (*The Butcher's Son* [2009]), directed by Josh Crook, looks at narratives of return as they relate to criminality, while the forthcoming documentary *Y este cuerpo también* (*This Body Too*), directed by Arisleyda Dilone, will continue to explore and challenge notions of womanhood and femininity in the director's Dominican/Dominican American family. By now you might be wondering, "What about *In the Heights*?" The recent release of *In the Heights* (2021), adapted from the musical play of the same name, directed by Jon M. Chu and written by Quiara Alegría-Hudes and Lin-Manuel Miranda, is a love letter to the Latinx community in the neighborhood of Washington Heights—mostly populated by Latinx of Dominican heritage. In spite of the incontestable criticism it received for its shortcomings in casting Afro-Latinx actors, *In the Heights* brings the dreams of a tight-knit community in the ethnic enclave of Washington Heights to Hollywood. It also makes a political statement by showing the resilience of various generations of Latinx in Uptown Manhattan amid their struggles with racism, discrimination, and the gradual gentrification of their community. Finally, by foregrounding the trope of return to the Dominican Republic through the character of Usnavi de la Vega (Anthony Ramos), *In the Heights* reflects upon the ways in which the longing for return to the Caribbean homeland informs and shapes Dominican diasporic identities in the United States.

**Sharina Maíllo-Pozo** *is Assistant Professor of Spanish and Latinx Studies in the Department of Romance Languages at the University of Georgia. Her work has appeared in* Ciberletras, Centro Journal, The Black Scholar, Chasqui: Revista de literatura latinoamericana, Small Axe, Cuadernos de literatura, Revista Estudios Sociales, *and various edited volumes on Caribbean and Dominican literature and cultural studies. She was the 2016–2017 National Supermarket Association Dominican Studies Fellow. She is currently at work on two book projects,* Beyond Borderlands: Popular Music in Contemporary Dominican/Dominican-York Literature and Performance *and (with Anne Roschelle)* Tracing the Legacy of Camila Henríquez Ureña through Translation and Beyond *(under contract with Biblioteca Nacional Pedro Henríquez Ureña Press).*

## BIBLIOGRAPHY

"BMCC Alumna and Documentary Filmmaker Carla Franchesca Robles Highlights 'Voices of the Unheard.'" *BMCC News*, 10 Mar. 2021, https://www.bmcc.cuny.edu/news/bmcc-alumna-and-documentary-filmmaker-carla-franchesca-robles-highlights-voices-of-the-unheard/.

Bustamante, Luis N., Antonio Flores, and Sono Shah. "Facts on Hispanics of Dominican Origin in the United States, 2017." *Pew Research Center*, 16 Sept. 2019, https://www.pewresearch.org/hispanic/fact-sheet/u-s-hispanics-facts-on-dominican-origin-latinos/.

García-Crespo, Naida. "Caribbean Transnational Films and National Culture, or how Puerto Rican or Dominican can you be in 'Nueba Yol'?" *CENTRO: Journal of the Center for Puerto Rican Studies*, vol. 28, no. 1, Spring 2016, pp. 146–75.

Goldman, Dara E. *Out of Bounds: Islands and the Demarcation of Identity in the Hispanic Caribbean*. Bucknell UP, 2008.

Lora, Félix M. "La corrupción institucional y la migración como parte del discurso de denuncia social en el cine de ficción dominicano." *Ciencia y sociedad*, vol. 42, no. 4, 2017, pp. 53–70.

Torres-Saillant, Silvio, and Ramona Hernández. *The Dominican Americans*. Greenwood Press, 1998.

## FILMOGRAPHY

*Buhoneros* (*Street Vendors*). Directed by Carla Franchesca, Rayoelú Films, 2016.

*De lo mío*. Directed by Diana Peralta, performances by Sasha Merci, Darlene Demorizi, and Héctor Aníbal, Rathaus Films and The Spirit Farm, 2019.

*In the Heights*. Directed by Jon M. Chu, performances by Anthony Ramos, Corey Hawkins, Leslie Grace, Melissa Barrera, Olga Merediz, and Jimmy Smits, Warner Bros, 5000 Broadway Productions, and Likely Story, 2021.

*Layers of a Baker*. Directed by Carla Franchesca, Rayoelú Films, 2019.

*Mad Hot Ballroom*. Directed by Marilyn Agrelo, Just One Productions, 2005.

*Mami y Yo y mi Gallito* (*Mom and Me and My Little Rooster*). Directed and produced by Arisleyda Dilone, 2015.

*My American Girls: A Dominican Story*. Directed by Aaron Matthews. PBS, 2001.

*Nueba Yol*. Directed by Ángel Muñiz, performances by Luisito Martí, Caridad Ravelo, Raúl Carbonell, and Rafael Villalona, Cigua Films and D'Pelicula, 1995.

*Un pasaje de ida* (*One Way Ticket*). Directed by Agliberto Meléndez, performances by Ángel Muñiz, Carlos Alfredo Fatule, Horacio Veloz, and Miguel Bucarelli, Producciones Testimonio, S.A., 1988.

*Raising Victor Vargas*. Directed by Peter Sollett, performances by Víctor Rasuk, Donna Maldonado, Kevin Rivera, Melonie Díaz, Krystal Rodríguez, and Judy Marte, Canal +, Forensic Films, and StudioCanal, 2002.

*La Soga* (*The Butcher's Son*). Directed by Josh Crook, performances by Manny Pérez, Denise Quiñones, Juan Fernández, and Paul Calderón, Antena Latina, 2009.

*Washington Heights*. Directed by Alfredo Rodríguez de Villa, performances by Tomás Milián, Manny Pérez, and Danny Hoch, Ex-Bo Productions, AsDuenDon, and Stolen Car Productions, 2002.

## FOR FURTHER STUDY

Cartelli, Philip. "Raising Victor Vargas in an Urban High School Classroom." *Radical Teacher*, vol. 84, 2009, pp. 71–72.

Dodds, Sherril. "*Mad Hot Ballroom* and the Politics of Transformation." *Decentring Dancing Texts*, edited by Janet Lansdale. Palgrave Macmillan, 2008, pp. 160–76.

Hoffnung-Garskof, Jesse. *"Nueba Yol": Migration and popular culture in Santo Domingo and New York, 1950–1992*. 2002. Princeton U, PhD dissertation, https://www.proquest.com/dissertations-theses/nueba-yol-migration-popular-culture-santo-domingo/docview/305499997/se-2?accountid=14537.

*Hookero* (*The Hookah Guy*). Directed by Carla Franchesca, Rayoelú Films, 2019.

Iturriza Mendía, Aitor, and Raisa Pimentel Mendoza. "El cine que emigra." *Arte y Políticas de Identidad*, vol. 13, 2015, pp. 197–213.

*Lorenzo*. Directed by Carla Franchesca, Rayoelú Films, 2018.

*New Dominican York*. Directed by Daniel Melguizo, Solaris Films, 2008.

*Nueba Yol 3. Bajo la nueva ley* (*New York 3: Under the New Law*). Directed by Ángel Muñiz, performances by Luisito Martí, Adalgisa Pantaleón, Raúl Carbonell, and Carlota Carretero, Cigua Films, D'Pelicula, and Kit Parker Films, 1997.

Roa Ogando, Gerardo. "Aspectos ideologizantes de las familias representadas en los largometrajes dominicanos: *Nueba Yol 1* (1995) Y *Yuniol 2* (2007)." *Ciencia y Sociedad*, vol. 43, no. 2, Apr. 2018, pp. 35–50.

*Savino*. Directed by Carla Franchesca, Rayoelú Films, 2018.

*La Soga: Salvation*. Directed by Manny Pérez, performances by Manny Pérez, Sarah Jorge León, Hada Vanessa, and Juan Fernández, Conuco Films, 2021.

*Two White Cars*. Directed and produced by Arisleyda Dilone, 2018.

Ulaby, Neda. "Raising Victor Vargas." *NPR.com,* Special Series, The DVD Room, 10 Dec. 2014, https://www.npr.org/templates/story/story.php?storyId=4212831.

*Veneno*. Directed by Tabaré Blanchard, performances by Manny Pérez, Pepe Sierra, Richard Douglas, Yamile Scheker, Frío Frío and La visual sonora, 2018

*Y este cuerpo también* (*This Body Too*). Directed by Arisleyda Dilone, produced by Ian Bell. Forthcoming.

# 15 The Central American Experience Onscreen

Jonathan Peraza Campos
(Georgia State University)

People of Mexican descent and Puerto Rican descent are the largest Latinx/Latin American groups in the United States, but following these two groups, Central Americans (also referred to as **Isthmians** in this chapter) comprise a significant portion of Latinx/Latin American communities across the country. Salvadorans and Guatemalans comprise the largest Central American populations in the United States relative to the other five countries, and they are the third and fourth largest Latin American nationality groups after Mexicans and Puerto Ricans. As many as 3,782,000 Central American migrants reside in the United States—the majority from Honduras, Guatemala, and El Salvador—a number that is increasing significantly as migration from the region escalates in response to intolerable violence, poverty, political instability, and natural disasters (Babich and Batalova). This number does not take into consideration the US-born children of Central American diasporas who comprise a large and increasing portion of Central American–descent people in the United States.

Central America is an isthmus, or land bridge, between Mexico and South America that includes the seven countries of Guatemala, Belize, El Salvador, Honduras, Nicaragua, Costa Rica, and Panama. It is a multiracial, multiethnic, and multilingual region with an approximate population of 182,036,000 across the region, according to United Nations figures ("Central America Population"). Central American countries and their peoples share many similarities as well as distinct historical, cultural, social, political, and economic circumstances that have shaped the lives and dynamics of the people who reside in the isthmus and those who migrate.

## ISTHMIANS IN MAINSTREAM AND ALTERNATIVE MEDIA

Dominant portrayals of Central Americans historically and in contemporary film and mass media demonstrate the power of representation for better and for worse. Alvarado, et al. write:

> Our migrant communities come from countries that have been made to occupy the geopolitical margins as some of the most geodisenfranchised and georacialized people within the Americas. This bottom placement within global hierarchies is reproduced at local levels, influencing representations of Central Americans as silent and invisible. Thus, economic underdevelopment is transposed onto the people, shaping stereotypes around the tropes of impoverishment and violence. (4)

Since the inception of films and television in the United States, stories and adventures, oftentimes in foreign lands with foreign people, onscreen have enamored the public. Other media, such as radio, newspapers, and, in the present-day, the Internet and social media, have continued to disseminate discourses, ideologies, and representations of Central Americans throughout the United States and the world.

**Mainstream (hegemonic) media** are the traditional and dominant form of media that are exclusively produced by professional media creators (e.g., journalists, filmmakers). They are hierarchically organized and monolithic in practice (Atton 492). Mainstream media, created by corporate media outlets, are focused on consumption by a wide audience with the intention of making a profit (Kenix 19). **Alternative media**, on the other hand, opposes the institutional and social order that mainstream media are embedded in; rather, they are invested in social change and challenging dominant structures (19–20). Usually under-resourced and beyond the commercial sphere, alternative media are produced by groups that have been historically and traditionally excluded by the mainstream media (19–20). Tropes of Central Americans in film and media from the Cold War era (1960s–1990s) to the 2010s illustrate the key historical and sociopolitical contexts around which representations of Central Americans in US films via Hollywood and in the mass media took shape. It is in these dominant portrayals in mainstream media that stereotypes of Central Americans have become deeply rooted in the American imagination. Throughout United States and Central American history, two master images and their iterations have crystalized in the film and mass media: servant or enemy.

Central Americans in US film and mass media have long been invisible and misrepresented, yet mainstream US media, as powerful and pervasive as they may be, have not entirely silenced the voices and stories of Isthmians. Through active cultural production, including films and mass media, Central Americans are responding to decades of controlling images, ideologies, and discourses that have spurred the drums of war, facilitated resource extraction and labor exploitation, and dismissed the complexity of Central Americans. Central American and Latinx filmmakers and media creators have produced humanizing Central Americans and authentic media representations that oppose damaging and distorted images of Isthmians in mainstream mass media. Alternative media produced by Central Americans and critical media creators challenge hegemonic Central American depictions in the United States and represent the diaspora in innovative film and media content. Most Hollywood and US productions fall into the category of mainstream media, though some attempts from Central and Latin American producers to tell Central American stories have complicated this binary as well. Alternative media is often produced by Central American creators themselves with varying budgets and resource availability, but the reconstruction of Central America and Central Americans in the media form is a significant disruption to dominant media portrayals. Through alternative media production, the bridge between continents and its peoples have refused to allow themselves to be trapped behind the lens of the imperialist, colonial White gaze; they have always pointed their cameras back.

## THE LATINA DOMESTIC IN AMERICAN CINEMA

Central American and Caribbean laborers of working-class, Afro-descendant, and Indigenous backgrounds comprised the primary working force in the inhospitable conditions of multinational corporate production and government projects since the nineteenth century and into the present. In the 1800s, US businessmen like William Walker, among others, aimed to conquer Central American land to expand slavery. With private paramilitary support, Walker and other filibusters of the era waged the Filibuster War that conquered Nicaragua in 1856 with eyes set on the neighboring countries. Walker became interim president of Nicaragua in 1856 until Central American militaries and the British resisted efforts for Walker's further expansion (Martelle; Zemler). The US multinational corporation the United Fruit Company (UFCO; now known as Chiquita) held land in Central and South America for banana plantation beginning in the 1900s (González). The construction of the Panama Canal directed by the US government between 1904 and 1914 also utilized Central American, Caribbean, and working-class US laborers. These historical precedents in the region laid the foundation for an ongoing relationship between the United States and Central America as boss and worker, master and servant (González; Martelle). The Latina domestic that has been present in US film is a continuation of this relationship of exploitation and servitude between the United States and Central America.

The domestic/maid trope is often associated with African American women (the "mammy") and Mexican working-class women. However, Central American, specifically Salvadoran domestic workers, were also caricatured with that trope in the US cinematic universe. In the 1995 film *Clueless*, wealthy, White socialite Cher (Alicia Silverstone) talks with her maid, Lucy (Aida Linares), about her inability to communicate with her gardener Jose because Cher does not "speak Mexican." Lucy responds angrily and with a heavy accent, "I not a Mexican," before storming off. Confused by Lucy's reaction, Cher's ex-step brother, Josh (Paul Rudd), corrects her: "Lucy is from El Salvador." Explicitly referencing the Central American nationality of the maid character in film and media matters insofar as to understand the "different baggage" (Arias 170) carried by Central Americans as a result of specific transnational connections and histories between the United States and the isthmus, according to Yajaira Padilla (43). Still, the sassy Salvadoran maid characters featured in *Clueless* and in the 1998 sitcom *Will & Grace* often refused to play a subordinate role, making the lead characters the butt of jokes while asserting their own selfhood as Salvadorans with richer personalities, particularly through Rosario Salazar's portrayal in *Will & Grace*.

Figure 15.1: Salvadoran maid Lucy (Aida Linares) responds angrily to the assumption of the main character Cher (Alicia Silverstone) that she is Mexican in *Clueless* (1995).

Source: DVD of *Clueless*
License: Fair Use

Salvadoran women arrived in Washington DC as early as the 1960s to work as domestic servants for US diplomats and their families (Repak 2). The gendered labor of domestic servants from Guatemala, El Salvador, and Nicaragua began before the civil wars in the region, but as more Central American women began to integrate into the gendered labor force as caretakers, nannies, and maids, this trope became further crystalized in the American imagination (44). US foreign policy brokered by the Washington DC bosses of many domestic servants influenced their migration and integration into the domestic labor force (Repak 2). The gendered and racialized representation of Latina/Central American women as domestic servants for a White upper class is a manifestation of imperialist interventions that created austerity in Latin America, resulting in the flow of prospective laborers from "backyard" colony to empire.

## REVOLUTIONS & RESTITUTION

After decades of direct intervention in the Global South during President Theodore Roosevelt's presidency (González 28), the United States changed its strategy from military invasion to covert operations that installed US allies in power (78). During the Cold War era between the Soviet Union (USSR; now Russia) and the United States from the mid to the late 1900s, the United States emphasized its moral and political authority over the Soviet Union and the specter of communism. Central America became a battleground for the Cold War and the United States' anti-communist crusade as Cuba and the Soviet Union established ties with leftist and anti-fascist groups in the region. A pivotal Cold War tactic by the United States that framed the future of US foreign policy in the region was the CIA-backed ousting of President Jacobo Árbenz in Guatemala in 1954. Árbenz aimed to implement land reforms that jeopardized the power and profits of prominent landholding elites, which alarmed the US government and UFCO. Accused of being a communist during the mid-twentieth century, the United States deployed its resources in collaboration with far-right co-conspirators to remove Árbenz from power, making him the first Latin American president to be ousted by US intervention. The broader context of US intervention in Central America and the ensuing migration of Central Americans from El Salvador, Guatemala, and Nicaragua is detailed in the film *Harvest of Empire* (2012), based on the book of the same name by Juan González and explored in the PBS documentary series *Latino Americans* (2013). The documentary series *The Houses are Full of Smoke* (1987) takes a closer look at each of the countries in conflict as well.

The longest civil war in Central America took place between 1960 and 1996 in Guatemala, with insurgency led largely by peasant and Indigenous groups. Then, between 1970 to 1990, Nicaragua was entrenched in its civil war between the authoritarian Somoza family and Sandinista rebels. In 1979, political-organizers-turned-guerilla-soldiers in El Salvador took up arms against the military dictatorship until the war's end in 1992 Grandin 88; Gonzalez 76). As satellite battlegrounds of the Cold War, the United States and Soviet Union pumped funding, training, and resources to the respective sides that they backed throughout these countries' conflicts. Beyond material support, the ideological work of the United States in particular entailed the production of films and media that boosted anti-communist propaganda in covert and overt ways. Film and TV media as well as news media facilitated Red Scare rhetoric that effectively convinced US citizens, particularly the White, middle- and upper-class populace, who their enemies were and who the US government must rescue from tyranny and bring to democracy (Herman & Chomsky). Despite Red Scare pressures, however, some filmmakers presented a critical stance on US intervention and war-mongering in the Global South (Landon).

## Films of the Salvadoran Civil War

The most canonical films about the Salvadoran civil war often did not feature Salvadoran actors and typically were not produced by Salvadorans themselves but by American and Mexican producers, but they provide necessary context to the era's circumstances. The 1989 film *Romero* portrays the tensions and the circumstances that eventually led to Salvadoran priest Óscar Romero's assassination during Catholic mass in 1980 after he organized peaceful protests against the government and spoke out against the military junta who ran the government. Often considered the spark that started the war, Priest Romero's life demonstrates how religious leaders were either complicit with the military dictatorship or resistant to it as Romero was, which ended with the killing of opponents of the regime. The Salvadoran film *Sobreviviendo Guazapa* (*Surviving Guazapa*) is a 2008 film produced in El Salvador about a military soldier and a guerilla rebel who band together to survive bombings and attacks with the goal of getting a young girl, who is stranded on the same mountain as them, to safety. Many Salvadorans did not know the war's motives and goals, or at the very least the intricacies of power that puppeteered the war, yet they were all victims to rampant militarized violence, especially as nearly 85% of acts of violence were committed by state agents (Commission). *Sobreviviendo Guazapa* is a Salvadoran depiction of the war time that is enriched further by documentary narratives like *Maria's Story: A Documentary Portrait of Love and Survival in El Salvador's Civil War* (1990). *Maria's Story* takes a close look at the life and efforts of guerilla soldier Maria Serrano to organize peasant communities during the war in her crusade as a Farabundo Martí Liberation Front (FMLN) combatant and educator to the guerilla rebels' children. This documentary demonstrates the critical role of women in the guerilla movement in El Salvador that is often relegated to the margins, and similarly, the documentary *¡Las Sandinistas!* (2018) focuses on the role of women combatants in the Sandinistas rebel group during the Nicaraguan civil war in taking down the US-backed Somoza regime and in present-day politics against misogyny and corruption in Nicaragua.

The renowned film *Voces inocentes* (*Innocent Voices* [2004]) illustrates the turmoil that families faced as military and guerilla soldiers recruited boy children during the decade-long Salvadoran civil war that killed nearly 75,000 people between 1979 to 1992 (Cuffe). Between daily storms of cross fires, bombs, and attacks between military soldiers—heavily supported by the US government—and rebels in the guerilla coalition FMLN, a young boy in a Salvadoran town, Chava (Carlos Padilla), tries to survive both the violence of the era and recruitment of boys primarily by military dictatorship forces and sometimes by guerilla rebels, as both ended the childhoods and lives of Chava's neighbors and friends. Eventually, after surviving the escalating violence that claims lives around him, Chava leaves the country to the United States to escape the fatal conditions that pushed thousands of Salvadorans from their country to the States and other countries.

## Films of the Guatemalan Civil War

In the case of Guatemala, the American-produced films *When the Mountains Tremble* (1983), *Granito: How to Nail a Dictator* (2011), and *500 Years: Life in Resistance* (2017) are a trio of documentaries that have portrayed the history of conflict, collaboration, and resistance between the Guatemalan government, US interventionism, working-class, and Indigenous Mayan communities. In *When the Mountains Tremble*, Mayan and human rights activist and leader Rigoberta Menchú narrates her family's history as well as the history of the Maya people in their struggle against racism, colonialism, and genocide in Guatemala. The more recent film, *500 Years*, elaborates on this context, emphasizing the history and development of the Mayan Indigenous peoples' resistance to ongoing inequality and the remnants of civil war's corruption and racism in modern-day Guatemala. *Granito* relies on rediscovered footage and evidence to build a case against the former dictator Efraín Ríos Montt, who presided over the genocide campaign during the Guatemalan civil war. Indigenous peoples, viewed as key enemies of the state during the civil war era, are largely featured in these documentary films as the survivors and leaders who resist racist state violence from the Guatemalan **mestizo** state and the US imperialist project.

Reaching the international stage from Guatemala, director Jayro Bustamante has produced acclaimed films with Indigenous lead actors and plots that revolve around the lives and histories of Guatemala's Indigenous peoples, including his award-winning films *Ixcanul* (Kaqchikel for "volcano," 2015) and *La Llorona* ("the Weeping Woman," 2019), both featuring Mayan Kaqchikel actress María Mercedes Coroy and other Indigenous lead actors in a country that seldom includes Indigenous peoples in its mainstream portrayals. *Ixcanul* focuses on the experiences of a young Kaqchikel woman in the highlands of western Guatemala where traditional Mayan life persists. She deals with the constraints of machismo, poverty, and structural racism as an Indigenous woman from a family of subsistence farmers. Migration also plays a role in the film as economic austerity pushes her love interest to leave Guatemala to the United States like many other Guatemalans have done in pursuit of opportunity. *La Llorona*, on the other hand, shuttles between modern Guatemala and the Guatemalan civil war and genocide. Relying on the folklore of *la llorona* about a ghostly woman seeking vengeance and closure, the family of a former president and alleged genocidal dictator (assumed to represent Efraín Ríos Montt) is frustrated by the protestors outside their home as he evades justice for his crimes against humanity during the war era. Beyond protests for justice, however, a supernatural force has entered the house as well after the hiring of a new servant woman (Mercedes Conroy), as ghostly appearances of those killed in the genocide fill the home and nightmares of genocidal violence begin to fill the family's psyche until the former general is killed by his wife, possessed by the spirit of a woman who fills her nightmares and reveals that she and her children were murdered by the general.

Figure 15.2: A Mayan survivor of rape and genocide gives her testimony in human rights court about her experiences during the civil war during the former general's trial in *La Llorona* (2019).

Source: DVD of *La Llorona*
License: Fair Use

Though El Salvador, Nicaragua, and Guatemala cinema deal with the Cold War conflicts and its consequences, recent films from these countries aim to revitalize domestic cinematic production and culture. According to Camilla Fojas, the *Festival Ícaro del Audiovisual Centroamericano* are institutions that aim "to support, promote, and sustain Central American cinemas in the recognition of shared histories of internal wars, military dictatorships, US intervention, and shared experiences of economic, social, and political instability" (98). However, more contemporary productions "deal with the postwar era, the construction of national identity, and the problems associated with social and economic instability" (99). One key example is the Central American International Film Festival, a transnational effort between Los Angeles and San Salvador "dedicated to showcasing Central American struggles, history, culture, and talent through the world of cinema" (*Central American International*) to make up for the lost time of the internal conflicts that curtailed cinematic productions. Though this chapter does not delve into cinematic production of other Central American countries—Honduras, Costa Rica, Panama, Belize, and Nicaragua—films from these nations have also aimed to expose the social conditions of racism, colonialism, sexism, homophobia, and poverty in these contexts. The diversity of Black, Indigenous, non-*mestizo*, and women actors and storylines is finding a niche in a growing film culture in these regions.

## THE MODERN REFUGEE CRISIS

In 2014, the news media became saturated with constant headlines announcing a border crisis in which migrants from El Salvador, Guatemala, and Honduras were filmed and interviewed constantly on TV. They shared their experiences with violence, poverty, political instability, and natural disasters in their home countries and why they joined the migrant caravans to the United States. Nicaraguans, too, have been fleeing political persecution and instability in their country under the Daniel Ortega regime, but most migrate into neighboring Costa Rica. This surge in immigrants from El Salvador, Guatemala, and Honduras has intensified the national debate about immigration control in the United States. Meanwhile, the Costa Rican government contends with Nicaraguan migrants, and Panama receives hundreds of migrants crossing through Panama to travel northward. The rise in Central American migration to the United States became overwhelming in 2014 and continued to escalate.

Many migrant justice advocates and lawyers pressured the US government to provide due process in asylum hearings for the many migrant children and asylum seekers. News media, photographs, articles, and sound clips of migrant children crying and pleading for their families in ICE facilities channeled the trope of the helpless refugee. Suffering migrant mothers and children are more prone to embody this controlling image, which can generate compassion and empathy that become politically useful in migrant advocacy and immigration litigation. However, the news media's fixed portrayal of Central American women and children as *only* defenseless refugees dismisses the resilience and agency that these migrants also possess. Central Americans' narratives of endurance and resourcefulness become obscured behind the helpless refugee trope that reduces migrants to a crying child and a suffering woman, nothing more (Lovato). Still, this image featured in national and global news media has called into question the United States's human rights leadership and generated calls for accountability and justice.

In capturing the migrant narrative in film, the canonical *El Norte* (1983), followed by the more recent film *La jaula de oro* (*The Golden Dream* [2013]; literally, "the golden cage," a title shared with a well-known **corrido** by Los Tigres del Norte), provides a fictional portrayal of the journey north to the United States from Guatemala. Then, the documentaries *Which Way Home* (2009) and the Central American–produced *Los Eternos Indocumentados* (*The Eternally Undocumented* [2020]) deal with the roots of migration and the perilous journey of those seeking refuge. *El Norte*, like *Innocent Voices*, is another example of American and Mexican productions that contain Guatemalan and Indigenous roles but often fail to cast Guatemalan and Indigenous actors, yet it provides impactful portrayals of Central American and Indigenous experiences with migration. Chicano director Gregory Nava tells the tale of Guatemalan Mayan siblings (played by Mexican actors Zaide Silvia Gutiérrez and David Villalpando) who escape the terror of the Guatemalan civil war and arrive in Los Angeles to pursue the American Dream. Mayan organizers agitate through a labor union for better conditions in their Guatemalan village only to be massacred by the Guatemalan army in response. After this ordeal, the siblings Rosa and Enrique migrate through Mexico to arrive in Los Angeles where they realize that arriving is only the first challenge. As undocumented migrants, Rosa and Enrique must navigate the precarious labor market for newly arrived undocumented workers like themselves, who must also be precautious and alert for signs of immigration enforcement that targets workers without legal status in '80s California.

Similarly, *The Golden Dream* follows the journey of three Guatemalan youth who become tired of their precarious condition in Guatemala. Based in the present, two of the youth, Juan (Brandon López) and Sara (Karen Noemí Martínez Pineda) come from the same town and plan to travel together until they meet Chauk (Rodolfo Domínguez), a Mayan youth who cannot speak Spanish. The three migrants set out to Mexico where they realize the dangers of being young and Guatemalan in Mexico, where officials crack down on Central American migrants. The language barriers between Chauk and the two others create some difficulty in comprehension, compounded by Juan's jealousy of the burgeoning friendship between Chauk and Sara. Sara becomes a victim of the gendered and sexual violence that women migrants endure at the hands of organized crime, and Chauk, almost nearing the end of the journey, is shot and killed by a border vigilante. Juan successfully arrives in the United States, though alone and bearing the weight of trauma, to work a job in a slaughterhouse that feels distant from the American Dream he gave up so much to acquire.

The documentaries *Which Way Home* and *The Eternally Undocumented* aim to humanize migrant narratives even further by demonstrating the factors behind migration through Mexico to the United States and the cruelty of the migration process. *Which Way Home* follows the journeys of Mexican, Salvadoran, and Honduran youth as they ride the top of trains and evade police along the way. They bounce between shelters to acquire a meal, a shower, and relief from the difficult trek, and in tragic cases, the children are never heard of again, with the hope that they arrived and the fear that they were deported, or worse, killed. Salvadoran American director Jennifer Cárcamo's documentary *The Eternally Undocumented* channels Salvadoran poet Roque Dalton's poetic image of the "eternally undocumented" to refer to the Central Americans who are caught in the crossfire of dictatorship, policy, and anti-immigrant attitudes. She interviews policymakers, activists, organizational leaders, and migrants themselves to understand the root causes of migration from Central America and the experiences of migrants in an anti-immigrant regime in the United States. Her work is used widely in Central American studies classrooms and for lessons on migration, paving a way for Central American voices to be centered in understanding the reality of Isthmians. The films discussed in this chapter are but few of the many titles that explore issues, experiences, and portrayals of Central Americans, but they are some of the most significant productions to deal with this diverse and multifaceted group of people.

Figure 15.3: A migrant smiles widely at the camera with a raised fist at a part of the border wall fencing in *The Eternally Undocumented* (2020).

Source: DVD of *The Eternally Undocumented*
License: Fair Use

## CENTRAL AMERICANS COUNTERING THE MAINSTREAM IN THE DIGITAL AGE

In response to mainstream media that "lacks genuine interest in Central American societies, disregards cultural notions, reveals biases, and oversimplifies phenomena" (Vida and Brown), Central Americans have engaged in alternative media production for more humanizing and critical narratives. During the Cold War era, revolutionary factions and social movements in El Salvador, Nicaragua, and Guatemala crafted an alternative narrative against US and right-wing propaganda that vilified guerilla soldiers and their cause (Chávez 5; McIntosh 12–13). The digital age and twenty-first-century cultural and media production are an opportunity to articulate "how the US diaspora views this particular spatial construct—Central America—as a site from which to assert their own sociopolitical claims" (Cardenas 6–7) rather than simply a peripheral and distant "backyard" for the United States to use as it pleases (5).

Recently developed resources have unified Central Americans in the United States and beyond through the online community of Central American Twitter (#CentralAmericanTwitter) toward the cause of representation and alternative media production. News media platform Central American News and social media pages such as Central American Beauty on Instagram (@centam_beauty) and the Central American Voices podcast have also amplified Central American issues, identities, and experiences in the digital sphere and soundscape. Additional social media pages and digital communities have been cultivated largely due to platforms like Central American Twitter that have provided a space for connection and storytelling online among Central Americans in diaspora (Vida). Twitter and

Instagram pages like Garifuna Market (@GarifunaMarket) and Blactina Media (@blactina) have provided space for doubly marginalized Black and Indigenous Central Americans in the face of *mestizo* hegemony in Central American spaces. Throughout history and across generations, if a platform for Central Americans to tell their stories did not exist, they have created it on their own and with each other. Central Americans are no longer marginal or invisible peoples. Their experiences, histories, narratives, and voices are central to the fabric of what is "American." Central American cultural production has long-challenged notions of Americanness, decentering the US rendition of its own exceptionalism, innocence, and superiority. Central Americans have never been silent and passive subjects; they have been revolutionaries, activists, artists, writers, creators, and filmmakers. Through diverse Central American narratives on the big screen and beyond, the people of the Isthmus continue to build bridges between borders and over walls.

*Jonathan Peraza Campos (he/him/él) is a 2018 graduate of Emory University, where he was a Mellon Mays Undergraduate Fellow and earned a bachelor's degree in Sociology. He has been active in struggles for racial, immigrant, and educational justice. Jonathan has a master's degree in Social Foundations of Education at Georgia State University and is now pursuing a master's in History and Latin American Studies at Georgia State University. He develops programs in metro-Atlanta to support Latinx and immigrant student success as an educator and educational consultant. He also organizes with the Abolitionist Teaching Network and the Buford Highway People's Hub for abolitionist education and liberation. As the Migration Curator for Central American News, he documents weekly current events related to migration and issues from Central American countries and in the United States.*

## BIBLIOGRAPHY

Alvarado, Karina O., Alicia I. Estrada, and Ester E. Hernández. "Introduction: US Central American (Un)Belongings." *US Central Americans: Reconstructing Memories, Struggles, and Communities of Resistance*, edited by Karina O. Alvarado, Alicia I. Estrada, and Ester E. Hernández, U of Arizona P, 2017, pp. 3–35.

Arias, Arturo. "Central American-Americans: Invisibility, Power and Representation in the US Latino World." *Latino Studies* vol. 1, no. 1, 2003, pp. 168–87.

Atton, Chris. "News Cultures and New Social Movements: Radical Journalism and the Mainstream Media." *Journalism Studies*, vol. 3, no. 4, 2002, pp. 491–505.

Babich, Erin, and Jeanne Batalova. "Central American Immigrants in the United States." *The Online Journal of the Migration Policy Institute*, 11 Aug. 2021, https://www.migrationpolicy.org/article/central-american-immigrants-united-states.

*The Central American International Film Festival*, https://centralamericanfilmfestival.com/.

*Central American News*, 2018, https://www.getrevue.co/profile/CentralAmericanNews.

Chávez, Joaquín M. *Poets and Prophets of the Resistance: Intellectuals and the Origins of El Salvador's Civil War*. Oxford UP, 2017.

Commission on the Truth for El Salvador. *Truth Commission: El Salvador. United States Institute of Peace*, 1 July 1992, https://www.usip.org/publications/1992/07/truth-commission-el-salvador.

Cuffe, Sandra. "War, Amputation, Refuge: A Salvadoran Migrant's Story." *Al Jazeera*, 11 Mar. 2019, https://www.aljazeera.com/features/2019/3/11/war-amputation-refuge-a-salvadoran-migrants-story.

Fojas, Camilla. "Cinemas of Central America." *Diálogo*, vol. 8, no. 1, 2004, pp. 98–99.

González, Juan. *Harvest of Empire: A History of Latinos in America*. Penguin, 2011.

Grandin, Greg. *Empire's Workshop: Latin America, the United States, and the Rise of the New Imperialism*. Metropolitan Books, 2006.

Kenix, Linda Jean. *Alternative and Mainstream Media: The Converging Spectrum*. A&C Black, 2011.

Landon, Phillip J. "Films of the Cold War: 1948-1990." *University of Maryland, Baltimore County*, https://userpages.umbc.edu/~landon/Local_Information_Files/Films of the Cold War.htm.

Lovato, Roberto. "Politics Pushes Central American Voices out of Child Separation Coverage." *Columbia Journalism Review*, Columbia Journalism Review, 26 June 2018, https://www.cjr.org/politics/child_separation_trump.php.

Martelle, Scott. *William Walker's Wars: How One Man's Private American Army Tried to Conquer Mexico, Nicaragua, and Honduras*. Chicago Review P, 2018.

McIntosh, Jane. "Radio and Revolution." *Index on Censorship* vol. 11, no. 5, 1982, pp. 12–13.

Padilla, Yajaira M. "Domesticating Rosario: Conflicting Representations of the Latina Maid in US Media." *Arizona Journal of Hispanic Cultural Studies*, vol. 13, 2009, pp. 41–59.

Repak, Terry. *Waiting on Washington: Central American Workers in the Nation's Capital*. Temple UP, 2010.

Vida, Melissa. "How #CentralAmericanTwitter Evolved Beyond a Hashtag Into a Much-Needed Community." *Remezcla*, 21 November 2017, https://remezcla.com/features/culture/central-american-twitter/.

Vida, Melissa, and Bree'ya Brown. "Central American News: The Diaspora's Media that Bridges Central America and Abroad." *Routed Magazine,* 23 June 2021, https://www.routedmagazine.com/central-american-news-diaspora.

Worldometer. "Central America Population (Live)." *Worldometer*, https://www.worldometers.info/world-population/central-america-population/.

Zemler, Jeffrey A. "The Texas Press and William Walker in Nicaragua." *East Texas Historical Journal* vol. 24, no. 1, 1986, pp. 27–38.

## FILMOGRAPHY

*500 Years: Life in Resistance*. Directed by Pamela Yates, Skylight Pictures, 2017.

*Clueless*. Directed by Amy Heckerling, performances by Alicia Silverstone, Paul Rudd, Stacey Dash, and Britney Murphy, Paramount, 1995.

*Los Eternos Indocumentados: Central American Refugees in the United States*. Directed by Jennifer Carcamo, 2018.

*Granito: How to Nail a Dictator*. Directed by Pamela Yates, Skylight Pictures, 2011.

*Harvest of Empire*. Directed by Peter Getzels and Eduardo Lopez, Onyx Films, EVS Communications, and Loquito Productions, 2012.

*The Houses are Full of Smoke*. Directed by Allan Francovitch, FOC Inc., 1987.

*Ixcanul*. Directed by Jayro Bustamente, performances by Maria Mercedes Coroy, Maria Telón, and Manuel Antun, La Casa de Producción and Tu Vas Voir Productions, 2015.

*La jaula de oro* (*The Golden Dream*). Directed by Diego Quemada Diez, performances by Brandon Lopez, Rodolfo Dominguez, and Karen Martinez, Animal de Luz Films, Castafiore Films, and Consejo Nacional para la Cultura y las Artes, 2013.

*La Llorona*. Directed by Jayro Busamante, performances by Maria Mercedes Coroy, Sabrina de la Hoz, and Margarita Kenefic, El Ministerio de Cultura y Deportes Guatemala, La Casa de Producción, and Le Film du Volcan, 2019.

*Latino Americans*. Directed by David Belton and Sonia Fritz, PBS, 2013.

*Maria's Story*. Directed by Pamela Cohen and Monona Wali, performances by Alma Martinez, Edward James Olmos, and Maria Serrano, Camino Film Projects, 1990.

*El Norte*. Directed by Gregory Nava, performances by Zaide Silvia Gutiérrez, David Villalpando, and Ernesto Gomez Cruz, American Playhouse, Channel Four Films, and Independent Productions, 1983.

*Romero*. Directed by John Duigan, performances by Raul Julia, Richard Jordan, and Ana Alicia, Warner Brothers 1989.

*Las Sandinistas*. Directed by Jenny Murray, performances by Dora Maria Tellez and Daisy Zamora, MCRM Productions, 2018.

*Sobreviviendo Guazapa* (*Surviving Guazapa*). Directed by Roberto d'Avila Alegria, performances by Roberto Jose Alegria, Geovanny Alvarado, and Salvador Bermudez, DVR Cineworks, Fundacine, and Digital 1, 2008.

*Voces Inocentes* (*Innocent Voices*). Directed by Luis Mandoki, performances by Carlos Padilla, Leonor Varela, and Xuna Primus, 20th Century Studios, 2004.

*When the Mountains Tremble*. Directors by Newton Thomas Sigel and Pamela Yates, performances by Rigoberta Menchú and Susan Sarandon, Skylight Pictures, 1983.

*Which Way Home*. Directed by Rebecca Cammisa, Documentress Films, Mr. Mudd, and Reason Pictures, 2009.

*Will & Grace*. Created by David Kohan and Max Mutchnick, NBC, 1998–2006.

## FOR FURTHER STUDY

*Ambiguity: Crónica de un Sueño Americano*. Directed by Grisel Wilson, performances by Hans Calderon, Juan Diego Rodriguez, Luigui Lanuza, and Maria Alejandra Solorzano, Humans & Fido Productions, 2015.

*America First: The Legacy of an Immigration Raid*, Directed by Almudena Toral and Andrea Patiño Contereras, Univision Interactive Media, 2018.

*Carla's Song*. Directed by Ken Loach, performances by Robert Carlyle, Oyanka Cabezas, Scott Glenn, and Salvador Espinoza, Channel Four Films, 1997.

*El Salvador: Another Vietnam*. Directed by Glenn Silber and Teté Vasconcellos, M J and E Productions, 1981.

*Malacrianza* (*The Crow's Nest*). Directed by Arturo Menendez, performances by Salvador Solís and Karla Valencia, Itaca Films, 2014.

*María's Story: A Documentary Portrait of Love and Survival in El Salvador's Civil War*. Directed by Monona Wali and Pamela Cohen, Camino Film Projects, 1990.

*El silencio de Neto* (*The Silence of Neto*). Directed by Luis Argueta, performances by Oscar Almengor and Pablo Arenales, Buenos Dias Productions, 1994.

# Part IV: Roundtable

# Latinx Media Today and Tomorrow: A Roundtable

Moderated and transcribed by
Leslie L. Marsh and Rielle Navitski

*The following conversation brings together four prominent scholars of Latinx media: Frederick Luis Aldama, Jillian Báez, Mary Beltrán, and Arcelia Gutiérrez, who offer their reflections on key trends in Latinx media and representation, leading tastemakers and changemakers in the field, and predictions about the future of Latinx media. This virtual roundtable originally took place on Zoom and was hosted by the Center for Latin American and Latino/a Studies at Georgia State University in March 2022. The discussion aims to complement the chapters included in this textbook and provides points of departure for further study of Latinx media.*

*This conversation has been edited for length and clarity.*

**LESLIE MARSH:** Thank you all for being here today for a roundtable on Latinx media, sponsored by the Center for Latin American Latino/a Studies at Georgia State University in Atlanta, Georgia.

**What do you view as the key trends in Latinx media and representation today? This could encompass production trends as well as more structural changes to film, radio/audio, TV, and digital media.**

FREDERICK LUIS ALDAMA: [It is] because of the grassroots efforts on the part of organizations like the [Latinx House](#), [ALLP](#) [Alliance for Latinx Leadership and Policy], [La Lista](#), and others that today we're seeing more Latino, Latina, Latinx [individuals] in the writers' rooms, we're seeing more showrunners, more exec[utive] producers, we're seeing more in those spaces in terms of the televisual media. But still not enough. So while we're about 19% of the population, we're still hovering anywhere between 2 and 3% representation across all media. So while I'm seeing more changes and also real vitality coming out of Afro-Latinx/Blatinx spaces in terms of storytelling, within TV, and especially comics, when it comes to cinema, it's almost like a complete wasteland from my perspective, still. And also, we just need more. So we are making a difference as scholars, as creatives, as [media] industry people, working together to make that difference. But the gatekeepers are still there, and they're still reproducing what I call in my latest volume, *Latinx TV in the Twenty-First Century,* the White oculi [gaze or perspective]. We're still not being given that space for us to be telling *our* stories, and the complexity of those stories, the joys and pleasures as well as the frustrations and difficulties of our different journeys.

JILLIAN BÁEZ: As I look at the media landscape today, I think, for me, what most defines that is that there is uneven development. So there has been a movement within the last fifteen to twenty years where I've seen that we've moved from severe under-representation, particularly in spaces like television, to something that's much more uneven. So what I mean by that is we have moments where we're seeing some programming that is interesting, there's some Latino talent both behind the camera and in front of it, but there's not necessarily sustainability there.

And so I think that it's a major inroad, but it's also a major challenge. I'm thinking about these developments both in the English-language media spaces but also the Spanish-language media spaces, and I say this because Spanish language and bilingual media still remains a stronghold from an industry standpoint. A lot of the Spanish-language industry, especially television, has been growing, both broadcast television but also nontraditional forms, like streaming platforms.

At the same time, one of the things that concerns me is that when we look at entertainment media, a lot of the content is in the form of reboots. Especially in terms of the English-language landscape. I'm thinking of shows like *Charmed* [2018–] or [*Roswell, New Mexico* (2019–)] that are spun now with Latina, Latino, Latinx characters and sometimes storylines. Or, in the case of Spanish-language media, there's a lot of adaptations of telenovelas, and sometimes there are creative conventions used in those reboots or in those adaptations, but what I want to emphasize here is that we really need more spaces for original programming. There are many, many talented writers and producers. Now we are in a moment where we've actually trained a lot of Latino students to produce this kind of work, both in news and entertainment content, but they're just not working. Not enough of them are working in real positions of power where they have decision-making [authority]. So that, I think, continues to be an issue.

And then the other concern that I'm seeing is particularly in terms of the news landscape as it intersects with social media with the issue of disinformation. I'm thinking, of course, about the last two years of the pandemic and thinking about information about COVID being circulated on social media, particularly amongst Spanish-dominant Latino audiences. In the last couple of weeks there's been a lot of coverage of a new program on Sirius XM called [*Americano*], which is a conservative radio program. There's a bit of concern there, there have been a number of articles questioning, Will this be the kind of space that will circulate disinformation as well? So I bring this up because we are in sort of a strange moment where there are more spaces for Latino voices, but at the same time, it raises the larger issue of, What is the quality of that content, and what are the implications of the kind of content that's being produced?

MARY BELTRÁN: In terms of key developments that I see, I appreciate everything that Frederick and Jillian just said. I think those are things that I agree with as well.

We are seeing more Latinx media-makers and executives, especially in writers' rooms, but the numbers are so much less than our [overall] numbers in the population. And as you all know, many of these [television] series are not lasting that long. So it can feel like one step forward, one step back all the time.

Some things that I see as key to progress have been the much more personal projects that we've seen get produced as series, like *Vida* [2018–2020] or *Gentefied* [2020–2021] or certainly *Los Espookys* [2019–], that are breaking out of the family sitcom box a bit more in the last decade and are shows that have been critically acclaimed. Certainly in the 2000s, *Ugly Betty* [2006–2010] in particular, I would say, got critical attention. *George Lopez* [2002–2007] was successful and, I think, a really important show, but it wasn't noticed quite as much by the critics, maybe because it looked much more like something that had been seen before, even though I think there's much more there than just a family sitcom. But I think that to have someone like Tanya Saracho, who was an award-winning playwright before she was able to be the showrunner of *Vida*, in some ways is showcasing more of the artistry of Latinx writers and producers than we'd seen in the past.

I'm also thinking of the sheer numbers of Latinx viewers that are out there in the potential viewing audiences for films, for TV shows, and so on. This is something that scholars of Latinx media have been saying forever: we're growing, we're going to have more impact. But I think at this point, at almost 20% of the audience and at least 25% of the youth audience, that we have to be responded to. For the survival of networks, they must think of Latino viewers. And I'm talking about English-language networks and certainly Spanish-language networks as well. I think it's going to be a matter of how they attempt to do that. We see certain types of strategies that might frustrate me more than please me, like seeing a show like *Charmed* just get remade with Latina actors in the roles and not much other focus on Latino cultures. We've seen attempted remakes of telenovelas that did not go well, that did not succeed like *Ugly Betty* and *Jane the Virgin* [2014–2019] [did]. We've also seen Latino actors sprinkled into White-centric shows, with no attention to cultural background at all. Some of these things are not progressive, but they are different types of attempts that we're seeing on the part of networks to try to appeal to Latinos while still often trying to appeal to other audiences as well.

And I do think on the part of the broader audience, the diverse audience, that there's more openness, I think, to Latino/Latina protagonists and narratives. Even among non-Latino viewers, [there's] more openness to Spanish and Spanglish on typically English-language networks [and channels]. So the fact that a show like *Los Espookys*, which is in Spanish and subtitled, to have been distributed on

HBO rather than HBO Latino, I think was a real step that we wouldn't have seen a decade ago.

And so I think there are a number of things happening. There are a few Latinx executives, especially at the middle level, not at the higher level, the greenlighting level. But we're getting in there where we were not before. Even now, there are still very few [Latinx] top-level executives, but we're closer. Those are some of the things that I see.

ARCELIA GUTIÉRREZ: In terms of television programming, I think we're starting to see more of an embrace of racially diverse casting, multi-ethnic and multi-racial casting, and more attention to LGBTQIA+ representation. We can think of, for example, *Pose* [2018–2021], a groundbreaking television series that was inspired by the documentary *Paris is Burning* [1990]. This TV series really centers the experiences of Black and Black Latinx trans and gender nonconforming characters. That's something that we hadn't really seen on television before in this way. And Stephen Canals is one of the co-creators of the series as well.

And in terms of multi-ethnic and multi-racial casting, I draw a comparison to Latin American–oriented telenovelas. We can think of *La reina del sur* [*The Queen of the South* (2011)] and its very multinational, multi-ethnic casting strategy that allows for the series to travel globally. It's going to travel well in Mexico and Colombia, parts of Africa, and Spain [Mexico, Colombia, and Spain were the three countries involved in the co-production, and the story is set principally in Mexico and Spain]. I think we're starting to see somewhat of a similar trend in Latinx television and the sense that we're getting this pan-ethnic, pan-racial casting that's very intentional. One example of that would be Amazon Prime's *With Love* [2021– ], which has this spectrum of ethnic and racial representation of Latinidad. We can talk about if that's actually a successful strategy or whether more culturally specific narratives are landing better, but it is a strategy that I'm currently seeing in Latinx television.

Something else [to consider] is the short-lived renaissance of Latinx content on over-the-top media, or streamers. I think their success has been mixed, largely due to the fact that Netflix and Hulu are predicated on the subscription model and growth has to come from [new] subscribers, thereby placing Latinx-oriented series in a predicament. I was reading an article about the cancellation of Netflix's *The Baby-Sitters Club* [2020–2021], and it mentions that Netflix already sees itself as having captured US-based subscribers, so growth isn't going to come from US subscribers but rather from other parts of the world. That negatively impacts Latinx series that are perceived as not traveling well. [We see] the demise of our stories because of the assumption they're not going to attract [international] subscribers. They're not marketed as universal stories but rather seen as more ethnically specific stories that don't travel well.

The other negative trend would be the failure of network television shows that are Latinx-oriented. We don't really have any, right? *The Baker and the Beauty*

[2020] on ABC was canceled. Five episodes of *Promised Land* [2022] aired on ABC, and then the series was moved to Hulu. I think that's a troublesome trend that we're seeing.

Latinx podcasting is going to be an area that's going to help positively transform the industry; there's going to be growth there. Right now we're seeing a boom that I think will continue to grow over the next years. We can think of podcasts like [Locatora Radio](), which is hugely popular, and Spanish-language podcast [Radio Ambulante](). [Futuro Studios]() is becoming a powerhouse and producing podcasting content such as [Anything for Selena](). They have a slate of diverse, pan-ethnically oriented podcasts that I think are going to be quite important.

Social media and digital media are areas that are often overlooked but where important content innovation is happening. The future trend, I think, is Generation Z and its relationship to TikTok. This entails how they engage on the platform, the content they produce and its reception, and issues surrounding algorithms and how they shape media consumption. These are trends that exemplify the future of social media entertainment.

**RIELLE NAVITSKI: Who do you see as the most important change-makers and tastemakers in the field of Latinx media today?**

FREDERICK LUIS ALDAMA: There are a number of really important innovators that are still working and have the courage to continue to do the work of keeping the little path we have cleared [open], because it's always kind of closing in on us. An interview I did recently with America Ferrera reminded me of this, and also Stephanie Beatriz reminded me of this. As Mary had mentioned and many of us had mentioned, when we are excited because, instead of these little moments, we're seeing, possibly, more of a *movement* toward [a greater] complexity spectrum [in media], you know, all of these things that we want. Yet in the end, America, Stephanie, Peter Marietta, a friend of mine, you know, they still have to put food on the table. I mention this because sometimes there are things that are happening in the industry that we can't see. We need to be kind of mindful of where we as scholars see a step back [in terms of representation], but in actual material practice it's by necessity. Therefore, we need to start thinking about what happens, for instance, in a reboot if, by necessity, that's the only space for re-inhabitation [by Latinx actors] for us. What can possibly happen in a *Party of Five* [a 2020 reboot of the 1990s TV show of the same name with a Latinx cast] that's new and innovative and interesting? So I think that's also something really important for us to be asking. People like America and Stephanie Beatriz, Alex Rivera in cinema, Gigi Saul Guerrero and Michael Peña, and others, you know that they've kind of been backed into situations [where they were cast in stereotypical roles] because that's happening, that's the reality. Now it's a question of, What are they able to do when they are backed into those situations? One of the questions I asked Stephanie Beatriz was why, when she was brought on to *Modern Family*, does she accept to play an even more caricatured version [of the Latina "spitfire" stereotype] than Sofía Vergara's Gloria, and she was totally upfront and frank about it: "I had to pay my bills." So I think that we need to see courage everywhere, is what I'm getting at. And, for those who are in these spaces, we also need to allow for a certain kind of grace of space in order for them to be able to do what they're doing in these media spaces.

JILLIAN BÁEZ: I think we're in a moment, where there are many individuals, especially in the social media space. I want to echo some of Arcelia's comments about what's happening on spaces like TikTok and emphasize that I think some of the most interesting work is done in the short form. Part of that is that it's easy to produce and circulate without having to go through these much bigger gatekeepers within media corporations. That's how we're seeing a lot of folks sort of infiltrating into the system—even folks that are on bigger platforms like [mitú](#) or, for example, on YouTube.

I would also emphasize here, too, that what is shaping this is that the Latino audience is a young audience. Mary pointed to this earlier—at least a fourth of the overall audience demographic in this century is young.

Children's media has always been ahead compared to adult programming, in terms of inclusion of Latinos, and I think that we're continuing to see that. As a trend it's something that we don't quite focus on—even as scholars, we tend to overlook it. But I want to just emphasize that, at the same time, there are bigger tastemakers who sometimes the industry might be listening to but audiences might have a more vexed relationship with.

One of the people that came to mind, as I was thinking through this question, is someone like Lin-Manuel Miranda. In the last few years we've seen a number of projects that he's done with really large media companies, for example, like Disney. I don't know how much agency he has—that's always unclear. How much agency do they have in terms of their creative work? I say this because he's someone who in many ways has some of the attention of these really, really top executives within industries and can make things happen that other creative folks cannot. But, at the same time, audiences have a bit of a frustrated relationship [with Miranda], depending on the project. Some more than others. I'm thinking, for example, about the response to *In the Heights* [2021] last year when the film adaptation was released [regarding the absence of Afro-Latinx actors in starring roles, despite the large Afro-Latinx population in New York City, where the film is set]. So, I think that it's really important, too, because there's sometimes a tension between who becomes a tastemaker and is able to break through to the mainstream, in this case both theater and film. But, also, how does that land with Latino audiences? In this case, it's a good example of someone to whom I think people have very mixed responses.

MARY BELTRÁN: These are great people that have been mentioned already, and I completely agree. I would add that I think that there are a number of performers who have now become writer-producers, or at least showrunners who are more symbolically in charge of projects. It's kind of a mixed thing, that these executive producers that are getting attention seem to have to first become celebrities in some other way. I don't know that that is the only way that people should have to be able to bring their creative projects forward. I mean, we can think of, in addition to America Ferrera [and] Tanya Saracho, Salma Hayek has also been a showrunner of some projects that have been successful. Fred Armisen also, in partnering with Ana Fabrega and Julio Torres. Armisen and Torres both came up through *Saturday Night Live,* actually, but they together [with Fabrega] are the EPs [executive producers] of *Los Espookys*.

Eva Longoria has actually also produced a number of important projects. I know she's one of the producers of the Hot Cheetos film that will be coming out [*Flamin' Hot*, directed by Longoria in 2021].

I think that we're seeing these individuals, who maybe originally came in to act, seeing a need to use the status that they've gained to do more to put Latinx projects out there and Latinx stories. I think that they are some of the key changemakers these days.

We could think of someone like Marta Fernandez, who was the executive at Starz, which greenlit *Vida* and also was working to try to nurture a few other Latinx projects at the same time. She moved from Starz, however, and *Vida* was canceled about a year later. We may gain champions, and we may lose them as well.

I also want to call attention to Latino Public Broadcasting. Luis Ortiz is one of the executive staff there who plays a major role in working to nurture talented writer-producers who want to try to get funding assistance and perhaps to get their [documentary film] premieres on public television. Some of these media-makers, like independent filmmaker Cristina Ibarra—she had the film *Las Marthas* [2014] debut on public television—will continue to produce more and more ambitious kinds of projects, I would think. Ortiz is creating a launching pad for new media-makers who want to make content about all different kinds of Latinx lives and cultures.

Christy Haubegger is an executive now at WarnerMedia who, many, many years ago, founded [Latina magazine](). She later worked to become a film producer and then an agent at CAA [[Creative Artists Agency,]() an influential sports and entertainment talent agency], where she ultimately pushed them to create a list of writers of color and other media-makers of color so that no one could ever say, "Oh, I didn't hire a Latinx writer, because I don't know that there are any." Now there's this list, and everyone can say, "Well, why didn't you go to the list?" She did that, and she also worked to create more avenues for staff writers, a kind of entry-level job in television, to create more avenues for people to get promoted to the mid-level and the executive producer level. So, she's been working from the inside to try to really push the industry to make changes that can make a difference. Now she's been hired by WarnerMedia to head some of their diversity efforts. Hopefully, she'll be able to have an effect there as well.

ARCELIA GUTIÉRREZ: One of the trends that I'm seeing currently is the rise of powerhouse Latina showrunners. Mary mentioned some of them: Tanya Saracho, the showrunner for Starz's *Vida*, landed an overall deal with Universal Content Productions—that's part of the NBCUniversal conglomerate—and so I think we're going to see programming coming in terms of television but also podcasting. Podcasting is part of that deal, so that's an interesting development. Gloria Calderón Kellett, who's known for *One Day at a Time* [2017–2020], landed an overall deal with Amazon Studios. Linda Yvette Chávez, who's one of the co-creators of *Gentefied*, is having a lot of crossover success, and now she's going into film with the Hot Cheetos movie [*Flamin' Hot*], so that's a really interesting development. And I think we're going to see the rise of Sierra Teller Ornelas, one of those showrunners for Peacock's *Rutherford Falls* [2021–]. If you haven't watched it, it's a hilarious sitcom that really centers Native history and offers a very savvy critique of settler colonialism, so I highly recommend that you check it out.

**RIELLE NAVITSKI: What are your predictions about where Latinx media is going in the future?**

FREDERICK LUIS ALDAMA: What I'm excited personally, selfishly, about is we're starting to see [exciting genre fare] . . . *Los Espookys* is just off-the-hook awesome. So if you haven't seen it and watched it carefully, please go do that. It's been mentioned a couple times by my amazing colleagues here. For all these incredible things that it's doing—not just [favoring] the Spanish dominant but the trans-hemispheric [approach], the collapsing of Chile [the shooting location] with LA in and through a kind of queer-goth-paranormal *Ghostbuster* forms. There's sci-fi, speculative fantasy, and within that, what I'd love to see more of, because this is my thing, is superheroes. I love *Raising Dion* [2019–]. And I especially love the character, [who is] not even the sidekick, because Esperanza Jiménez is kind of Dion's copilot. They're "tweensters" and they're saving the world. I love that in *Stargirl* [2020–], even though it was a White protagonist-focused series, we got our Yolanda Montez [who plays the character of Wildcat], our Latina kick-ass, misfit boxer who gets a whole arc of her own within that space. I love that we've got in *The Umbrella Academy* [2019–], especially season 2 where we finally get Diego [played by David Castañeda] getting a lot of air time and a lot of complexity. *Doom Patrol* [2019–] is another one where Diane Guerrero re-inhabits a White character from the comic book and does something really interesting with that. Of course, in the past, we had *Dark Angel* [starring Jessica Alba; 2000–2002]. We also have Rosario Dawson as Night Nurse [in several Marvel Cinematic Universe shows produced by Netflix]. For me, I would love to see us really push into the space of speculative storytelling.

JILLIAN BÁEZ: I definitely see a continued push for more racial inclusivity within Latino representation. Here, I'm talking about more images and more stories that center Afro-Latino characters, that really foreground Blackness. But also Indigeneity. We haven't seen as much of a push for that, at least in media spaces. But I think that's definitely something that already is happening on the ground level, that we will begin to hopefully see start to seep into production and representation.

These questions about the future are always so hard—I'm not a fortune teller. But, I do think that the future is now. It starts now. I think that demographic shifts are also going to play a role in some of the developments that we see in terms of Latino media. We've really emphasized, for example, the youth and the fact that they are so much of the audience.

I also want to emphasize thinking more about Central American stories. I think it's really important to emphasize that Salvadorans are now the third largest group in terms of Latinos in the US. Although we've seen some coverage of Salvadorans, I would say more so in terms of news media or, every once in a while, in terms of crime stories that are centered in Central America, particularly El Salvador and sometimes Guatemala. I think that we're going to see much more of a push for more representations from that particular part of the population that push back against the limited kind of border narratives, because really those are part of a larger border story now. But people really don't know who Central Americans are or even realize how much of a second-generation population there is here now in the US. That's one of the shifts that we will begin to see. I don't know how long that will take, but definitely that's something where I feel like the seeds are in the ground right now.

MARY BELTRÁN: One thing that I learned as I did research for my recent book, *Latino TV: A History* [NYU Press, 2022], is that there was a real shift among the Latinx TV writing community in the 2010s. A few things have shifted. One is that we've had many more women begin to enter the industry and be quite successful. A few of them have been quite successful, like Gloria Calderón Kellett and Tanya Saracho. And the women that have worked on *Queen of the South* [2016–2021], the English-language remake of *La reina del sur*.

Also, a few things that were part of the shift that we've seen is that, for the first time, we've had Latina and Latino writers get overall deals. An overall deal is basically an offer from a network or studio that is multi-year. So, it might be, for example, that they want them to create three different series for us over five years. It offers a kind of financial stability to creatives that they don't always have. It often allows them to hire other people to work with them. Sometimes it even allows them to have a deal where they can actually help someone else create a new show. It just depends on what kind of deal they have. But Latino writers weren't getting those. Initially, it was only White writers and then a few African American writers. Now, finally, some Latino writers—and it's just turned out that women actually have gotten them more than men lately. What get these kinds of deals does is, it encourages more community among the creatives. They don't have to compete in the same way. It's not like ABC has their one Latino show, so we're all going to compete to try to get that one. There's a little more of an opportunity for veteran writers to support new writers.

And, we're seeing some professional support groups are being created. [Untitled Latinx Project](#), which I think Fede [Frederick Luis Aldama] mentioned, was created by Tanya Saracho and Gloria Calderón Kellett and some other women working in the industry. They are now working to push the industry to be more inclusive, to "put their money where their mouth is," and saying they really care about Latinx narratives on television. I'm sure there must be sometimes a fear of being seen as too much of an activist while you're working within the industry because you might be seen as a troublemaker who should not be hired again. I think this kind of thing at least helps individuals working as professionals to focus on their career but also focus on trying to make the industry better for all Latina/Latino and Latinx narratives and professionals. I'm seeing some shifts in that way.

But there's still a lot of frustration and a lot of effort that can get put in without a lot of payback. Latinos need to show that we will support Latino projects. This is something anyone who studies Latinx media has probably been saying for decades now, but it's still important. Yet I know it's a little harder when it's a streaming media outlet that doesn't even release its figures, as has been the case for Netflix. I know that the people that worked on *One Day at A Time* were never given accurate statistics about who was watching the show as they were being told that it might not get renewed. There's still this issue of us needing to show that Latinos want to see Latino protagonists.

ARCELIA GUTIÉRREZ: For the future, something exciting is a renewed attention to systemic inequities in media industries broadly. I think #OscarsSoWhite and the #MeToo movement opened up that discursive change. Before there was attention paid, but not as much. I think, because of these movements, [these issues are] on the minds of a lot more people and seen as something that's important and that we need to advocate for. That's an important shift that's just happened within the last few years. And I tie that to the work that Congressperson Joaquin Castro is doing to hold various media industries accountable to Latinx inclusion, from public broadcasting to studios to television. My hope is that changemakers, media activist organizations like the [National Hispanic Media Coalition](#) and NALIP [[National Association of Latino Independent Producers](#)] , and we as audiences and viewers can push to hold industries accountable for the representation that we want and the inclusion that we deserve.

**Frederick Luis Aldama** is the Jacob & Frances Sanger Mossiker Chair in the Humanities at the University of Texas, Austin. He also holds a Faculty Affiliate appointment with UT Austin's Radio-Television-Film department and is an Adjunct Professor at The Ohio State University. He is the award-winning author of over forty-eight books, including an Eisner Award for *Latinx Superheroes in*

Mainstream Comics *(University of Arizona Press, 2017)*. *He is editor and co-editor of nine academic press book series, including the editor of* Latinographix *that publishes Latinx comics. He is the creator of the first documentary on the history of Latinx superheroes and founder and director of UT's Latinx Pop Lab.*

**Jillian Báez** *is an Associate Professor of Africana and Puerto Rican/Latino Studies at Hunter College. She is also an affiliated faculty member at the CUNY Mexican Studies Institute and the Center for the Study of Women and Society at the CUNY Graduate Center. Trained as a media studies and cultural studies scholar, her research expertise lies in Latinx media and popular culture, transnational feminisms, and issues of belonging and citizenship. She is the author* of In Search of Belonging: Latinas, Media and Citizenship *(University of Illinois Press, 2018).*

**Mary Beltrán** *is an Associate Professor of Radio-Television-Film and Associate Director and former Founding Director of the Moody College of Communication's Latino Media Arts & Studies Program at the University of Texas at Austin. Dr. Beltrán's scholarship has explored such topics as the evolution of Latina/o film and television production and stardom since the 1920s, the implications of the rising visibility of mixed-race actors and characters, and strategies on the part of television networks to appeal to more diverse audiences. She is the author of* Latina/o Stars in US Eyes *(University of Illinois Press, 2009), co-editor, with Camilla Fojas, of* Mixed Race Hollywood *(New York University Press, 2008), and author of* Latino TV: A History *(NYU Press, January 2022).*

**Arcelia Gutiérrez** *is an Assistant Professor in the Department of Film and Media Studies at the University of California, Irvine. She specializes in Latinx studies, media studies, media activism, and media industries. Her current book manuscript, tentatively titled "Deploying Latinidad: The Politics of Contemporary Media Activism," traces how Latinx media activists have navigated processes of deregulation and neo-liberalization and the strategies they've used to push for the inclusion of Latinxs in television, film, and radio. Dr. Gutiérrez serves as the co-chair of the Society for Cinema and Media Studies' Latino/a Caucus. She also served as curator of the Latin America exhibit for the "Unlocking the Airwaves: Revitalizing an Early Public and Educational Radio Collection" project, a comprehensive online collection of early educational public radio content from the National Association of Educational Broadcasters (NAEB).*

# Part V: Key Creatives

This section offers brief profiles of the life and work of significant Latina/o/x media makers, such as directors, screenwriters, showrunners, and actors. These profiles are designed for classroom use in two capacities. First, they can be used as concise introductions to the work of individuals who are frequently studied in Latinx media courses. Second, they can serve as models for an assignment that uses the principles of open pedagogy. Rather than asking students to complete work that will only be read by the instructor and, in some cases, by fellow students, open pedagogy guides students in creating informative resources for the public at large. These resources can be incorporated into open educational resources like this textbook or shared in other ways. We have included sample profiles by scholars that use both traditional academic sources and non-traditional sources, as well as examples of student-created profiles.

After reading a Key Creatives profile, students should be able to do the following:
- Provide an overview of the individual's background, formative experiences, and collaborations.
- Provide an overview of the individual's professional trajectory, including key works, recurring themes or preoccupations, and major shifts in their approach or mode of production over time.
- Explain the significance of their work within Latinx media history and/or in relation to key issues or debates such as race, gender, sexuality, class, or politics.

# SAMPLE PROFILE:
# TRADITIONAL ACADEMIC SOURCES
## LOURDES PORTILLO

Rielle Navitski
(University of Georgia)

Lourdes Portillo is perhaps the most prominent filmmaker working at the intersection of documentary cinema and feminist politics, and between Latin America and the United States. Her eclectic body of work takes a critical look at the human costs of political repression and global inequality, particularly in the US–Mexico border region. In two of the most impactful works of Portillo's forty-year career, the courage of women in the face of unthinkable acts emerges as a persistent theme. Her Oscar-nominated feature *Las Madres: The Mothers of the Plaza de Mayo* (1986), co-directed with Susana Muñoz, documents the activism of grieving mothers whose children became victims of enforced disappearance during the "Dirty War" waged by Argentina's military dictatorship between 1976 and 1983. *Señorita extraviada* (*Missing Young Woman*, 2001) investigates another series of devastating disappearances: the kidnapping, sexual assault, and presumed murder of hundreds of young women in Ciudad Juárez, just across the border from El Paso, Texas.

Other entries in Portillo's filmography portray individual acts of violence that nonetheless reverberate in the US–Mexico borderlands and beyond. In *El diablo nunca duerme* (*The Devil Never Sleeps* [1994]), the mysterious death of Portillo's uncle, a politician and real estate developer in her home state of Chihuahua, triggers an obsessive investigation into family secrets that also uncovers the corruption and ecological damage (namely, the draining of underground water reserves for agriculture) underlying the border region's rapid economic growth. *Corpus: A Home Movie for Selena* (1999) depicts the murder of Tejana music idol Selena Quintanilla by the president of her fan club as both a private family tragedy and a watershed moment for Latino visibility and Latina self-expression, communicated through public acts of mourning and the aspirations of many of Selena's fans to become performers themselves.

The very format of the text you are reading, the filmmaker profile, tends to reinforce common ideas about the director as a lone genius. Yet Portillo herself has stressed the importance of her longstanding collaborations with cinematographer Kyle Kibbe, sound recordist José Araújo, and editor Vivien Hillgrove, as well the role of in-depth conversations with her crew in defining a film's concept before shooting begins (Fregoso, *Lourdes Portillo* 27–28, 33–34; Torres 66; Martínez 25, 29). *The Devil Never Sleeps* even includes a moment where members of the film's crew are revealed to be accompanying Portillo as she records a phone call with her uncle's widow, who declined to be interviewed on camera. Kibbe and Araújo also appear as members of a documentary film crew in Portillo's documentary-fiction hybrid *Al más allá* (*Beyond the Beyond* [2008]), further blurring the boundary between fact and fantasy, while the central role of a filmmaker reminiscent of Portillo is played by professional actor Ofelia Medina. As these self-referential techniques suggest, Portillo's films draw attention to the act of representation and the subjective, incomplete nature of knowledge, rather than presenting documentary as a straightforward and definitive truth.

Portillo identifies as **Chicana**—a term that indicates both Mexican-American origin and a political commitment to the liberation of the Mexican-American community—and as a lesbian, though her relationship to both those identities has evolved over time (Hidalgo-de la Riva 83; Velasco 247). Born in Chihuahua City in 1944, Portillo moved with her family to Los Angeles in the late 1950s and quickly felt the impacts of racial discrimination in her daily life (Hidalgo-de la Riva 79; Velasco 246). With film production taking place all around her, Portillo first ventured into the industry as a production assistant at the age of twenty-one and quickly came to feel she had found her calling (Torres 66; Martínez 25). However, Portillo "never thought [she] could fit into Hollywood" (Martínez 28) as a Chicana. She reflected in an interview, "It was the 1970s and if I went into the offices of the funders, or whomever was in charge, I'd probably look like their maid and they wouldn't trust me with a million dollars [to make a film]" (Hidalgo-de la Riva 80–81). As a result, Portillo relocated to San Francisco, where she joined the leftist filmmaking collective Cine Manifest and later earned an MFA in film from the San Francisco Art Institute (Fusco 22; Hidalgo-de la Riva 81). Working at a distance both from Hollywood and the critical mass of LA-based Chicano filmmakers that positioned themselves in opposition to it, Portillo cultivated a unique style of independent filmmaking (Hidalgo-de la Riva 80–82). Her work has circulated largely on public television, at film festivals, and in alternative venues rather than being exhibited commercially, and has been supported by public media organizations, government agencies like the National Endowment for the Arts, and major charitable foundations.

Portillo made her directorial debut with *Después del terremoto* (*After the Earthquake* [1979]), a fictional, black-and-white short she co-directed with Nina Serrano. *After the Earthquake* is a portrait of a young woman named Irene (Vilma Coronado), who has fled Nicaragua in the aftermath of the 1972 earthquake that devastated the nation's capital Managua. The disaster fueled opposition to the dictatorship of Anastasio Somoza Debayle, who misappropriated international aid to enrich himself and cracked down on the leftist Sandinistas who sought to oust him from power. This group of dissidents is represented in the film by the character of Irene's former fiancé Julio (Agnelo Guzmán), who has just arrived in the United States after being imprisoned and tortured. Irene is poised to choose between the individual choices privileged by American consumer culture—represented by her purchase of a television set early in the film—and a life with the idealistic Julio, whose idea of revolution does not seem to incorporate feminist values (Fregoso, *The Bronze Screen* 96). The film's open-ended structure deliberately offers no clear resolution to these tensions. Yet some viewers were skeptical of the way it seems to privilege feminism over Nicaraguan nationalism and leftist politics (Fregoso, *The Bronze Screen* 153).

Figure 17.1: Irene (Vilma Coronado) signs paperwork to purchase a television on layaway, a symbolic act of financial independence and participation in US consumer culture, in *After the Earthquake* (1979).

Source: DVD of *Después del terremoto*
License: Fair Use

As Ana Patricia Rodríguez points out, *After the Earthquake* was part of a broader trend in the work of Chicana writers and filmmakers who sought to express their solidarity with Central Americans fighting against the effects of colonialism and the Cold War—including the United States' backing of right-wing dictatorships in the region and its funding of the *contras*, armed groups that sought to overthrow the Sandinistas who came to power in Nicaragua in 1979—but often erased the specifics of Central American experiences in the process (199–200). Portillo's next film *Las Madres: The Mothers of the Plaza de Mayo* also dealt with a human rights crisis in Latin America that led many Latinos living in the United States to speak up in solidarity: namely, the violence and torture perpetrated by Argentina's military dictatorship, which was also aligned with the United States under its Cold War policy of suppressing socialism at any cost.

Working with the Argentine-born filmmaker Susana Muñoz, Portillo registered the harrowing testimonies of a group of mothers searching for answers about the fate of their children who, despite being branded as extremists and terrorists by the government, were merely idealistic young people seeking greater social equality. Despite suffering arrests, torture, and disappearances themselves, Las Madres became the most visible symbols of resistance to the military dictatorship. Largely unadorned in its style—it mostly consists of "talking head" interviews with the families of the disappeared—*Las Madres* exemplifies Portillo's approach as she defined it in a 1998 interview: "rather than try to convey political oppression, economic oppression, I think what I'm trying to do is, I'm trying to touch people's humanity with the humanity I'm trying to portray [ . . . ] We want feelings and hope that, in creating this love and this feeling of humanity amongst the viewer, the film creates compassion" (Fregoso, *Lourdes Portillo* 28–29).

In an effort to recover from the emotionally difficult process of filming *Las Madres*, Portillo turned to the creation of *La Ofrenda: The Days of the Dead* (1988). Also co-directed with Susana Muñoz, the film explores how death is typically viewed in Mexican culture as an integral part of daily life rather than a threat to be feared (Martínez 27). *La Ofrenda* documents the rituals surrounding the Day of the Dead, when deceased loved ones are believed to visit those left behind, both in Mexico and in Chicano communities.

*The Devil Never Sleeps*, one of Portillo's best-known and critically acclaimed works, also explores the topic of death, but through a deeply personal lens. The film attempts not only to unravel the mystery of the death of Portillo's uncle Oscar Ruiz Almeida by gunshot wound—while it was ruled a suicide, some family members suspected murder—but also to sort through conflicting accounts of what he was like as a person. Ultimately, the film suggests that truth is always partial and knowledge subjective and incomplete. As rumors of business deals gone wrong, adultery (Ruiz Almeida remarried just two months after the death of his first wife), child abuse, and homosexuality fly, the film cuts between interviews with her uncle's family and friends and footage of Mexican telenovelas whose emotional intensity, it's suggested, is only slightly greater than the real-life drama. Highlighting the selective nature of any documentary account, the film's compositions emphasize the intervention of media technologies, including the visible edges of television screens (a motif that reappears in *Missing Young Woman*) and reflections of the footage Portillo is reviewing in mirrored sunglasses.

**Figure 17.2:** Portillo films herself reviewing footage in *The Devil Never Sleeps* (1994) in a sly commentary on filmic mediation.

Source: DVD of *The Devil Never Sleeps*
License: Fair Use

Like *The Devil Never Sleeps*, *Missing Young Woman* delves into a seemingly unsolvable mystery, in this case one of truly horrifying scope and proportions: the murders of hundreds of young women in Ciudad Juárez beginning in the 1990s. As a result of police incompetence, corruption, and even involvement in the rape and murder of women, the killings continued, despite the arrest of the alleged killer. The official explanation was that he paid accomplices to continue the murders while behind bars; yet the systemic nature of the horrendous crimes was never addressed by the authorities. *Missing Young Woman* is at once a chronicle of the flawed police investigation, an elegy for the disappeared—who had been further dehumanized through the circulation of graphic imagery of their bodies (Portillo 254; Driver 221)—and a document of their family members' desperate search for their loved ones.

The majority of the missing women were employed in ***maquiladoras***—US-owned factories that sprung up after the North American Free Trade Agreement lifted US trade barriers to goods made in Mexico—signaling the deadly consequences that can accompany economic growth. As Portillo states in the film's voiceover over dizzying time-lapse images of the city, "Juárez is the city of the future. As a model of globalization, Ciudad Juárez is spinning out of control." Portillo's denunciation of the deadly conditions created by Juárez's status as a node of both legal and illicit commerce (in the form of drug trafficking) foreshadowed the tidal wave of violence unleashed by President Felipe Calderón's frontal assault on organized crime beginning in 2006, which has not subsided as of this writing in 2022. *Missing Young Woman* became an organizing tool for families seeking justice in Mexico (Driver 221), and Portillo embraced the role of "human rights worker," touring internationally with the film (Portillo 258–62). This work consumed her energies for several years. Completed seven years after the release of *Missing Young Woman*, Portillo's next film *Beyond the Beyond* continued to explore the social toll of the drug trade and the economic disparity between the US and Mexico, represented by the presence of wealthy expats and tourists in an undeveloped area. Filmed on the Yucatán Peninsula, *Beyond the Beyond*'s creative mix of fiction and nonfiction gently pokes fun at the hubris of documentary filmmakers as they attempt to draw firm conclusions about complex social realities from an outsider's vantage point.

Figure 17.3: *Missing Young Woman* connects the murders and disappearances in Ciudad Juárez to the abuses of global capitalism, stressing the vulnerability of the largely female population of maquiladora workers such as the woman pictured here.

Source: DVD of *Missing Young Woman*
License: Fair Use

Now in her late seventies, Portillo recently made the animated short *State of Grace* (2020), which grapples with her cancer diagnosis while evoking the emotional strength she draws from her family and ancestors. Even as she delves into the violence that marks colonialism, capitalist exploitation, and even intimate family dynamics, Portillo illuminates the creativity, resilience, and activism of Latin American and Latinx communities and their transformative power.

***Rielle Navitski*** *is an Associate Professor in the Department of Theatre and Film Studies at the University of Georgia. She is the author of* Public Spectacles of Violence: Sensational Cinema and Journalism in Early Twentieth-Century Mexico and Brazil *(Duke University Press, 2017) and co-editor of* Cosmopolitan Film Cultures in Latin America, 1896-1960 *(Indiana University Press, 2017). Currently she is working on a book manuscript entitled "Transatlantic Cinephilia: Networks of Film Culture Between Latin America and France, 1945-1965" (under contract, University of California Press).*

## BIBLIOGRAPHY

Driver, Alice. "Feminicide and the Disintegration of the Family Fabric in Ciudad Juárez: An Interview with Lourdes Portillo." *Studies in Latin American Popular Culture*, vol. 30, 2012, pp. 215–25.

Fregoso, Rosa-Linda. *The Bronze Screen: Chicana and Chicano Film Culture*. U of Minnesota P, 1993.

---. (ed.). *Lourdes Portillo*: The Devil Never Sleeps *and Other Films*. U of Texas P, 2001.

Fusco, Coco. "An Interview with Susana Muñoz and Lourdes Portillo." *Cinéaste*, vol. 15. no. 1, 1986, pp. 22–25.

Martínez, Michelle J. "Cinema Chicana: An Interview with Lourdes Portillo." *Journal of Film and Video* vol. 62, no. 1/2, pp. 23–30.

Portillo, Lourdes. "Tracking the Monster: Thoughts on *Señorita extraviada*." *Born of Resistance: Cara a Cara Encounters with Chicana/o Visual Culture*, edited by Scott L. Baugh and Víctor A. Sorell, U of Arizona P, 2015, pp. 254–62.

Rodríguez, Ana Patricia. "The Fiction of Solidarity: Transfronterista Feminisms and Anti-Imperialist Struggles in Central American Transnational Narratives." *Feminist Studies* vol. 34, no. 1/2, 2008, pp. 199–226.

Torres, Hector A. "A Conversation with Lourdes Portillo." *Film & History*, vol. 34, no. 1, 2004, pp. 66–72.

Velasco, Juan. "The Cultural Legacy of Self-Consciousness: An Interview with Lourdes Portillo." *Journal of Latinos and Education*, vol. 1, no. 4, pp. 245–53.

# SAMPLE PROFILE: TRADITIONAL ACADEMIC SOURCES
## ALEX RIVERA

Sarah Ann Wells
(University of Wisconsin, Madison)

Alex Rivera, the son of a Peruvian immigrant, has made films since 1995. His work ranges from shorts to feature-length documentary and fiction films, and moves beyond cinema in the traditional sense to include other screen media: webpages, memes, satirical trailers, and music videos for activist campaigns (Schreiber; Aldama 380). He was one of the founders of the Latinx filmmaking distribution collective SubCine, and his films have screened in top venues, including the Sundance and Berlin film festivals, Getty Museum, and the Guggenheim Museum Bilbao; in 2021, he was named a MacArthur "Genius" Fellow. He has also been artist-in-residence at various universities and at the National Day Laborer Organizing Network (NDLON). His work is identified by three interwoven elements: first, a focus on immigrants and their labor; second, a multi-platform approach to screen media and solidarity, including engaging with diverse communities (activists, students, intellectuals, film critics); and third, an interest in satire or parody. Together, these elements constitute a project of "hacking" or remixing—or, as Rivera and several critics have put forth, a *rasquache* Latinx aesthetic (Decena et al.; Castillo; Lozano). **Rasquache** describes how people irreverently produce art from daily life—for example, with cars or buildings—through the use of cheap or discarded materials refashioned for new, creative uses.

Rivera often cites and distorts US media coverage and popular culture to highlight its anti-immigrant premises. He also frequently deploys operational images (logistical images not intended for viewing) against themselves to criticize practices of surveillance.

Figure 18.1: X-ray surveillance footage of migrants, deployed in the documentary short *A Visible Border* (2003).

Source: DVD of *A Visible Border*
License: Fair Use

Figure 18.2: Surveillance footage from the US–Mexico border in the opening sequence of *The Infiltrators* (2019)

Source: DVD of *The Infiltrators*
License: Fair Use

In this context, Rivera draws on models from "hactivists," especially Ricardo Dominguez, a conceptual artist, programmer, and activist focused on the US–Mexico border (Castillo 9–10). Similarly, Rivera frequently plays with or "hacks" genres, as in his spoof on industrial films created by companies for promotional or training purposes, the web-based short *Why Cybraceros?* (1997). Anticipating his feature-length film *Sleep Dealer* (2008), *Why Cybraceros?* updates a promotional film by the Council of California Growers, *Why Braceros?* (1959), for the age of the Internet by imagining how underpaid manual labor could be performed by Mexicans remotely. Instituted in 1942, the Bracero program was designed to fill a shortage of labor in the United States when many young men were fighting in the Second World War by temporarily hiring Mexican guest workers. The same year, he released two other satirical shorts about the border, *Animaquiladora* ("the animation sweatshop"), which features vignettes spoofing negative portrayals of Latinx people, and a mock trailer, *Día de la independencia*, which parodies the alien invasion genre and its underlying xenophobia, as in the blockbuster *Independence Day* (1996).

Rivera's first film, based in an undergraduate thesis, was the creative documentary *Papapapá* (1995). The title is a play on the similarly spelled Spanish words for potato (*papa*) and Dad (*papá*): Rivera's father is an immigrant from Peru, where the potato is a central crop. Highly experimental, *Papapapá* can be characterized as both an essay film (exploring the intersection of personal and political issues) and a "mockumentary" poking fun at traditional ethnographic documentary; it combines home video footage, talking head interviews, 16mm experimental images, stop-motion animation, snippets of fake/satirical gameshows, audio recordings from the state department, and more (Carroll).

Rivera's father went in search of better opportunities in the United States, only to be disillusioned by the discrimination he faced here. Papa Rivera now remains connected to his fellow Latinx community only through the television screen, where he is filmed endlessly consuming **telenovelas**. (Worth noting is that the film was made in a pre-Internet era.) The titular father has become a "couch potato"—a visual and verbal pun that works especially well for Spanish-English bilinguals like Rivera. The film interweaves the story of his father with the longer trajectory of the potato. An early product of globalization, potatoes originated in the Andes as a staple food central to the way of life of the Incas; subsequently, they were exported to Europe and later became a quintessentially "American" food—the potato chip.

*Papapapá* anticipates most of the major themes and strategies that will characterize Rivera's future filmography. In 2003, Rivera released several short documentaries exploring different facets of immigration in a less experimental and less personal vein. All were commissioned by PBS's Point of View (POV) documentary series and appeared both on television and various websites.

Three very short films comprise the Borders Trilogy. While different in style, viewed together they explore who or what gets to travel under global capitalism and current US policy. In *Love on the Line*, separated families and partners reunite on the border for moments of communion: to eat, talk, and kiss. Meanwhile, *Container City* continues *Papapapá*'s interest in global commodities by focusing on a shipping container facility in New Jersey, showing how objects are allowed to traffic more freely than human beings. The most disturbing of the three shorts is *A Visible Border*, which consists of a single, initially unclear, sequence of a black-and-white photographic negative. As the camera lens zooms out, we learn that the image was taken from real surveillance technology utilized at the Mexico–Guatemala border; we begin to recognize these shapes as the ghostly outlines of bodies who are attempting to become part of the informal, "underground" US economy. Rivera employs governmental surveillance technologies to reveal the violence experienced by workers attempting to immigrate.

A separate documentary released the same year, *The Sixth Section* (2003), tells the story of Grupo Unión, a solidarity network of Mexican immigrants. Rivera explores how this group of mostly undocumented men based in Newburgh, New York, sustain links with their hometown of Boquerón in Puebla, Mexico. Their energy and conviction have enormous ramifications for the people of their hometown, including reshaping infrastructures—water treatment facilities, an ambulance, and a community center for sports. Demonstrating, like in *Love on the Line*, how attachments transcend entrenched borders, the film underscores the growing autonomy of the group. Newburgh has become a flourishing, if partially hidden, "sixth section," or additional jurisdiction of their hometown in Mexico. Toward the end of the film, we learn that this group is one of over one thousand similar organizations, challenging ideas of "homeland," "immigrant," and "national economy."

Migrant labor and virtual networks of solidarity are also key themes in *Sleep Dealer* (2008), Rivera's most well-known film (co-written with David Riker). It is also his first, and thus far only, feature-length fiction film, and his only project exclusively in Spanish. Filmed mostly in Mexico with a **transnational** cast, it received the Alfred P. Sloan Prize for best film focusing on technology and science at the Sundance Film Festival in 2008. *Sleep Dealer* is set in a world where water has become the new oil, rigidly controlled by corporations and security forces based in the United States, and farming communities in Mexico are being devastated.

The physical border between the two nations is now all but impenetrable, especially those seeking to head North. Memo (Luis Fernando Peña), a young man from the Oaxaca region, is forced to migrate to the border town of Tijuana to work in the *infomaquiladoras*, factories that exploit migrant labor through computerized technology and interfaces called nodes that allow the workers to manipulate robots on the US side of the border. In this way, the film invokes the phenomenon known as the **maquiladoras**—transnational factories often built along border regions to evade national tax laws and reduce tariffs and labor costs (Rivera).

Figure 18.3: In the near-future world of the science fiction film *Sleep Dealer* (2008), water in Mexico is policed by security forces working for multinational corporations.

Source: DVD of *Sleep Dealer*
License: Fair Use

On the way to Tijuana, Memo meets Luz (Leonor Varela), a blogger-journalist interested in capturing his story. Meanwhile, Rudy (Jacob Vargas), the Chicanx drone pilot who has assassinated Memo's father after mistaking him for an "aqua terrorist" (a reference to real-life social movements in Latin America, for example, in both Mexico and Bolivia) is searching for Memo and lands on his story through Luz's virtual platform. The film charts Memo's experience of debilitating work in the sleep dealers, his relationship with Luz, and the eventual uniting of Rudy, Memo, and Luz, who conspire together to strike back against water privatization.

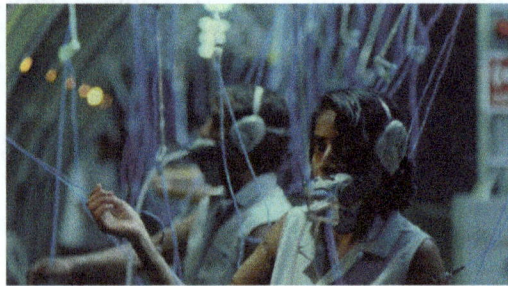

Figure 18.4: The *infomaquiladoras* of *Sleep Dealer* draw on histories of the exploitation of Mexican manual laborers to create a dystopic future.

Source: DVD of *Sleep Dealer*
License: Fair Use

*Sleep Dealer* tackles not only the depiction of migrants but also the problem of visibility within science fiction itself. By imagining a Latin American "unskilled" worker in the role of science fiction protagonist,

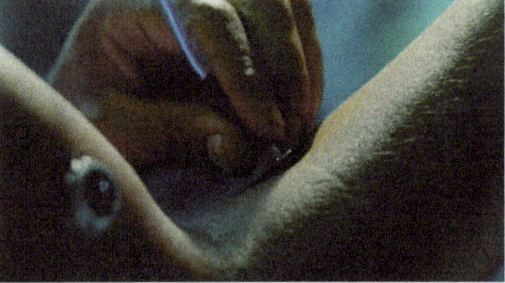

Figure 18.5: Detail shot of "connecting" through cybernetic nodes in *Sleep Dealer*.

Source: DVD of *Sleep Dealer*
License: Fair Use

and by making Tijuana the center of the action, Rivera reworks the genre (Wells). Traditionally, science fiction requires large budgets to execute its characteristic special effects; facing low budgets, filmmakers must devise creative solutions, including initial experiments with short films (Frelik), as Rivera did with *Why Cybraceros?* Rivera and his crew also employed real Apache helicopter communications (available through the public domain) to imagine the drones. In the decade or more since *Sleep Dealer* was released, the surveillance of the US–Mexico border has increased, making the film each year less a science fiction and more a documentary of our world, with its drones and militarized video games, man-made droughts, call centers located in India, a rigid border wall, and workers who never "unplug." After *Sleep Dealer*, Rivera continued to explore the relationship between humans, technology, and labor in his short episode "A *Robot Walks Into a Bar*" (2014), which aired on PBS's *FutureStates* series. Featuring an all-Latinx cast, Rivera approaches issues of automation and workplace obsolescence with an empathy for both the titular robot and the workers he displaces.

With his most recent feature film, the experimental documentary *The Infiltrators* (2019)—co-directed and co-authored with his partner, Latinx documentary filmmaker Cristina Ibarra—Rivera once again pursues his interest in practices of "disruption." Like *Sleep Dealer*, this film examines groups who come together to reroute systems of control and oppression and create alternative communities. *The Infiltrators* won an Audience Award and the NEXT Innovator Award at the Sundance Film Festival. It has been described as "docufiction" (Flores Ruiz), "docu-thriller" (Bugbee), and a "reverse heist" (Schindel). The film follows young DACA (Deferred Action for Childhood Arrivals) activists in the National Immigrant Youth Alliance (NIYA, an organization no longer active) from 2012 to 2016 in their plan to infiltrate a detention center to help detained immigrants by providing them with legal information and, at the same time, drawing public attention to their cases. The activists chose a "model" detention facility, the Broward Transitional Center (Florida), run by a private corporation, which held immigrants not charged with crimes—counter to the claims of the then-Obama administration that only criminals were being deported.

While they originally conceived *The Infiltrators* as a more traditional documentary (Schindel), the filmmakers lacked access to what took place within the detention center, sites notoriously opaque to filmmakers and the general public (Rossipal). Thus, they turned to reenactment—filming in a former mental institution and drawing on the activists' memories through workshops (Flores Ruiz; Schindel)—to explain the infiltration strategies and to make them gripping and suspenseful. The filmmakers used contrasting strategies (lighting, framing, pacing, and camera work) to produce two parallel ways of presenting the present. The result is a new mode of documentary filmmaking that opposes what Rivera deems the "extractive" model: "producing narratives out of a process where filmmakers drop in and capture material and walk away" (Flores Ruiz). At one point in the film, one of the activist-infiltrators states in voiceover, "In every family I've been able to see my own family." *The Infiltrators* suggests that together these activists are also developing a new, diverse family inside and beyond the detention center, with the filmmakers themselves joining them. In positing new forms of community engagement in a transnational frame, Alex Rivera and his collaborators reimagine what Latinx screen media offers the world.

**Figure 18.6:** DACA activist Marco Saavedra protesting, as seen in *The Infiltrators* (2019).
Source: DVD of *The Infiltrators*
License: Fair Use

**Sarah Ann Wells** *is Associate Professor of Literary Studies at the University of Wisconsin, Madison. She is the author of* Media Laboratories: Late Modernist Authorship in South America *(Northwestern University Press, 2017) and co-editor of* Simultaneous Worlds: Global Science Fiction Cinema *(University of Minnesota Press, 2015). Her research and teaching focus on literature and cinema of the Americas, and on the relationship between artistic and political movements.*

## BIBLIOGRAPHY

Aldama, Frederick Luis. "Towards a Transfrontera-LattinX aesthetic: An interview with filmmaker Alex Rivera." *Latino Studies*, vol. 15, no. 3, 2017, pp. 373–80.

Bugbee, Teo. "The Infiltrators' Review: Immigrant Activists Slip Into Detention." *New York Times*, 30 April 2020, https://www.nytimes.com/2020/04/30/movies/the-infiltrators-review.html. Accessed 15 May 2021.

Carroll, Amy Sara. "From *Papapapá* to *Sleep Dealer*: Alex Rivera's Undocumentary Poetics." *Social Identities*, vol. 19, no. 3-4, 2013, pp. 485–500.

Castillo, Debra Ann. "Rasquache aesthetics in Alex Rivera's '*Why Cybraceros?*'" *Nordlit*, no. 31, 2014, pp. 7–23.

Decena, Carlos Ulises, Alex Rivera, and Margaret Gray. "Putting Transnationalism to Work: An Interview with Filmmaker Alex Rivera." *Social Text,* no. 88, 2006, pp. 131–38.

Flores Ruiz, Diana. "Interview with Cristina Ibarra and Alex Rivera." *Film Quarterly*, vol. 78, no. 1, 2019, pp. 54–63, https://filmquarterly.org/2019/09/10/by-radical-means-necessary-interview-with-cristina-ibarra-and-alex-rivera/.

Frelik, Pawel. "Famous for Fifteen Minutes: Permutations of Science Fiction Short Films." *Simultaneous Worlds: Global Science Fiction Cinema,* edited by Jennifer L. Feeley and Sarah Ann Wells, Minnesota UP, 2015, pp. 47–61.

Lozano, Jennifer M. "Digital Rasquachismo: Alex Rivera's Multimedia Storytelling, Humor, and Transborder Latinx Futurity." *Latinx Ciné in the Twenty-First Century,* edited by Frederick Luis Aldama, Arizona UP, 2019, pp. 267–79.

Rivera, Lysa. "Future Histories and Cyborg Labor: Reading Borderlands Science Fiction after NAFTA." *Science Fiction Studies*, vol. 39, no. 3, 2012, pp. 415–36.

Rossipal, Christian. "The Black Box of Detention: Migration, Documentary, and the Logistics of the Moving Image." *The Global South,* vol. 13, no. 2, 2019, pp. 104–29.

Schindel, Dan. "The Undocumented Activists Who Turned Themselves in to Infiltrate ICE." *Hyperallergic*, 6 Oct. 2020, https://hyperallergic.com/592417/the-infiltrators-pbs-documentary-interview/.

Schreiber, Rebecca M. "The Undocumented Everyday: Migrant Rights and Visual Strategies in the work of Alex Rivera." *Journal of American Studies,* vol. 50, no. 2, 2016, pp. 305–27.

Wells, Sarah Ann. "The Scar and the Node: Border Science Fiction and the *Mise-en-Scène* of Globalized Labor." *The Global South*, vol. 8, no. 1, 2014, pp. 69–90.

# SAMPLE PROFILE: NON-TRADITIONAL SOURCES
## ROBERT RODRIGUEZ

Charles Ramírez Berg
(University of Texas at Austin)

Robert Rodriguez began filmmaking by creating Mexican American children's comedies. Growing up in San Antonio, Texas, he became consumed with making films in his early teens. Using his father's VHS camera, he made dozens of short family comedies starring his nine brothers and sisters (Black). By the time he was accepted to the University of Texas at Austin, he had thousands of hours of movie writing, directing, shooting, and editing experience. Not surprisingly, the final project in his first film production class was another comedic Rodriguez family short, *Bedhead* (1990). It went on to win five Best Short Film awards, including one from the prestigious Black Maria Film Festival (*"Bedhead"*, IMDb).

Figure 19.1: David (David Rodriguez) teases and torments his sister Rebecca (Rebecca Rodriguez) in the short film *Bedhead* (1990).

Source: DVD of *Bedhead*
License: Fair Use

Figure 19.2: Rebecca summons special powers to turn the tables on David in *Bedhead*.

Source: DVD of *Bedhead*
License: Fair Use

Deciding to make a feature-length film next, Rodriguez raised seven thousand dollars by volunteering for a month-long medical trial and spent the summer before his senior year shooting *El Mariachi* (1992). It was filmed using a friend's 16mm camera in Ciudad Acuña, across the Rio Grande from Del Rio, Texas, where

Rodriguez's high school friend, Carlos Gallardo, lived. Carlos played the Mariachi and was the movie's co-producer, assisting Rodriguez by finding locations (a bar, brothel, jail, ranch house), props (a pickup truck, a city bus, an antique bathtub), and getting his hometown buddies to play most of the parts. Rodriguez did everything else: he wrote the script, lit, shot, sound recorded, and directed the film, then edited the footage into a finished feature (Rodriguez, *Rebel*).

**Figure 19.3: In a memorable chase scene in *El Mariachi* (1992), the Mariachi (Carlos Gallardo) escapes the bad guys by swinging from a hotel terrace onto a passing bus.**
Source: DVD of *El Mariachi*
License: Fair Use

His sensible if ambitious plan for *El Mariachi* was to sell it to one of the Spanish-language straight-to-video companies in Hollywood for fifteen thousand dollars, use that money to make a second film, then repeat the process. Making three back-to-back films single-handedly in this way would be his film school. But the scheme failed because *El Mariachi* was too good. While waiting for a response from the Spanish-language home video company, he dropped off a VHS copy of *Bedhead* containing a two-minute trailer for *El Mariachi* at International Creative Management (ICM), a top talent and literary agency. One of the agents watched the video, was intrigued, and asked to see *El Mariachi*. When he did, he was so impressed that he quickly signed Rodriguez with ICM. In a matter of weeks, the agency had brokered a deal for Rodriguez to direct two features for Columbia Pictures (Rodriguez, *Rebel*).

It was the beginning of a long and very active movie-making career. And those two early films, *Bedhead* and *El Mariachi*, were early indicators of the two entertaining sides of Rodriguez's creative output: light-hearted children's comedy-adventures on the one hand and hard-hitting adult action flicks on the other. Looking at each group in turn is a useful way to appreciate his filmmaking output.

If you've ever sat on the floor to play with a four- or five-year-old, you know that the operative word for the session is "pretend." Once the child says that, "real world" rules are suspended and anything imaginable is possible. What makes Rodriguez's children's films different from anybody else's is his ability to access his five-year-old brain and pretend without limitations. Films like "The Misbehavers" episode in *Four Rooms* (1995), *Spy Kids* (2001) and its three sequels (2002; 2003; 2011), *The Adventures of Sharkboy and Lavagirl* (2005), *Shorts* (2009), and *We Can Be Heroes* (2020) are not only about kids who possess that boundless world view, they are written and directed by Rodriguez from that anything-is-possible perspective.

As opposed to most studio-produced children's fare, which are made by adults trying to remember childhood, Rodriguez's films completely inhabit that worldview. If his kid flicks are often messier, noisier, and less coherent than a typical family film, they truly do resemble a movie made by a post-toddler unaware of the rules of storytelling and moviemaking. They are more like, well, playing on the floor with a five-year-old—and that is part of their charm.

**Figure 19.4: Robert Rodriguez collaborated with his sons Racer and Rebel and daughter Rhiannon to create *We Can Be Heroes* (2020), a "pretend" story about the children of superheroes who possess their own superpowers.**

Source: Screen capture of *We Can Be Heroes*
License: Fair Use

As for the full-tilt, hard-core action films, they are R-rated because they're pushing the genre in new, unexpected directions. Films such as the Quentin Tarantino–scripted criminals-on-the-run-plus-vampire flick *From Dusk Till Dawn* (1996), the exploitation-movie celebration *Planet Terror* (2007), his violent and sexy collaborations with graphic novelist Frank Miller's *Sin City* (2005) and its 2014 sequel, the explosive set-in-Mexico adventures *Desperado* (1995) and *Once Upon a Time in Mexico* (2003), the gritty revenge duo *Machete* (2010) and *Machete Kills* (2013), the manga-inspired *Alita: Battle Angel* (2018), and even his recent PG-rated *El Mariachi*-meets-*Star Wars* episode "The Tragedy" from *The Mandalorian* (2020) all operate on the basic premise driving the best action movies, namely the need to push familiar genre elements—fights, chases, rescues, shootouts, killings—beyond anything ever seen before.

Two more aspects of Rodriguez's filmmaking deserve mention. First, his technological wizardry has made him a cinematic innovator. Along with George Lucas, he was one of the first filmmakers to switch to digital movie making in 2001 (Rodriguez, "Film Is Dead"). The adoption of high-definition digital video allowed him to set up his editing suite in his garage in Austin, Texas, and edit his films at home on his own—a move soon copied by other directors, beginning with his friend James Cameron ("FULL SPEECH"). Additional benefits of moving to digital technology were that it made his filmmaking process easier and cheaper. For example, his first released digital film, *Spy Kids 2: The Island of Lost Dreams* (2002), contained twice the number of special effects as the original for the same cost (Lee).

Digital also allowed him to make movies he couldn't have made on film, such as *Sin City*. Rodriguez admired Frank Miller's graphic novel so much that he was determined to make a film that preserved the high-contrast black-and-white look of the book. He managed to capture the graphic novel's distinctive look by shooting in digital with green screen technology then refining those images with special effects post production (Rodriguez, *Sin City Director's Commentary*). Furthermore, the artistic and financial success of *Sin City* was a major factor in shifting filmmaking toward more special-effects-heavy films, from Zack Snyder's historical epic *300* (2007) to the many superhero adventures that have followed.

**Figure 19.5: To capture the look of Frank Miller's graphic novel, Robert Rodriguez shot *Sin City* (2005) with digital cameras and perfected green screen technology, pioneering a new era of special effects moviemaking.**

Source: DVD of *Sin City*
License: Fair Use

Finally, one little-recognized facet of Rodriguez's body of work, and one that makes him unique in film history, is his career-long dedication to teaching young—especially Latinx—filmmakers. By continually demystifying the process for the last thirty years, he has encouraged aspiring moviemakers to make their films. It started with the *El Mariachi* DVD. His director's comments were entirely devoted to explaining—step by step, shot by shot—how he made the movie for seven thousand dollars and telling wannabe directors that if he did it, they could too. That DVD also inaugurated a regular Rodriguez DVD feature, the "10-Minute Film School," where he reveals how he solved tricky filmmaking problems. Other examples of his willingness to pull the curtain back to divulge his filmmaking process are his books, such as *Rebel Without a Crew*, the diary of his making of *El Mariachi* that became a sort of DIY bible for beginning independent filmmakers, and *Sin City: The Making of the Movie*, co-authored with Frank Miller, a detailed description of how he used green screen technology to bring Miller's graphic novel to the screen (Miller and Rodriguez). In addition, there are his many online interviews and numerous appearances at film festivals, fan conventions, and conferences such as Comic-Con and South by Southwest (SXSW).

His most recent and educationally ambitious filmmaking-teaching project was a series he developed for his cable channel El Rey. First of all, a word about his 2013 founding of El Rey, which was conceived of as the first Latinx cable channel (Perren). Besides providing programming for a younger generation of Latinx viewers, Rodriguez has said that one of his main goals in creating the channel was to give budding Latinx filmmakers inspiration by providing them with a creative destination, somewhere they could send their work ("FULL SPEECH").

In 2018 he conceived a youths-making-films series for El Rey. He selected five young filmmakers to support as they made their first feature films, holding them to the same constraints he had when he made *El Mariachi*—a seven-thousand-dollar budget and a fourteen-day schedule. Their journey would be recorded by an El Rey film crew, forming the basis for a series titled *Rebel Without a Crew: The Series*. At the same time, Rodriguez would join them and make his own seven-thousand-dollar feature, *Red 11* (2019). On top of that, he produced a making-of documentary feature covering how he made *Red 11*. Both films premiered at SXSW in the spring of 2019, and the series aired on El Rey later that year. (Ramírez Berg)

**Figure 19.6:** Robert Rodriguez at the premiere of *Rebel Without a Crew: The Series* and his seven-thousand-dollar feature *Red 11*, at South by Southwest, 2019.

Source: Charles Ramírez Berg
Attribution: Charles Ramírez Berg
License: © Charles Ramírez Berg. Used with permission.

Contributing considerably to American film history, innovating the medium as he did, sharing his filmmaking knowledge with others, and never losing sight of his Mexican American identity, Robert Rodriguez is an inspirational example of a Latinx filmmaker.

**Charles Ramírez Berg** *is the author of several books, including* Latino Images in Film: Stereotypes, Subversion and Resistance *(University of Texas Press, 2002) and* The Classical Mexican Cinema: The Poetics of the Exceptional Golden Age Films *(University of Texas Press, 2015). He has also written articles and book chapters on Latinos in US films, film history, and narratology, Mexican cinema, as well as entries for* The World Film Encyclopedia, The International Dictionary of Films and Filmmakers, *and* The Oxford Encyclopedia of Latinos and Latinas in the United States. *Most recently he published a photo essay on Robert Rodriguez titled "Robert Rodriguez: Teaching Creativity" in* Texas Studies in Literature and Language.

## BIBLIOGRAPHY

"*Bedhead*." IMDb, https://www.imdb.com/title/tt0165634/?ref_=nm_flmg_dr_50.

Black, Louis. "Sibling Revelry," *Texas Monthly*, Aug. 1992, https://www.texasmonthly.com/articles/sibling-revelry-2/.

"FULL SPEECH—Filmmaker Robert Rodriguez talks about 'El Rey,' his upcoming new cable channel." *YouTube*, uploaded by Moody College of Communication (The University of Texas at Austin), 22 May 2012, http://www.youtube.com/watch?v=w4raIL0jZOA.

Lee, Patrick. "Robert Rodriguez spies on the stars of his *Spy Kids* sequel," *SciFi*, 3 June 2008, https://web.archive.org/web/20080603060037/http://www.scifi.com/sfw/issue277/interview.html.

Miller, Frank, and Robert Rodriguez. *Sin City: The Making of the Movie*. Troublemaker Publishing, 2005.

Perren, Alisa. "El Rey: Latino Indie Auteur as Channel Identity." *From Networks to Netflix: A Guide to Changing Channels*, edited by Derek Johnson, Routledge, 2018.

Ramírez Berg, Charles. "Robert Rodriguez: Teaching Creativity." *Texas Studies in Literature and Language*, vol. 63, no. 2, Summer 2021, pp. 173–98.

Rodriguez, Robert. "Film Is Dead: An Evening with Robert Rodriguez." 17 July 2003, Sony Pictures Studio Cary Grant Theater, Los Angeles, CA. https://www.youtube.com/watch?v=Ag7eNNtJLMQ.

---. *Rebel Without a Crew: Or How a 23-Year-Old Filmmaker with $7,000 Became a Hollywood Player*. Dutton, 1995.

---. *Sin City* Director's Commentary. *Sin City* DVD Extended Edition, Theatrical and Recut Versions. Miramax, 2005. Online audio version uploaded by IDP at https://www.youtube.com/watch?v=8c0TokXZf8E.

# Student Key Creatives Profiles

## AURORA GUERRERO

Katie Morgan

Aurora Guerrero, the daughter of two Mexican immigrants, began her journey by first studying her own community at UC Berkeley (Tribeca Film Institute). She looked into Chicano studies and psychology, graduating first with a Bachelor of Arts, and then later received a Master's degree for filmmaking from Cal Arts (Tribeca Film Institute). Guerrero says a large inspiration for her own work was the writings of Chicana feminists Gloria Anzaldúa and Cherríe Moraga, who pushed her to pursue intersectional subjects of her films (Tribeca Film Institute). Her filmmaking work has ranged from short films to TV episodes to full-length films, with pieces of not only her identity as a Chicana, but also as a queer woman threading through these films. The first film Guerrero worked on was assisting Patricia Cardoso in her feminist Latinx film, *Real Women Have Curves* (2002), a coming-of-age story featuring a plus-sized Latina who struggles with her future, family, and sexist societal pressures (Launius 16). Guerrero, along with co-founders Dalila Mendez, Maritza Alvarez and Claudia Mercado, created Womyn Image Makers (WIM), a collective that sought to embrace the community of filmmaking as well as the founders' shared identities as Chicanas (Díaz-Sánchez 96). Guerrero directed the short film *Pura Lengua* (2005) through WIM, as well as *Viernes Girl* (2005), a short film featuring same-sex attraction between two Latinas (Díaz-Sánchez 96). The short follows the main character, a Latina woman, who is living with her brother, and deals with the antics of him bringing girls around to their house. Finally, on Friday (hence the name *Viernes Girl*), the girl her brother brought over sends him to get her horchata so she can spend time with his sister. The girls dance together in her room, laughing and joking that "she does know how to dance, like a true Salvadorean." The short ends with the girls kissing and the brother throws the horchata against the wall in frustration. Throughout the dance scene, Guerrero uses close ups on the girls' hands as they touch and share this moment, showing their fingers intertwined, touching each other's waists and hips. Both short films debuted at the Sundance Film Festival, picking up attention from Sundance as well as Tribeca and Film Independent. The next time Guerrero debuted a film at the Sundance film festival, it was perhaps her most influential film to date, *Mosquita y Mari* (Díaz-Sánchez 96).

*Mosquita y Mari* (2012) is a full-length film which follows the relationship between two teenaged Latinas as they explore their same-sex attraction in a subtle, slow-burn romance (Holden). The film delves into the uncertainty and exploration that comes with lesbian relationships, especially between young women who have never considered their own sexuality before (Díaz-Sánchez 98). The main character, Yoli (Fenessa Pineda), is a high school sophomore with nearly perfect grades and heavy pressure from her immigrant parents to succeed in school (Holden). She crosses paths with Mari (Venecia Troncoso), a troubled neighbor who is doing poorly in school, and offers to help her study. As their friendship blossoms, the girls become very close and share quite a few romantic moments with each other (Morales 72). *Mosquita y Mari* is set in the Southern Californian city of Huntington Park, whose Latinx population is 97.1% (Data USA), and the film features an entirely Latinx cast. The setting itself acts as a narrative device, as the girls claim the city as their own over the course of the movie, specifically making a hideaway of their own that they visit while they spend time together (Díaz-Sánchez 99). A theme throughout the film is the ability to have freedom and authority over one's space, often referencing Mari's desire to become a truck driver to have freedom of mobility, and the use of the bicycle as the girls ride around Huntington Park (Díaz-Sánchez 99-100).

Guerrero focuses on the subtle moments between Yoli and Mari, marked by unmet glances at each other, physical closeness, and moments of tension between the characters, without the two acting on their desire forwardly. This is a stark contrast between many other explorations of lesbian sexuality in which their attraction may be oversexualized or even facilitated for the male gaze (Alanis and Kompalic 85). *Mosquita y Mari* captures the intimacy that Guerrero herself confirms is based on her own experiences exploring her sexuality as a young Latina (Alanis and Kompalic 86).

Stylistically, the film creates a soft, emotional feeling to it using many techniques. Close ups on the girls' hands are used frequently as they nervously fidget with things, work on homework together, and share intimate moments of physical touch. These shots give the audience clues as to how the characters are feeling as well as guide their focus along with the character's. For example, while Mari stands in the mirror to change, the camera follows what can be inferred as Yoli's gaze, creating an intimate feeling for the scene and giving the viewer insight as to her feelings about Mari. Another stylistic choice in *Mosquita y Mari* is the use of focus to draw the viewer's eye and create specific feelings. In one scene, the two main characters talk at sunset with shallow focus on them, creating a soft, colorful effect with the lights behind them yet keeping the viewers' attention on the characters. Many of these intimate moments are accompanied by warm, contemplative music that adds to the romantic, close feeling of these scenes.

*Mosquita y Mari* also explores class and financial struggle, as Mari and her family are poor and she often mentions struggles with money, specifically mentioning how this is made harder by her lack of citizenship. Toward the end of the film, Yoli walks in on Mari prostituting herself in order to support her family. This moment captures the desperation Mari feels as she uses the hideaway that she and Yoli created to keep her family financially afloat. Although it was Mari's decision to allow this breach of both her body and her refuge from the world, she does this out of desperation. The build-up throughout the film of Yoli and Mari's soft, subtle, mutually desired relationship is harshly contrasted with this invasion of the metaphorical and literal space as Mari sells her favors to the older man (Aldama 126).

*Mosquita y Mari* went on to be shown in over one hundred film festivals, and amassed many awards and nominations. Following the success of *Mosquita y Mari*, Guerrero directed an episode of *Queen Sugar* (2017), a TV series following a Black family struggling to navigate their futures and assets after a family tragedy, further solidifying Guerrero's history of focusing on stories of people of color (Alanis and Kompalic 90). The episode centers around the romance and sexuality between the characters Violet (Tina Lifford) and Hollywood (Omar J. Dorsey).

Guerrero's directing style for *Queen Sugar* had quite a few stylistic similarities to *Mosquita y Mari*, including use of shallow focus to draw the viewer's attention and create an intimate, emotional feeling. Often the shots would be framed to have a lot of the background visible behind the characters, although out of focus. This episode, however, did not share the use of close ups on hands and other movements like *Mosquita y Mari* or *Viernes Girl*, highlighting the difference in the way Guerrero portrays heterosexual and lesbian intimacy.

Aurora Guerrero has also collaborated with Lin Manuel-Miranda to direct a short film for a song from the Hamilton Mixtape, *Andra Day: Burn* (2018). The short film follows a woman coping with her partner cheating on her.

Guerrero's work provides an important, unrepresented perspective for the film community. The intersectionality of race, gender, sexuality, and class are all explored in her work, highlighting her own unique experience as a queer Chicana feminist, and drawing from the works of Anzaldúa and Moraga with themes of intersecting identities that build upon one another. Not only does she share the stories of Latinas, but queer Latinas, often intersecting with themes of class struggle and immigration status (Gopinath 12). Her portrayal of queer Latinas is romantic and not hypersexualized or centered toward the male gaze as many depictions of lesbian relationships in media are (Alanis and Kompalic 85) By centering her stories on mostly Latinx people and other people of color, Guerrero is able to exhibit intersectional stories and characters and provide representation to those who are usually extremely unrepresented in film.

**Katie Morgan** is a third-year student at the University of Georgia working towards a bachelor's degree in marine biology. She is specifically interested in studying sharks and other cartilaginous fish, and plans to graduate in spring of 2023.

## Bibliography

Alanis, Diana, and Verónica González Kompalic. "Aurora Guerrero on *Mosquita y Mari*: 'My Experience Is Just a Fraction of What We've Lived [and] What Our Community Goes Through.'" *Film Matters*, vol. 9, no. 2, Fall 2018, pp. 85–91.

Aldama, Arturo J. "Decolonizing Predatory Masculinities in *Breaking Bad* and *Mosquita y Mari*." *Decolonizing Latinx Masculinities*, edited by Arturo J. Aldama and Frederick Luis Aldama. U of Arizona P, 2020, pp. 117–130.

Data USA, "Huntington Park, CA." https://datausa.io/profile/geo/huntington-park-ca/.

Díaz-Sánchez, Micaela Jamaica. "Re-Mapping Queer Desire(s) on Greater Los Angeles: The Decolonial Topographies of Aurora Guerrero and Dalila Paola Méndez." *Chicana/Latina Studies* vol. 17, no. 1, 2017, pp. 94–117.

"Five Major Influences For Aurora Guerrero." *Tribeca Film Institute*, https://www.tfiny.org/blog/detail/five_major_influences_for_aurora_guerrero.

Gopinath, Gayatri. *Unruly Visions: The Aesthetic Practices of Queer Diaspora*. Duke University Press, 2018.

Holden, Stephen. "Bravado and Caresses: Girls on the Way to Life." *New York Times*, 3 Aug 2012, C7(L).

Launius, Christie. "*Real Women Have Curves*: A Feminist Narrative of Upward Mobility." *American Drama*, vol. 16, no. 2, 2007, pp. 15–27.

Morales, Nicole. "*Mosquita y Mari*." *Bitch Magazine*, no. 55, Summer 2012, p. 72.

# LIN-MANUEL MIRANDA

Grace Kennedy

Lin-Manuel Miranda grew up in a predominantly Spanish-speaking, immigrant neighborhood in northern Manhattan in New York City. He was born to immigrant parents who moved from Puerto Rico to New York City in order to provide a new life and opportunities for their children. From a young age, Miranda experienced the isolation that is expressed by many first-generation Latinx individuals: a feeling of being different from his white, English-speaking classmates while also feeling separate from other Latinx children in his neighborhood and his family back in Puerto Rico. He grappled with these feelings throughout the majority of his teenage years (Norman 9-12).

Miranda began his career on the stage in musical theater. He began directing, writing, and acting in short plays and musicals while still in middle school, continuing to do so until he graduated from high school. He first got the idea for his first musical, *In the Heights*, while still in college, and he dedicated months of his time to creating the first rendition of the musical. He has described the process of developing the original version of the show, explaining that it really allowed him to better connect to his Latinx background and that the entire experience brought him closer to his cultural roots (Schwartz 10-13). After leaving college, Miranda began to develop the project more, bringing together a diverse set of writers, producers, and cast members to work on expanding the story and characters. The original cast consisted of a wide array of different first-generation Americans, many of whom had at least one parent coming from a Latin American country. Miranda and his writing partner, Quiara Alegría Hudes, fleshed out the story, explaining that they "wanted to give more realistic, rounded portrayals of Latinx characters" (Norman 25). *In the Heights* opened on Broadway in March of 2008, launching the beginning of a very successful career for Miranda. In the same year, he began working on his next project, a musical centered around one of the founding fathers, Alexander Hamilton. The release of *Hamilton* in 2015 was viewed as a revolutionary moment on Broadway because of its unique hip-hop approach—inspired by music Miranda listened to in his neighborhood growing up—as well as its diverse cast of characters, contributing to a "definite upward trend in the casting of minority actors" (Craft).

While he worked on a variety of small TV and film roles in addition to his musical theater work, Miranda's major transition to the big screen was seen in 2021 with the release of the film adaptation of *In the Heights*. He also composed the music for several Disney movies, helped research and develop the story for Disney's *Encanto*, and had his directorial debut with the Netflix original movie, *Tick, Tick... Boom!* (2021). Through all of the works done by Miranda—whether they be on the stage or on the big screen—one common theme that permeates is the discussion of immigration and the generational trauma that often comes with it. This can be observed in both *In the Heights* and *Encanto,* with both films discussing different implications of the aforementioned generational trauma.

*In the Heights (2021)* follows the lives of several different individuals in the Washington Heights neighborhood of New York City, focusing specifically on local bodega owner, Usnavi de la Vega (Anthony Ramos). Usnavi is the son of Dominican immigrants and has a dream to move to the Dominican Republic in order to better connect with his heritage. His story is intertwined with that of several other characters, all with their own dreams, motivations, and internal battles with their backgrounds. Nina Rosario (Leslie Grace) is both a first-generation American and a first-generation college student, grappling with the weight of being the "success story" for immigrants in the community. Sonny (Gregory Diaz IV) is Usnavi's younger cousin who has a passion for social justice and desire for education and is held back by his immigration status. These stories all tie in together to display the unique experiences and struggles faced by different Latinx individuals.

Stylistically, the film pays homage to the original musical through its musical numbers involving massive dance scenes, shot using a series of crane shots and long shots to fully capture the entire cast within the frame. The camera movements in these musical scenes are set apart from the stage with their camera movements and framing; on a stage, one can only use stage movements and lighting to create the different movements and emphasis. In the film, the camera uses rapid movements and zooms to establish the high-energy, fast-paced nature of the neighborhood and match the energy of the soundtrack.

Miranda played the roles of actor, composer, producer, and writer for the film, though we will be focusing on his roles as writer and producer. While writing the script for the film, Miranda wanted to create a story that Latinx individuals could connect with while highlighting key issues such as immigration, the generational trauma that comes with immigration, and the gentrification faced by immigrant communities. Gabriela Cázares describes the story as an experience "written by a Latinx about the Latinx experience, specifically with respect to gentrification" (90). Like previously mentioned, the characters within the film are all either the children of immigrants or immigrants themselves. The story addresses the different manifestations of this trauma within the different characters. As mentioned before, Nina deals with the pressure and expectations as a first-generation student at a prestigious college while also struggling to fit in with her peers; her father (Jimmy Smits) unknowingly projects his expectations of a better life onto her by giving up everything he has in order for her to succeed, putting even greater pressure onto her as she tries to navigate the disconnect with her identity and community. Usnavi, having lost his parents at a young age, is left only with idealized stories of the Dominican Republic to remember them by; he spends his time dedicated to connecting with his parents and culture by hyperfixating on returning to where they had come from.

The discussion of gentrification arises in several instances throughout the story. The neighborhood *piragüero*, or shaved-ice vendor (Lin-Manuel Miranda), describes how he is being put out of business by the Mister Softee truck in the song "Piragua." Nina's father, Kevin, has a similar experience with a neighboring business owner looking to buy out his office with a large sum of money; Kevin caves and sells his business in order to pay for Nina's tuition. In the song "96,000", Usnavi describes that if he won the lottery, the money would be needed "just to save [his] ass from financial ruin." All of these storylines address the issues faced in many immigrant communities: larger corporations will always come in and buy out local businesses, taking advantage of the financial desperation of lower income communities, or the prices in these areas will continue to rise until people can no longer afford to live there.

The other high-profile film Miranda worked on is the Disney-Pixar animated film, *Encanto*. The film is set in a fictional nation, inspired heavily by Colombia. The film's producer, Clark Spencer, describes the choice of setting, stating "Colombia is really the crossroads of Latin America. The people are Spanish, they're Black, they're Indigenous . . . you can get everything you want and more from Latin America" (Rifkin). It follows the magical Madrigal family, made up of multiple generations of magic users, as they navigate complex familial relationships and expectations.

Miranda acted as a composer and story-contributor for the film; he worked very closely with the writers and producers to make the representation of the culture and dynamics as authentic as possible, keeping in mind the imaginary nature of the setting. He went on research expeditions to Colombia in order to better understand the culture and create music that best fits the sounds and experiences of the country.

Despite being a children's movie, *Encanto* really highlights the dangerous conditions that push communities to immigrate, the long-lasting trauma that comes from those experiences, and the impact that it has on future generations. The elder matriarch of the Madrigals, Abuela Alma (voiced by María Cecilia Botero), was forced to flee her original home with her three newborn babies and her husband as men ransacked their town, burning and destroying everything in their sight. In the process, Alma's husband was killed, leaving her to raise her children alone in an unfamiliar area. This depiction in the film leaves the attackers very ambiguous, with no real identifying features really being shown. This deliberately allows viewers to project their own experiences with persecution onto the film.

The film discusses how Abuela Alma's concerns have been projected onto her entire family. Alma cast out her own son Bruno (voiced by John Leguizamo) because his abilities weren't conducive to her ideal, perfect family structure. She constantly isolates and excludes Mirabel (Stephanie Beatriz) because she lacks the gifts that are the identifying feature of their family, she projects her need for perfection onto Luisa (voiced by Jessica Darrow) until she breaks down from overworking herself, and forces Isabela (voiced by Diane Guerrero) into a life as the perfect child—similar to Nina from *In the Heights*—despite that not being the life she wants for herself.

Lin-Manuel Miranda, despite being relatively new to film, has already begun to make a name for himself and use his extensive platform to create content for

Latinx viewers that allows them to see characters that share their appearances, experiences, and backgrounds while also discussing complex topics such as generational trauma and the lives of immigrants.

**Grace Kennedy** *is a criminal justice student who also studies sociology and culture. She enjoys examining sociological and cultural concepts in pop-culture media like film and television to see various portrayals and discuss the implications of different kind of representation.*

## Bibliography

Aguilar, Carlos. "'In the Heights': How Cinematographer Alice Brooks Captured a Hollywood Musical on Location." *IndieWire*, 11 June 2021, https://www.indiewire.com/2021/06/in-the-heights-cinematography-alice-brooks-shooting-on-location-1234643923/.

Craft, Elizabeth Titrington. "Can We 'Leave behind the World We Know'?" *The Routledge Companion to the Contemporary Musical*, edited by Jessica Sternfield and Elizabeth L. Wollman. Routledge, 2019, pp. 216–225.

Cázares, Gabriela. "Resisting Gentrification in Quiara Alegría Hudes and Lin-Manuel Miranda's *In the Heights* and Ernesto Quiñonez's *Bodega Dreams*." *American Studies*, vol. 56, no. 2, 2017, pp. 89–107.

Hans, Simran. "*Encanto* Review – Disney Musical Casts Its Spell with a Little Help from Lin-Manuel Miranda." *The Guardian*, 27 Nov. 2021, https://www.theguardian.com/film/2021/nov/27/encanto-review-disney-musical-animation-lin-manuel-miranda.

Nelson, Rajczak Kristen. *Lin-Manuel Miranda: From Broadway to the Big Screen*. Lucent Press, 2019.

Rifkin, Jesse. "Cinematic Enchantment: Disney Reunites with Lin-Manual Miranda for Animated Musical Encanto." *Boxoffice*, 28 Nov. 2021, https://www.boxofficepro.com/encanto-disney-lin-manual-miranda/.

Schwartz, Heather E. *Lin-Manuel Miranda: Revolutionary Playwright, Composer, and Actor*. Lerner Publications, 2020.

# GREGORY NAVA

Zayna Khan

Gregory Nava is a widely known director and screenwriter of Mexican and Basque heritage who directed *El Norte, Selena, Mi Familia, Bordertown*, and other award-winning and nominated films (Raab 178). He grew up on the border of Mexico and the United States (West 26), alternating between living in San Diego and Tijuana on his grandfather's ranch (Portillo and Harrington). The experiences he and his family went through because of where they are from influenced Nava's work as he grew older. For example, he deals with the issue of deportation in the film *Mi Familia* because his grandfather was deported back to Mexico even though he was an American citizen (Portillo and Harrington). Another example are the hospital scenes in his work; he was very close to his Aunt Lucy and draws from his traumatic experience with her death in his films (Portillo and Harrington). In *El Norte* Rosa dies in a hospital, and in *Mi Familia*, Isabelle dies in childbirth. There is also the scene in *Selena* where she dies in the hospital after getting shot. Because Gregory Nava lived on the border, he saw the contrast between a first world city and a city filled with poverty. In addition, to finding inspiration in his family, his work was also influenced by the families he observed around him that lived on the border (West 26). In an interview by the Academy of Motion Picture Arts and Sciences, Nava calls these experiences "powerful images" and implies that they are the reason why he has such good artistic capabilities when making films (Portillo and Harrington).

Nava was involved in film from an early age. His family shot many home movies (Portillo and Harrington), so Nava was often being recorded as a child. In high school he made a movie with his brother's Bolex 8 mm camera named *The Day 100,000 People Vanished*. He then attended UC Berkeley for college (Portillo and Harrington), later transferring to UCLA film school, where he made his first film called *The Journal of Diego Rodríguez Silva* (Raab 178). The film was about Spanish poet Federico García Lorca and played with the themes of betrayal because he was influenced by what was going on around him. There were betrayals during the student movements that were happening, and his uncle betrayed his grandfather by stealing his ranch (Portillo and Harrington). Nava shot the entire movie by himself; he was the only person in the film production crew. He also chose exactly where the film should be in Mexico because he had lived there for much of his life (Portillo and Harrington). *The Journal of Diego Rodríguez Silva* won the National Student Film Festival Drama Award in 1972. The next film Nava made got slightly more recognition and was shown at the Chicago Film Festival (Portillo and Harrington). It was called *The Confessions of Amans*. The film was about a scholar in medieval Spain, and it established his reputation as a credible filmmaker (Raab 178).

After the release of his first two movies, Nava got to work on a film focused on Latinos called *El Norte* (1983). Nava's wife, Anna Thomas, helped him write the screenplay, but when he sent the script around, nobody wanted to work on it because there were no white people in the movie (Portillo and Harrington). *El Norte* follows two Mayan siblings from Guatemala as they go to Mexico and try to cross the border to America, and Nava was against adding a white hero to his film that would essentially "save" the siblings from their home country and bring them to the idyllic America because he didn't want the story to be colonized (Barrera 233). Nava used a concept that he would later include in his more recent films as well, and he structured the story on Indigenous mythology. He took inspiration from the Popol Vuh, a Mayan text, in which a set of twins must go through trials before being able to achieve their goal. He also includes mythical and magical imagery as in a scene with the white butterflies in *El Norte*. Nava believed taking influences from myths would allow his work to strike his audience more emotionally (Barrera 233). *El Norte* includes the theme of family, which can be seen when Enrique (David Villalpando) must decide whether to stay with Rosa (Zaide Silvia Gutiérrez) in the hospital or go to Chicago in order to make money, and he eventually gives up his materialistic desires to stay with his sister.

Because Nava wanted Indigenous Mayans to be the main characters (even though the actors who play them are non-Indigenous Mexicans), the movie needed to include three languages: Quiché Mayan, Spanish, and English (Williams 57). Initially, Nava had to shelve the project when he couldn't find anybody to finance his movie. However, eventually Lindsey Law, the vice president of American Playhouse (a venture of four public television stations that helped finance feature films in exchange for the rights to broadcast them on PBS), liked the script and Nava had enough money to continue making the film. The movie included around sixty speaking parts (Rosen 254). Similar to how he filmed *The Journal of Diego Rodriguez Silva* (Portillo and Harrington), Nava chose locations all around Mexico. However, he did also film in the United States. *El Norte* premiered at the Telluride Film Festival, and it was rather successful, receiving many offers to distribute the movie in theaters (Rosen 254). While *El Norte* included three languages, Spanish was the only language used during plot development to cater to the Latinx audience more than Indigenous audiences or US viewers who only spoke English (Williams 59).

Nava's next project was *Mi Familia* (1995), a movie that follows the Sánchez family from Mexico to America beginning around 1920 and ending in 1978 (Raab 182). Nava collaborated with the well-known producer and director Francis Ford Coppola, who helped him get a budget for the movie and a studio to accept the script. On the same film, Nava also worked with Ed Lachman, an Oscar-nominated cinematographer. Lachman then went on to work with Nava for his next two films, *Selena* and *Why do Fools Fall in Love*. Editor Nancy Richardson also first worked with Nava on *Mi Familia* and now cuts most of his films. When working on *Mi Familia*, Richardson had to change her editing style three times because the movie follows three generations that have their own distinct time periods (Portillo and Harrington).

Nava's *Mi Familia* is a significant film because it not only increased the visibility of Chicanos, but also veered away from the negative stereotypes that are often associated with Latinos. Nava wasn't the first director to try and change the perception Americans had of people of Hispanic heritage, but he did help popularize the inclusion of Indigenous mythology in films, referencing the Mayan, Aztec, and other pre-Columbian roots of many Chicanos (West 27). *Mi Familia* is often regarded as Nava's response to social issues involving Chicanos and their struggle for rights and equality (Serrato 69). Additionally, people see *Mi Familia* as a representation of Nava's own family, and in an interview, he stated that he made the narrator's father strong, supportive, and loving to resemble his own father (Portillo and Harrington). One criticism of this film is that it forces Chicanos into a narrow definition because the family lives in East Los Angeles, which is famously known for having a high population of Mexican Americans. That region of California was also correlated with poverty and crime, so having the family live there seemed to perpetuate stereotypes. However, East Los Angeles was not portrayed how white people in America perceived it; the community shown in *Mi Familia* represents the Mexican American identity and authenticity. *Mi Familia* touches on the fact that much of the southwestern United States was once a part of Mexico. One of the characters in the movie is called El Californio, because he was born in Mexico. However, his birthplace is now called Los Angeles, playing with the idea that the people some Americans call illegal have more historical claim to the land than U.S. citizens. A constraint on Nava's creative agency is that he had to be careful in what messages he conveyed because as one of the filmmakers to create popular Latinx films with large Chicano casts, he acted as an authority on the subject of Chicano identity, and it was very easy for him to do damage to the perception of Mexican Americans with his portrayal of them in his film. Therefore, it was important for him to stray from the then normalized negative stereotypes of impoverished, violent Latinos (Serrato 74-75).

One of Nava's most recent films is *Bordertown* (2007), which is a thriller about the murders of many women working in American factories in a town called Juárez near the border. This film deals with the political issue of the influence of the North American Free Trade Agreement (NAFTA) on Mexico and the social issue of the working conditions inside American-owned factories or **maquiladoras**. NAFTA allowed trade between the United States, Canada, and Mexico to happen without trade barriers like tariffs and quotas. However, this agreement negatively impacted workers because now that people could trade without limits, more factories were set up in Mexico with lower wages and no concern for the workers' safety. In addition, most of the workers were women because companies found that they were more willing to accept lower wages. Women would work in the factories while passing through the cities near the border, hoping to be able to cross the border soon. These women were targeted by men and murdered (Monnet 200-206). Business owners in America benefited from the suffering going on in these factories because they were making money selling the products made in the factories. *Bordertown* focuses on the murders of women, an issue that was kept quiet for a long time because it was in the best interests of the Mexican government and US corporations. This led to Nava was receiving death threats; ultimately, he had to film the rest of the movie somewhere else (Raab 188).

A major shift within Nava's film style as he filmed *El Norte*, *Mi Familia*, and *Bordertown* is how Chicanos were viewed in terms of "otherness" and "outsidedness" (Raab 179). While Nava does develop his themes and style as he makes more films, he keeps certain aspects constant such as his use of mainly Latinx actors, the theme of family, and resisting the use of stereotypes (Agostinelli 47). In *El Norte* and *Mi Familia*, which were Nava's earlier films, the Latinx characters are defined as the "others," meaning they are shown as being different from the rest of the population. For example, in *El Norte,* Rosa speaks a different language from the other Latinos in the film, who only speak Spanish. In addition, a lot of mythical Mayan elements are associated with Rosa, marking her as different. In *Mi Familia*, the otherness that the Sánchez family experiences is less because while they are shown to be culturally different from those around them, they are also shown to have the same human attributes that everyone else has. In *Bordertown*, which is one of Nava's much later works, the white owners of the factories are associated with this concept of otherness (Raab 190). Throughout all these films, Nava makes sure that most of the cast is Latinx and that he is portraying them in a positive light without making use of harmful stereotypes. In addition, family is a theme seen often in his films through the sibling bond between Rosa and Enrique and the support that the Sánchez family gives each other.

**Zayna Khan** *is a first-year student at UGA studying biology with the goal to go to medical school. She is also looking to minor in either computer science or math. Her hobbies include watching films, reading, and calligraphy. She enjoys travelling and plans to study abroad next Spring.*

## Bibliography

Agostinelli, Gianni. "A Mexican American Journey of Generations: *My Family: Three Generations of Dreams.*" *Migration World Magazine*, vol. 23, no. 3, 1995, p. 47.

Barrera, Mario. "Story Structure in Latino Feature Films." *Chicanos in Film: Essays on Chicano Representation and Resistance*, edited by Chon A. Noriega, Garland Publishing, 1992, pp. 218–40.

Monnet, Agnieszka Soltysik. "Border Gothic: Gregory Nava's *Bordertown* and the Dark Side of the NAFTA." *Neoliberal Gothic: International Gothic in the Neoliberal Age,* edited by Linnie Blake and Agnieszka Soltysik Monnet, Manchester University Press, 2017, pp. 200–14.

Portillo, Lourdes and Harrington, Ellen. "Gregory Nava, Academy Visual History." *Academy of Motion Picture Arts and Sciences*, 2016, https://pstlala.oscars.org/interview/gregory-nava/.

Raab, Josef. "Latinos and Otherness: The Films of Gregory Nava." *E Pluribus Unum? National and Transnational Identities in the Americas,* edited by Sebastian Thies and Josef Raab, Bilingual Press, 2009, pp. 175–92.

Rosen, David. "Crossover: Hispanic Specialty Films in the U.S. Movie Marketplace." *Chicanos in Film: Essays on Chicano Representation and Resistance*, edited by Chon A. Noriega, Garland Publishing, 1992, pp. 241–60.

Serrato, Phillip. "Just the Tip of the Iceberg: The Truncation of Mexican American Identity in *My Family/Mi Familia.*" *Mester*, vol. 33, no. 1, 2004, pp. 68–90.

West, Dennis and Nava, Gregory. "Filming the Chicano Family Saga: An Interview with Gregory Nava." *Cinéaste*, vol. 21, no. 4, 1995, pp. 26–28.

Williams, Bruce. "The Bridges of Los Angeles County: Marketing Language in the Chicano Cinema of Gregory Nava." *Canadian Journal of Film Studies*, vol. 14, no. 2, 2005, pp. 54–70.

## DANNY TREJO

Chris Borg

Danny Trejo is an actor who has been working in the film industry since 1983. Trejo has dozens of acting credits as of 2021, according to his website dannytrejo.com. More than anything, Trejo is known for his demeanor as "a stocky, long-haired, often mustachioed, craggy-faced American of Mexican descent covered in prison tattoos from his previous life as a violent offender" (Meeuf 117). As an actor, Trejo has worked with mostly action directors such as Michael Mann, Robert Rodriguez, Rob Zombie, and John Frankenheimer, among many others.

Born in Los Angeles in 1944 to Mexican American parents, Trejo's adolescent years were marred with constant run-ins with law enforcement which started as young as when the actor was ten (Trejo 19). Trejo was moved around to five high schools in Los Angeles in a year (Trejo 20) and became known for his hot-headed temper and knack for fighting. Eventually, his involvement in crime such as dealing drugs and collecting debts (Trejo 74-75) landed him in jail multiple times, culminating with a final stint at Soledad State Prison prior to his release in 1969 (Trejo 116). In 1968, his last year in prison, Trejo made the decision to sober up (Trejo 109). Trejo also completed a twelve-step rehab program and became a drug counselor for a local rehab program, something that he continues to volunteer for (Bowles).

Trejo did not begin acting until his late thirties and this new career path could be described as a massive coincidence. In prison, Trejo made a name for himself among inmates and guards as a competitive boxer (Trejo 73). It was these martial arts skills paired with Trejo's threatening demeanor that gave him his first film acting role in the 1985 film *Runaway Train*. It was the film's director, Andrei Konchalovsky, who took a liking to Trejo and offered him a role in the film as a prison boxer who has to fight Eric Roberts' character. On top of an acting role, Trejo was also given the job of training Eric Roberts with his boxing skills (Trejo, 222). Following this role in *Runaway Train*, the former convict decided to pivot to a career in acting. Trejo was given his first speaking role in *Death Wish 4: The Crackdown* (1987) and continued to appreciate more and more minor acting roles each subsequent year. In the documentary *Inmate #1: The Rise of Danny Trejo*, Trejo remarks "I trained at San Quentin Drama Arts", a tongue-in-cheek joke about the fact that he never had any professional acting lessons (Harvey).

Another key work in Danny Trejo's filmography that harkens back to his earlier roles is the 1995 Michael Mann-directed film *Heat*. A blockbuster film like *Heat* is indicative of not only the action movies that Trejo chooses to act in but also his characters' tendency to die violent deaths, akin to the roles played by actor Sean Bean. *Con Air* (1997), *Reindeer Games* (2000), *Anaconda* (1997), and *The Hidden* (1987) are just a few among the myriad of films where Trejo is slain. In *Heat*, Trejo plays a substantial role as a professional criminal who is part of a heist crew led by Neil McCauley (Robert De Niro). Trejo's character (also named Trejo) as well as the two other members of the crew, Waingro (Kevin Gage) and Michael Cherrito (Tom Sizemore), are introduced to the audience separately during the first robbery sequence. This "differentiates the collective of mavericks from the unified groups of men in films by John Ford or Howard Hawks" and Trejo gives off a "don't mess with me" criminal attitude (Rybin, 138). Trejo had complained that in his previous film, *Desperado* (1995) director Robert Rodriguez would not let him speak in his role as Navajas because his face said more "than most actors can do with a page of dialogue" (VladTV), but in *Heat* that was not the case. When McCauley finds Trejo bloodied and dying, Trejo reveals Waingro's betrayal of the other members of the crew before asking to be put out of his misery by McCauley. Michael Mann scholar Steven Rybin discusses how Mann and cinematographer Dante Spinotti utilize the empty spaces of the Los Angeles skyline at night. The skyline is enormous, intangible, and infinite in its possibilities (Rybin, 139). The execution of Trejo by McCauley is no different, as the camera cuts away to the LA skyline while the muzzle flash is seen and gunshot is heard. The overall quiet sound-mixing of the city, briefly interrupted by a loud noise is juxtaposed with a depiction of the city as vast, spread out, and atomizing to its residents (Rybin 137). The way that Mann depicts Los Angeles in *Heat* is a society where Danny Trejo's character is still bound to the film archetypes of the past, just like Kevin Gage and Tom Sizemore's characters are. But Trejo's character name even suggests a sense of otherness compared to the two other members of the heist crew. Considering that his character name is "Trejo", the same as his actual last name suggests that the actor "is playing himself when he takes on roles as career criminals" (Meeuf 125).

What makes Danny Trejo's work significant as a Chicano actor is how the image of Latino machismo that the actor projects has shifted since he began acting in the eighties to the present day. Like many other character actors, the possible cult appeal could lie in Trejo's embodiment of difference and otherness "emblematic of a recognizable, but personally distinct social position" (Thomas 3). Trejo's rise to fame as an actor included him affirming many of the stereotypes that plague Latino men as hyper-masculine, violent criminals (Meeuf 117). In the book *Rebellious Bodies: Stardom, Citizenship, and the New Body Politics*, Russell Meeuf remarks how the characters that Trejo has portrayed in his film career also have changed as Latino visibility has increased in the past few decades (118). Since the mid-2000s, the roles Trejo has chosen depict his menacing, violent characters as figures that are compulsory in reforming whiteness as well as mocking outdated stereotypes (Meeuf 118-119). These critiques of how certain white Americans view the Latinx population are represented in films like *Machete* (2010) constitute "a joke about how silly violent Latino machismo is while simultaneously expressing a deep longing for such masculinities" (Meeuf 120).

2010's *Machete* marks Trejo's first leading role, given to him by his longtime collaborator, second cousin, and friend Robert Rodriguez. Rodriguez had worked with Trejo on six films before giving the actor top billing at the age of sixty-six.

*Machete* is inspired by the hyperviolent "grindhouse" exploitation films of the 1970s, but this time helmed by a Latino protagonist. In the film, the titular ex-*Federale* agent Machete (Danny Trejo) is forced by businessman Michel Booth (Jeff Fahey) to assassinate Texas State Senator John McLaughlin (Robert De Niro), who is running on a protectionist re-election platform of deporting illegal immigrants. This ends up all being a false flag operation in which Machete is set up to botch the assassination attempt of McLaughlin as a way for the Senator to gain more support in the polls. Academic William Orchard notes that "scholars have viewed [*Machete*] as a fantasy response to the political persecution of Latin@s, one in which the film's hero fulfills the wish for justice through spectacular acts of violence" (222) but the analysis of the film's significance should be broader in scope. Machete's actions in the film show a character of traditional heroism, masculinity, and rugged individualism (Orchard 226). He stands apart from the film's depiction of a network to resettle illegal immigrants and elude oppressors such as Immigration and Customs Enforcement (ICE). Machete's rugged and old-fashioned character is less concerned with the plight of the migrants rather than his own predicament of being pursued by people who want him dead for attempting to assassinate, against his will, a politician who happens to hold strong anti-immigrant views.

Danny Trejo is a rare case of someone who has grown in star power even as he reached senior citizen status. His pride in his Chicano heritage also represents the shifting visibility of these identities as Hollywood has continued to progress to become a more inclusive space. One thing is for sure: with over a dozen projects in production, Danny Trejo is not going away any time soon.

**Chris Borg** *is an undergraduate student at the University of Georgia majoring in political science and film studies. Chris' academic pursuits surround the overlap between historic political movements and how they were shaped by cinema. Some of his favorite films include* Medium Cool *(1969),* Koyaanisqatsi *(1982), and* Lost in America *(1985).*

## Bibliography

Bowles, Scott. "Machete' Star Danny Trejo Is an Illustrated Man, in Many Ways." *USA Today*, 3 Sept 2010, https://usatoday30.usatoday.com/life/movies/news/2010-09-03-trejo03_st_N.htm.

Harvey, Brett, director. *Inmate #1: The Rise of Danny Trejo. ITunes*, Universal Studios, 2019, https://itunes.apple.com/us/movie/inmate-1-the-rise-of-danny-trejo/id1518094623.

Meeuf, Russell. *Rebellious Bodies: Stardom, Citizenship, and the New Body Politics*. U of Texas P, 2017.

Orchard, William. "Machete Don't Text." *Aztlan: Journal of Chicano Studies*, vol. 41, no. 1, 2016, pp. 235–249.

Rybin, Steven. *Michael Mann: Crime Auteur*. Scarecrow Press, 2013.

Thomas, Sarah. "'Marginal Moments of Spectacle': Character Actors, Cult Stardom and Hollywood Cinema." *Cult Film Stardom*, edited by Kate Egan and Sarah Thomas, Palgrave Macmillan, 2013, pp. 37–54.

Trejo, Danny. *Trejo: My Life of Crime, Redemption, and Hollywood*. Atria Books, 2021.

VladTV, "Danny Trejo on Doing 'Heat' with Al Pacino and Robert De Niro (Part 9)."*YouTube*, 29 May 2019, https://www.youtube.com/watch?v=DD_E3taRvBg.

# LUIS VALDEZ

Andrew Phipps

Luis Valdez is a Chicano playwright and director and is regarded as the father of Chicano theater. While best known for writing and directing the films *Zoot Suit* and *La Bamba,* Valdez has been involved in the film and theater industry since 1963 when he staged his first play. Through his work, Valdez has fought for the civil rights of Chicanos by rallying workers to fight for better working conditions and putting on display the struggles and discrimination felt by Chicanos in America.

Luis Valdez was born in Delano, California in 1940 to migrant farm worker parents from Mexico. Being the second child of a family of 12, Valdez began helping his parents in the fields at the age of six (D'Souza). In addition, his family moved frequently as they followed the seasonal harvests. Due to this, it comes as no surprise that later in his early adult life Valdez would focus on improving the lives of farmworkers through his work. Despite the struggles in his early life, he did well in school, taking a liking to performance early on, and eventually going on to produce his first full-length play, "The Shrunken Head of Pancho Villa," while in college (Nelson 493).

After college, Valdez began his career in the San Francisco Mime Troupe, a theatre group that produces political satire. A farmworkers' movement had risen up in California, with one of the most notable groups established being the National Farm Workers Association (NFWA), now known as the **United Farm Workers**. During his stay with the troupe, Valdez formulated the idea of "a theatre group for the Valley," however he recognized he "didn't have the resources" (Bagby 73). After attending a march in the Delano Grape Strike on September 8, 1965, Valdez spoke with Dolores Huerta, the co-founder of the NFWA, about creating a farm workers theatre (Bagby 74). Huerta and Cesar Chávez, the other co-founder of the NFWA, encouraged Luis to return to Delano and after some test trials, El Teatro Campesino (The Farmworkers' Theater) was formed later that year (Bagby 74-75).

El Teatro Campesino acted as the cultural arm of the NFWA, contesting inadequate working conditions, raising money for the strike, and gaining the union new members (Elam 3). In the beginning, performances were often improvisational, largely relying on physical comedy and expressive gestures and body movements (Elam 3). As the group grew, Valdez incorporated *mitos* (myths) and *corridos* (ballads) into the performances (Nelson 494). These elements emphasized the social justice struggle and served to affirm cultural consciousness or Chicanismo to their largely Chicano audiences (Elam 47; Nelson 494). These musical elements seen in the *corridos* of the plays would also be seen in Valdez's later work such as *Zoot Suit* and *La Bamba*.

While at first, the members of El Teatro Campesino were seen as "*payasos*" (clowns), the theater quickly gained popularity and was effective at lifting the spirits of the strikers while focusing attention on the strike breakers (Valdez 38-39). In fact, the group became so popular that it would later break away from the

NFWA and tour both the United States and Europe (Nelson 494). Along with this growth in popularity came a growth in influence. El Teatro Campesino managed to convince thousands of farm workers to join the strike and in 1970, along with the NFWA (now the UFW after merging with another labor group), would pressure agribusiness to sign the first union contract with farm workers in American history (Valdez 43).

Valdez would later begin breaking away from El Teatro Campesino in 1978 during the first production of the play *Zoot Suit*. Similar to the *corridos*, the play features music and singing. However, unlike his previous work in the *actos* (political skits), *mitos*, and *corridos* of El Teatro Campesino, *Zoot Suit* was based on extensive research into a historical event: the Sleepy Lagoon murder trial, an incident that drew attention to the police brutality, discrimination, and injustice felt by the Chicano community. The play broke box office records in Los Angeles theater and would go on to be one of the first Chicano plays to open on Broadway (Valdez and Huerta 11). As a result of *Zoot Suit*'s success, Valdez signed a deal with Universal Pictures, adapting the play into a film as its director.

While *Zoot Suit*'s content contrasted with Luis Valdez's projects with El Teatro Campesino, thematically and stylistically the film is a culmination of his previous work, tackling issues of civil rights in the Chicano community. Aspects of the *actos, mitos,* and *corridos* can be seen throughout the film. The *acto* is seen in the film's presentational style, as it presents the social ills and discrimination felt by the Chicano community in a sort of dramatized documentary (Valdez and Huerta 13-14). Meanwhile, the *mito* and *corrido* can both be seen in the character of El Pachuco (Edward James Olmos), who often breaks into song (though musically, these are not corridos) and exercises his "mythic" powers to freeze time. In addition, El Pachuco also invokes the image of an Aztec in the scene where he is stripped of his zoot suit (Valdez and Huerta 14-15; Galens 274).

The theme of civil rights and the cultural clash between Chicanos and the predominant Anglo culture is repeatedly shown in *Zoot Suit*. This is seen both in the content of the film, but also through the use of style. For instance, the baggy style of dress for which the film is named serves to draw a contrast between Chicano culture and the Anglo mainstream. A sensationalistic press treats the style as evidence of Chicanos' disruptive and violent nature, ultimately leading to a mass arrest and a highly biased trial of the protagonist Hank Reyna (Daniel Valdez) and his friends (Galens 274-275). The absurdity of the discriminatory nature of the justice system is depicted by the sped-up footage of Hank and his friends standing and sitting as their names are mentioned as stipulated by the prosecuting attorney. The theme of cultural clash is depicted stylistically most often in the dance hall scenes, where the mise-en-scène and accelerated shot pace draw a contrast between Hank and his gang and white couples.

Following *Zoot Suit*, Valdez went on to write and direct the movie *La Bamba*. Unlike *Zoot Suit*, *La Bamba* was a commercial success. Like *Zoot Suit*, *La Bamba* incorporates music and dance, as it is based on the life of the Chicano rock 'n' roll star Richard Valenzuela, known professionally as Ritchie Valens (Lou Diamond Philips). Once again, Valdez's film draws attention to discrimination and the struggles of those in the Chicano community as we follow Ritchie Valens through his rags-to-riches tale. Throughout the film, Ritchie deals with discrimination in the film in the form of his White girlfriend Donna (Danielle von Zerneck)'s father, who opposes their being together on account of his race. Similar to *Zoot Suit*, the character of Ritchie's half-brother Bob (Esai Morales) serves as a foil to the protagonist, embodying a symbol of Chicanismo that includes its negative side, akin to El Pachuco (Fregoso 41). This contrast between Ritchie and Bob also serves to critique assimilation into Anglo culture. Bob represents those who have retained their cultural identity or "Chicanismo," and as a result have had their social mobility barred; on the other hand, Ritchie, who is largely assimilated, has greater social mobility (Fregoso 46). All the while, the film still reaffirms cultural consciousness of Chicanos, not unlike El Teatro Campesino, by showing how it was through Ritchie's trip to Tijuana that he was able to discover the song "La Bamba," which later topped the charts.

Stylistically, *La Bamba* is more subdued than *Zoot Suit*, with Valdez sticking to more conventional Hollywood technique. Despite this, the film still utilizes different stylistic choices to build upon its themes. For instance, the contrast between the good, assimilated Ritchie and the bad, *machista* Bob is seen in the stares Bob gets when he returns home, shown via **point-of-view** (POV) shots from Bob's perspective and the POV shots as he gets into a fight during a concert. Ritchie's struggle to make it in America as a musician is shown through his different performances with **eyeline matches** from members of the crowd and Ritchie and their evolution from playing around the campfire, to the garage, to big performances. The theme of cultural consciousness is built on during Bob and Ritchie's trip to Tijuana, where Ritchie rediscovers his roots. An example of this is the contrast of the close-ups of the women at a brothel versus the close-ups of the band that catch Ritchie's attention when they start playing the Mexican folk song "La Bamba."

In short, Luis Valdez was (and still is) an influential member of the Chicano film and theater communities. Through his work in El Teatro Campesino, films, and plays he has managed to make strides in Chicano civil rights by bringing attention to issues of discrimination, injustice in the judicial system, and the importance of cultural consciousness in the Chicano community.

*Andrew Phipps earned a bachelor's degree in Computer Science with a minor in Film Studies from the University of Georgia in 2021.*

## BIBLIOGRAPHY

D'Souza, Karen. "Luis Valdez: the Father of Chicano Theater." The Mercury News, 5 Feb. 2018, https://www.mercurynews.com/2007/11/04/luis-valdez-the-father-of-chicano-theater/.

Nelson, Emmanuel S. *Ethnic American Literature: An Encyclopedia for Students*. ABC-CLIO, 2015.

Bagby, Beth, and Luis Valdez. "El Teatro Campesino: Interviews with Luis Valdez." *The Tulane Drama Review*, vol. 11, no. 4, 1967, pp. 70–80.

Elam, Harry Justin. *Taking It to the Streets: The Social Protest Theater of Luis Valdez and Amiri Baraka*. U of Michigan P, 2005.

Valdez, Luis. *Theatre of the Sphere: The Vibrant Being*. Routledge, 2021.

Valdez, Luis, and Jorge A. Huerta. *Zoot Suit and Other Plays*. Arte Público Press, 1992.

Galens, David. *Drama For Students: Volume 5*. Gale, 1999.

Fregoso, Rosa Linda. *The Bronze Screen: Chicana and Chicano Film Culture*. U of Minnesota P, 2007.

# Glossary

**1965 Immigration Act:** a law representing the first major change to US immigration policy since 1924. Significant aspects the law included the elimination of national origins quotas that had heavily favored Northern European countries while discouraging immigration from other parts of Europe and had banned immigration from much of Asia outright. Each country would henceforth have the same yearly quota for immigrants to the United States, regardless of demand in each country. The law also established paths for individuals to sponsor close family members abroad to immigrate to the United States.

**Advertising-based video on demand (AVOD):** a streaming service that is free to consumers if they watch short commercials.

**Alternative media:** media productions that oppose the institutional and social order of the mainstream media and create media with the goals of social change and challenging dominant media portrayals beyond the commercial sphere. This media is often produced by historically excluded groups of people.

***Antihaitianismo*:** based on traditional racist notions of *negra/o* (Black) inferiority, in the Dominican Republic those notions are structured around their views of, and in relation to, Haiti. Much of Dominican identity is therefore formed in juxtaposition to how Dominicans racialize Haitians as the ones who are truly "Black." And in order to provide that necessary separation from Haitians, African descent is obscured under a claim of being racially Indigenous (or *indio*). For Afro-Dominicans to consider themselves Black or of African descent means that they share a common heritage with Haitians, a population they see as racially and socially inferior to themselves.

**Anti-miscegenation laws:** laws prohibiting marriage between individuals considered to be from different racial groups.

**Balsero crisis:** a sharp increase in the number of Cubans attempting to reach the United States on rafts or boats (totaling over 30,000) in 1994. The immediate cause was economic collapse in Cuba in the wake of the 1991 fall of the Soviet Union, Cuba's main trading partner.

**Bay of Pigs Invasion**: a 1961 attack carried out by CIA-trained and -supported Cuban exiles with the intention of overthrowing Fidel Castro's government.

**BIPOC:** an abbreviation meaning Black, Indigenous, Person of Color.

**Boricua:** a person from Puerto Rico by birth or descent.

**Brown Berets:** a youth organization fighting for Chicano civil rights and community development, founded in 1967 and inspired by the Black Panthers.

**Cable equipment:** an electronic set-up box. This piece of equipment receives TV signals from a cable television system and sends them to a television.

**Camera angle:** the orientation of the camera in relation to its subject, including high angle (the camera is tilted down at a height from the main subject of the shot), low angle (the camera is tilted up from a low position relative to the main subject of the shot), and straight-on angle (the camera is level with the main subject).

**Camera distance:** the apparent distance between the camera and the main subject of the shot, often a human figure. Common terms used to describe camera distance are extreme close-up (a detail of a face or an object fills the frame), close-up (the character's face or another object fills the frame), medium close-up (characters are framed from the shoulders up), medium shot (characters are framed from the waist up), long shot (the full length of characters' bodies are visible in the frame), and extreme long shot (characters appear tiny in relation to the setting). Also known as shot scale.

**Camera movement:** visible changes in the orientation of the camera toward the objects/setting that appear onscreen created by moving the camera during filming.

**Casting:** the process of assembling a group of actors to appear in a film or television project, including not only stars but also the rest of the cast and extras.

**Chicana/o/x:** formerly a derogatory term referring to Mexican Americans, the term was reclaimed during the Chicano Movement of the 1960s and 1970s and refers to Mexican Americans born in the United States.

**Chicano Student Movement to Aztlán (Movimiento Estudiantil Chicano de Aztlán; MEChA):** a student activist group, founded at the University of California, Santa Barbara in 1969.

**Circular migration:** the tendency of individuals to leave their point of origin, migrate to the United States, and return to their point of origin in a cyclical manner.

**Coalition/coalitional:** a coalition refers to a formal or informal political alliance between groups that may not necessarily share all the same interests or goals in order to create a more powerful voting or organizing bloc. Coalitional is the adjective used to describe this type of political strategy.

**Colorblind ideologies:** a set of beliefs that disregards racial and ethnic differences and the realities of discrimination by suggesting we simply need to treat everyone equally, often criticized by advocates for social justice.

**Colorism:** the practice of giving preferential treatment to individuals with lighter skin or more European features.

**Commercial broadcasting:** a form of radio and television sustained financially by advertisers and sponsors rather than through government funding or nonprofit corporations, a system known as public broadcasting.

**Composition:** in the context of film, the arrangement of shapes, colors, and contrasts of light and shadow within the frame in a particular shot.

*Corrido:* a type of folk ballad that emerged in the US-Mexico border region, dedicated to narrating current events. Corridos, including narcocorridos about the exploits of drug traffickers, remain a popular musical genre today.

**Crane shot:** shots that involve the camera being lifted through space, moving freely on a device similar to a construction crane.

**Creator:** in the context of television, a person who develops the idea for a series. The creator is often an executive producer and in some cases a writer-producer. The creator may also be the showrunner, but does not have to be.

*Cuadros de castas:* "caste paintings" that offered terms for and visual representations of specific categories of multiracial individuals, arranging them in an imagined social hierarchy.

**Cuban Adjustment Act:** a 1966 law that granted permanent residency to any Cuban who had lived in the United States for a year or more.

**Data:** in the context of digital media studies, all information collected by users of online media. It is important to remember that data is not an abstract set of values that are then put through a process of categorization. Data is social. Data is produced and sorted by people—it is socially constructed.

**Degeneration:** the idea that unfavorable genetic material or social conditions can lead to physical and/or mental weakness or other problems in an individual or population; linked to flawed, now debunked ideas about human evolution and genetics.

**Diasporic:** pertaining to a dispersed group of people living outside their original homeland due to migration or forced relocation.

**Diegetic sound:** sound that we understand to be emanating from the fictional world of a film that could be heard by the characters.

**Digital divide**: unequal access to new media technologies and infrastructures. This concept has limitations, however. Critical Internet studies has critiqued the notion that simply increasing access serves as a solution to power disparities.

**Digital video recorder (DVR):** a digital video recording device used to record, save, and play back television. It also has the option to fast-forward, often used during a commercial.

**Distribution:** the business deals, marketing, and logistics needed for films to be shown to the public.

**Division of Community Education (División de Educación de la Comunidad; DIVEDCO):** an initiative of the government of Puerto Rico that aimed to educate the population about topics such as public health, economic prosperity, and participation in a democratic political system.

**Docudrama**: a type of fiction film that uses some documentary strategies, often dramatizing real-life events or issues.

**Dominicanyork**: an individual of Dominican origin or descent based in New York City.

**DREAMer**: a term used to refer to an undocumented individual who was brought to the United States as a child. The term is derived from the Development, Relief, and Education for Alien Minors Act, a proposal for a law that would have provided a path to citizenship for people in this situation.

**Editing:** the assembly of the many shots that make up a film or television show.

**Episodic television:** shows whose entire plot, conflict, and resolution unfolds in a single episode in a three-act structure. Episodic is the opposite of seriality. The TV show will reveal all the necessary information to understand the situation or conflict at hand and solve it all in one episode.

**Essential/essentialism:** An understanding of identity that regards it as rooted in biology rather than being socially constructed as the majority of social and natural scientists believe. For example, the notion of the "essential Black subject" assumes that there is an essence to Blackness that is shared by all of those of African descent; a "fixed transcultural or transcendental" understanding of Blackness rooted in biology or nature.

*Estado Libre Asociado* **(commonwealth)**: the political status of Puerto Rico since 1952, which includes some aspects of nationhood, such as a constitution, while lacking others. Somewhat confusingly, Puerto Rico is considered a commonwealth (territory) rather than a free associated state of the United States (a semi-independent nation under the protection of another), which is the status of Palau, Micronesia, and the Marshall Islands in relation to the United States.

**Ethnicity:** a social category based on cultural characteristics such as religion, language, and customs.

**Eugenics:** the effort to "improve" the human race by careful control of reproduction, which was linked with deeply problematic attitudes about race and disability.

**Exhibition:** the presentation of films in theaters and on television, home video, and streaming services.

**Eyeline match**: a component of shot-reverse shot structure that gives the impression the actors are looking at each other, usually because one is looking to the right of the frame and another to the left and their gazes cross.

**Film cycle:** a group of films made around the same time that share thematic concerns.

**Film sound:** the dialogue, ambient noise/sound effects, and music used in a film.

**Film style:** audio and visual choices made by a film's creative team.

**Frame:** the visible portion of a film or television image at any given moment; can also refer to the individual images on a film strip that together create the illusion of motion.

**"Freedom Flights":** twice-daily flights operated via an agreement between the Cuban and US governments that brought about 300,000 Cuban refugees to the United States between 1965 and 1973.

**Good Neighbor Policy**: a program designed to improve US–Latin American relations and draw Latin American countries into the United States' sphere of influence, using film as a key way to spread the message of hemispheric solidarity.

***La gran familia puertorriquena***: the distinct and specific Puerto Rican ethnoracial mixture consisting of Taíno Indian, Spanish, and African descents. Specifically, this construction implies the unsubstantiated idea that unlike the United States, where there is racism and racial stratification, Puerto Rico has a racial democracy.

**Greaser film cycle:** a cluster of films made between 1908–1914 that featured a stereotypical Mexican male character, referred to by the derogatory term greaser.

**Great Migration:** in the context of US–Puerto Rico relations, a surge in migration from Puerto Rico to the US mainland that peaked during the 1950s, totaling an estimated 470,000 individuals during that decade. The expansion of air travel and the impact of Operation Bootstrap contributed to this exodus.

**Hashtag activism**: the use of online platforms as digital public spaces for political organization, particularly the use of hashtags to enhance the discoverability of online media content.

***Hijas de Cuauhtémoc*:** a Chicana feminist student newspaper founded at California State University Long Beach in 1971.

**Hispano:** a person descended from Spanish settlers in the Southwest before it became part of the United States.

**Hypodescent:** the practice of determining the classification of a child of mixed-race ancestry by assigning the child the race of their more socially subordinate parent.

**Ideology of whitening:** the inaccurate belief, often held by Latin American elites, that the genetic heritage of white people would eventually "win out" over Indigenous and African heritage in national populations due to the false assumption of white superiority; often linked with efforts to encourage immigration from Europe to hasten this process.

**Indigeneity**: refers broadly to shared characteristics of global Indigenous populations, namely ancestral, historical, and cultural connections to home territories that predate colonial societies.

**Interface:** online functionalities and/or design that structures user interaction.

**Intersectional/intersectionality:** an analytical lens that considers how overlapping forms of oppression based on identity categories such as race, gender, and sexuality compound each other to shape individuals' life outcomes. The term "intersectionality" was coined by legal scholar Kimberlé Crenshaw in 1989. "Intersectional" is the adjective used to identify such an approach.

**Intersex:** a physical condition experienced by an estimated 1%–2% of the population in which an individual's genetic material and anatomy do not follow the common XX/female or XY/male patterns.

**Intertitles:** slides inserted at specific points in a film that convey narrative information or dialogue.

**Isthmian:** an alternative term to refer to people originating from or descending from the Central American region that privileges a sense of being tied to the land rather than nation-states and geopolitical constructions.

**Jones-Shafroth Act:** a 1917 law that, among other provisions, made all Puerto Ricans born in or after 1899 citizens of the United States, a status they had not previously held. The timing of the law is often viewed as suspect, given that the conferral of citizenship made Puerto Rican men subject to the draft just as the United States entered World War I.

**Latin look:** the popularly represented Latino/Hispanic identity creates a Latina/o type that is physically adherent to what Rodriguez calls the "Latin look"—characterized by tan/olive skin with dark hair and eyes—and seems to acknowledge only the Spanish and Indigenous heritages of US Latinas/os, not their African or Asian roots.

**Latinidad:** Latino-ness; or discourses and subjectivities of Latina/o/x identity.

**Laugh track:** a pre-recorded soundtrack that contains the laughter of an audience, often used in sitcoms.

**League of United Latin American Citizens (LULAC)**: the oldest Hispanic/Latino/Latinx civil rights organization in the United States. Founded in 1929, LULAC focuses on voting rights and voter participation and issues of educational and economic opportunity.

**Mainstream (hegemonic) media:** traditional and dominant media productions that are hierarchically organized and usually created by corporate media outlets to generate profit from mass consumption.

*Maquiladoras*: factories, usually owned by US business, built along the US–Mexico border region to avoid higher taxes and labor costs in the United States. After the passage of the North American Free Trade Agreement in 1994, goods made in Mexico could enter the United States without paying the tariffs previously in place, making this business model highly profitable.

**Mariel Boatlift:** the 1980 exodus of approximately 125,000 Cubans who reached the United States in privately chartered boats after Fidel Castro exceptionally allowed individuals to leave Cuba without express permission from the government.

*Marimacha*: an insulting slang term for lesbian.

**Medium specificity:** the ways that film, television, and digital media allow for different forms of storytelling or aesthetic expression that are particular to the stylistic and narrative properties of that medium.

*Mestizaje*: the process of racial, ethnic, and cultural mixing.

***Mestizo:*** a person of mixed Indigenous and white descent.

**Mise-en-scène:** the elements of film borrowed from theater, including set design, locations, costume design, and lighting.

**Multi-sited:** involving more than one location.

**Network era:** the first period (early 1950s to mid-1980s) of broadcast television, which was dominated by the Big Three television networks: ABC, CBS, and NBC.

**Networked public:** the online space and imagined relationships that emerge from the intersection of users, technology, and everyday practices.

**New Queer Cinema:** a filmmaking movement that took shape during the early 1990s, which was characterized by an unapologetic, even nihilistic approach to LGBTQ identity and experiences and a self-referential, often ironic approach to pop culture.

**Newsreel:** weekly compilations of footage of current events.

**Niche audience:** a particular subset of an audience, like women, Latinx, or queer folks instead of a broader audience.

**Non-diegetic sound:** sound that is understood to originate from outside the fictional world of the film and would not be heard by the character, most notably orchestral scoring.

**Nuyorican:** an individual of Puerto Rican origin or descent based in New York City.

**Offscreen sound:** sound without a visible source onscreen.

**One-drop rule:** the belief that an individual with any known or visible African ancestry should be considered Black, which was enshrined in law in several US states.

**Onscreen sound:** sound with a visible source onscreen.

**Operation Bootstrap:** a collaboration between the Puerto Rican and US federal government to rapidly transform the island's economy from an agrarian system into an industrial one.

**Operation Peter Pan**: an initiative to bring 14,000 unaccompanied Cuban minors to the United States for resettlement implemented by the Catholic Welfare Bureau with some backing from the US government, between 1960 and 1962.

**Over-the-shoulder shot**: a type of shot composition used in shot-reverse shot structure in which the camera is positioned behind one of the actors and a sliver of their body, typically a shoulder, is visible, helping to clarify where the characters are positioned relative to each other.

***Pachucos:*** members of a Mexican American youth subculture. The *pachuco* subculture arose from the social issues Mexican American youth experienced during the later decades of the nineteenth century and early decades of the twentieth century.

**Pan:** side-to-side movements of the camera pivoting on a fixed point, typically a tripod.

**Pan-ethnic:** referring to a social category that groups individuals of different national origins together, such as Latino or Asian.

**Pan-Latinidad:** the notion that all US residents of Latin American origin share a cultural kinship that trumps identification with a particular national origin.

**Parallel editing:** an editing pattern that alternates shots of actions happening in different locations, implying that they are happening simultaneously. Also known as cross-cutting.

*Pata*: an insulting slang term for lesbian.

**Performative/performativity:** referring to the learned, culturally coded nature of everyday behaviors that might appear natural on the surface. Performative is the adjective used to describe these qualities.

**Point-of-view shot structure:** a shot of a character looking followed by a view, typically from the reverse angle, that is implied to be through their eyes.

**Post-network era:** the second and ongoing period (mid-1980s to present). Due to technological changes impacting the transmission of television, US TV transitioned from a business model controlled by only a few networks into an era where television became multi-channeled with a shift from "free" broadcast television to paid commercial content.

**Production:** the creation of a media product, broadly defined; can be further divided into the following stages: development (the process of going from an idea to a complete script and then to a viable project with a director, main actors, and financing lined up), pre-production (the completion of casting and other aspects of mise-en-scène), shooting (the creation of the raw footage for a film or television show), and post-production (processes like editing, color correction, and sound mixing that are necessary to assemble and polish the footage created during shooting to create a finished product).

**Race:** a socially constructed grouping based on individuals' physical characteristics, which does not correspond to meaningful biological differences between groups.

*Rasquache*: a specifically Mexican American or Latinx aesthetic that is rooted in the resourceful repurposing of discarded or devalued materials and defies conventional notions of "good taste," often using bright colors and bold choices.

**Ratings sweep:** a brief period each year where Nielsen, the company responsible for calculating television ratings, consults detailed records of the viewing patterns of selected households. Networks tend to concentrate exciting programming during this time to attract the largest possible audience.

*La raza cósmica*/**the cosmic race:** in the writings of José Vasconcelos, a future race of humans that would unite all the existing races. While praising racial mixture, the idea of a cosmic race was premised on the disappearance of African and Indigenous peoples. Vasconcelos also made denigrating comments about Asians in his discussion of the concept.

**La Raza Unida:** a political party founded in Crystal City, Texas, in 1970 as an effort to mobilize Chicano/Latino voters to support Latino candidates rather than candidates fielded by the Republican or Democratic parties, which rarely prioritized issues affecting Latino communities.

**Reception:** the response of audiences and critics to a media product.

**Reverse angle:** an editing pattern involving a 180-degree change in perspective between two shots.

**Satellite:** a technology that allows for the simultaneous airing of programs from coast to coast and the expansion of available channels beyond network TV.

**Scientific racism:** the effort to find evidence for the imagined superiority of whites to other racial groups, based in practices such as phrenology that were considered valid in the 1800s but have been debunked as pseudoscience.

**Second-wave feminism:** a surge of feminist activism in the 1960s and 1970s focused on issues such as equality in the workforce, reproductive rights, and the effort to overturn patriarchal dynamics in personal relationships.

**Serial television:** shows whose story unfolds over multiple episodes, seasons, or even during the duration of an entire length of series. A TV series may reveal parts of plot, conflict, or character developments in each new episode. Sometimes this occurs weekly or daily in a soap opera or telenovela, depending on the genre's format.

**Shot:** an unbroken run of the camera.

**Shot-reverse shot:** a common pattern in film editing that combines images of two individuals who are facing each other, each shot with a 180-degree change in the placement of the camera.

**Showrunner:** a person who has overall creative authority and management responsibility for a TV program. This person is responsible for overseeing all areas of writing and production on a television series, ensuring that each episode is delivered on time and on a budget for the production studio that produces the show and the network or platform that airs it. The word showrunner is often used synonymously with writer-producer or creator of a TV series, but these three terms refer to different roles, although an individual can hold more than one of them.

**Single reel film:** during the silent period film lengths were measured in reels of approximately 10,000 feet or approximately ten minutes each.

**Sitcom:** a distinctive TV genre primarily defined by its structure and the central role of comedy.

**Slave codes:** a series of laws that assigned Black servants a lower social status than their White counterparts and progressively stripped them of rights.

**Social media:** social networking sites such as Twitter and Facebook, blogs, video sharing sites such as YouTube, and any other online platform that allows users to create their own content and facilitates interaction between groups of people in much of the same way as other public spaces have done and continue to do so.

**Social problem film:** a type of film made in the 1940s–1960s that tackled issues such as racism, assimilation, and inequality.

**Spanish-language film production:** a short-lived phenomenon in Hollywood during the transition to sound in the late twenties and early thirties, in which movies were shot in both English and Spanish versions. This practice began when dubbing was not yet practical and subtitles were not widely accepted. It was also used for other languages such as French and German.

**Star persona:** the combination a performer's onscreen roles and the way they are represented in the press.

**Stereotypes:** widely held but oversimplified images of a person or group.

**Subscription video on demand (SVOD):** streaming services such as Netflix, HBO Max, and Disney + that have a flat rate per month, allowing the viewer to self-determine how much content they want to view each month without paying more.

**Technological affordances:** characteristics of online environments which make possible certain types of social interactions. Sometimes, affordances are designed to specifically encourage certain interactions. However, online practices can often develop in ways not predicted or intended through design choices.

**Telenovelas:** episodic dramas with some similarities to soap operas. However, they are typically broadcast during primetime hours and their storylines have a definite endpoint, unlike US soap operas.

**Third world cinema:** a mode of politically charged filmmaking that challenges the dominance of Hollywood by developing alternative forms of film narrative and style.

**Three-camera setup (or multiple-camera setup):** a method of TV production commonly used in sports events, news, soap operas, talk and game shows, and most sitcoms. It involves using three simultaneously recording cameras instead of one, taking footage from various angles, and maximizing filming time, which is essential when recording shows with a live audience like talk and game shows.

**Tilt:** upward or downward movements of a camera pivoting on a fixed point, typically a tripod.

**Tracking shot:** a shot involving movement forward, backward, or parallel to the plane of the frame, using train-like tracks or a dolly with wheels.

**Transactional video on demand (TVOD):** the opposite of monthly subscription video. Here, consumers can purchase content on a pay-per-view basis, such as buying a single TV series season or film.

**Transnational:** a phenomenon that unfolds across one or more national borders. For instance, transnational identity can be defined as a multi-geographical view of identity wherein a person identifies with both the local or national identity of their place of origin and with the local or national identity of the place in which they currently reside.

**Traveling shot:** a shot that combines different types of camera movement. Traveling shots are often produced using a Steadicam (a camera mount worn on the operator's body, consisting of a mechanical arm that helps buffer the camera from sudden movements, producing a smoother final image).

**TV anthologies:** shows whose situation, conflict, and resolution happen within one episode but each with a different set of characters.

**United Farm Workers:** a union for agricultural workers founded by César Chávez and Dolores Huerta in California's Central Valley in 1962. Originally known as the National Farm Workers Association, the organization led several influential marches and boycotts during the sixties and seventies for the right to unionize and for better wages and working conditions.

**Vertical integration:** control by one company of multiple stages in the lifecycle of a particular product, which can help maximize profit. In the context of the film industry, vertical integration refers to a single company being involved in production, distribution, and exhibition, essentially giving it a guaranteed outlet for its media products.

**Volstead Act:** the law that instituted Prohibition in the United States between 1920 and 1933, forbidding the manufacture, transportation, and sale of alcohol.

**West Indian:** the primary term used to refer to those from Caribbean Islands that have a British colonial history. As a term used to refer to the Caribbean Islands, "West Indies" is based on the legacy of Christopher Columbus's assumption that he had landed in what is now called the East Indies (an area off the mainland of continental Asia).

**Wet foot, dry foot policy:** a 1995 change to the Cuban Adjustment Act that granted Cuban immigrants the right to stay in the United States if they made it to US soil. If they were intercepted at sea between Cuba and the United States, they would be turned back.

**Writer-producer:** a person who helps write and produce a TV show.

**Young Lords:** a youth organization fighting for Puerto Rican civil rights and communities, founded in Chicago in 1968. The Young Lords modeled some aspects of their community engagement and political tactics on the Black Panthers, with whom they sometimes collaborated closely.

**Zoot suits**: the customary dress of *pachucos* (members of a Mexican American youth subculture). A zoot suit consists of high-waisted pants and long blazers, with excess fabric through the width of the pants and arms sleeves in defiance of wartime restrictions on the use of cloth. The suits are often accompanied with fedoras and chains hanging from the waist. *Pachucas* also had a signature style. This consisted of elements like longer coats that often reached their fingertips, draped slacks or a short skirt, and high socks.